FDR V. THE CONSTITUTION

# FDR v. The Constitution

## The Court-Packing Fight
## and the Triumph of Democracy

BURT SOLOMON

Walker & Company
New York

Published by Walker Publishing Company, Inc., New York

All papers used by Walker & Company are natural, recyclable products
made from wood grown in well-managed forests. The manufacturing processes
conform to the environmental regulations of the country of origin.

LIBRARY OF CONGRESS CATALOGING-IN-PUBLICATION DATA

Solomon, Burt.
    FDR v. the Constitution : the court-packing fight and the triumph of democracy / Burt
Solomon.—1st U.S. ed.
        p.    cm.
    Includes bibliographical references and index.
    ISBN-13: 978-0-8027-1589-0
    ISBN-10: 0-8027-1589-3
    1. Roosevelt, Franklin D. (Franklin Delano), 1882–1945.    2. United States. Supreme Court—
History—20th century.    3. Judges—Selection and appointment—United States—History—
20th century.    4. Law—Political aspects—United States—History—20th century.    5. Executive
power—United States—History—20th century.    6. Separation of powers—United States—
History—20th century.    7. United States—Politics and government—1933–1945.
8. Constitutional history—United States.    9. Democracy—United States—History—20th century.
10. Political culture—Washington (D. C.)—History—20th century.    I. Title.    II. Title:
FDR versus the Constitution.
    KF8742.S585 2009
    347.73'2609—dc22

                                                                                2008033222

Visit Walker & Company's Web site at www.walkerbooks.com

First U.S. edition 2009

1 3 5 7 9 10 8 6 4 2

Typeset by Westchester Book Group
Printed in the United States of America by Quebecor World Fairfield

To Nancy

# CONTENTS

# PROLOGUE

THE COLD, DRIVING rain presented the nastiest weather for a presidential inaugural since 1909, when a blizzard had forced William Howard Taft to move his inside. When someone suggested to Franklin Delano Roosevelt that he do the same, on the twentieth of January in 1937, he shot back, "If those people can take it, I can, too." He meant the thousands upon thousands of Americans who had flocked to Washington to celebrate the beginning of his second term in the White House.

The president had ridden to the Capitol in an open car and had willed his nearly useless legs across the roofed platform, leaning on the arm of his eldest son, James. He stood and faced Charles Evans Hughes, the chief justice of the United States; both men were bareheaded in the swirling rain. His family's old Dutch Bible was covered in cellophane, and he placed his hand on top. In repeating the full oath of office, forsaking the traditional response of "I do," he spoke slowly and with emphasis as he swore to "protect and defend the Constitution of the United States."

Then he stepped to the podium, wearing a winged collar, a gray cutaway suit, and an overcoat. His hair was grayer and sparser and his features were heavier than four years before. Gone from his muscular face was any trace of his famously sunny smile. Below, the umbrella-covered crowd had thinned as the spectators sought shelter. At the east front of the Capitol, in a plaza that could hold a hundred thousand, no more than eight thousand onlookers remained, ankle-deep in mud. The few of those who could hear him found it hard to applaud with an umbrella in hand.

"My fellow countrymen . . ." This was not the salutation that radio listeners had learned to expect; in his fireside chats he always began, "My friends." Yet there was an unfailing cheerfulness to his tenor, even as the wind whipped across his cheeks.

"This year marks the one hundred and fiftieth anniversary of the constitutional convention which made us a nation . . ." The Founding Fathers had designed a means of escaping from the chaos of the Revolution—"a strong government, with the powers of united action sufficient then and now to solve problems utterly beyond individual or local action. A century and a half ago they established the federal government in order to promote the general welfare and secure the blessings of liberty to the American people. *Today* we invoke those *same* powers of government to achieve the *same* objective."*

The weather may have been gloomy, but the nation's outlook was sunnier than it had been four years earlier, when Roosevelt first stood at the east front of the Capitol after the most pitiless four months in the nation's economic history. He had recently spent his reelection campaign telling the public how he had mastered the "economic royalists," the malefactors he had assailed in accepting his party's nomination for a second term, and how the New Deal had salved the Great Depression by supplying farm subsidies, public works jobs, an assurance of collective bargaining, rural electricity, jobless benefits, old-age pensions, a guarantee for frightened bank depositors. More than anything, the New Deal—and the man behind it, the thirty-second president—had given the citizenry a spirit of hope. "The only thing we have to fear is fear itself," he had famously asserted. Economics, with its graphs and statistics, was an expression of mass psychology, the aggregation of how millions of people—producers, transporters, consumers—acted and interacted at a moment in time. The economy was something more than a soulless machine; it was amenable to human influence.

Roosevelt had satisfied enough of the voters that they rewarded him with the greatest presidential landslide since 1820, when James Monroe ran unopposed. Forty-six states, all but Maine and Vermont, had cast a majority of their votes for the Democrat in the White House.

"But *here* is the challenge to our democracy!" The president had personally scratched his speechwriters' suggested colon into an exclamation

---

*In his reading copy, Roosevelt had underlined the italicized words.

point. "I see millions of families trying to live on incomes so meager that the pall of family disaster hangs over them day by day. I see millions whose daily lives in city and on farm continue under conditions *labeled indecent.*"

He raised his voice and sped up his cadence as the rain pounded down. The tuba player in the marine band at the base of the podium tilted his instrument and dumped the water out. Twice, the president brushed the rain from his face. "I see millions lacking the means to buy the products of farm and factory and by their poverty denying work and productiveness to many other millions. I see one-third of a nation ill-housed, ill-clad, ill-nourished."

Despite his lordly upbringing and his presumption of privilege, the squire of a Hudson Valley estate had never forgotten the forgotten man. Within blocks of where he was standing, hidden along the alleyways near Capitol Hill, stood the dreariest and the most fearsome of slums. Among the thousands of letters that the White House received day in and day out, he could hear the cries of pain that would move even the most hardened politician:

> Dear President Winter is coming and we have no coal I haven't got a suit of clothes, to where to church . . . We will have to face the winter naked, hungry . . . it is hard to try and feed 8 children on bread & milk . . . My father he staying home. All the time he's crying because he can't find work . . . I have no shoe and we are suffin . . . i have four boys going to school and this makes the second week they stay home for they do not have any clothes or shoes to wear . . . All I want is a chance . . . Mrs. Roosevelt this nation is hanging over a giant powder keg just waiting for someone to light a match . . . PRESIDENT ROSEFELT WE WISH YOU WERE DICTATOR FOR AWHILE . . . If you could only know how I feel. I am most frantic with depression.

Not since the North and the South had taken up arms, brother against brother, had the nation known a sadder time. This was a war without bayonets or bullets, rife with suffering but allowing only the slowest death. Since the railroads had crossed the rugged country soon after the Civil War, and since the factories had sprung up across the land like wild rice, the softer rhythms of a pastoral America had been fading into the past, drowned out by the whir of machinery, the screeches of metal, the whistles at the changes of shift, the muffled resentments in the company towns, the sighs of the sweatshop, the shouts of the strikers, the crackle of fright and despair. An industrial America was a belching and belligerent place.

The United States, to be sure, had never been truly united, but the nature of the disunity had changed. In the past, the nation had found itself divided by region or by race or, in sophisticated cities, by breeding and birth. Those now seemed quaint. The lines had grown uglier, crasser, more intensely separating economic classes between capital and labor. Capitalists had created the wealth of a powerful industrial nation, but on the backs of the workingman and at the price of the poor. Twice before, the rising anger had erupted into movements for reform; first the agrarian-based populist movement of the 1890s and then the more urban and cerebral Progressives of the 1910s and 1920s tried to apply the government's power to fix the nation's ills. Occasionally they succeeded—busting trusts, instituting an income tax, regulating the nation's railroads and the safety of its food and drugs.

This was before catastrophe struck. During the Great Depression, following the stock market crash of 1929, the world had seemed to spin out of control. The surge of economic instability and the political devastation that it provoked had been splashed across every front page. In Europe, where democracy had been born in ancient Greece, the democracies proved unequal to the assault. Hitler had risen to dictatorial power in Germany, Mussolini preceding him in Italy; in Spain, Franco was marching on Madrid while militarism settled onto Japan. Stalin had consolidated dictatorial power in the Soviet Union, while in Brazil, a dictatorship had supplanted a republic. Almost inevitably, it seemed, a nation that watched its economy collapse soon saw its democracy succumb. Even within the United States, dangers lurked. Huey Long had built a virtual dictatorship in Louisiana and became the Kingfish in the vast Mississippi Valley before he was assassinated in 1935. Father Coughlin had taken his fascist-worthy invective to the radio airwaves throughout industrial America and, before his superiors reined him in, had drawn an unsettling response.

The nation had been battling over the nature of its democracy since its inception. Its primordial philosophical dispute pitted Thomas Jefferson against Alexander Hamilton. The Sage of Monticello envisioned a society of hardy individuals who controlled their own fates; the best government was the one that governed the least and in closest proximity to the people. Hamilton was the entrepreneurial immigrant, the ambitious New Yorker, who craved a national government strong enough to encourage prosperity and improve its citizens' lives. For a century and a half, this rift had sliced through the republic's affairs without ever being resolved. Now the suffering of the Depression had become the irresistible force in compelling the popularly elected national government to side with the people. The dispute over philosophy had turned into a crisis because of an immovable judicial object.

The president had been expected to say something in his inaugural address about the Supreme Court. The nation's highest court had long been a bulwark of property owners and an enforcer of laissez-faire. It had already struck down a dozen New Deal laws after aggrieved parties filed lawsuits that provided the Court an opportunity to act, and it was soon to deliver its verdict on most of the rest. Two weeks earlier, in addressing Congress on the state of the union, the president had said, "Means must be found to adapt our legal forms and our judicial interpretation to the actual present national needs," becoming the first sitting president since Abraham Lincoln to criticize the nation's highest court openly, if not by name.

At this grander podium, in the opening moments of his second term, President Roosevelt looked out across First Street at the Court's new quarters, little more than a year old, an island of white even in the darkened rain. He said nothing about the Court explicitly, though he made himself clear. "The Constitution of 1787 did not make our democracy impotent," he shouted into the rain, with the emphases he had planned with his pencil. The people, he went on, "will insist that *every* agency of popular government use effective instruments to carry out their will." The chief justice was seated just behind the podium, and there was no doubt, according to a presidential confidant who was watching his face, that he understood what FDR meant.

Everyone else would learn soon enough. Sixteen days later, President Roosevelt touched off an epic battle over the Supreme Court. His plan to enlarge the Court from nine justices to as many as fifteen—to "pack" it, as the opponents decried—was, by all accounts, constitutional. The nation's founding document was silent about the Court's size; only since 1870, within the living memory of some of the current justices, had the seats on the nation's highest bench numbered nine. But for the next 168 days, the fight over expanding the Court played out over the radio airwaves, across dinner tables all over America, and inside the august and serene chambers of the nation's capital.

In 1937, the stakes could not have been higher. They extended beyond the makeup of the Court or even the fate of the New Deal. For one thing, the president's proposal would undoubtedly jeopardize the constitutional balance within the federal government in favor of the elected branches, by increasing their leverage over the judiciary through the appointment of additional justices. Anyone who listened to Lowell Thomas or H. V. Kaltenborn on the radio about the disturbing events overseas, anyone who watched a newsreel or read a newspaper, would recognize the danger of tyranny as far more than theoretical. By effect, if not by intention, in hopes of avoiding any such outcome in America, the president was proposing to subvert the Constitution.

Something else of grave importance was at stake—the sort of nation that the world's oldest constitutional democracy was to become. Would it remain the land of laissez-faire, in which the corporate interest was treated as tantamount to the national interest, or should the national government be allowed to champion the majority's needs? Which would rule: property, or, as in the opening words of the Constitution, "We, the People"?

No one suspected after his electoral landslide in 1936 that the masterful politician would so swiftly fall from grace, that he would be denied the instrument he insisted he needed to make the country whole again. But that was before a judicial pragmatist and a legislator of principle joined the fight—a swing justice of inscrutable views and a maverick senator who never backed down. Together they inflicted the worst defeat on the century's greatest president.

Yet Roosevelt's failure to pack the Supreme Court did not mean that property had won. Even as FDR lost, he had gained his objective—a liberal-minded Court, one that would endure for seven decades or more.

# CHAPTER ONE

# Nine Old Men

THE JUSTICES OF the Supreme Court of the United States were soon to arrive at the White House for the final formal dinner of the winter's social season. Upstairs, Franklin Roosevelt gathered with three of his intimates and mixed the martinis or old-fashioneds in his enigmatic proportions. The second-floor study, his favorite room in the presidential mansion, was crammed with books and stacks of papers and well-worn leather seats and paintings of ships under full sail and one of a young Eleanor, his wife. The president loved gossip and reminiscences as respites from the rigors of the day, but tonight's conversation was less frothy than usual. The president's companions, his personal secretary Missy LeHand and his ghost speechwriter (and New York judge) Sam Rosenman and his wife, were all in on the secret that he would spring on the capital—and on the nation—in three more days.

"The time for action with respect to the Supreme Court really cannot be postponed," the president said, "and unpleasant as it is, I think we have to face it."

He pretended to be dreading the dinner, but his friends knew he would enjoy it. They drank a toast to the Supreme Court—as it was and as they hoped it would soon become.

On this cold and clear evening of February 2, 1937, eighty-five guests assembled downstairs to partake in the president's annual dinner for the Supreme Court justices. Woodrow Wilson's widow had accepted the invitation, along with the handsome ex-boxer Gene Tunney and his pretty socialite wife, the congressional barons who regarded the judiciary as their own preserve, a rear admiral, a major general, the Pittsburgh judge who had crusaded against intoxicated drivers—the president had personally added him to the invitation list—and almost a dozen millionaires named by the party treasurer as having helped "financially and in other ways during the recent campaign." These were in addition to seven of the Nine Old Men, as a recent ill-natured best seller had described this evening's guests of honor.

Everyone had gathered in the East Room. Just that morning, Mrs. Roosevelt had announced that the room's elderly draperies of gold damask, which her aunt had chosen when *she* was the first lady, were soon to be replaced, along with the gold-leafed piano. Charles Evans Hughes, the chief justice, noticed Senator William Borah across the East Room and strode over. The wavy-haired dean of the Senate, the Lion of Idaho, had a massive forehead, a chiseled face, and a mind of his own. The one-time Shakespearean actor, an unpredictable progressive, preferred the magnificently lost cause to quiet victory. The evening before, he had delivered a nationwide radio speech that defended the Court's independence against the president's recent public criticism. "A great speech," the chief justice told him as they shook hands.

For FDR, the dinner for the justices was almost a necessity. Approaching the fifth year of his tenure, he remained the first president since Andrew Johnson who had lacked the opportunity to nominate a single justice. William Howard Taft, in his single presidential term, had named five of them, and that was before he joined the bench himself. President Roosevelt had sought to ingratiate himself in private with as many as three or four of the sitting justices, but they had proved immune to his blandishments. This left the annual dinner as his best chance to hobnob with the secluded jurists who had been thwarting his programs.

The president was wheeled into the State Dining Room in his reconfigured kitchen chair, and the chief justice's wife strolled in the place of honor at his side. Just behind them, Charles Evans Hughes escorted Eleanor Roosevelt. Hughes looked like a chief justice, as if Cecil B. DeMille had imagined him for the silver screen, with his piercing gray eyes, the snowy sweep of his mustache, and his luscious, parted white beard that lent him a chilly dignity concealing his private good cheer.

Tonight he was as jovial as his public nature permitted. He loved his own voice, and he could take forever to get to the point. But he was no longer the human icicle he had seemed to the citizenry in 1916, when he had gone to bed on Election Night thinking he was the president-elect and had awakened to find that Woodrow Wilson had won instead. Later there was much talk of a "new Hughes," a jocular Hughes, one who read Balzac and played golf, though not everyone had gone away convinced. "First, is he human?" a magazine writer who had known Hughes as a youth once asked, and then answered: "Mr. Hughes is unquestionably of human origin."

The eldest justice, eighty-year-old Louis D. Brandeis, and his wife had declined the invitation following their physician's advice—they never ventured out at night—and Harlan Fiske Stone had returned too recently to Washington from his lengthy convalescence in the South. But all of the other justices showed up, even James McReynolds, a rude and caustic conservative who "detested the very name 'Roosevelt,'" according to his law clerk. For George Sutherland, courtly and cultured but equally conservative, this was the only dinner invitation he accepted all year.

The justices joined Roosevelt in the State Dining Room at the horseshoe-shaped table, decorated with red roses, white snapdragons, and maidenhair ferns, and set with the gold-edged china (bearing the Roosevelt coat of arms and the presidential seal) that he and Eleanor had acquired. He waved his cigarette holder as he regaled his listeners with stories and chortled at everyone's wit.

After dinner, once the ladies had retired to the Blue and Green rooms, the men smoked cigars, sipped brandy, and bantered. There was much to discuss. Troops armed with machine guns and bayonets had surrounded General Motors' two Fisher Body factories in Flint, Michigan, where the sit-down strikers vowed to defy a state judge's order to vacate the property. The U.S. Senate was debating at length its policy of neutrality amid the rising tensions of Europe. The stage actress Tallulah Bankhead, who was the House Speaker's daughter, had just announced an extra matinee of *Reflected Glory* at the National Theater, three blocks from the White House, as a benefit for the thousands of flood victims along the Ohio and Mississippi rivers. The president had asked Congress to accept Andrew Mellon's $50 million collection of art, to be housed in a Roman-domed gallery on the national Mall. A boxing match between the heavyweight champion, James J. Braddock, and the aspirant Joe Louis, the Brown Bomber, seemed assured for Chicago. The only subject apparently off limits was the one on everyone's mind: the Supreme Court itself.

The chief justice chatted and laughed with the president. They had much in common and every reason to get along. Both had been born along the Hudson River and had served as reform-style governors of New York. They called each other "Governor"—a young FDR had crossed party lines to vote for Hughes, a progressive Republican—and though they hailed from different parties, neither was dogmatic about what he believed. Their similarities extended to their shared practice of using all three of their given names. More often than not, the chief justice had found himself agreeing with the president that the Constitution had to be interpreted to fit the needs of the times. Within the quiet confines of the Court, he had applied his diplomatic skills toward just such an end, albeit unproductively to date, as much as anyone could tell.

Their shared experience had not advanced their relationship nearly as far, however, as the president would have liked. During his four years in the governor's mansion in Albany, Roosevelt had consulted on occasion with the state's preeminent jurists about the constitutionality of a bill before it became a law. He was hoping for a similar informality in Washington. There was precedent. James Buchanan, while the president-elect, pushed for a decision on the *Dred Scott* case and lobbied a northern justice to join the Court's southern majority. After Taft became the only ex-president ever to become the chief justice, he often conferred with President Coolidge and members of his cabinet. FDR, as the president-elect, suggested "the same type of delightful relations" to Justice Benjamin Cardozo, who had served as the chief judge on New York's highest court, and also once or twice to Brandeis, and he had evidently broached the idea with Hughes himself, though the chief justice later denied it. Hughes found himself explaining to Roosevelt that the judiciary was an independent branch of the government and must be treated as one. Inevitably, the other justices learned of the approaches and, liberals and conservatives alike, were horrified, leaving Roosevelt without any real friend on the Court.

Clusters of notables gathered at other tables. Justice Owen J. Roberts sat with Donald Richberg, a friend who had run the National Recovery Administration before its premature death at the Court's hands. Roberts "did not hesitate to rag me," Richberg recounted, about the NRA chief's recent speech to a legal society in Philadelphia, Roberts's hometown, criticizing the justice's controversial opinion that had struck down the New Deal's Agricultural Adjustment Act.

All evening the president's spirits ran high, no doubt fueled by the secret he was keeping. For nearly two years he had wondered what to do about the Supreme Court. Nothing in the Constitution gave the Court the power to strike down a law, but John Marshall, its third and greatest chief justice, had simply asserted the right of judicial review in 1803, and the Court had been exercising it at plaintiffs' behest ever since—lately, with a vengeance. During the previous two years, the Court toppled pillar after pillar of the New Deal, and more of the president's favorite legislation faced a clear and present danger.

But the few others who were in the know felt uneasy. "I wish this message were over and delivered," Homer Cummings, the attorney general, whispered to Sam Rosenman. "I feel too much like a conspirator."

"I wish it were over too," Rosenman replied.

Jimmy Roosevelt, the president's eldest son, savored the irony. The twenty-nine-year-old had been an insurance executive and the head of a yeast company when his father recently named him, over Eleanor's objections, as one of his three White House assistants. He was to be the confidant that the president had been missing since Louis Howe, his longtime strategist and alter ego, died. "The President had fun with the Justices last night," Jimmy wrote in his diary the next day. "I am wondering how they will like him thirty days from now."

He would not need to wait nearly so long to find out.

THREE DAYS LATER, the president's physician was stationed by the door to the Cabinet Room, in case anyone fainted or skipped a heartbeat. This was meant as a joke, yet the glint of melodrama was deliberate.

The White House stenographers had been summoned at six thirty that Friday morning, February 5, allowing them no time to spread the word. They were put to work typing and then mimeographing the six legal-size pages of the president's message to Congress and the attorney general's six-page cover letter, including the statistical tables. A special cabinet meeting had been called for ten o'clock, instead of the usual two o'clock, on a subject that the cabinet officers had been told was confidential in the extreme. John Nance Garner attended, as usual, unlike most of the vice presidents before him (though President Wilson had first allowed it). Five leaders of Congress, all Democrats, also had been invited. The president had personally telephoned the House Speaker, William Bankhead of Alabama, and the Senate majority leader, Joe Robinson of Arkansas.

Everyone crowded into the low-ceilinged Cabinet Room, which was undecorated save for portraits of Thomas Jefferson, Andrew Jackson, and Woodrow Wilson, the rare heroes of the Democratic Party's pallid past. The Republicans had dominated in Washington since the Civil War, and especially since the 1890s, when hard economic times had made them the majority party. Yet the recent election had produced a potent Democratic majority, one that would dominate the far-flung nation for the next four decades. Factory workers and farmers, Catholics and Jews, big-city political machines, white southerners and the descendants of slaves—they joined in the most disparate coalition imaginable. Black voters, long loyal to the party of Lincoln, had backed Herbert Hoover, the failed Republican, for reelection against Roosevelt in 1932 by even grander majorities than in 1928, despite the Great Depression that had intervened. By 1936, they had come to understand where their true interests lay.

Through the French doors of the Cabinet Room lay one of the capital's loveliest sights, framed by the massive magnolia tree that Andrew Jackson had planted a century before and, toward the right, the south lawn of the White House, rolling down toward the alabaster obelisk of the Washington Monument. The nation's leaders sat around the table with eight unequal sides, designed so that the president might see everyone at once. They listened as he talked—and talked.

"Delay in the administration of justice is the outstanding defect of our federal judicial system," the president began, and for forty minutes he went on. He read first from the attorney general's cover letter and then from the message he was sending to Congress, which outlined the problems with the judiciary and his plan to fix it—"our plan," as he referred to it, gesturing toward his attorney general, Homer Cummings. Bald and paunchy, a beaked nose on his doughy face, Cummings restrained a smile and twirled his pince-nez with a monocle cord. That his Justice Department had made a name for itself in the public eye had mainly been the doing of his publicity-savvy young subordinate J. Edgar Hoover, the director of the Federal Bureau of Investigation and its famous G-men. Nor did the department's higher profile conceal that Cummings was a political animal, as a three-term mayor (of Stamford, Connecticut), a national Democratic committeeman, a convention keynoter, the party's national chairman for a few harrowing months, a dark-horse candidate for the presidency who had never come close. He had gained his seat in the cabinet after diligently lobbying for it, only because the man originally named had suddenly died.

"Of course, everyone except myself," Cummings boasted to his diary, "was taken completely by surprise." Secretary of Labor Frances Perkins, the first woman ever to join a president's cabinet, told him afterward that he had looked like the cat that swallowed the canary.

The president described the highlights of the message that was to be delivered to Congress at noon. For a while, his listeners were puzzled about what he had in mind. He told them he had ruled out trying for a constitutional amendment that might force the Court's hand—"Give me ten million dollars," he said, "and I can prevent any amendment to the Constitution from being ratified by the necessary number of states"—or seeking legislation to alter judicial procedure, such as requiring agreement from two thirds of the justices to strike down a law. He detailed the judiciary's rising case loads and its overstuffed dockets and the Supreme Court's unwillingness to hear most of the appeals—87 percent of them—that came its way. He alluded to a recommendation by earlier attorneys general—who, he did not bother to say—that a supplementary judge be appointed for every septuagenarian on the bench who refused to retire.

"The personnel of the federal judiciary is insufficient to meet the business," the president read aloud, then added a flourish of poetry to his legalistic recitation. "Modern complexities call also for a constant infusion of new blood in the courts," he went on. "Little by little, new facts become blurred through old glasses fitted, as it were, for the needs of another generation."

Only when he burrowed into the legalisms of the accompanying draft legislation did he make his solution plain. For any judge on a federal court who had spent ten years on the bench and failed to retire by the age of seventy and a half, the president could name another one, though not without limit. The number of justices could rise no higher than fifteen; the prospect of six more seats just happened to match the number of the Supreme Court's sitting justices who were older than seventy.

The Constitution had left it to Congress to set the size of the Supreme Court, and eight times during the first eighty-one years, the legislators had exercised their discretion. Sometimes it was for practical reasons, back when the justices on horseback rode circuits to hear judicial appeals through a nation that was spreading west. But at least as often, politics was involved. In 1801, the outgoing Federalist-controlled Congress passed a law to reduce the number of justices from the original six to five, to prevent the incoming president, Thomas Jefferson, from replacing a justice expected to die, until an anti-Federalist Congress repealed it in 1802. In 1863, Abraham Lincoln prevailed on Congress to expand the number of justices from nine to ten, after the Court upheld the legality of measures to fight the Civil War on a too-narrow five-to-four vote. After the Civil War, politics also explained why the Radical Republicans in charge of Congress trimmed the number of seats from ten to seven, to block the southern-sympathizing president, Andrew Johnson, from filling the vacancies, and then raised it to nine once Ulysses S. Grant, a Republican hero, entered the White House. The Court had been fixed at nine justices ever since.

But never had any president proposed such a transformation of the Court. The most zealous New Dealers at the cabinet table showed their delight with the president's proposal. Even the cantankerous and conservative vice president, so often at odds with the president, screwed up his leprechaun-ish face before he seemed to relax and wink at Homer Cummings, which the attorney general took to mean "there is no doubt about his wholehearted support." Cummings concluded the same about Hatton Sumners—that the chairman of the House Judiciary Committee looked "well-pleased"—and he was equally inaccurate in his conclusion.

The congressional leaders, Joe Robinson and Speaker Bankhead, kept poker faces. Throughout his first term in office, in extracting a historic number of landmark laws at a record-breaking pace, the president had worked attentively with members of Congress, soliciting their advice, dickering with them, twisting their arms, occasionally stealing their thunder, but making them feel as if he valued their presence, whether he did or not. He had once been a legislator himself, and even as Woodrow Wilson's assistant secretary of the navy, he had learned how to fawn over legislators to meet their needs, leaving unpunctured their sense of self-importance. The recent election had added another dozen Democrats to the Senate and more than a hundred in the House of Representatives, to build the most lopsided majorities that a president's party had seen since just after the Civil War. The Seventy-fifth Congress stood "in awe of President Roosevelt's popularity," Hearst's longtime Washington columnist had written as the lawmakers convened a month earlier. "There is no opposition worth mentioning. None is likely to develop."

This time, however, the president had not conferred with congressional leaders. Cocky over his monumental mandate at the polls, this morning he invited no discussion. He had kept the reporters waiting a half hour in the West Wing lobby, and after delivering his plan he wheeled himself out of the Cabinet Room and into his office.

More reporters than usual, as many as two hundred, gathered for the president's regular Friday morning press conference. The night before, at a reception, the president had teased Arthur Krock of the *New York Times*, "There will be big news tomorrow," but would say nothing more. The early arrivals had seen the shiny square-backed limousines in the White House driveway and intuited that something momentous was afoot. Their suspicions grew when the cabinet secretaries and congressional leaders hurried past them on their way out, saying only that the president had a statement to make, fearing his wrath if they divulged anything more.

Minutes later, the door to the president's Oval Office swung open and the correspondents rushed in. Despite the gray-green walls, the dark green curtains, the heavy pediments over the doors, and the Great Seal in the ceiling, the room had a certain lightness. The Currier & Ives lithographs of the Hudson River and the ship models on the mantel, the indirect lighting and the unembarrassed clutter, lent the Oval Office what a historian later described as "the usual Rooseveltian country-house informality."

The reporters jostled for position on three sides of the long desk, which was orderly except for the menagerie of knickknacks—donkey figurines, a mule made from pipe cleaners and nuts, a mashed bullet, a pottery pitcher of a miniature pig, a *World Almanac*. The president sat at the desk, flanked by flags, in front of windows that looked out on the last snow melting in the crotches of the elm trees. His three secretaries sat behind him and a stenographer at his side. When Charlie Michelson, the Democratic Party's publicity man, strolled in and took a seat behind the desk, Joe Robinson greeted him with a mournful shake of the head.

"All in," the doorkeeper announced. It was five minutes to eleven.

Lacking his usual smile, the president fumbled with some papers in his lap. He wore a blue suit, a white shirt with a soft collar—a change from his predecessors' starched collars—and a gray tie. He lit a Camel in his amber holder and cleared his throat. Even seated, he could hold the attention of a room.

"I have a somewhat important matter to take up with you today," he started. His press secretary, Steve Early, had suggested that he order the reporters to tell no one outside of their news organizations until noon, to prevent them from prowling Capitol Hill for reactions. "Copies will be given to you as you go out," the president said—"and don't anybody go out until that time."

"We brought our lunches," a reporter called out.

"I am glad you did," the president said, leading the laughter.

President Roosevelt's relations with the White House correspondents had been genial, even affectionate, from the first. He was far more open with them than his immediate predecessors had been. Calvin Coolidge and Herbert Hoover had met regularly with the press, but they required that the questions be submitted in advance and they left unanswered any that they disliked; nor could anything be attributed to them directly. FDR, upon taking office, had abandoned these formalities and proved casual and voluble with the press, following the example of his illustrious fifth cousin, Theodore Roosevelt, who as president had invited reporters in to watch him shave.

Most of the patrician newspaper publishers detested "that man" in the White House as a traitor to his class, and the editorial pages reflected their disgust. But the reporters, by and large, had emerged from the lesser classes; journalism was regarded not as a profession but as a working-class trade, even if its practitioners in Washington were prone to refer to themselves as "journalists" instead of "reporters." They instinctively sympathized with the New Deal, even before the president took steps to seduce them. In the spring he traditionally put on a White House dance for the press, featuring barrels of beer in a corridor and a midnight buffet in the

State Dining Room. A death in a reporter's family brought flowers and possibly a presidential telephone call. Far more consequential to the reporters than the niceties was the unprecedented access he gave them. Herbert Hoover had stood behind a podium and was businesslike and brief. Franklin Roosevelt let his questioners gather around, talking on and on, and allowing the correspondents to attribute the substance of his remarks (and occasionally, a quotation) directly to him, rather than to the "spokesman" who had veiled his predecessors. Best of all, he liked them—or seemed to, which served equally well.

The reporters were aware of the calculation behind the kindness. The president could shape their coverage by what he said and how he said it. He understood how to harness the powers of publicity to establish the terms of debate—something else he had learned from his cousin. Yet the reporters could only rejoice in the bargain. Day after day, in exchange for being used, they got to write another front-page, newspaper-selling, potentially salary-raising dispatch. In no one's memory had the White House mattered more, and therefore neither had the reporters who covered it.

"I will just touch the high spots," Roosevelt said, as he started to read from the attorney general's letter.

The pitch of his tenor strained a tone or two higher than usual at first, but as he continued to read, he relaxed. He showed "an almost voluptuous pleasure in being dramatic," the most conservative of columnists sneered the next day. Twice, he digressed to make jokes, and often he leaned back and smiled; once, he laughed out loud. The reporters stayed for an hour, twice their customary time, and he told them more than he had shared with the eminences of the cabinet and Congress. When he cited the suggestions by past attorneys general to name a new lower-court judge for every sitting septuagenarian, he volunteered to "end the suspense" as to their identities. The original recommendation had come from Woodrow Wilson's attorney general, none other than James McReynolds, now the most obstreperous of the president's nemeses on the Court. This touched off the merriest laughter yet.

Like any dramatist who understood what motivated men, the president sensed when a fact was most usefully withheld. In exceptional cases, he explained to his audience, judges might remain vigorous until an advanced age, but others who were unable to see their own infirmities "seem to be tenacious of the appearance of adequacy." Amid the laughter he noted that he was quoting "a very important judge" but would not furnish the name. "You will have to find out," he said, thereby guaranteeing that every newspaper would identify the author as the seventy-four-year-old chief justice, Charles Evans Hughes.

The president took pains to bury the lead, waiting until nearly the end to explain that his solution to judicial congestion included the appointment of a new jurist for any sitting judge older than seventy and a half and that this included the Supreme Court, which would be allowed as many as fifteen members—permanently. Only then did the reporters understand the magnitude of his proposal. A president who named six new justices to the nation's highest court would surely control it.

"And that is all the news," he finished blandly.

"Mr. President," said a reporter, "this question is for background, but is this intended to take care of cases where the appointee has lost the mental capacity to resign?"

The reply—"That is all"—was lost in the laughter.

"Thank you, Mr. President."

The reporters grabbed for the mimeographed documents and raced for their typewriters and telephones, to tell the world. The president went off to eat lunch with the newsreels' favorite, the young leader of the FBI, the up-and-coming J. Edgar Hoover.


YOUNG TOMMY CORCORAN, as the president's messenger, arrived at the Supreme Court building just before noon. The edifice that housed the third branch of the national government was believed to contain more marble than any public building in the world, counting its corridors, the black fireplace in every justice's office, and an exterior so white that on sunny days the guards wore tinted glasses. "The Ark of the Constitution," *American Mercury* had called it.

The shocking whiteness of the marble had helped to change the look of the national capital. Before the railroads, the cost to transport marble from the quarries to Washington, D.C., was exorbitant, and the city had mostly made do with local brick and sandstone. Not many decades had passed since Washington was a city of red, exuding a warmth and welcome— the Smithsonian castle on the Mall, the Renwick Gallery across from the

White House, the Pension Building, most of the homes on Capitol Hill and beyond. The construction of Union Station in 1908, with its Roman arches and Ionic columns, as the railroad's imposing entrance to a newly imperial city revived Washington as a city of white. This was the white of the White House, of the Capitol, of the Washington Monument, of the Senate office building, of the Lincoln Memorial—of the Supreme Court. Already on architects' drawing boards were a marble monument to Thomas Jefferson and another for housing Andrew Mellon's artwork on the Mall. Washington was becoming a cold, neoclassical city, as if to emulate the self-conscious grandeur of Greece and Rome.

Tommy Corcoran felt at home in the neoclassical Washington. He read Aeschylus in the original Greek and could recite his beloved Dante at length, even persuading the president to quote the Italian poet in accepting the Democratic nomination the summer before. Corcoran had come to Washington in early 1932, for a job at the Reconstruction Finance Corporation, but he probably would have left after three months had he not been dissuaded by the man he was about to see.

He was visiting the Court with the president's permission, intending (as he told an administration colleague) "to soften the blow." He followed along the marble corridors and into the justices' robing room, a rather plain facility furnished with nine gymnasium-style green lockers (without locks) and straight-backed chairs. He was looking for the justice known affectionately around the White House as "old Isaiah," and when he found Louis D. Brandeis, just before the Court convened, he delivered what he knew would be unwelcome news.

The physical contrast between the thirty-six-year-old Corcoran and the octogenarian Brandeis belonged to vaudeville. The short and pugnacious Irishman—James Cagney would be a natural for the role—gazed up at the tall, thin-faced Jew with delicate features, large soft eyes, a nimbus of wild whitish hair, and recently, a stoop to his walk. The two Harvard Law School graduates had known each other since Corcoran's first stint in Washington, during the High Court's 1926–27 term, and they had revered the same man, the late Oliver Wendell Holmes Jr.

Perhaps the greatest associate justice in the history of the Supreme Court, Holmes had been eighty-five years old when he hired Tommy Corcoran as his personal secretary, the equivalent of a law clerk. Corcoran was the latest in a procession of brilliant graduates of Harvard Law School whom Felix Frankfurter, a strenuously well-connected professor, dispatched to Holmes's chambers.* Quickly the young Rhode Islander had become more than a law clerk to Holmes. He read aloud to the old man—Dante's *Divine Comedy,* the entire Old Testament, all of Montaigne's essays, Greek poetry in ancient Greek. After he returned to Washington, he would stop by Holmes's house on I Street, near the White House, and read to him weekly; in 1935, he sat by his deathbed.

If Corcoran had been like a grandson to Holmes, Brandeis was like a precocious younger brother. "Holmes and Brandeis dissenting"—it became a refrain in the Court's opinions for fifteen years, until the ninety-year-old Holmes retired in 1932. The two justices, however, had never been of a single mind. Holmes believed, to an extreme, that legislatures might do whatever they wished on the people's behalf unless the Constitution expressly forbade it. His philosophical indifference to the substance of a legislature's wishes prompted his succession of dissents against a conservative majority that saw the devil's hand in progressive-minded laws, but it contrasted with Brandeis's passion about the policy outcome. Brandeis was inclined to decide first on his conclusion and then to find the legal arguments to fit. Almost invariably, though, they reached the same result, and the hopelessness of their opposition to the Court's conservative majority had bound them close. Every morning they had ridden to the Court together. Even after Holmes retired, they took walks in the late afternoon.

Tommy Corcoran and Louis Brandeis, beyond their shared devotion to Justice Holmes, had developed a friendship of their own. Brandeis had always enjoyed the company of youth. He trolled the law schools for the brightest students, though his wife's frail health had forced him to suspend his famous Monday afternoon teas attended by the bright young men and women drawn to the capital. (Each had gotten ten or fifteen minutes in the chair by the justice's side, until Alice Brandeis eased one out and beckoned the next one in.) Brandeis had impressed upon Corcoran, while Herbert Hoover was still in the White House, that it was his duty to remain in the government's service. They had been friends ever since, even as Tommy

---

*Another brilliant young man, named Alger Hiss, filled the post three years later.

the Cork—the president had bestowed the nickname—came to be considered the most accomplished of the ambitious and idealistic young men who filled the ranks of the New Deal. He had remained on the payroll of the Reconstruction Finance Corporation but performed whichever tasks—drafting a policy, writing a speech, twisting an arm—the president wanted him to do.

When Corcoran explained to his old friend what the president had proposed, their friendship mattered for naught. Neither did the justice's own disgust with the Court's conservative course. No man had a better claim than Brandeis to being "in a sense, the original New Dealer," as Robert Jackson, one of the newer New Dealers, believed. Before joining the Court, Louis Brandeis had been famed as "the people's lawyer," having spent decades fighting for the common man, and as a justice he had voted to uphold all but one of the New Deal laws.

But the imputation that any justice older than seventy was judicially unfit upset Brandeis—and hurt him. Though the president's real motivation centered on the Court's conservative decisions, the substance of its constitutional interpretation, Brandeis felt sure that the president's disingenuous emphasis on age was aimed at him. He thought it unfair, cruel, and worst of all, a shortcut—an attempt to hasten the customary workings of Father Time.

"Tell the president that he's gone too far this time," Brandeis told his young friend, "and that he's making a great mistake."

There was no time to dwell on it further. Chief Justice Hughes was a fiend about promptness, and at the stroke of noon, he nodded to a page in blue knickers and black cotton stockings, then pressed a buzzer that signaled the Court crier to announce: "The honorable, the chief justice and the associate justices of the Supreme Court of the United States."* Hughes was the first to pass between the wine-colored velvet curtains and into the courtroom. Willis Van Devanter led the line of associate justices, followed by Brandeis and the rest, in order of seniority. Each wore a black silk robe, tailored in Albany, which rustled like a petticoat when it swayed. They

---

*For twenty-three years, the Court crier had uttered the very same words, but because of his periodic dreams in which he recited "Little Jack Horner" or the Gettysburg Address, he kept them written in a loose-leaf notebook on the table before him.

constituted the oldest bench of justices—on average, seventy-one years old—that the Court had ever known. They stood behind their nine distinctive chairs as the Court crier proclaimed, "Oyez, oyez, oyez, all persons having business before the honorable, the Supreme Court of the United States are admonished to draw near and give their attention, for the Court is now sitting. God save the United States and this honorable Court." At the crack of a gavel, the justices took their seats, and the spectators in the pews did the same.

Hushed and dignified, the courtroom was almost a perfect cube, from its marble floor and walls to its high ceiling of Greek-patterned florets. Around the top of the walls, ringing the room, the marble friezes portrayed history's lawgivers—Hammurabi and Confucius, Moses and Muhammad, Charlemagne and Napoléon, John Marshall alone. The mahogany bench stretched majestically across the front; along each wall, four pillars of Italian marble gave off the warmest of hues, a creamy cappuccino veined in rose, gray, and blue. No place in Washington felt more solemn or serene.

The Court resumed the oral argument it had started the afternoon before, over the inequities in pay cuts for tenured teachers in a New Jersey town. As the lawyers argued, a page boy passed behind the bench and placed a copy of the president's message in front of every justice.

Virtually all of the time, Charles Evans Hughes played his role to perfection, handsome and magnificent in the center seat, utterly upright, never leaning to either side, as if he were marble himself. But now he fidgeted as he read the mimeographed pages on the bench. Justices Sutherland and Stone skimmed the document but betrayed no reaction, while Benjamin Cardozo read some and laid it back down. Owen Roberts thumbed through the pages and pored over one in particular. Pierce Butler leaned over to him and whispered, and both men chuckled.

At the rostrum facing the bench, the lawyer looked startled by the justices' inattention.


AS THEY EMERGED from the White House, the congressional leaders looked as glum as the grayish Treasury Building next door. "We were all so stunned we hardly spoke," the vice president recounted. Only in the taxi back to the Capitol did they feel free to speak. Hatton Sumners, the House judiciary chairman, was an old and foxy Texan who had supported the president's policies more often than he would have preferred. He had been alone among the Democratic congressional leaders in believing his ears about the president's intentions during the State of the Union address the previous month. Now he knew for certain what the president had meant.

"Boys," he announced to his colleagues, "here's where I cash in my chips."

They arrived at the Capitol too late to break the news. Upon entering the House of Representatives, the legislators had already noticed the radio microphones that had been hastily installed. As word spread, even though it was a Friday, the number of members on the floor grew from seventy-five to more than two hundred, half of the House.

At the White House, the president sat in Missy LeHand's office, adjacent to his, with his son Jimmy, Steve Early, and another aide. They listened over the radio at ten past noon as South Trimble began to read the message from the president. The clerk of the House was a former congressman, for three terms long ago, and he understood the tactics of politics. He had made sure of the legislators' attention by declining to distribute the mimeographed copies until he was done. As he droned on in his Kentucky mountain twang, he was interrupted twice with applause, and again at the end.

In the northern wing of the Capitol, in the Senate chamber, eighty-three of the ninety-six senators answered the quorum call, even without the allure of radio microphones. As the clerk read the president's message aloud, the senators followed along line by line on the mimeographed copies that were waiting at their desks. These were men—and one woman, Hattie Caraway of Arkansas, the first ever to serve in the Senate for more than a day—who took themselves seriously. The swarthy marble pillars across the front of the chamber and the vast oval blue-and-green skylight in the soaring ceiling—in a hailstorm, the senators could hear nothing else—were apt to remind them of the Senate's glorious past. The Founding Fathers had created the upper house, with its six-year terms, as the saucer in which the people's passions might cool. Alexis de Tocqueville, the Frenchman who had written *Democracy in America* a century before, admired the Senate's "eloquent advocates, distinguished generals, wise magistrates, and statesmen of note." Senators still occupied the compact mahogany desks with a *Webster* or a *Clay* scratched inside the drawer, even if they made little use anymore of the spittoons between every two desks. Time and again, the Senate had stood its ground against the president—"against the possibility of executive tyranny," as a historian wrote—and prevailed. Most recently, in 1919, its refusal to ratify the Treaty of Versailles and to consent to U.S. entry into the League of Nations had driven Woodrow Wilson, the uncompromising second-term president, into a grueling cross-country campaign that ended when he suffered a massive stroke.

Yet by 1937, the Senate's stature, and that of Congress, had fallen low. In part, the world had passed it by. The awful events within memory—a world war, the Depression—had demanded a decisiveness and a specialist's speed that was bound to favor the executive over a legislature that was sluggish by design. Still, the Senate bore considerable responsibility for its own decline. Letting the people directly elect the senators in place of the states' legendarily venal legislatures, starting in 1914, had not noticeably improved—or diminished—the quality. The news would soon break that the American Tobacco Company had paid fifteen senators $1,000 apiece to join Gary Cooper, Carole Lombard, and Cary Grant in endorsing Lucky Strikes (*U.S. Senator Reynolds says: "Luckies are considerate of my throat"*), but only three of them felt embarrassed enough to give the money back. The Senate's troubles were also institutional. Its meager staffs, the stingy salaries, and the proud antiquity of its parliamentary rules had left it vulnerable to a president who was truly determined and had the people behind him. The torrent of legislation from the Democrat in the White House, supported by a people in distress, had turned the lopsidedly Democratic Congress into little more than a rubber stamp, much as its Republican-run predecessors had acquiesced to the popular Republican presidents during the 1920s.

The clerk had barely finished his recitation when Joe Robinson jumped to his feet at the majority leader's desk in the front row, on the center aisle. This was no easy feat for the fifth-term senator from Arkansas, with his massive frame.

"I ask that the message of the president," he bellowed, "together with the letter of the attorney general, draft of a bill, and other accompanying papers be referred to the Committee on the Judiciary."

The majority leader could not be certain if the senators had grasped the meaning in the president's obfuscation. Just three weeks earlier, the president had proposed a reorganization of the entire executive branch, to create two new cabinet agencies, the Department of Social Welfare and the Department of Public Works, and to plant all of the independent regulatory commissions within the cabinet's—that is, the president's—purview; but Congress was balking at granting the president the additional authority. Word of the new proposal—and its new presidential authority—was already spreading among the anxious senators, and Joe Robinson was taking no chances on an impromptu debate.

"Without objection, it is so ordered," John Nance Garner decreed. The vice president, in the presiding officer's chair, was exercising his sole constitutional power, other than voting to break a Senate tie. A tie seemed improbable in a Senate that now included so many Democrats—seventy-six—after the landslide election that thirteen of the party's junior senators were consigned to desks in the back two rows on the Republican side of the aisle, along with the two Minnesotans in the Farmer-Labor Party. The sixteen Republicans were the party's fewest since before Lincoln took office.

The Senate was rich in procedures for sidestepping whatever it wished to ignore, and Garner took refuge in the routine. That day, he added a senator from Massachusetts to a special committee investigating the production and marketing of wool; delivered the pleas from the legislatures in Montana (to furnish seed grain for needy farmers), in Minnesota (to allot money to needy Indians), and in Iowa (to name a battleship the USS *Iowa*); and presented the interior secretary's drafts of legislation to pay a former superintendent of the Zuni Indians and to divide up the Mission Tribe's California lands into individual parcels.

As soon as he could, Garner slipped out of the high-backed chair, left the rostrum, and ducked into the Democratic cloakroom. A canny old pol, "Cactus Jack" was short and sturdy, with shaggy white eyebrows and startlingly blue eyes at a slant, and had earned his ruddy face both in the rugged hills of southwestern Texas and indoors, with a glass in his fist. As the House Speaker, he had hosted the late-afternoon "Board of Education," a gathering of the chamber's leaders who charted its course with tumblers of whiskey in hand—"striking a blow for liberty," Garner liked to say. He had been conscientious in managing the House and had run for president in 1932, seriously enough for Roosevelt to trade the vice presidency for his support and thereby break a stalemate and assure Roosevelt the two-thirds vote he needed to secure the nomination. Garner had never wanted the job as vice president—he had first accepted it out of party obligation and presumably the second time with the hope of succeeding the incumbent. Yet he had become one of the most influential vice presidents in history, not only on Capitol Hill, but also, on occasion, with the president. His shift in duties—from primacy in the House to subservience in the White House—had never cured his habit of saying what he thought, even to the man he now addressed as "Boss."

The cloakroom stretched behind the Senate chamber like a Pullman car, with a rounded ceiling and a disarray of leather seats. No one exerted more influence over the upper chamber than Garner, the longtime denizen of the House. As an assistant to the attorney general watched from across the room, the vice president huddled in conversation with several senators and jabbed one hand thumb-down toward the floor. Then, with his other hand, he held his nose.

When the story reached the president, he smiled.

# CHAPTER TWO

# Laissez-faire

HOW SIMPLE — HOW SAFE — the 1920s had seemed, especially in retrospect. The senseless slaughter of the Great War, fought for reasons that no one could clearly recall, begat a normalcy that spiraled into self-indulgence. And why not? Precious few Americans knew a flapper or guzzled bathtub gin, but every dot on the map had a speakeasy, for the pleasure of its adventurous citizens and the profit of Al Capone and his ilk. The material pleasures of life vaulted ahead—telephones, refrigerators, rayon, Chaplin in the movies, cigarettes, automobiles. In 1927, Henry Ford enthralled the nation into a state of suspense when he unveiled the Model A, as competition for the slicker Chevrolet, by splashing five days of advertising across two *thousand* daily newspapers. Americans adored their possessions and gushed over their heroes—plucky Charles Lindbergh, the fast-living Babe Ruth. It was the Age of Gatsby, of conspicuous consumption, of unembarrassed wealth. Insouciance was admired; life was to be lived.

That was before the stock market crashed in 1929 and the economic depression spread over the globe. Everywhere, not only in America, there was unrest. In India, a man in a loincloth was ready to give up the path of nonresistance, though not of nonviolence, and launch an active campaign against British colonial rule. A new Japanese cabinet that appeared to be moderate failed to conceal the triumph of the imperialists who coveted China. The Italian Army was about to capture and drag Haile Selassie's son-in-law before a firing squad to end the last resistance to the occupation of Ethiopia. In Moscow, the execution of thirteen Trotskyists, after their leader had fled to Mexico, climaxed Stalin's second show trial. In Spain,

Generalissimo Franco's artillery unleashed the heaviest bombardment of Madrid since his siege had begun. In Paris, food workers were threatening a general strike. In Berlin, Hitler declared to the impotent parliament that the Nazis' "beautiful democracy" would last a thousand years, even as he repudiated Germany's willingness to accept blame in the Treaty of Versailles, which had ended the catastrophic Great War.

"Each year, since Versailles, we have moved farther from peace," a columnist bewailed.

The United States, though protected by oceans, was hardly immune. Seventy percent of Americans now believed it had been a mistake to enter the world war, and even more of them told pollsters they expected another. In country after country, the economic upheavals and the social despair had driven democracy out. The United States had so far been spared. Huey Long was dead, along with his iron grip on Louisiana, but the populist anger that he reflected lived on. Father Coughlin, the Radio Priest, who reached as many as forty million Americans, had turned against President Roosevelt and the New Deal (for "leaning toward international socialism or sovietism") while praising Hitler and Mussolini. In the national capital, a retired marine general with an impeccable record had already testified to Congress in 1933 of a Wall Street plot to wage a military coup that would have reduced FDR, at best, to a figurehead.

American society seemed in upheaval, often out of control. Sit-down strikes had erupted first in Akron in the spring of 1936 and then burst upon the national scene in December, when the unionized workers at almost a score of General Motors factories, mainly in Michigan, sat down at their assembly lines and, week after week, refused to leave. The workers at a factory in Flint slung rocks, bottles, and door hinges, drawing the tear gas and pistols of the police; only by the grace of a workingman's God was nobody killed. The violation of property horrified anyone who believed in laissez-faire.

The nation seemed to be slipping away from stability, and not only along the barricades between capital and labor. The society's moral order was under assault. Syphilis was more prevalent than tuberculosis and twice as common as scarlet fever. Parent and Teacher Associations were urged to worry about marijuana in the schools, because of its presumed link to sex crimes. (*Reefer Madness*, a film shot by a church group in 1936, connected the drug to rape, murder, and suicide.) Half of the white women in America practiced birth control, and a clear majority of Americans told pollsters that prostitution ought to be legalized as a means of controlling venereal disease. But any public easing of morals provoked a reaction. The sexually suggestive movies that had made Mae West the highest-paid American in 1934, other than William Randolph Hearst, spurred Hollywood to self-censorship, with a production code that banned not only prurience from the movies but also anything that fostered disrespect for the law. In Washington, at a policewoman's behest, the Civic Theater's production of *Lysistrata*, the antiwar comedy of ancient Greece, deleted "brothel," "pregnant," and "rape" from the script and softened a scene centered on a mattress. The 2,348-year-old play had been banned in Los Angeles.

The end of Prohibition had done little to stanch the gangland slayings and the surges of crime. The FBI had shot John Dillinger to death and then Pretty Boy Floyd; G-men captured bank robbers and racketeers with an eye for publicity; and in the spring of 1936, after J. Edgar Hoover had personally arrested Alvin Karpis in New Orleans (though by Karpis's account, other G-men had seized him first), the FBI director and his young agency became household names. Nearly a year after Bruno Hauptmann's execution for the abduction and murder of Charles Lindbergh's baby son, his ashes remained at a crematorium in Queens, even as kidnapping had become popular as a get-rich-quick crime. "Bank-robbing ain't the soft racket it used to be," a crook in Brooklyn admitted before he was sent to the new federal prison on Alcatraz. The latest kidnapping, of a prominent surgeon's ten-year-old son in Tacoma, Washington, had ended in the boy's funeral. Hoover sent a pillow of gardenias and roses.

The Coolidge prosperity had fueled the decade's bull market, but nearly seven years of sustained prosperity had masked the underlying deficiencies of an economy in optimism's thrall—the skewed distribution of wealth, the absence of regulation, a structure of banking and of corporate holding companies that made it easy for trouble to spread, the desperate years for farmers unable to buy what the factories produced, the advice of economists that invariably made everything worse. Confidence had fed on itself, and as hemlines rose with the stock market, anyone with a work ethic could climb from poverty to riches. The pushcart peddlers on the East Side of Manhattan pitched in to buy a share of stock in General

Motors and kept a close eye on the listings. Men of business saw themselves, journalist Frederick Lewis Allen recounted, "as men of vision with eyes steadfastly fixed on the long future." The business of America was business—this was the theology as stated by Calvin Coolidge, who likened a factory to a temple—and the nation's secular faith was laissez-faire.

Laissez-faire. The word was French and its philosopher-king was a Scotsman, but no nation had ever believed in it as ardently as America. Adam Smith published *Wealth of Nations* the same year that America achieved its independence. What else was the Revolution—indeed, the invention of America—than a casting off of government's heavy hand? The principle that the government ought to leave the marketplace alone, that the actions of countless buyers and sellers served as an "invisible hand" that allowed the market to regulate itself, was a natural fit for a young and energetic nation. It suited the pioneer experience of the hardy individuals who had fought their way west, as well as the self-selected, entrepreneurial immigrants, desperate or brave, who arrived on American shores. Laissez-faire reflected America's faith in the individual, in the right of anyone to pursue happiness, to make something of oneself, applying talent and hard work.

It remained an article of faith even as the realities of the society evolved. The invisible hand was intended for a society of yeomanry, like the one in Thomas Jefferson's mind's eye, in which each of the farmers owned some land and exercised a certain leverage in the marketplace. But if America had ever truly been as Jefferson imagined, it was not to last. In the wake of the Civil War, as the railroads crossed the nation, the boom in industry and commerce—oil, steel, coal—gave birth to the Gilded Age, the era of robber barons and their Fifth Avenue mansions. Along the Hudson River, the Vanderbilt mansion, built with the railroad fortune, made the Roosevelt family's home two miles south look like a bungalow. Industrialization stretched the distinction between rich and poor. Among the men of position, the concept of "survival of the fittest," philosopher Herbert Spencer's application of Darwin's theory of evolution to the organism of society, counted as a self-evident truth. To the wealthy, wealth defined the measure of a man.

Some capitalists proved fitter than others, and as their wealth became increasingly unequal, so did their leverage in the marketplace, which made them richer still. The railroads took advantage of their monopoly to gouge the farmers who had no alternative in moving their crops and live-stock to market. The industrial trusts of the 1890s only exacerbated the disparities in power over an economy that was becoming truly national in scope. The mismatch in economic might between factory owners and workers kept wages low and provoked a succession of strikes that too often ended with nightsticks or gunshots. The excesses of laissez-faire, climaxed by a run on the nation's supply of gold, brought on the Panic of 1893, the worst economic depression the nation had seen yet. This only exacerbated the powerlessness of workers and farmers and incited successive move-ments for reform.

The prosperity of the 1920s had concealed the distance that economic realities had drifted from Adam Smith's image of capitalism. The decade saw a torrent of corporate mergers, so that by 1929, two hundred corpora-tions controlled nearly half of the nation's industrial wealth. "Clearly a major cause of the unstable foundation beneath the prosperity decade," a historian would write, "was the dichotomy between the reality of massive concentration in American business and the classical economic model upon which policy was still being based."

After the economy collapsed, President Hoover labeled the downturn a "depression," thinking that it sounded more soothing than "crisis" or "panic," the epithets preferred in the past. By whatever name, the farmers had been trapped in it for years, throughout the 1920s, the result of heavy debt and the loss of foreign markets because of overproduction worldwide. Between 1929 and 1933, farm prices tumbled further, by half or more, to their lowest level since the Civil War. (A bushel of wheat that sold for al-most three dollars in 1920 went for thirty cents in 1932.) The farmers' cash income shrank by more than two thirds, causing bankruptcy, foreclosures, and eruptions of violence. The four best-selling novels of the 1930s told stories about surviving on the land. Of every nine Americans, four of them still lived in the countryside, and FDR blamed their lack of purchasing power for funneling the stock market crash into a full-fledged Depression.

A quarter of America's workforce, nearly thirteen million Ameri-cans, were out of work. Between 1929 and 1933, the gross national prod-uct plunged by half, and the total business investment by seven eighths. Technology took the place of workers—telephones with dials that put two thirds of the operators out of work, or the talkies, which cost musicians their jobs. Cigarette manufacturers and shoemakers, suppliers of the necessities of hard times, lost only a little of their business, but the markets for discretionary items crumbled. Automobile production fell by two thirds and housing construction by four fifths, which devastated the demand for workers in steel, coal, lumber, bricklaying, and plumbing.

The statistics only started to depict the suffering. "It was simply a gut issue then: eating or not eating, living or not living," the son of a coal miner recalled. The number of weddings declined by a fifth. Fathers who lost their jobs also lost their self-respect in front of their children. Faith in the future was gone. The promise of America lay in ashes, a historian noted, leaving "the human wreckage of a century of pell-mell buccaneering, no-holds-barred, free-market industrial and agricultural capitalism."

Worse than the material scarcity, perhaps, was the deadening of the spirit. When Mrs. Roosevelt's close friend Lorena Hickok traveled to her native North Dakota in the fall of 1933, she mourned for "the terrible, crushing drabness of life." No matter how hard the breadwinners tried, and through no fault of their own, their children might yet go to bed hungry. A man was no longer the master of his fate. As the hopelessness stretched from months into years, it was natural for desperation to set in. In some quarters, the election of 1932 was considered the nation's last chance to salvage its system of capitalism—and of democracy—by peaceful means.

FRANKLIN DELANO ROOSEVELT'S ancestors had arrived on American shores more than a century before a wilderness became a nation. The Delanos, the family of his mother, Sara, claimed to be descended from at least seven passengers on the *Mayflower* and linked themselves later to the Astors. The first Roosevelt—van Rozenvelt—had left Holland in the mid-1600s, and his son was elected to public office, as an alderman in New York City, in 1700. Two of the politician's sons, a merchant and a real estate investor, respectively, sired the two branches of the family. The merchant's descendants were drawn to Long Island, with their country homes at Oyster Bay, while the landowner's heirs persisted in buying land toward the north, as gentleman farmers along the Hudson River. By 1866, this included an estate of 110 acres with a rickety seventeen-room house in Hyde Park, acquired by James Roosevelt, Franklin's father, who spent his career managing his inheritance and otherwise living a life of ease. The Roosevelt family occasionally crept within sight of momentous events (Franklin's great-great-grandfather had cofounded the Bank of New York with Alexander Hamilton), but not until the turn of the twentieth century, in its sixth generation in America, did anyone in either branch make much of a mark.

Mindful of the family's blue blood, Sam Rosenman struggled over the years to understand the source of Franklin D. Roosevelt's feeling for the common man; he asked friends, family, and Franklin himself but never found a satisfying answer. "The reason was born," Rosenman concluded, "when he was born: it was in the heart and soul of the man, in his love of people, his own sense of social justice, his hatred of greed and of exploitation of the weak, his contempt for the bully."

Part of it was undoubtedly a matter of noblesse oblige, the penchant by the later generations of well-established families to feel a sympathy, if rarely an empathy, for the low-born. It was a trait that his mother, Sara, had bequeathed. At Groton, the teenage Franklin fell under the spell of the Reverend Endicott Peabody, the headmaster, a crusader for a muscular Christianity, who preached to the sons of the wealthy that the privileged must serve. But maybe more than anything, both Franklin and Eleanor had learned what it was to suffer. Eleanor, a member of the family's Oyster Bay branch, had endured a lonely girlhood, as the daughter of a chaotic marriage, an orphan by age ten. Apt to regard herself as the ugly duckling, she aspired to usefulness as the surest path to joy. Franklin's empathy for the victims of fate blossomed on a summer's afternoon in 1921, at his family's retreat on Campobello Island, the last time he would ever walk unaided. Frances Perkins, who had worked with him since his days as governor, observed, "Having been to the depths of trouble, he understood the problems of people in trouble." But that explained only so much. Even while he could walk he had been a liberal, in favor of helping people who could not help themselves. "The seed," as Rosenman insisted, "was there long before."

Later it was suggested that FDR "saw the New Deal as applied Christianity." He first suggested that government had a "social duty" to use its resources to help the unfortunate as the governor of New York, in a speech to the legislature in 1931. The following summer, in accepting the Democratic nomination for the presidency, he pledged himself and his party "to a new deal for the American people." His approach to government acquired a name, though precisely what it encompassed was harder to say.

During the winter of 1932–33, as the economy sank lower still, the nation waited for four long, dark months until the president-elect entered the White House.* Three thousand "hunger marchers" arrived in the capital, and as many as a hundred thousand Washingtonians lined the streets on their lunch hour to watch as a red-clad band playing the *Internationale* led them to the Capitol, where they delivered petitions calling for the enactment of unemployment insurance. They followed the Bonus Army, the war veterans who had set up camp in Washington the summer before to demand the bonuses that Congress had long promised but never paid, and the hunger marchers had just as little success.

"You just hand me your petition—you needn't make any speech," the outgoing vice president, Charles Curtis, snapped. "I have only a few minutes' time."

AS THE PRESIDENT-ELECT, Roosevelt had ignored his predecessor's plea for help in containing the runs on beleaguered banks, preferring to let the problem fester. Five thousand banks had failed between the crash and his inauguration, and on the first weekday of his presidency, when he declared a bank "holiday"—with its festive undertone—the public was enthralled. His decisiveness, along with his willingness to confer with congressional leaders (and even the nation's governors, in Washington for the inauguration), evoked a surge in support. The House of Representatives took thirty-eight minutes to pass the new president's banking legislation, which few of the members had seen, allowing the banks to reopen once properly licensed and empowering the treasury secretary to avert the hoarding of gold; less than eight hours after the bill was introduced, it was

---

*During the interregnum, enough states ratified a constitutional amendment to move subsequent inaugurals from March 4 to January 20.

signed into law. Once the banks felt safe again, the stock market registered the greatest one-day leap in its history.

Thus began the famed first hundred days of his presidency, perhaps the most dramatic spell in the nation's capital since the British burned the White House and the Capitol in 1814. Between March 9, 1933, when the session was convened, and the early hours of June 16, when it adjourned, Congress received fifteen legislative messages from the president and passed fifteen consequential laws. The proliferation of alphabetical agencies would forever change the face of the national government and of the city that was its home.

Early in the New Deal, a philosophical schism emerged over competing approaches that an activist government could pursue. Some of the president's advisers adhered to a Jeffersonian vision, long identified with Louis Brandeis, in which bigness was considered a problem in itself, whether in business, in labor unions, or in government. The government, they believed, ought to use the antitrust laws to assure that power was decentralized, dispersed across society, and that decisions were left as often as possible in individuals' hands. Harder-headed New Dealers found this easy to mock—"if America could once more become a nation of small proprietors, of corner grocers and smithies under spreading chestnut trees," one of them said, "we should have solved the problems of American life." They saw a genuinely national economy and believed that the intensity of society's problems argued for a centralized, purposefully managed response.

The president himself held no abstract or consistent—or even particularly coherent—view of how to proceed. Asked about his political philosophy, he replied, "Philosophy? Philosophy? I am a Christian and a Democrat—that's all." He held a single, central idea: that the government ought to help the people in distress. He believed in relying on managed capitalism, not on collectivism, to further the general welfare, but beyond that, he cared little about how it was done. George Creel, a prominent journalist who had the president's ear, interviewed him after the 1936 election and wrote in *Collier's*, "The whole of his first term was an open rebellion against discredited dogmas and moldy formulas." Ideology bored him, and he reveled in inconsistency. His mind, a biographer judged, "was open to almost any idea and absolutely committed to almost none." Apt to veer back and forth, in hopes of keeping his opponents guessing, he likened himself to a quarterback who could not possibly know until he ran the next play which play should follow. He was willing to try whatever seemed likely to succeed. And whatever worked, he could feel certain, the public would like. In a democracy, little else counted. People who had suffered on their own for years at last had someone on their side. Soon he would be loved by untold millions as few presidents are ever loved, and for far longer.

Having rescued the banking system, FDR next addressed the plight of the farmers. To Roosevelt, this was a matter of sentiment as well as of economics. He had known farmers as his neighbors all his life, and during his weeks and months in Warm Springs, Georgia, as he struggled to surmount his paralysis, he drove all over the countryside in his automobile fitted with hand controls and learned firsthand about the miseries of the subsistence farmer. Far from bringing an equilibrium to agricultural markets, laissez-faire had made many lives worse. If the price of cotton or corn or hogs started to drop because of an oversupply, individual farmers were naturally inclined to bolster their income by producing more—on more acreage, spraying more fertilizers, using a tractor—but this depressed prices even further. The desire for self-improvement that was presumed to drive Adam Smith's invisible hand had only served to send the imbalance between supply and demand into a tailspin.

The Roosevelt administration's solution to this quandary was the Agricultural Adjustment Act (AAA), which concocted a Rube Goldberg mechanism that was meant to raise the prices of crops and livestock by inducing a scarcity. Twice during the 1920s, Congress had passed legislation to provide subsidies to farmers in distress, but both times it was killed by President Coolidge's veto. Roosevelt's latest apparatus imposed a tax on cotton mills, beef packagers, and other processors of whatever the farmers produced, and the revenue was paid to the farmers, who in turn agreed to leave their acreage fallow and to limit their livestock. Farmers had always relied on their own strong backs and on the caprices of nature for success or failure, and the notion of a government-arranged bailout was startling indeed. Now that government had taken the responsibility for the prices of what farmers produced, a part of laissez-faire had died.

The craziest thing about the AAA scheme was that it worked. More than three million farmers signed contracts with the government, which paid them more than $1 billion in two and a half years to perform less of their life's work. Remarkably, the prices of farm goods shot up, saving many of the farmers from bankruptcy. Yet for the public, indelible images remained: of the plowing under of ten million acres of cotton and the slaughter of six million piglets and two hundred thousand sows. In every city, and even on farms, where Americans were going hungry and dressing in rags, it was obvious that the world had stopped making sense.

The AAA was the first of the truly New Deal laws proposed to Congress by a president who had promised during his campaign to pursue "bold, persistent experimentation." Some of the new programs were intended simply to put the jobless back to work, though in innovative ways, such as the Civilian Conservation Corps (CCC), FDR's own idea. The CCC ultimately hired three million young men for $1 a day in almost twenty-five hundred camps, planting trees, digging reservoirs, and otherwise conserving nature. This put money in their pockets and in those of their families, for they were required to send most of it home. It also supplied the young city dwellers with a breath of pure air, while reforesting the land, as Roosevelt himself had done on his family's fifteen hundred acres in Hyde Park.

Even more breathtaking, in its conception and its reach, was the Tennessee Valley Authority (TVA). The president had long believed in publicly owned electricity, and he adopted the Progressives' long-held idea of having the federal government operate a power plant at Muscle Shoals, in northern Alabama. He then expanded it to encompass the proponents' fondest hopes, by including the entire Tennessee Valley. Its purpose went beyond introducing lights, radios, refrigeration, and irrigation to help lift the power-starved region out of its ingrained poverty. It was also to serve as a yardstick to measure—and thereby constrain—the price of electricity that the privately owned utilities generated. Asked to describe the political philosophy behind the TVA, the president replied, "It's neither fish nor fowl but whatever it is, it will taste awfully good to the people of the Tennessee Valley."

In those first hundred days, an ambitious president and a willing Congress created agencies that would become familiar parts of Washington's life: the Securities and Exchange Commission, intended to keep corporations sufficiently honest for wary investors to trust their dollars; the Federal

Deposit Insurance Corporation, which protected banks by guaranteeing depositors against the loss of their funds; and the Farm Credit Administration, to handle the government's loans to flailing farmers.

The least imaginative venture of the hundred days also turned out to be the least effective. The Federal Emergency Relief Act funneled money to the state governments to be redistributed to the unemployed and their dependents, in the hope of salvaging lives and goading consumption. Its $500 million in federal money, however, barely made a dent in the problem of the millions of unemployed, and the humiliations of its means test and the local administrators' contempt undermined any psychological benefit. Equally straightforward as a means of helping the jobless, and showing greater results, was the Public Works Administration (PWA). FDR was wary about a program that turned federal dollars into concrete and jobs, because he suspected that many of the projects had little merit on their own. But he acceded to the political pressure, and billions of dollars were spent, with consequences as widespread—and as beneficial—as the Grand Coulee and other huge dams, the Florida causeway to Key West, and New York City's Triborough Bridge. Later the PWA was overshadowed by the far more ambitious Works Progress Administration (WPA), which built thousands upon thousands of schools, courthouses, city halls, libraries, airports, parks, roadways, and sewers in almost every county coast to coast, an infrastructure that would last for generations.

In the wee hours of the morning on June 16, 1933, on the hundredth day since the Seventy-third Congress had convened, came the final act of the New Deal's opening days. The National Industrial Recovery Act had been hastily drafted as a countermeasure to deter something more radical, the proposal by Senator Hugo Black of Alabama to limit the workweek to thirty hours. As the president signed the bill just before noon the same day, he extolled "the most important and far-reaching legislation ever enacted by the American Congress." He was exaggerating no more than any ambitious president would.

The NRA, as it came to be known, for the National Recovery Administration that it created, was meant to increase workers' wages, and thus their purchasing power, and to spread the work by shortening the hours. Its mechanism was the government-sanctioned cartel. In each industry, a trade group that spoke for management would negotiate with labor's representatives and draw up an "industrial code," which set minimum wages, maximum hours, and production quotas once the president approved. In industries such as oil and coal, where cutthroat competition had wreaked havoc, it could also set acceptable prices—the antitrust laws be damned. More than seven hundred industries joined in, extending even to the burlesque shows in the nation's capital, and the foray into a managed economy succeeded, to an extent. It added roughly two million workers to the nation's payrolls, raised wages, and delivered a fleeting sense of national unity. The NRA's emblem, the Blue Eagle, appeared in countless store windows, as an indication of a commitment to the common good. The NRA's impact, however, proved more problematic, for prices rose faster than wages, and big companies were given license to dominate the small. The image that the NRA inspired was less that of the Three Musketeers—one for all and all for one—than of Mussolini's corporate state, run by syndicates of owners and workers, "heaving toward some sort of national control," as a writer in *Harper's* fretted.

The AAA, as the program developed, imposed a similarly monopolistic effect, favoring the corporate farmers, the recipients of the biggest payments, over the family farmers struggling to survive. Across the South, the AAA made the most vulnerable farmers' plight all the worse; to gain subsidies, many landowners cut back on production by driving landless sharecroppers off their land. Again and again, the New Dealers of a Jeffersonian bent, the admirers of Brandeis, found themselves shunted aside. The conflict, of historic dimensions, pitted a competitive economy that reflected the simple individualism of the past against the national economy of the present and the future. Beyond human scale, immense corporations faced the national labor unions, with a bureaucratic government as the referee.

Or so the president had decreed, as had a compliant Congress. But this left one branch of the government yet to be convinced. The heavier hand of government, meant to rescue a nation in distress, relied on a broader interpretation of the Constitution—in particular, of the clause that granted Congress the power to regulate commerce between the states—than the Supreme Court had been willing to concede for nearly four decades.

# CHAPTER THREE

# The Third Branch

THE MEN WHO wrote the U.S. Constitution in 1787 designed the judiciary as the weakest branch of the federal government. They consigned it to Article III of the national blueprint, behind the legislative and the executive branches, for it was presumed to exert its legal judgment and nothing more. The Supreme Court "has no influence over either the sword or the purse," Alexander Hamilton noted in the *Federalist Papers*. Nor had it any troops to enforce its decrees or, indeed, power beyond its moral suasion to compel recalcitrants and nullifiers to obey. The first chief justice, John Jay, served as a special ambassador to England without relinquishing his judicial post, and he ran twice for the governorship of New York before he won and stepped down from the Court. (Later, he declined reappointment.) Small wonder that Pierre L'Enfant had not bothered to specify a location for the Supreme Court in the world's first custom-designed capital.

Yet the Founding Fathers saw the judiciary as vital to the success of a workable democracy. Because no other institution of government remained so distant from the people's electoral reach, only the judiciary could prevent the president and Congress from aspiring to a dictatorship on the people's behalf—or on their own. "An impenetrable bulwark against every assumption of power in the legislative or executive," the Father of the Constitution, James Madison, described the High Court.

A bulwark, that is, against the people.

As men of property and education, the Founding Fathers had taken pains to protect their liberty and their wealth from the depredations of the masses. It was the people's passion they feared, should it sweep through the body politic, whether fueled by suffering, envy, greed, or patriotism. The Founding Fathers had thrown off a tyranny and had no stomach for another, and they sought to prevent any one person or interest or even a democratic majority from exercising untrammeled control. They designed a government of checks and balances, one that fragmented power not only between the states and the federal government but also among the three branches of government, so that no single mortal or group could wield too much of it. The Supreme Court was to act as a check on the power of the popularly elected officials to intrude on the rights of citizens. "The peace, the prosperity and the very existence of the Union are placed in the hands of the Judges"—so concluded Alexis de Tocqueville, among his observations of America in the 1830s. "Without their active cooperation, the Constitution would be a dead letter."

Just how powerful an institution the Supreme Court should become had been a matter of contention from the first. During George Washington's presidency, the belligerency between Alexander Hamilton and Thomas Jefferson—respectively, the treasury secretary and the secretary of state—over the proper scope of the national government extended to the reach of the Supreme Court. Hamilton suggested that the justices wear white powdered wigs, but the only justice who put one on found boys hooting at him in the street. The very idea of it horrified Jefferson, who saw an august judiciary as an obstacle to the majority's will.

Jefferson's fear of the Court became a reality after he was elected as the nation's third president. The departing president, John Adams, was a Federalist who disagreed with Jefferson on the fundamentals of government and politics. To replace the chief justice, who had resigned because of ill health, Adams unexpectedly named his secretary of state, and the lame-duck Senate hurriedly confirmed him. A second cousin of Jefferson but a political ally of Adams, John Marshall believed in the Federalist goals of a stronger national government and an independent judiciary. Unwilling to wear a wig, he was nonetheless ambitious in his vision of the Court. In 1803, in the historic case of *Marbury v. Madison*, he established the Court's grandest power, one that the Constitution had never made clear, the right of judicial review. From then on, the Supreme Court could strike down any law that Congress had passed and the president had signed if somebody challenged it in court and a majority of the justices determined that it conflicted with the Constitution.

For most of the Court's first century, however, the judiciary was nothing close to an equal branch of the government. After *Marbury v.*

*Madison*, fifty-four years passed before the Court struck down another law as unconstitutional, in the *Dred Scott* case, thereby protecting slavery and hastening the outbreak of the Civil War. All the while, the Court's quarters shifted from one borrowed home to another, all of them inside the Capitol (except for the five years after the British burned Washington). From a small basement room beneath the House chamber, to a courtroom below the Senate, and then to the Senate's own abandoned chamber, the Court worked under the roof of the government's preeminent branch. Its prestige slipped further after the Civil War, when it swiftly reversed itself in a landmark case, on allowing greenbacks to be used as legal tender, shortly after President Grant named two new justices—"a serious mistake," according to a future chief justice, Charles Evans Hughes.

The tumult of the Industrial Revolution and the suffering it caused throughout the lower reaches of society ultimately pushed the Supreme Court to the fore. Bloody battles erupted between capital and labor, which the forces of capital ordinarily won, occasionally tempting legislators, state or federal, to step in and regulate business on the workers'—and voters'—behalf. The judiciary could not help but become involved.

The unlikely mechanism of the Court's ascendancy was the Fourteenth Amendment to the Constitution. Passed in the wake of the Civil War, it had assured the freed slaves that no state could "deprive any person of life, liberty, or property, without due process of law." In 1873, the Supreme Court affirmed that the Fourteenth Amendment was meant to apply to the freed slaves and to nobody else, but as was so often the case, the constitutional future was revealed in a justice's seminal dissent. Stephen J. Field of California had been Lincoln's politically adroit choice for the Court ten years before, as an inducement to keep the western states contentedly within the Union. A onetime seeker for gold, a man of obstinate and creative opinions, Field saw something in the Fourteenth Amendment that had nothing to do with slaves—indeed, that eventually worked to the former slaves' disadvantage. Starting in 1886, in the case of a railroad trying to avoid a property tax, the Court regarded a corporation as a "person," in the eyes of the law, and therefore deserving of the Fourteenth Amendment's protections. In a succession of dissents as the Gilded Age rolled on, Field interpreted the amendment's guarantee of due process as one that applied not only to the fairness of the legal procedure but also to the substance of the results. The notion that emerged—called "substantive due process," in legal shorthand—regarded any attempt by government to restrain a corporation's treatment of its employees or customers as equivalent to the taking of private property without a judicial proceeding.

Not until after Stephen Field had left the bench in 1897, already senile—he insisted on staying until he bested John Marshall's record of more than thirty-four years on the Court—did a majority of justices accept his interpretation. "Liberty of contract"—this was the truth the Court discerned in the Fourteenth Amendment—was becoming the law of the land. By 1905, in the famous *Lochner* case, the Court ruled on a five-to-four vote that the State of New York had no right to force a bakery owner in Rochester to limit his workers to sixty hours a week because it intruded on "the freedom of master and employee to contract with each other," as if both sides had the same power to bargain.

Thus began the so-called *Lochner* era of laissez-faire jurisprudence, in which it was no longer considered the proper business of government to tell business what to do unless it involved a state's narrowly defined "police power" to assure its citizens' safety and health. The Court relied on more than its contortion of the Fourteenth Amendment to achieve such an end. It had decided as early as 1873, in the so-called *Slaughterhouse* cases, that the Fourteenth Amendment's guarantee of "equal protection of the laws" offered no protection at all against a monopoly or, as of 1896, against a black man's separate but equal seating in a railroad car. In the sugar trust case of 1895, eight of the nine justices had decreed that a sugar refinery was not, in itself, involved in interstate commerce, even if the sugar was to be sold in another state. Gone was John Marshall's expansive view of Congress's authority over commerce "among the several States." Instead, the Court ruled, because a factory or a mine or a farm was confined to a single place, it was only "indirectly" involved in interstate commerce, and therefore its behavior lay beyond Congress's regulatory authority. Only when a product was being transported from one state to another did it come within Washington's reach.

The Supreme Court was only embodying the ethos of the age, reflecting what the body politic seemed to want. Decades of Republican presidents who believed in laissez-faire had assured this by appointing justices who accepted the principles of capitalism as their own. They obeyed the wisdom that Mr. Dooley, as the humorist Finley Peter Dunne named his fictional bartender-philosopher, proffered after the justices' sugar trust

decision and before their dictum in *Lochner*, that "th' Supreme Court follows th' illiction returns."

The Court made itself into the champion—indeed, the protector—of
laissez-faire. The justices' approach to the Constitution was more than a
passive matter of interpretation. They saw in the Constitution what they
wanted to see. They believed in a world in which property was sacrosanct,
economic regulation was taboo, and the survival of the fittest—social
Darwinism—was a nation's natural route to prosperity and power. In the
1880s and 1890s, federal judges began to overturn hundreds of state laws,
those that controlled railroad rates and the like, and by century's end the
High Court was doing the same. With pride of purpose, the justices struck
down the laws they did not like—the income tax in 1895, the child labor
law in 1913, a minimum wage for women in 1923. During its first seventy
years in existence, the Supreme Court had deemed only two congressional
statutes to be unconstitutional, but in its next seventy years it struck down
fifty-eight. Once the twentieth century began, as a Court historian recounted, "judicial *review* became judicial *supremacy*."

Having openly taken sides, the Court laid the legal foundations that
established laissez-faire as the nation's guiding doctrine—treating Adam
Smith's economic views, a later justice would write, "as though the Framers
had enshrined them in the Constitution." Even before he became the chief
justice in 1921, William Howard Taft praised the Court as "the bulwark to
enforce the guaranty that no man shall be deprived of his property without
due process of law." On the bench, Taft and his majority of conservatives
treated property rights as beyond the reach of a democracy's experimentation. And their faith was amply rewarded, as the triumph of laissez-faire
fueled the economic boom of the 1920s. By 1937, however, the boom was a
painful memory, while the Court remained the "super-legislature" that Justice Brandeis had decried in 1924. Brandeis had been appointed by the era's
lone Democratic president, Woodrow Wilson; Holmes, by the current president's progressive cousin. Otherwise, the latest president Roosevelt had
good reason to conclude that the Supreme Court had already been packed.


EVEN WHILE HE was living in the White House, nursing a secret
ambition since boyhood for a justice's seat, William Howard Taft had

quietly tried to correct L'Enfant's oversight by finding a location for the Supreme Court. Once he occupied the Court's center seat himself, Taft was politically pragmatic enough to push for a site that Congress had favored for decades, on the high ground across the street from the Capitol, in symmetrical arrangement with the Library of Congress. Taft was larger than life—three hundred pounds or more—and he liked things that way, so he hired an architect who knew how to think big. Cass Gilbert had designed the Woolworth Building in New York City, the world's tallest and most elegant skyscraper. Traveling in Greece in 1927, in search of inspiration for the judiciary's new home, he mailed a postcard to Taft: "The visit to Athens has been well worth while." By the time the "$9,000,000 Parthenon," as the newspapers dubbed it, opened in the fall of 1935, Taft had been dead for five years, though his figure had been carved—reclining, barechested—in the pediment over the building's grand entrance.

The new building employed a special police force answering only to the Court. Alone among the lawmen in Washington, its members sported a Sam Browne belt, with its leather shoulder strap, such as Hitler favored. But on the morning after President Roosevelt unleashed his assault on the Court, there was no policeman on duty inside, at the bronze latticework door that led to the justices' chambers, and newspapermen who could hardly claim to be gentlemen passed through.

The justices were to gather at noon for their Saturday conference. Each of the justices was given a three-room suite, plain and none too large, yet tasteful in unpolished white oak. Only two of the justices bothered to work in their chambers instead of at home. The reporters were fortunate to find both of them in Justice Sutherland's office.

George Sutherland was a tall, slender, scholarly, unfailingly conservative ex-senator, born in England but reared in Utah, who had gained his seat on the Court in return for his service as the one-man brain trust in Warren G. Harding's 1920 front-porch campaign. As the Court's literary stylist, with a sweet nature and a modest demeanor, he never sought to outargue his colleagues at their weekly conference. Yet his pince-nez and his disciplined white beard suited his position as the intellectual leader of the Court's laissez-faire bloc. This morning he was conversing with the fifth and least reliable of the Court's conservatives, Owen J. Roberts. Square-jawed and husky, with the mien of an athlete, the sixty-one-year-old Roberts was the youngest justice, second to last in seniority, and in his philosophy of jurisprudence, the least formed. Both jurists were affable toward the intruding newspapermen, while offering no opinion on the president's recommendations. Nonetheless, that afternoon, the Court's marshal issued an order barring reporters or anyone else from entering the justices' wing, except by special appointment.

The justices looked cheerful as they entered the conference room. Chief Justice Hughes was seated at the head of the long table and, one by one, brought up the cases that had been argued during the previous week. For each, he summarized the facts and the issues of law, then asked each of the associate justices to offer his opinion, in the order of seniority, starting with Willis Van Devanter, the longest-serving, and finishing with Benjamin Cardozo, who had filled the vacancy caused by Oliver Wendell Holmes's retirement in 1932. When the discussion of a case ended, the tentative voting began, the junior justice first, so as not to feel coerced. After Justice Van Devanter made his judgment known, the chief justice cast the final vote, and sometimes the decisive one. Later in the evening, a Court courier would arrive at the justices' homes with assignments to write opinions for the Court.

Occasionally, the backs-and-forths could grow as stormy as in Congress across the street; a contentious case could prolong the conference beyond its usual closing time of four thirty or five o'clock (though Brandeis left by five, no matter what). But that was not the case on this particular Saturday. Most of the nine disputes they had heard during the week were easy and unexciting—involving a district court's jurisdiction over a probate case in Alaska, for instance, or the ban in Texas on using natural gas that was pure enough to heat homes for the manufacture of carbon black. Only two of the week's cases provoked dissents. The meatier case posed a question that was bound to affect millions of employees in state and local governments: did the federal government have the constitutional right to tax the salary of the chief water engineer for New York City? Seven justices thought this violated the independence of the states, but Justice Roberts disagreed. He argued that it was "essentially unfair," as he would write in his dissent, to let the municipal engineer escape from paying federal taxes while anyone who performed the equivalent job for a private company could not. This was a moral principle he was advancing, more than a point of law. Only one other justice joined his dissent, and an unlikely couple they made, Roberts and the Court's staunchest liberal, Louis Brandeis.

The justices also voted on another case, one that had been argued and tentatively decided in mid-December, but awaited Harlan Fiske Stone's return. Weeks later, when the five-to-four vote decision became known—indeed, famous—it would reshape the political battle over the Court that had just begun. But the chief justice would hold off on the announcement for a while, to escape any accusation that the Court was acting at the president's behest.

The Supreme Court was in a fix of its own making. Its steadfast and heartfelt refusal over so many years to understand the world from the vantage point of the laborer or the farmer or anyone who lacked leverage in a ruthless marketplace had not mattered very much while prosperity reigned. But now that the nation was deep into the Depression, if the Court was seen to be blocking the people's will, it endangered its standing with the public. This mattered to Hughes, if not to the rest of the Court. The previous year, he had published a book on the Supreme Court in which he lamented "three notable instances the Court has suffered severely from self-inflicted wounds"—its decision on *Dred Scott*, its reversal in the legal tender case, and its striking down of the income tax—and, as a consequence, a years-long loss of prestige. In a constitutional system of checks and balances, an extended reign of unpopularity will bring down the people's wrath, even upon an unelected branch of government. The Court's inveterate divisiveness carried a similar risk, at least in the chief justice's mind. Hughes hated dissents. Like many a chief justice, he seemed to believe that the Court's best hope for restoring its moral authority with the public—and assuring his own reputation—was by issuing unanimous, or at least lopsided, decisions. No politically minded man wanted to be part of an institution that the public disrespected, much less occupy its center seat. Yet a Court exposed as a nakedly political institution would subject itself to the checks and balances that the Constitution reserved for any branch of government that overreached.

In the conference room, Hughes radiated authority. With his commanding presence, his photographic memory, and his analytical agility, he dominated the discussions. He forced his colleagues to a conclusion, at times annoying them. ("It seems to be more important nowadays to rush our work than to do it right," Justice Stone had complained to a friend.) Justices were careful to avoid frivolous comments for fear of Hughes's penetrating mind. "You just didn't like to talk," Felix Frankfurter said after he joined the Court, "unless you were dead sure of your ground." Whether by brilliance or by brusqueness, by force of his personality or by the logic of his argument, by reframing the legal question or by trying to reconcile irreconcilable views, Hughes labored hard—and with only occasional success—to keep the justices working as one.

Charles Evans Hughes had taken himself seriously all of his life. As a five-year-old, the only child of a Baptist preacher, he wrote an essay, "The Evils of Light Literature." At age six, he trained himself not to wriggle while reciting lessons to his mother, and he made—and kept—a promise to his father never to read a novel until he finished college, third in his class at Brown. As a young man, the other parents in his church held him up as someone for their sons to emulate—shoulders back, head held high, his hands always free of his pockets. In the courtroom, Hughes held speakers precisely to their allotted time, once interrupting an eminent New York lawyer (as it was recounted only half in jest) in the middle of "if." Having placed his faith in efficiency, in not wasting time, Hughes was an easy man to admire but hard to love.

It was neither his efficiency nor his intelligence that the Court needed the most, but rather his skill at diplomacy. Hughes's marvelous résumé showed him as an interrogator for the New York legislature, a two-term governor, an associate justice of the Supreme Court, almost a president, and supposedly the greatest trial lawyer of his generation. But the most serviceable entry for the task that lay before him was his four years as the nation's secretary of state. As Harding's chief diplomat and then as Calvin Coolidge's, he applied his realism and intellectual clarity in drafting a treaty acceptable both to Germany and to the U.S. Senate that formally ended the Great War. Then he conceived and shepherded an international conference in Washington that limited naval armaments and, albeit ever more tenuously, had kept the peace. Hughes had shown a knack for crafting a consensus out of chaos.

The diplomatic challenge that faced him on the Supreme Court was every bit as delicate as anything he had accomplished as secretary of state. By 1937, these same nine justices had served together for five years, but the stretch of stability had only sharpened the confrontation. The justices had formed themselves into two competing cliques that began as ideological in nature and then became personal. The three reliably liberal justices—Brandeis, Stone, and Cardozo—often left the courtroom together, in smiling conversation, and they met every week at Brandeis's apartment on Friday afternoon to prepare for the Saturday conference. Two of the steadiest conservatives, Willis Van Devanter and Pierce Butler, liked to share a round of golf on Sundays at Burning Tree Country Club, past the Maryland line. And all four of them, including James McReynolds, ordinarily rode together home from the Court in Justice Sutherland's machine.

The hostility between the liberals and the conservatives betrayed itself in open court whenever the justices wrestled over the constitutional provocations of the New Deal. If any of the liberals read a dissent, Justice McReynolds was apt to read a newspaper or stand up and leave the bench, while irritation might cross Pierce Butler's or Owen Roberts's face. Unfortunately for Hughes's hopes of finding a whole in the parts, the justices' incompatibility reached deeper than manners or personality or even ideology or any differences that might conceivably be split.

The newspapers called the conservatives the Four Horsemen, alluding less to the biblical Apocalypse and its agents of destruction—famine, pestilence, destruction, and death—than to Notre Dame's starting backfield on the gridiron of 1924. The name had stuck. All four conservative justices had been born within a year or two of the Civil War and had come to manhood amid the political and economic stability of the Gilded Age. At heart they had remained nineteenth-century men, imbued with an unquestioned faith in laissez-faire economics. Even as the stalwart of a prominent Salt Lake City law firm, George Sutherland believed that "the rules which govern [judges'] deliberations and decisions are to a large extent fixed and permanent." He and two of the others, named by Republican presidents, had found their fortunes on the western frontier, not as rugged individualists but as lawyers for the railroads or other corporations. Willis Van Devanter, in pursuit of adventure, had left Indiana at age twenty-five and, by thirty, served as the chief justice in Wyoming Territory, where cattle rustling and gunplay were the rule; after statehood, in practicing law, he represented the Union Pacific Railroad, hunted with Buffalo Bill

Cody, and involved himself in Republican politics that brought him to Washington. Pierce Butler was born in a log cabin in Minnesota after Indians had burned down his parents' first home; after Butler spent years as the chief lawyer for the Chicago, St. Paul, Minneapolis, and Omaha Railroad, famed for his ruthless cross-examinations, Chief Justice Taft whispered on his behalf in President Harding's ear.

Alone among the Four Horsemen, James McReynolds hailed from an older frontier, as the son of a plantation owner in the hills of Kentucky, a southern Democrat—a trust-buster, no less—who served as Woodrow Wilson's first attorney general. In the cabinet, his arrogance and temper in dealing with Congress quickly earned him a kick upstairs to the Court, where, to the Wilsonian progressives' horror, he revealed himself as business's dearest friend. In private, Justice McReynolds was candid about the world he hoped to sustain. "If it were not for the Court," he had recently told his law clerk, "this country would go too far down the road to socialism ever to return." He despised women with red nail polish, men who wore wristwatches, and "lady lawyers of both sexes." This "savage," as Oliver Wendell Holmes had described him, believed that black people were inferior and Jews, beneath contempt. The only Jew who had ever entered his apartment on Sixteenth Street, NW, was the owner of Garfinckel's, the capital's classiest department store. For three years he had refused to talk to Louis Brandeis, the first Jew on the Court, or even to sit near him. Nor was he on speaking terms with Benjamin Cardozo—"another one," he had muttered as he read a newspaper during the second Jewish justice's swearing-in.

The most illuminating contrast between the Court's ideological factions was the chasm that separated McReynolds from the other justice who had been born and raised in Kentucky, Louis D. Brandeis. The gulf between them was more than simply a matter of religion or ideology, but rather of life experience—more than anything, of culture. McReynolds, on his father's plantation, had absorbed the assumptions of the Old South while Brandeis, born and raised in Louisville, the son of immigrants from Prague, was thoroughly urban and progressive in his sense of self. After Harvard Law School, he practiced law in St. Louis and then in Boston, and, by 1910, he achieved national fame as "the people's attorney," a reformer, the scourge of monopolies and big business. In 1913 he published *Other*

*People's Money*, a study of interlocking corporate directorates, a development he regarded as both morally offensive and unfriendly to innovation. The controversy his work had caused prompted the newly elected Woodrow Wilson to pass over Brandeis as his attorney general—and to choose McReynolds instead.

Brandeis's vision of America, in which individuals exerted control over their destinies, bore a curious similarity to that of the conservatives. But his version took into account the unpalatable realities of twentieth-century life, in hopes of reaching moral judgments that were grounded in the facts. Brandeis revered facts. He absorbed them in tomes, economic or sociological, on the structure of electric utilities, the plight of sharecroppers in the South, the joblessness among Negroes in Chicago. Brandeis, above all, was a realist. The nation that he knew bore no resemblance to the mythic world of the frontier; instead, its economy was dominated by mighty corporations that exercised a leverage none of its employees or customers could match. He believed, as a result, that business and financial interests had to be subordinated, if necessary, to the popular will.

All three of the Court's liberals were men of the East, of modern outlook, urban by choice if not by birth, born in the nineteenth century but comfortably at home in the twentieth. Harlan Fiske Stone was a son of New Hampshire, an outdoorsman, sturdy in body and mind, who had found himself drawn to New York City both for its bare-knuckled legal practice and, as the dean of Columbia Law School, its intellectual delights. Benjamin Cardozo was a native of New York City, a man of delicacy and learning, so brilliant a jurist that a Republican president, Herbert Hoover, had been persuaded to appoint the kindliest of liberals out of sheer merit. (When Hoover questioned the prospect of having three New Yorkers on the Court, counting Hughes and Stone, Stone replied he would gladly resign to open up a seat.) They believed that a society must be free to experiment and that a constitution written in the days of tallow candles and scattered hamlets had to allow it.

"It is not a contest between conservatism and radicalism," Stone had once explained to Felix Frankfurter, "nearly so much as it is a difference arising from an inadequate understanding of the relation of the law to the social and economic forces which control society." The modernists accepted what legal scholars portrayed as a "living Constitution." Only a political system that was able to adapt, they believed, could hope to help its citizens survive the hard times and thereby dissuade them from pursuing some other, undoubtedly more severe, style of government.

The Court's philosophical factions differed on the fundamentals—on the essence of how a society should function, of how a government should act—and the chief justice's strokes of diplomacy were bound to fall short. This was hardly enough. John Knox, who was McReynolds's law clerk for the 1936–37 term, had heard that "the chief justice was even forced to give two annual dinners each year—instead of a single dinner—so that Brandeis would be invited to one function and McReynolds to the other. In this way, McReynolds could still avoid meeting Brandeis socially and Hughes could still keep an uneasy peace among his brethren."

In trying to bring order to the Court, the chief justice had more than diplomacy at his disposal. The division between the Four Horsemen and the three dependable liberals, on the nine-justice Court, left the remaining two justices with the balance of power. Few justices in history, a scholar concluded later, had "more successfully eluded" characterization as either a liberal or a conservative than Hughes himself. Ida Tarbell and the journalistic muckrakers of the Progressive Era had esteemed his time as a legislative investigator of the gas and insurance industries and his two terms as New York's governor; during his 1910–16 stint as an associate justice, he had led the Court's liberal minority. Still, the Senate's liberals had objected in 1930 to his return to the Court as chief justice, wary of the well-heeled corporations he had represented—for enormous fees—in most of his fifty-four appearances before the Court he would lead. The senators had been skeptical that he had acted solely as a lawyer, on a client's behalf. But once he had returned to the Court, this time in the center seat, Hughes championed civil liberties and, on questions of the government's authority over business, voted more often with the liberals than the Senate's progressives had feared.

Hughes, in fact, seemed to care less about a philosophy of jurisprudence or a particular constitutional worldview than about the institutional health of the Court—and, Stone suspected, about the size of his "throne," and not only figuratively. (Stone had served on the committee that purchased the furniture for the Court's new home.) Hughes had reason to worry about the public's loss of confidence in a Supreme Court that obstructed the popular New Deal. If the Court declined in the public's estimation, its chief justice would, too.

His yearning for consensus left him at the mercy of the Court's least predictable justice, Owen J. Roberts. The Four Horsemen could not prevail without the vote of either Roberts or Hughes, nor could the liberals win without both. And Hughes, in closely contested decisions, needed Roberts's vote either to reach a majority or to expand it beyond the slimmest of margins. With rare exceptions, whatever Roberts did, Hughes felt compelled to support in the name of consensus.

But as to precisely what Roberts would support, in a particular case, no one could ever feel sure. Since joining the Court three months after Hughes, he had bounced back and forth between the factions. Originally touted as a conservative, he had voted often with the liberals at first. In the spring of 1934, he had heartened New Dealers with a breathtaking opinion in the precedent-shattering case of *Nebbia v. New York*, which seemed to open the way for state legislators to regulate the economy on the public's behalf as they saw fit. But a year later he jumped to the conservatives' camp and joined in decimating the New Deal, and he had never bothered to explain his shift. His legal reasoning had proved wildly inconsistent, even within a single opinion. He was a man of dueling impulses—comfortable in a tuxedo or in overalls, in the city or on the farm, who seemed to believe in just about everything, but in no one thing above all. He stalked moose in the Maine woods but refused to shoot them. He kept his own counsel, and nobody could quite figure him out.

Only one thing about him was certain: on the bitterly divided Court, his opinion mattered the most. It had been that way since he joined it. *The Christian Century* had wondered in a headline in 1931: "Is Justice Roberts the Real Ruler of the United States?" Six years later, the most mysterious of the Nine Old Men still held the meaning of the Constitution in his hands.

# CHAPTER FOUR

# The Swing Vote

EVEN AS A boy, Owen Josephus Roberts had been self-contained. "Ownie," as he was called almost until manhood, was big for his age, and his friends would try to pry him away from his studies to play football or baseball at school. Instead, the copper-haired youngster spent the afternoons curled up with his books in his third-floor bedroom of the house on shady Fisher's Lane in Germantown, an up-and-coming neighborhood near the edge of Philadelphia.

The boy's father, Josephus Roberts, was a man on the rise. The Welsh immigrant's son had started as a wagonmaker—a manual laborer—and soon co-owned a wholesale hardware business in Center City. Then he spent two terms (and declined a third) on the city's Common Council, as a reform Republican. He would never be rich, but he was a man of affairs, a successful businessman comfortable enough to assure his only son the wherewithal to keep rising, to find the route to the top.

"He was an ambitious boy," his father later told a newspaper reporter with obvious pride. As a two-year-old he asked for books, and at four he cried because he was too young for school. He received the education of a Philadelphia blueblood, first at the elite Germantown Academy and, starting at age sixteen, at the city's—and state's—preeminent educational institution, the University of Pennsylvania.

At Penn, Owen Roberts found his place. Ben Franklin's inspiration was a practical-minded university, interested less in teaching theology, Greek or Latin, or other otherworldly pursuits—the specialties at Harvard and Yale—than in the study of science, modern languages, history, political economy, and psychology. Franklin called it "a school adapted to such a

country as ours." As Owen Roberts was entering the Class of 1895, the
university required a rigid and classical curriculum, devoid of electives for
the first two years, in the belief (as a writer in *Harper's* explained) that "the
experience of the University is wiser than that of a Freshman or a Sophomore." But as soon as he could, the young Roberts gravitated toward the
ethereal, majoring in Greek and choosing classes in Latin, English literature, philosophy, ethics, and astronomy, performing well enough to join
Phi Beta Kappa.

His ambitions, however, were not confined to his studies. He was a
self-possessed, sturdily built, smolderingly handsome young man with
deep-set bluish-gray eyes and thick dark hair that he parted at the side—not
in the middle, as was the fashion. He found the time to compile a record of
extracurricular activities that fell a single word short of the longest yearbook caption for any member of his eighty-man class. He served as the
editor in chief of the student newspaper, the chairman of the yearbook
committee, the class historian, the president of one debating society and
the treasurer of the other, the corresponding secretary for the YMCA, the
toastmaster at the Senior Supper, a sports judge, and the assistant marshal
at the Washington's Birthday celebration, and he belonged to the Republican Club, the Six-Foot Club, and the Sophomore Cremation Committee,
which burned effigies of the dullest professors. The class poem exalted
"Roberts, our Pooh Bah of to-day." But even his own yearbook staff saw
that he was trying too hard. "After Roberts got himself elected president,"
it was noted in chronicling the Zeloscopic debating society, "he attended
the remaining meetings in spirit only." Unashamed of his ambitiousness,
he selected a quotation from Sir Walter Raleigh—"Fain would I climb"—
beneath his name in the yearbook.

His next step was law school, also at Penn. He had originally wanted
to teach school, but the decision was not his to make. His argumentative-
ness as a boy had persuaded his father that his son should be a lawyer instead, and when Ownie disagreed, his father asked the headmaster at
Germantown Academy, William Kershaw, to arbitrate.

"Your father is right," Kershaw adjudged. "You will be a lawyer, Owen."

"But can I be a lawyer and be honest?" the boy replied.

The headmaster stood and put his hand on his student's shoulder.
"Owen, you can be honest at anything."

At law school he was invited to join the staff of the law review and, more important, completed his entry into "the University crowd" that could assure his worldly success in socially insular Philadelphia. With his knack for attracting mentors, he learned corporate and insurance law from George Wharton Pepper, a well-born Philadelphian, then served with him for many years on Penn's law faculty. Another law school friend became Philadelphia's district attorney and hired Roberts as the top assistant on his staff. As a prosecutor, he was a natural, a problem-solver more than a thinker. Willing to work night and day, he won most of his criminal trials and earned headlines by securing the convictions of politically connected contractors who had defrauded the city. In the courtroom, he proved fast on his feet and hypnotic with juries, and the six-footer found that "a good big man can usually get the better of a good small man." He told a friend that his ambition was to do "something big for my city, something big for my state, and something big for my nation."

Having turned his prosecutorial talents toward defending the city's powerful streetcar company against the victims of accidents, imagined or real, he left the public payroll in 1905 and lawyered for Philadelphia Rapid Transit directly. In 1912 he started a law firm with two well-connected friends, luring the streetcar company as a client along with the bluest-chip corporations in the city and state—the Pennsylvania Railroad, Bell Telephone of Pennsylvania, the investment firm Drexel & Company, Equitable Life Assurance, Philadelphia's chamber of commerce. Soon he was sitting on several corporate boards, as well as on the municipal panel that managed the trust funds that Philadelphians bequeathed to the city, and he belonged to five of the city's most exclusive clubs. He conducted civil trials of every description, involving negligence cases or contested wills, representing building contractors or the architects the contractors sued, and occasionally criminal cases, notably that of an ex-governor charged with defrauding the company he ran. During the Great War, as a special deputy attorney general, a temporary federal post, he sent several editors at the city's German and Lithuanian newspapers to prison for sedition.

By 1924 the firm of Roberts, Montgomery & McKeehan was believed to be earning a prodigious $150,000 a year. With his extravagant income, Roberts and his wife, Elsie, and their daughter, Elizabeth, could live well. He purchased an elegant four-story town house, the only one on the long block with a fancy bowed front, near lofty Rittenhouse Square. His success as an attorney brought privileges and profits. During the stock market boom of 1929, he was invited along with Charles Lindbergh, John J. Pershing, and scores of prominent businessmen and politicians to buy a special allotment of stock at a steep discount, courtesy of his client Drexel & Company, an affiliate of J. P. Morgan & Company. The benefit came to light in a Senate investigation of Morgan only after Roberts joined the Court.

Still in his forties, Roberts had reached the uppermost rank of Philadelphia's estimable bar. Raised as a Baptist, he had become an Episcopalian—Elsie's doing, but Owen's pleasure. He devoted himself to church, family, and the law. No stranger to life's tragedies—two stillborn sons and a two-day-old daughter's death—he took solace as he could. ("I was very, very spoiled rotten," recalled Elizabeth, the only child who survived.) But he had never rebelled and rarely, it seemed, had he questioned. In his father's life and in his own, the Protestant ethic had shown the promised results. By dint of self-reliance, hard work, and the cultivation of connections, his family had seen the American success story come true. To Owen Roberts, a conventional man of conventional outlook, the American dream was nothing less than a fact of life.

His opinions, at least in public, were no less conventional. At a dinner in 1923 for bankers at the Waldorf-Astoria in New York, he praised "old-fashioned Anglo-Saxon individualism" and denounced socialism for its "suppression of ambition." He drew cheers for defending the $100,000-plus salaries of Standard Oil executives for having increased the production of oil and reduced the price to consumers. The government had drifted in its proper role, he argued, away from what the Founding Fathers had foreseen, so that "noisy minorities are running to the legislators every year for government and state regulation of all sorts of businesses which the government has no concern whatsoever . . . The businessman in America today feels he is doing business with a minion of the government looking over his shoulder with an upraised arm and threatening scowl."

His opinions were safe and his friends had reached high stations. One day in February 1924, George Wharton Pepper, in his third year as a senator, called from the White House and summoned his protégé to Washington. Owen and his wife left immediately, and that evening Pepper ushered his friend into the White House to meet the president of the United States.

Calvin Coolidge was in a difficult position as the 1924 elections approached: his predecessor had left him a scandal. Only after Warren G. Harding's unexpected death of an undetermined illness in 1923 did the corruption of his cronies become more than a rumor. Soon the playfully shaped rock formation atop a Wyoming oilfield known as Teapot Dome became synonymous with allegations of bribes and criminals near the presidency. Coolidge, known for his quiet rectitude, wanted to hire a pair of irreproachable special prosecutors, a Republican and a Democrat, to separate himself from any imputations. His original Republican nominee had withdrawn once it was discovered that he was a director of the bank that had floated bonds for the oil company accused of bribing the interior secretary. Pepper had not been alone in suggesting Owen Roberts for the post; so had Coolidge's old college chum Harlan Fiske Stone, who was practicing law in New York City, after he turned down the job himself. Coolidge's holdover secretary of state, Charles Evans Hughes, had seconded the choice.

At age forty-eight, Roberts's plainspoken manner inspired confidence. As Roberts answered President Coolidge's probing questions, Pepper rephrased one he thought was unclear; the president interjected, "He knows what I mean." At last the president turned to Pepper and said, "I don't see any reason why I shouldn't appoint this man." And thus, as the *Literary Digest* announced, "fame struck Owen J. Roberts with the swiftness of lightning."

The senators charged with voting on his nomination worried about his lack of a national reputation for such a high-profile job and his ignorance of public land law. ("I think that in an hour's time I could get the necessary details," he told the Senate Committee on Public Lands and Surveys.) But it was his speech the previous year in Standard Oil's defense that, more than anything, gave some of the senators pause. The Wisconsin progressive Robert La Follette made sure that the newspaper account of the nominee's praise for oil executives was placed on every senator's chair. It was oil executives, after all, who were alleged to have bribed Secretary of the Interior Albert Fall to lease federal oil properties in Wyoming and California without competitive bidding. The gravest governmental scandal since the days of Ulysses S. Grant crystallized the public's anxieties over corporate corruption and power that had festered ever since the munitions industry had urged a reluctant nation into the Great War. Still, only eight members of the Republican-controlled Senate voted against Roberts's nomination, five fewer than opposed the Democratic nominee, Atlee Pomerene of Ohio—a former senator, no less.

"We will make haste," Roberts announced after his confirmation, "but we will make haste slowly, for whatever we do we wish to be as nearly uncriticized as possible." He could never have guessed that the prosecution would go on for six years.

ROBERTS TOOK CHARGE of the prosecution. A tenacious investigator, relentless in court, he did most of the work and advanced the money for his own expenses. This prosecution was far more complicated than the trials for sedition he had conducted during the war. To trace the $304,000 in Liberty Bonds allegedly paid to Fall, he became "a Sherlock Holmes as well as a lawyer," as a newspaper noted, secretly dispatching Treasury agents to New York, then to Toronto and to Pueblo, Colorado, then to El Paso and back to Washington. Finally, in October 1929, the ailing interior secretary sat in a Washington courtroom, slumped in a Morris chair, convicted of accepting a $100,000 bribe, the first former cabinet member ever imprisoned for his actions in office.

For Roberts, the timing of the triumphant headlines could not have proved more opportune, for a few months later another Republican president, Herbert Hoover, found himself in a quandary. On his way to the Court one morning in March 1930, Justice Edward Sanford, who belonged to the club of conservatives who met at Chief Justice Taft's home on Saturday afternoons, had stopped off to have a tooth pulled, then collapsed as he stood up from the dentist's chair. By noon, he was dead.

The Teapot Dome prosecutor was mentioned in the press as a possible nominee, but President Hoover settled on John J. Parker, highly regarded as a federal appeals court judge from North Carolina. However, labor unions loathed him because of his judicial assent to employment contracts that outlawed workers from joining a union. More problematical was a statement that Parker had made during his 1920 gubernatorial campaign—"the participation of the Negro in politics is a source of evil and danger to both races"—which rankled the Republican senators from the North and Midwest who counted on the votes of slaves' descendants. After a vitriolic debate, Parker's nomination was defeated by two votes.

This was Hoover's second confirmation battle within less than three months. Taft had resigned as the chief justice because of illness, and the choice of Charles Evans Hughes to succeed him had provoked a pitched battle before the Senate acquiesced. Already vexed by an economy unable to recover from the stock market crash, Hoover had no stomach for yet another clash over the Court, and he had no time to spare. Yet again, Owen Roberts emerged as a panicky president's second choice, readily acceptable to both sides.

The Senate's conservatives deemed him safe, a corporate lawyer who was presumed to believe in his bones the accepted truths of laissez-faire. To liberals, Hoover had nominated the hero of Teapot Dome, the prosecutor of Republican corruption, probably as tolerable a nominee as the Republican president was likely to name. Indeed, this was the core of Roberts's appeal: People could see in him whatever they liked, and to a remarkable extent, they were right. He was a conservative in Philadelphia's conservative bar, a denizen of corporate boards of directors, who had discouraged friends from lobbying for his appointment so that he might resume his lucrative practice of law. Yet there was more to Owen J. Roberts than this. As the prosecutor for Teapot Dome, he had often shared a table with reporters in Washington at a dingy basement lunchroom near the courthouse, chatting about politics, poetry, and baseball, and they had wound up believing he had progressive sympathies—"both a heart and a head," as one of them wrote. He was a churchgoing man who talked little about his faith but, by all accounts, felt it deeply. Recently he had accepted the chairmanship of a new committee to lobby for America's entry into the World Court. This was hardly his only glimmer of idealism, his quiet but high-minded conception of how the world ought to be. His work with Philadelphia's Board of City Trusts had involved him with a school for orphaned boys, as the chairman of its instruction committee, while Lincoln University, in nearby Chester County, had recently named him as a trustee.* "Knowing him as I do," a member of the National Association for the Advancement of Colored People wired a friend about Roberts, "I am confident he is not

---

*The oldest college of arts and sciences anywhere in the world for boys of African descent was about to graduate a promising young Baltimorean, Thurgood Marshall, who was destined to become the first of his race on the Supreme Court.

only devoid of prejudices but is a friend of Negroes as he is of every minority group and every humanitarian cause." Even labor had kind words. The American Federation of Labor's president, William Green, endorsed the nominee as someone able to understand the "profound social and economic problems" that ensued from the war between capital and labor.

"There is a good deal of talk about 'conservative' and 'liberal,'" Felix Frankfurter wrote in a congratulatory note to the justice-to-be. "The characterizations don't describe anybody because we are all a compound of both. What divides men much more decisively is the extent to which they are free, free from a dogmatic outlook on life, free from fears. That is what cheers me most about your appointment, for you have, no doubt, no skeletons in the closet of your mind and are a servant neither of a blind traditionalism nor a blind indifference to historic wisdom."

But nobody knew what Owen Roberts believed about the Constitution and its principles, about its balance of powers and rights, much less his vision of a working democracy. And nobody had occasion to ask. Only once before had the Senate ever summoned a Court nominee to testify; five years earlier, Harlan Fiske Stone was examined because of his role as the attorney general in approving the indictment of Senator Burton Wheeler. But this time they were too tired of the acrimony to invite the nominee in. Ten days after the president nominated Roberts on May 9, 1930, the Senate Judiciary Committee approved it unanimously. The next afternoon, in less than a minute, without debate or even a vote, the Senate did the same.

Before he left for Washington, Roberts told his friends in Philadelphia that he intended to be his own man on the Court, that he would decide each case on the merits, with complete independence, and would refrain from identifying himself with either ideological faction.

THE POPULATION OF the nation's capital had almost doubled in the course of the Great War, but culturally it was a backwater in 1930, with an orchestra of its own but nothing in the way of homegrown theater or art; most of the patrons at the art galleries were tourists. The women of sophistication in Washington would travel to Baltimore for a decent lunch, to Philadelphia for a concert, to New York to see a play.

Construction in the city was everywhere. Just beyond Fourteenth

Street, the new Commerce Department building was rising, with its endless lines of Ionic columns. It was to be the largest office building in the world, once it opened in 1932, more spacious than the Empire State Building, completed in 1931. Two blocks farther east, the Internal Revenue Service building, also of a classic Greek design, had opened already. In 1935, a repository for the National Archives replaced the old Center Market, with its exotic red towers and its jumble of vendors outside. The government also was ready to start building new homes for the departments of Justice and Labor—a dozen huge government buildings altogether, spread over seventy acres, supplanting the warehouses, lumberyards, garages, and saloons bordered by Fifteenth Street, Avenue B (soon to be broadened and renamed Constitution Avenue), and the hypotenuse of Pennsylvania Avenue. The Federal Triangle, as the locale was to be known, heralded a federal government that had begun to expand as the Depression took hold, to serve a growing, despairing population.

Owen Roberts decided to live in Georgetown, the only neighborhood in the city that was older than the capital itself. Georgetown was run-down and still of a low social repute, hardly the fanciest place for a man of distinction to live. But its similarities to Philadelphia, in looks and demeanor, were unmistakable: narrow streets, crammed-together brick town houses, uneven sidewalks, an intimate scale. The Robertses leased one of Georgetown's oldest and largest residences, a white clapboard house at the corner of Thirty-first and O streets, featuring old-fashioned galleries along the first and second floors (including an art studio upstairs for Elizabeth) and a garage that had once housed slaves.

Roberts liked to ride the streetcar down to the Court, along Pennsylvania Avenue into the center of Washington—a throwback, in effect, to the earliest justices, especially John Marshall, who would stop to gossip with the common citizenry while shopping for provisions in the marketplace. In Marshall's day, the justices all shared a boardinghouse in Washington and drank the chief justice's Madeira until the wee hours. The shabbily dressed chief justice blurred the boundary between the High Court and the general public. But such informality was long gone, for as the Court had ascended in importance since the 1890s, justices had made themselves physically remote. The danger that a conversation in Washington might turn to something political or judicial had discouraged most of the justices from a public presence. Only by keeping themselves apart from everyone else could they maintain what a journalist mocked as their "mystical halo of dignity, almost of sanctity."

Owen Roberts would have none of this. Sometimes he carried his lunch to work, a sandwich and a thermos of coffee in a paper bag, and one noontime as a new justice he strolled into the public section of the Senate restaurant and ordered his lunch. When the headwaiter rushed over and suggested that he move to the section reserved for the senators, Roberts smiled and shook his head. During recesses of the Court, he liked to stroll around the Capitol grounds, chatting with messengers and tourists, puffing on the briar pipe he always clenched between his teeth.

Soon the capital's society pages chronicled the comings and goings of the junior justice and his family—the luncheons in Elsie's honor, her publicity work for the Community Chest, the family's box at the National Capital Horse Show, Elizabeth's visit to the opera, Elsie as cohostess for a luncheon of the English-Speaking Union, Elsie and Elizabeth in Mrs. Hoover's box for a musicale at the Mayflower Hotel, Elsie at Frances Perkins's luncheon for Mrs. Roosevelt. Owen and Elsie attended the dedication of the Folger Shakespeare Library, a National Theatre premiere, the Soviet Union's first official Washington reception, and affairs given by the British, Swiss, and Czech ambassadors and the Bulgarian chargé d'affaires, and they served as host and hostess for the departing ambassador from Brazil.

Owen Roberts quickly drew close to Harlan Fiske Stone and Charles Evans Hughes. Even before the Senate had taken up Roberts's nomination, Stone wrote to recommend a real estate agent and a stenographic secretary. "We shall look forward to counting you among our friends," he added, for his wife and himself. Harlan and Agnes Stone invited the Robertses to their box at Constitution Hall for the National Symphony; the two couples were considered to conduct the sprightliest social lives on the Court.

Roberts's friendship with Hughes was more than merely polite from the first. The chief justice's warm note of welcome to the justice-designate "touched me deeply," Roberts replied in his easygoing and legible hand. "I view the responsibility with trepidation, but I know I can count on your sympathetic aid." Hughes simply liked the younger man with the amiable personality, and Roberts would come to think of the chief justice as something of a father.

These efforts at friendship also concealed ulterior motives. As one of the three outnumbered liberals, Stone was in search of another ally, and Hughes sought to restore comity to the Court. For Roberts, too, his enthusiasm for the capital's social whirl hinted at something more than just an outgoing nature. Not long after joining the Court, in an interview with a Philadelphia newspaper reporter, he described the job of a modern legal practitioner as someone who was hardly hidebound in the law. A lawyer, he said, "must be trained to think things out for himself and not look at the past for his material. A lawyer should have no need, especially in economics and in psychology, to call in an economist every time he has a case dealing with a new problem of business. He should have no need to call in a psychologist when he is faced with an unusual human problem."

At first, the newest justice seemed like the answer to the judicial liberals' prayers. During his opening term on the bench, Roberts joined with Stone, Brandeis, Oliver Wendell Holmes Jr., and Chief Justice Hughes in striking down a Minnesota law that banned a scandal sheet from going to press and, again, in upholding Indiana's right to protect mom-and-pop shops by imposing a tax on chain stores. The completion of the Court's 1930–31 term prompted the *Literary Digest*, the favorite of the eastern elites, to herald "The Supreme Court's Shift to Liberalism." Nonetheless, true to his vow to his friends, Justice Roberts had voted about half the time with the liberals and otherwise with the Four Horsemen. Neither camp could claim him.

Possibly he had revealed his truest instinct in the first opinion he wrote. At his inaugural Saturday conference, he selected *Poe v. Seaborn* as his subject—"a tidy little case," another justice remarked, though one fraught with political complications. At the behest of John Nance Garner, then a powerful congressman from Texas, the Treasury Department had pursued a Court decision on whether husbands and wives in community-property states (such as Texas) could file their federal income taxes separately. Competing lines of judicial precedent suggested opposite conclusions. Roberts ruled against the Treasury position. Examining the words of the federal statute—the word "of" in particular—he hewed to the letter of the law in ruling that "the use of the word 'of' denotes ownership" that the state law in question conferred on wives. He acted as a lawyer's lawyer, without a thought of justice.

It was the Court's custom to accept a new justice's maiden opinion unanimously. But in *Poe v. Seaborn*, both Hughes and Stone declined to participate, without explanation. Rumor had it that they had considered writing a dissent but refrained, so as not to embarrass their newest brother on the bench.

THREE YEARS LATER, in the early hours of a cold morning in December 1933, Owen Roberts was pacing the floor of his home in Georgetown, wrestling with the issues posed by the case of *Nebbia v. New York*, which involved a trivial incident but a major point of law. Leo Nebbia was a grocer in Rochester, New York, who had sold a customer two quarts of milk for nine cents apiece and had thrown in a five-cent loaf of bread for free. A competitor may have turned him in—a wagon driver whose willingness to deliver milk for free provided a competitive advantage in selling the price-controlled wares. A $5 fine was imposed for violating the state law that fixed the price of milk high enough for dairy farmers to survive. The law arguably trampled Leo Nebbia's due process rights by forbidding him to sell his milk at whatever price he wished, such as by charging nothing for a loaf of bread. "If I want to give it away," the grocer had pleaded in his defense, "who is hurt but myself?" The state argued for the public's larger interest that undercutting the price of milk damaged the welfare of struggling dairy farmers in their effort to turn a profit and thereby to stay on their land. The outcome was crucial to determining the power of state governments to ease the suffering of the Great Depression and, by extension, the likelihood that the New Deal laws would survive the Court's scrutiny.

The public did not learn the results of Justice Roberts's deliberation until the first Monday in March 1934. The Court was still meeting in the Capitol, in the Old Senate Chamber, which the upper house of Congress had abandoned in 1859 and handed down to its lesser branch of the government. In the stuffy, lushly decorated chamber, the dramatically arched ceiling, the subdued lighting, and the spectators' pews enhanced the ecclesiastical air. There was a hushed silence as Justice Roberts, seated farthest to the spectators' left, started to read. With his broad shoulders and strongly cut face, he filled up the high-backed swivel chair.

"During 1932 the prices received by farmers for milk were much below the cost of production." Roberts outlined the agricultural dynamics.
This was a subject he had learned firsthand. In 1929 he had acquired the
farm he had dreamed of since boyhood—some seven hundred acres of
rolling fields and meadows in Chester County, Pennsylvania, near Valley
Forge, thirty miles northwest of Center City. With the help of a resident
foreman, he grew alfalfa, barley, wheat, corn, oats, and string beans, and
experimented with raising chickens and hogs before turning to cows. At
first he lost a good deal of money, but eventually he built a herd of thirty
Guernseys, each of which he knew by name, and he sold the milk in Phoenixville until finding a better price in nearby Mont Clare. He insisted on
running the farm like a business, in hopes that the revenue from milk and
alfalfa, mainly, would cover the operating costs. "I'm a city farmer," he later
explained.

*Nebbia v. New York* was a case that a city farmer would understand,
and Roberts posed the constitutional quandary directly: did the Fourteenth Amendment's guarantee of due process trump the dairy farmers'
despair? Then he answered boldly. "[T]his court from the earliest days
affirmed that the power to promote the general welfare is inherent in
government," he wrote. "Under our form of government, the use of property and the making of contracts are normally matters of private and not
of public concern. The general rule is that both shall be free of governmental interference. But neither property rights nor contract rights are
absolute"—the courtroom was hushed—"for government cannot exist if
the citizen may at will use his property to the detriment of his fellows, or
exercise his freedom of contract to work them harm. Equally fundamental
with the private right is that of the public to regulate it in the common
interest."

For sixty years, the Court had decreed that a state could regulate the
prices in businesses "affected with the public interest," but this was a narrowly drawn category that had never included anything like milk. That
standard was now obsolete. Instead, legislatures had been accorded the
constitutional power to balance the "common interest"—the public good—
against the property owner's rights, then to act as it saw fit. As long as the
law was "neither arbitrary nor discriminatory," Roberts reasoned, the grocer's right of due process had been satisfied, and "a state is free to adopt

whatever economic policy may reasonably be deemed to promote public welfare." Presumably Congress was, too.

The sweeping decision, wrenching the Supreme Court away from its decades of defending property rights, was adopted by the narrowest of margins, on a five-to-four vote. Over the Four Horsemen's objections, the majority had swept away a bulwark of the conservatives' jurisprudence. Roberts's opinion heralded a revolution in due process jurisprudence that would extend well beyond the confines of price regulation. American justice had placed humans, at long last, ahead of property.

Roberts included nothing in his legal argument that the Court's venerable liberals, back to Holmes, had not invoked in their earlier dissents. The difference, of course, was that this was not a dissent. Roberts was speaking for a majority of justices, for the Court as a whole—for the nation. "Another historic liberalization of the court's construction of the Constitution," the *Washington Post* reported, "another 'modernization' of judicial interpretation."

"Certain fundamentals have been set beyond experimentation," Justice McReynolds wailed in his dissent. "If now liberty or property may be struck down by difficult circumstances, we must expect that hereafter every right must yield to the voice of an impatient majority . . . All rights will be subject to the caprice of the hour; government by stable laws will pass." The Four Horsemen understood the stakes. For more than a generation, conservatives had dominated the Supreme Court, but with this ruling the Court had, at least for the moment, transformed its understanding of how much the Constitution allowed the government to do for the people it ruled.

# CHAPTER FIVE

# The Conservative Court

ELSIE ROBERTS HAD a round face, black curly hair, a reserved manner, and strong opinions that she mostly kept to herself. On a Monday fourteen months later, in May 1935, she was sitting in the section of the Old Senate Chamber reserved for family and friends, as she always did when her husband was to perform. As usual, he did not disappoint. Justice Roberts glanced around at the audience, crossed his arms over his black-robed chest, folded them on the bench, and leaned forward to emphasize his points as he recited the Supreme Court's majority opinion on the constitutionality of the 1934 federal law that required railroads to establish pensions for employees. Soon the spectators noticed that he was reciting from memory. They also realized that in this pivotal case, he had jumped sides.

Roberts had voted with the liberals in February when, by a five-to-four vote, the Court upheld the New Deal legislation that authorized the use of paper dollars to satisfy a debt even if the contract called for repayment in gold. Homer Cummings had personally argued for the "gold clause" before the Court, and the possibility of losing had been the president's worst nightmare. This time the issue before the Court was the Railroad Retirement Act passed by Congress the June before. By requiring the railroads to offer pensions, the New Deal law was intended to persuade older workers to retire, thereby opening up jobs for the unemployed.

The railroad unions had been thrilled with the prospect of a hundred thousand newly vacated posts, despite the statute's 2 percent bite from workers' paychecks to pay for pensions. The railroads, however, which contributed twice as much, were up in arms. Most of the big railroads paid pensions already, but being forced to—this was worse. Soon 134 railroads joined in a lawsuit, and when their lawyers wound up facing the former railroad lawyers on the High Court, the reception was warmer than they might have anticipated in any forgotten man's home.

Everyone acknowledged that the statute was, as President Roosevelt had admitted even as he signed it, "crudely drawn" and in need of a future Congress's ministrations. Nor did it adequately provide for the inevitably higher costs as additional workers retired. Still, the sweep of Roberts's opinion was a shock. Unless the pensions had an impact on a railroad's operations as it crossed state lines, he reasoned, the law "obviously" lay beyond Congress's constitutional power. "We search in vain for any assertion that the feature under discussion will promote economy, efficiency, or safety . . . It is an attempt for social ends to impose by sheer fiat"—he spoke with an uncustomary vehemence—"a means of assuring a particular class of employees against old age dependency." In a five-to-four majority, Roberts had sided with the Four Horsemen, with a tone that suggested more was to come.

Charles Evans Hughes delivered the dissent himself, with palpable frustration. "The gravest aspect of the decision," the chief justice began, "is that it does not rest simply upon a condemnation of particular features of the Railroad Retirement Act, but denies to Congress the power to pass any compulsory pension act for railroad employees"—and the power to pass so much else. Many or most of the New Deal laws that Congress had passed during the Hundred Days and afterward, such as this one, relied for their constitutional authority on a commonsense understanding of interstate commerce, one that counted factories, mines, and railroads as inherently involved in the movement of goods across state lines, with an impact on the national interest. If Congress had so little power to correct the injustices of Darwinian commerce, clearly the Social Security bill that was still mired in Congress would die at the hands of the Court, should it ever be enacted.

The liberals, so recently Roberts's allies, were aghast. "About the worst performance of the Court since the Bake Shop case," Harlan Stone sputtered to Felix Frankfurter, referring to the *Lochner* decision in 1905. In the tradition of Oliver Wendell Holmes, Stone believed in the principle of judicial self-restraint, in allowing the legislature to act as it saw fit. "The bill, it is true, was a bad one, and if I had been a member of Congress I am certain I should have voted against it," he wrote, "but to say that it is beyond the range of constitutional power puts us back at least thirty years. A bad matter was made worse by the cocksure assumption that we could determine judicially that there was nothing for the congressional judgment to act upon. How arrogant it must all seem to those unaccustomed to judicial omniscience."

By nature, Owen Roberts was anything but arrogant. Why he had joined with the conservatives, or how long he would stay, nobody could say for sure, though the speculation was rife. His law clerk insisted that the justice's approach to each case was pragmatic, not theoretical, but liberals suspected that it was personal. On the bench, Roberts was often seen to share a chuckle with Pierce Butler, the conservative in the adjacent seat and a frequent visitor to Roberts at home. He had also drawn close to the unsociable McReynolds, who was genial to the few people he liked; the two of them, along with Sutherland, had formed a club of sorts. Edward Corwin of Princeton, a political scientist who was the nation's leading scholar of constitutional history—and also an adviser to the administration—felt certain that Roberts had fallen "much under Justice Sutherland's influence."

The notion that friendships on the bench or political ambition could alter the course of judicial history was difficult even for cynics to believe, but evidence was available for anyone who wished to find some. Owen Roberts's name had bubbled up as a Republican presidential dark horse before the party's 1928 and 1932 national conventions, and he was considered a long shot for 1936, behind William Borah, Alf Landon, and the second coming of Herbert Hoover. Striking down the Railroad Retirement Act might have helped him among Republicans, but in a general election, or so he joked to a newspaper friend, "I figure that cost about three million votes."

Elsie had argued against any thoughts of the presidency, for she believed that the position he already occupied was weightier still. After his ruling on railroad pensions, a *News-Week* profile titled "The Supreme Court's Hard-Working Balance-Wheel" anointed him "the most important man in Washington." Instead of pursuing the presidency, Elsie told members of the family, "Owen's duty is to use his position to stabilize the country."

This was grandiose, but she was probably correct. Elsie disliked the New Deal, and Roberts had come to oppose it as well. His traditionalist upbringing had taught him that every man ought to make his own way in life. He cautioned a gathering of Boy Scout leaders in 1936 near his Pennsylvania farm that the Depression had made people "soft," for it had given many Americans the idea that if they leaned hard enough on the government, it would support them. Roberts privately believed, or so a Court insider later divulged to a reporter, that the Roosevelt administration was grabbing the country's resources "and plunging them down the sewer." Thus, in the spring of 1935, the Court's swing vote swung to the conservatives' side.

THREE MONDAYS AFTER the Supreme Court derailed the Railroad Retirement Act, it met for the next-to-last time, on a hot and sunny day, in its hand-me-down quarters in the Capitol. Charles Evans Hughes had never looked more Zeus-like as he stroked his beard and rocked back and forth in his seat. Two decisions had been announced, neither of them consequential, both of them unanimously, each a blow to the White House. The spectators were rustling to leave when the chief justice called out a docket number. A sigh went up, out of pleasure and suspense.

This was the case everyone had been waiting for. The National Industrial Recovery Act, the climactic achievement of the Hundred Days, was under review in *Schechter Brothers v. United States.* "In some people's minds the New Deal and NRA were almost the same thing," Frances Perkins exclaimed. The Blue Eagle had soared in popularity at first, because of the additional jobs and the rising wages in its wake. But then job creation slowed, and increases in prices outpaced the higher pay, sometimes from the start. The industrial codes, as they developed, allowed the big companies to exploit their leverage against their smaller competitors, prompting the famed criminal lawyer Clarence Darrow to condemn the NRA—the National Recovery Administration—as an instrument of monopoly. The statute was an agglomeration of ill-fitting ventures that had been rushed to passage on Capitol Hill, having been drafted so haphazardly that the president, in signing it, had acknowledged that Congress would need to fix it. Beyond the section that authorized $3.3 billion in public works spending and the language that assured the workers' right to collective bargaining, the main part of the law radically altered the dynamics of the U.S. economy. It replaced a system of unchecked—and often destructive—competition with the presumed efficiencies of cooperation, by means of the presidentially approved industrial codes that bound employers to pay minimum wages, limit each worker's hours, and accept common standards of production.

The four Schechter brothers, the proprietors of a kosher poultry wholesaler in Brooklyn, had been fined and sentenced to jail for multiple violations of the New York Metropolitan Area Live Poultry Code. The city's kosher butchers had agreed to pay employees at least fifty cents an hour and to limit workweeks to forty-eight hours. But after a month-long investigation, presumably prompted by a rival's complaint, a federal grand jury indicted the Schechter brothers for sixty alleged violations, including selling diseased chickens, paying the workers too little, and keeping them too long at their posts. In the subsequent trial, they were found guilty on nineteen counts, and when a federal appeals court overturned the convictions on minimum wages and maximum hours, Justice Department lawyers appealed the case as its vehicle for testing the NRA's constitutionality before the Supreme Court.

The chief justice read the decision for the Court in his sonorous baritone. The NRA was unconstitutional, he ruled, on two counts. For one thing, the Constitution did not grant Congress the right to delegate to the president the power to approve the industrial codes hammered out by management and labor. His other reason was far more consequential, in its potential damage to the New Deal. Hardly a word had been uttered during the Constitutional Convention in 1787 about the clause that gave Congress the authority to regulate interstate commerce. Since 1895, the Court had distinguished between business with a "direct" impact on interstate commerce, and thus subject to congressional involvement, versus business that affected interstate commerce only indirectly, which was off-limits to federal control, and had considered this a difference of kind and not of degree. In assessing the NRA, Hughes held strictly to precedent: Congress had no power to impose its will on any business that was involved only indirectly in interstate commerce, including a kosher poultry wholesaler in Brooklyn. The distinction, he decreed, was fundamental.

"Hot dog!" a spectator exclaimed near the back of the courtroom. A court official started toward him.

The audience sat stunned, not only because of the decision itself but even more because of the justices' unanimity. The centerpiece of the New Deal had succumbed without a single dissent. Even the Court's three reliable liberals had turned against the New Deal, at least this farthest outpost. The three of them plus Hughes had seen in the Railroad Retirement Act a commonsense understanding of interstate commerce. But the NRA reached beyond what the liberals accepted as liberalism, in which the federal government intervened to protect the individual. Brandeis, in particular, the apostle of a decentralized democracy, was bound to feel repulsed by a Mussolini-style system of government-approved industrial cartels. The New Deal, it seemed, had gone too far.

In the audience, the NRA's bald, big-boned administrator, Donald Richberg, turned pale. Tommy Corcoran also sat among the spectators, and as the session ended, a Court page tapped him on the shoulder and led him out of the courtroom and across a Capitol corridor into the justices' robing room. With its stately old furniture, a crystal chandelier, and the paintings of noble predecessors, the justices used the room as an informal retreat, a place to smoke or read a newspaper or crack a joke. But today they were in no joking mood. As Corcoran arrived, a page was removing Louis Brandeis's robe, and the justice stood with his arms outstretched—in Corcoran's mind, like a black-winged angel of destruction. Brandeis had summoned his cocky friend.

"This is the end of this business of centralization," the justice told the young man who had FDR's ear, "and I want you to go back and tell the president that we're not going to let this government centralize everything. It's come to an end." Jeffersonian justice had inspired the New Deal, and Brandeis had voted to uphold every one of its laws, until now. He and the New Deal were parting ways. "The president has been living in a fool's paradise," he told Corcoran.

Among New Dealers, the twenty-seventh of May in 1935 would forever be known as Black Monday.


"YOU MEAN IT was unanimous against us?" the president marveled to Don Richberg over the telephone. "Where was old Isaiah?"

Richberg told him.

"What about Ben Cardozo?" The absence of dissent shook him up.

Attorney General Homer Cummings was sitting in his spacious office at the Justice Department's neoclassical new building on Constitution Avenue, eating a ham sandwich, when the word arrived. He spent the afternoon studying the decision, and then he rushed over to the White House. For two hours, he and the president conferred in the study upstairs, along with Richberg, who was now out of a job, and Stanley Reed, the solicitor general, who had argued the case before the Court. The president feared for the fate of the other New Deal laws. They agreed to suspend the NRA's operations at once, and when Richberg delivered the news to a batch of impatient reporters, his usual smile had grown grim.

"Today was a bad day," Homer Cummings said with a snarl into a Dictaphone for his diary that night. "If this decision stands and is not met in some way, it is going to be impossible for the government to devise any system which will effectively deal with the disorganized industries of the country, or rout out, by any affirmative action, manifest evils, sweatshop conditions, child labor, or any other unsocial or anti-social aspects of the economic system." He was angry—and quite certain—that the justices had exceeded their powers. "A good many people are saying that either the Supreme Court was wrong, or the Constitution was wrong, and this has revived talk about constitutional amendments, or other methods of endeavoring to prevent the Supreme Court from thwarting the purposes of the people."

The news traveled abroad. "La Mort du Bleu," a French newspaper trumpeted its obituary for the Blue Eagle's death. In the White House, Roosevelt tried to turn his judicial misfortunes into a political opportunity. The NRA decision had created a sensation, and within ten days the AFL announced that at least a million workers had seen their wages cut and others stood in fear of losing their jobs. Seeking to turn to his political advantage the public's anger toward the Court's antipathy for the New Deal, the president championed a bill that he had long resisted, sponsored by Senator Robert F. Wagner, a slum-reared Democrat from New York, to force employers to negotiate with their workers' unions. Roosevelt also used the uproar to increase the pressure on Congress to break the impasse over the Social Security Act. A surge of legislation followed, not only the Wagner Act and the Social Security Act but also a law to curb the power of utility companies, a "wealth-sharing" tax bill, and legislation that bolstered federal banking rules and strengthened the TVA—the so-called Second New Deal that historians saw as the beginnings of an American welfare state.

Roosevelt wasted no time in urging the public to support his own constitutional vision and to share his disdain for the Court's. Four mornings after the NRA bombshell, he was dressing for his regular Friday session with reporters when Steve Early, the press secretary, mentioned his brother-in-law's comment during their morning commute into the city. "George says that those boys up there," Early recounted, alluding to the justices, "think that this is still the horse-and-buggy age." The president offered no reply.

The correspondents crowded into the Oval Office, and Roosevelt smiled as he twisted a cigarette into his holder. "The implications of this decision," he declared, "are much more important than almost certainly any decision of my lifetime or yours, more important than any decision probably since the Dred Scott case." Then he spoke for almost an hour and a half, without interruption, in the longest press conference of his presidency to date. In detail, he explained that such a constricted view of interstate commerce that excluded factories, mines, and farms left the federal government jurisdiction over little beyond the goods actually in transit. This would dump the problems of a national economy onto the shoulders of the individual states—an attitude that made more sense in 1787, when the Constitution was drafted.

"The country was in the horse-and-buggy age when that clause was written," the president said. Communities then were self-sufficient, and the purpose of granting Congress control over the commerce between states was to protect any state from taking advantage of another. "Since that time," he argued, "because of the improvement in transportation, because of the fact that, as we know, what happens in one state has a good deal of influence on the people in another state, we have developed an entirely different philosophy. The prosperity of the farmer *does* have an effect today on the manufacturer in Pittsburgh. The prosperity of the clothing worker in the City of New York has an effect on the prosperity of the farmer in Wisconsin, and so it goes. We are interdependent—we are tied in together."

When the president finished, Francis Stephenson of the Associated

Press asked, "Can we use the direct quotation on that 'horse-and-buggy stage?'"

"I think so."

Steve Early jumped in: "Just the phrase."

Newspapers across the country quoted the president's characterization of the Court as stuck in the past.

SOON A LESS enduring term entered the political lexicon, contributed by Henry A. Wallace, the agriculture secretary with a mystical streak. One day in the fall of 1935, he speculated with reporters about the judicial fate of the Agricultural Adjustment Administration, with its convoluted apparatus for taxing the mills and packagers that processed whatever the farmers produced, then using the revenue to pay the farmers to produce less. The processors' outrage had propelled the case through the lower courts to the nation's highest bench. Wallace began, "If we are Schechtered . . ."

The Supreme Court had not ruled on a New Deal law since moving into its majestic new building. On the first Monday of 1936, the courtroom was jammed to capacity, and long lines had formed outside. The Court had been in recess since before Christmas, and a decision was expected on the AAA.

"I have number four-oh-one," Justice Roberts announced as he fiddled with his glasses, "the United States against William M. Butler et al., receivers of the Hoosac Mills Corporation." An electricity ran through the crowd—this was the AAA case, *United States v. Butler.* That Roberts was to read the majority opinion came as a surprise, though nobody in the audience quite knew what it meant. A gentleman farmer who had never received a penny from the AAA, Roberts had spent the holiday, as usual, on his Pennsylvania farm, writing and rewriting the opinion he now began to recite. He barely glanced at the twenty pages in front of him on the mahogany bench as he boomed out sentences and paragraphs almost verbatim.

Some of the Court's opinions were written in recognizable English, lucid enough for nonlawyers to understand. This one was as convoluted as the program it described. Roberts, chin on hand, spoke in a conversational yet resonant voice, so that despite the courtroom's haphazard acoustics, everyone could hear his words. But understanding them was something else. As he finished half of the opinion, the eight men who sat to his left were still the only ones in the courtroom who knew which way he would rule.

He started by taking up an argument over constitutional interpretation—again, between Hamilton and the Jeffersonians—that had endured since the Constitution began. Specifically at issue was the Constitution's clause that empowered Congress to raise taxes "to provide for . . . the general Welfare of the United States." James Madison, like Jefferson, believed in a weak central government, and he had argued that the authority to tax the citizenry was limited to the purposes and powers that the Constitution had expressly granted to Congress. To Hamilton, who envisioned a government with teeth, this was nonsense. Congress could define the general welfare for itself, he believed, unless the Constitution barred the way.

"This court has noticed the question," Roberts said, "but has never found it necessary to decide which is the true construction." Now, however, it did. "The power of Congress to authorize expenditure of public moneys for public purposes," he decreed, "is not limited by the direct grants of legislative power found in the Constitution." He seemed to favor Hamilton and the New Deal. But in the very next sentence, he backed away. Even the government's broader authority to spend money on the general welfare, he noted, was subject to the Constitution's limitations, including a familiar one, rooted in the Court's pinched definition of interstate commerce. Congress had no power to involve itself in agriculture, Roberts reasoned, because growing a crop or tending an animal was a local activity, even if the harvest was to be sold in another state. Even so, the tax itself might have been constitutionally tolerable, he went on, except that in the elaborately contrived mechanism of the AAA, the tax was not truly a tax. Instead, the tax that processors paid, to be redistributed to the farmers who agreed to produce less, was in reality a cog in a federal regulatory scheme meant to coerce farmers to act as the government wished, in violation of the Tenth Amendment, which limited the powers that the federal government could apply. This left the AAA's power to tax and spend, Roberts concluded, as nothing more than "means to an unconstitutional end." The verdict, at last, stood revealed, as another blow to the New Deal. The audience, as one, let out a sigh.

The law reviews would soon mock Roberts's sinuous reasoning—"a novel approach," as the *Harvard Law Review* archly described it. Surely more hurtful was the judgment of the journal he had once served as an editor. "[T]he Court while purporting to adopt a liberal construction of the federal government's taxing power has in effect created merely an indefinite limitation on the exercise of this power, the extent of which is known only to the Court itself," the *University of Pennsylvania Law Review* decried. "The dangers inherent in such a situation might seem less real were they not so strongly expressed by the vigorous dissenting opinion of one-third of the Supreme Court."

"I think the judgment should be reversed." The blunt opening sentence of Harlan Fiske Stone's dissent suited him. The sixty-four-year-old justice had the thickset body of an aging athlete, and the farmer's son from New Hampshire was without pretense. A sign on his desk described a New England Yankee's four rules of life: "Eat it up; Wear it out; Make it do; Do without it." He had been expelled from Massachusetts Agricultural College for assaulting a chaplain during a brawl, prompting his transfer to Amherst College, in the same town. There he became a bone-crushing lineman, one of the college's all-time gridiron greats, and pals with a Vermonter in the class behind him, Calvin Coolidge. In 1924, embroiled in his predecessor's scandal, President Coolidge prevailed on his old friend, recently the dean of Columbia Law School, to join his cabinet as an incorruptible attorney general. Nine months later, Coolidge named him to the Court.

An outdoorsman, Stone often seemed restless on the bench. He was the most gregarious of justices and probably the frankest—the only one unafraid, it was said, of blurting something about a pending case. He also had a prankish sense of humor. In his library at home, at the touch of a button, a bookcase swiveled open as an entrance into a secret study, where he could work undisturbed. He enjoyed hobnobbing with musicians and young artists, and at least once a week he typed a loving and candid letter to one or both—"Dear Youngsters"—of his grown sons. Another justice's law clerk lauded "the warmth of Stone's personality [and] the greatness of his heart."

On this sleety midday in January 1936, Harlan Stone was anything but warm. Veteran Court-watchers could not remember such sarcasm expressed from the bench, delivered by Roberts's erstwhile friend. "A tortured construction of the Constitution," he railed, leaving no doubt about the identity of the torturer. He accused the majority of judicial arrogance. "While unconstitutional exercise of power by the executive and legislative branches of the government is subject to judicial restraint," he cautioned, "the only check upon our own exercise of power is our own sense of self-restraint." The Court had no authority to rule on the wisdom of a law, he argued, only on Congress's right to pass it.

"The joke of it," he wrote to his sons, "is that I haven't very much confidence in the A.A.A."

He and Roberts had argued heatedly in the Saturday conference, or so the president regaled his cabinet when the gossip reached his eager ears. Stone had grilled Roberts, asking him again and again to admit that the federal government had the constitutional power to pay citizens to act in society's interests. Each time, Roberts had refused to say. In the courtroom, Stone's shrewd eyes flashed as he ridiculed the majority's reasoning. A tax was no less a tax, he argued, if it was spent in a way that imposed conditions on its recipients. Concluding otherwise, he said, "must lead to absurd consequences. The government may give seeds to farmers, but may not condition the gift upon their being planted where they are most needed or even planted at all. The government may give money to the unemployed, but may not ask that those who get it shall give labor in return." Justices Brandeis and Cardozo had joined Stone in his dissent.

Once it was realized that Chief Justice Hughes had sided with the conservatives in the six-to-three vote, rumors soon started, and persisted, that he had initially voted with the liberals but switched sides—perhaps to avoid another politically unpalatable five-to-four vote, or to let him exercise the chief justice's prerogative in assigning Roberts to write the Court's opinion. But years later, constitutional scholars shared Stone's disdain for Roberts's jurisprudence—its "House-that-Jack-Built reasoning," "a wretchedly argued opinion," "a rather lumbering affair." They reserved their greatest scorn for an aside in the twenty-six-page opinion in which Roberts described his approach to judicial review. In deciding if a law passed constitutional muster, the Court had only one duty: "to lay the article of the Constitution which is invoked beside the statute which is challenged and to decide whether the latter squares with the former." Roscoe Pound, the legendary dean at Harvard Law School, had derided such a simplistic conception years earlier as the "slot machine" theory of judicial review, for implying that the Constitution was no more challenging to decipher than determining if three lemons had lined up side by side.

Legal sages knew better. "Of the 6,000-odd words of the constitutional document, at least 39 out of every 40 are totally irrelevant to the vast majority, as well as to the most important, of the problems which the Court handles each term in the field of constitutional interpretation," Edward Corwin of Princeton explained. "Or to put the same thought a little differently, about 150 words serve to articulate the bulk of our constitutional law." Most of these momentous words were simple enough for a child to understand, but artfully—and evocatively—indefinite: *liberty, general welfare, equal protection, persons, cruel and unusual, necessary and proper, among the several States, due process, no law* . . . Reasonable people could understand them differently, and their meaning was bound to shift at different stages in a nation's life. "Since most of the words and phrases dealing with the powers and the limits of government are vague and must in practice be interpreted by human beings," the famed historian Charles Beard penned for an academic symposium that was published that spring, "it follows that the Constitution as practice is a living thing." A constitution that defined its terms with too much precision could become a straitjacket as the decades and centuries passed. In judicial liberals' thinking, it was the brilliant ambiguities in America's Constitution that explained its endurance, by allowing its meaning to evolve—much as John Marshall had hoped—to suit whatever the nation needed at the time. Surely the Founding Fathers, who were so farsighted in so many ways, had anticipated that the accepted understanding of the Constitution should continue to stay current as the dynamic nation developed.

Roberts's opinion that abolished the AAA sparked outrage all over the country. A spokesman for Kansas farmers pronounced it a "national calamity." On a highway near Iowa State College, in the agricultural heartland, the authorities found six life-size figures—cardboard, in black robes—hanged in effigy. "Heartbreaking," said New York City's mayor, Fiorello La Guardia, though the AAA had increased what his constituents paid for food. "If the American farmer is prosperous," he elucidated, "American industry is prosperous, and American workers have jobs." The feelings ran high on both sides. "I doubt if any action of the Supreme Court," Stone confided to his sons, echoing Roosevelt's response to the NRA's demise, "has stirred the country so deeply since the Dred Scot [*sic*] decision. My mail is full of letters—some abusive and condemnatory." At a social reception in Washington, he saw Alice Roosevelt Longworth, the sharp-tongued daughter of Theodore Roosevelt and the widow of Nicholas Longworth, a powerful House Speaker. "Recreant," she accused Stone for his ardent dissent, using her gussied-up word for a traitor.

THE UPROAR DID not deter the Court's conservatives, who kept dealing the New Deal a thrashing. In May, Owen Roberts joined the Four Horsemen once again to strike down the entire statute that regulated the prices and wages in the coal industry, on the grounds that governmental discipline over wages was reserved to the states. Of the ten New Deal laws that had come before the Supreme Court, the justices had overturned eight. Only the TVA and the gold-clause law had survived.

On the first of June 1936, the Court met for the final session of its persistently conservative term. The only major case still pending involved the state law in New York that set a minimum wage for women. The justices had barely taken their seats when Pierce Butler started to speak. A hulk of a man with piercing blue eyes, the Court's only Catholic—in every way a conservative—still wore eyeglasses with old-fashioned metal frames. Because of his doggedness in conference and his sour disposition, Hughes considered him the most difficult man on the Court.

For nearly forty-five minutes, Justice Butler lumbered on. The three-year-old law in New York was similar to statutes in sixteen other states. Joseph Tipaldo, the manager of the Spotlight Laundry in Brooklyn, had refused to pay his female employees the required weekly wage of $13.42, on average, and had falsified his records. Butler found the issue straightforward, a matter of settled precedent. "The right to make contracts about one's affairs," he declared, "is a part of the liberty protected by the due process clause," for the employers as well as for the employed. The Court had settled this question already, he noted, in the *Adkins* case in 1923, when it struck down a federal statute that set a minimum wage for women in Washington, D.C. Though the *Tipaldo* case involved a state law, not a federal law, Butler saw no distinction in the circumstances that applied to the laundry in Brooklyn, and the other three Horsemen—and Owen Roberts—had agreed.

Justice Stone's dissent, yet again, was scathing. "It is difficult to imagine any grounds, other than our own personal economic predilections," he charged, "for saying that the contract of employment is any the less an appropriate subject of legislation than are scores of others," ones the Court had allowed. He denigrated *Adkins* as the controlling precedent, arguing that society had learned quite a lot since then about whether an employer beset by ruthless competitors and a worker reduced to desperate straits were truly free to bargain. "There is grim irony in speaking of the freedom of contract of those who, because of their economic necessities, give their services for less than is needful to keep body and soul together," Stone implored. "Because of their nature and extent these are public problems. A generation ago they were for the individual to solve; today they are the burden of the nation." The proper precedent, he insisted, his rapier flashing, was not *Adkins* in 1923 but rather the *Nebbia* case in 1934, in which Roberts had concluded that a legislature—New York's, as it happened—could regulate the economy pretty much as it liked. Stone made a point of quoting Roberts's own words that a state could adopt any economic policy likely to further the public welfare as long as it has "a reasonable relation to a proper legislative purpose."

Privately, Stone was even more distraught. He was already troubled by the Court's zigzags, such as in upholding the TVA, with just a single dissent, after killing the AAA. "I think there has never been a time in the history of the Court when there has been so little intelligible, recognizable pattern in its judicial performance as in the last few years," he had written to Frankfurter on the February day the Court accepted the TVA. "It just seems as though, in some of these cases, the writer and those who united with him didn't care what was said, as long as the opinion seemed plausible on its face." With the *Tipaldo* case, Stone wrote to his sister, the Court was finishing "the most disastrous term in its history." The Court, which had already determined the federal government lacked the constitutional authority to protect the health and well-being of its most vulnerable workers, was now barring the state governments from protecting them as well. Despite the millions of unemployed and the persistence of bread lines and hunger, the Supreme Court had decided that no government, on any level, had the power to address the citizens' most wrenching needs. No matter what the people wanted or who they elected, they were on their own.

AROUND WASHINGTON AND across the nation, the reaction was merciless. Organized labor was horrified. George Meany, the young president of New York's labor federation, warned that working people might soon regard the Court "as an instrument of oppression." Even the Court's customary champions rebelled. "It is hard to find a good word spoken for the majority decision, even among conservatives," *Kiplinger's Letter* told its business subscribers. An editorial in the *Boston Herald* called it "a shocking blow to enlightened conservatives." Of the 344 newspaper editorials around the country, only 10 endorsed the decision. "The law that would jail any laundryman for having an underfed horse," a Republican newspaper in upstate New York scowled, "should jail him for having an underfed girl employee."

The timing of the decision, shortly before the political parties' 1936 national conventions, added to the tumult. On his way to Cleveland the following week for the Republicans' convention, even Herbert Hoover conceded that "something should be done to give back to the states the powers they thought they already had." The party's platform asserted that state laws to set minimum wages and maximum hours for women and children could be "done within the Constitution as it stands now."

In the course of its past two terms, the Supreme Court had faithfully thwarted the efforts of the president and Congress, of the governors and legislatures, to succor the Depression-stricken voters who had put them into office. The unelected Court was remote from the people, but it was not beyond their reach. And now it had gone too far.

# CHAPTER SIX

# The Court Plan

AS THE REPORTERS crowded around the president's desk, one of them asked if he saw any means of accomplishing the New Deal's goals "within the existing framework of the Constitution," in light of the Court's minimum-wage decision the day before.

"I think I will have to reframe your question," the president replied with a smile. "'Have you any comment on the Supreme Court decision?'" Then he provided one. He reminded the reporters that New York's legislature had debated the minimum-wage law while he was the governor and had enacted it since Herbert Lehman had taken his place. "It seems to be fairly clear as a result of this decision and former decisions," he said, "that the no-man's-land where no government can function is being more clearly defined." He inhaled on his cigarette. The phrase "no-man's-land" had become notorious during the Great War as the stretch of certain death between the trenches. In invoking it as an epithet for the Court's unwillingness to allow any level of government to come to the rescue, the president had lifted it from an editorial in the *St. Louis Star-Times*. "A state cannot do it," he said, "and the federal government cannot do it."

"How can you meet that situation?" a reporter asked.

"I think that is about all there is to say on it."

"I think there are dangers"—another reporter tried—"in the existence of that no-man's-land."

"I think that is all there is to say about it."

The president was under pressure to do something about the Court. The head of the Democratic Club in Stockton, California, wrote him on June 3, "By another 4 to 5 decision on the part of the JUDOCRACY, *one*

84

*man* has been able . . . to nullify the progress of half a century along humanitarian lines." Reforms that had taken decades to materialize were endangered by a few callous men. At the same time, the Social Security Act and the Wagner Act, the capstones of economic progressivism, were making their way onto the docket of the Court just as the 1936 election was approaching, with FDR's prospects for reelection looking less than certain. The untried Gallup poll allotted him a slim summertime lead of only 5 percentage points, and the *Literary Digest* survey, which had never been wrong, found Alf Landon a sure thing. The president knew he needed to campaign on the New Deal's accomplishments, not on the divisive issue of the Supreme Court. Indeed, the Democratic platform that year suggested only "a clarifying amendment" to the Constitution, if needed to assure Congress and the state legislatures the power to act. In the course of the presidential campaign, a single timid reference was made to the Court—by Landon. For the moment, the president followed the advice that Henry Fountain Ashurst, the cunning chairman of the Senate Judiciary Committee, had volunteered a second time after the Court struck down the AAA. He had told the president, "Father Time, with his scythe, is on your side."

LOCKING HORNS WITH the Supreme Court was a presidential sport almost as old as the Court itself. Thomas Jefferson wrestled with a Court packed with his Federalist opponents, and he tried but failed to have one ousted from office. Andrew Jackson had dared the Court to make him obey: "John Marshall has made his decision," he reportedly stated—"let him enforce it now if he can." Abraham Lincoln had defied it during the Civil War, when he ignored its objections and suspended the right of habeas corpus, temporarily driving the Court into eclipse. ("If the policy of the government, upon vital questions affecting the whole people, is to be irrevocably fixed by decisions of the Supreme Court," he declared in 1861, "the people will have ceased to be their own rulers.") Theodore Roosevelt, as an ex-president in 1912, called for letting the public override Court decisions by referendum. "I may not know much about law," he said, "but I do know one can put the fear of God into judges."

On May 28, 1935, the day after the Court's unanimous rejection of the NRA, the president had summoned Homer Cummings back to the White House, and again the next day, to discuss the possibilities of changing the Constitution—or the Court. The two men had worked together for many years in the political vineyards. At the 1920 Democratic national convention, the well-born and Yale-educated Cummings, then the party chairman, delivered the keynote address, a tribute to the stricken outgoing president, Woodrow Wilson. It proved so eloquent that the thirty-eight-year-old FDR, then the assistant navy secretary and a delegate from New York, was inspired to snatch his state's standard out of a Tammany delegate's hands and to parade it around the hall, drawing the Wilsonites' gratitude and some welcome attention to himself. Before the convention ended, he found himself as the party's vice presidential nominee on the ticket with Ohio's reformist but colorless governor, James Cox.

Homer Cummings, more than anything, was a loyalist. The practiced politician, also a Mason, an Elk, and an Odd Fellow, was "a man who would play ball," as a home-county Connecticut newspaper described him. He had supported Roosevelt for the presidency starting in 1931 and delivered the most passionate speech of the 1932 convention, establishing Roosevelt as the liberal heir of William Jennings Bryan and Woodrow Wilson. After Roosevelt won the election, Cummings campaigned even harder for the post of attorney general. When the president-elect instead selected Thomas Walsh, Montana's populist senior senator, Cummings's consolation prize was the governor-generalship of the Philippines. After the election, he stopped off in Washington on his way overseas, when Providence intervened. Walsh, a seventy-three-year-old widower, was on the train back to Washington from his honeymoon in Miami, after his sudden marriage to a Cuban sugar heiress far younger than he. Two mornings before the new president's inauguration, the attorney general–designate was found dead on his stateroom floor—of a heart attack, the doctor guessed, though no autopsy was performed. (The senator's son-in-law later told friends that he suspected the new widow's maid of poisoning him.) And thus, at Missy LeHand's suggestion, Homer Cummings secured the job of his dreams.

The new attorney general was far more of a politician than a practicing lawyer, much less an expert on the Constitution, but Roosevelt had explained, "I think he's a shrewd, level-headed fellow." Nor was he much of a New Dealer. He liked to think of himself as neither liberal nor conservative but rather a conservative liberal, to the extent that he had ideological feelings at all. It had been assumed at the start that he would not stay long in the cabinet, but he had performed serviceably in the job. For one thing, the federal government's crime-fighting role had burgeoned under his tenure. He had launched the War on Crime, persuading Congress to declare bank robbery, racketeering, and kidnapping as federal crimes, replacing the old military prison on Alcatraz, refashioning his department's Bureau of Investigation into the Federal Bureau of Investigation, and keeping its director, J. Edgar Hoover, under a semblance of bureaucratic control.

The president simply liked Homer Cummings and his lively and quick-witted wife. Cecilia Cummings would send the president small gifts ("I am afraid I did not tell you the other day how much I liked my handkerchiefs," he once wrote back) and affectionate notes, often graced with a tiny self-portrait of her Betty Boop hairdo. But the president valued Cummings for more than his wife, his political skills, or even his presumed competence. Rather than cataloging the reasons why the president could not do what he wished, Cummings tried to find a way it could be done while conforming to the Constitution.

After a second day of discussions, Cummings saw a reason for optimism in the defeats the New Deal had suffered at the Court. "Personally, I cannot help but feel that, while in a certain sense they are a setback for America," he wrote in his diary, "they are a godsend to the administration. The whole scene is shifted. We are no longer on the defensive." Cummings felt something had to be done—"either a liberalized interpretation of the Constitution, or some drastic method of change," he suggested. "It is impossible to put America into a legalistic straitjacket. It simply cannot be done." When the president instructed him to figure out a solution, Cummings eagerly obliged.

The possibilities were endless—"literally thousands," by a newspaperman's calculations. A constitutional amendment could expand the federal government's powers to intervene in the economy, such as by assuring Congress's power over interstate commerce or by clarifying its authority to promote the general welfare or by disentangling the procedural rights of due process from the judicial protection of laissez-faire. The president fancied an amendment that would permit Congress to trump the judiciary by repassing a law that the Court had struck down after an election had intervened. But Cummings had learned enough about constitutional law to understand that to draft any of these amendments "implies a very delicate surgical operation," in finding just the right words to empower Washington sufficiently to relieve the citizenry's distress but not so much that the states might lapse into impotence. Even if the drafters found the precise wording that could attract enough political support, an amendment was easy to stymie—because of the Constitution itself. The cumbersome process, requiring two-thirds approval in each chamber of Congress and then ratification by the legislatures in three fourths of the states, would undoubtedly take two years or more. A few million dollars spent in thirteen small states could probably block anything. Twelve years after Congress had proposed a constitutional amendment to outlaw child labor, its ratification had stalled twelve states short. Nor did a constitutional amendment match Cummings's understanding of the problem at hand. "The real difficulty is not with the Constitution," he wrote to the president after the Court had squelched the AAA, "but with the Judges who interpret it." He considered an amendment requiring that "all Federal Judges, or, at least, all Supreme Court Judges" retire at age seventy. This would leave intact the Court's jurisdiction and the balance of power within the government and "would merely insure the exercise of the powers of Court by Judges less likely to be horrified by new ideas."

Legislation was a possibility, too. The Constitution specified next to nothing about the "one supreme Court," leaving its jurisdiction, its procedures—even its makeup—in Congress's hands. Congress could pass a law requiring the vote of six or seven justices to declare a statute unconstitutional—though the Court could declare *that* law unconstitutional. Or Congress could strip the Court of its authority over particular kinds of appeals or otherwise somehow meddle with its workings. In the course of 1936, members of Congress had proposed more than a hundred bills meant to rebalance the powers of government, though none of them survived the legislative labyrinth.

There matters lay until after the election. It was the angriest campaign the nation had seen since 1896, when the populist William Jennings Bryan led the workingman and the farmer—the have-nots—against the haves. The conservative columnist David Lawrence saw the 1936 election as the climax of "a titanic struggle between conservative and liberal forces," the belief in laissez-faire versus the welcoming of government-mandated restraint. The unemployed and insecure Americans, still in need of a new deal, confronted the economic royalists—the capitalists and tycoons. During the campaign, the president was pleased to be booed on Wall Street and at Harvard, his alma mater, for it helped to remove any question that the aristocrat from Hyde Park—more than the Kansas governor, Alf Landon, from America's heartland—was truly the man of the people. Only in the campaign's last rally, at Madison Square Garden, did Roosevelt allow his bitterness to seep through. "I would like to have it said of my first administration that in it the forces of selfishness and of lust for power met their match," he declaimed. "I should like to have it said of my second administration that in it these forces met their master." He thought of the election as a referendum on himself—"and the people must be either for me or against me," he told an aide.

Unambiguously, the people decided. During the fall, Roosevelt kept gaining in voters' favor, and any doubts they may have entertained about the New Deal or the continuing—though ever-lighter—Depression gave way to their trust in a proven and empathetic leader. On Election Day, Alf Landon failed to take any state other than Maine and Vermont, including his own. Afterward, the reelected president portrayed the election results as an expression of the national will, a ringing endorsement not only of himself but also of the AAA, the Wagner Act, the Social Security Act—the New Deal.

The Sunday evening after the election, upon his return to Washington from Hyde Park, the president summoned his attorney general to the White House. For an hour they bantered about the reelection campaign. The president joked about the attorney general's rumored bender upon learning of the Democratic victory in Stamford, Connecticut, his reliably Republican hometown. Then the conversation moved on to the subject of the Supreme Court—"weighing pro and con, the question of constitutional amendments of one kind or another," as Cummings confided to his diary, "or possibly changes in the Supreme Court or additions thereto."

The president told his interior secretary, Harold Ickes, over lunch a few days later that he doubted that any of the justices would ever resign. And none, so far, had died. Yet he already seemed to glimpse a solution. He regaled Ickes with the story of how, two decades earlier, the British House of Lords kept refusing to approve legislation that the House of Commons sent up, but when the successive prime ministers Herbert Asquith and David Lloyd George threatened to appoint several hundred more peers, the chamber bowed to the leaders' will.

The idea of expanding the size of the Court had first come to the president's attention on a January night in 1935. Cummings had argued the gold-clause cases that afternoon, and the president was alarmed at the tenor of the justices' questions. Robert Jackson, an up-and-coming Treasury Department lawyer, described an article he had read in *Political Science Quarterly* that recalled how President Grant had nominated two additional justices to the Court—"for the purpose of reversing," as Jackson recounted the tale, its 1870 decision that barred the use of greenbacks as legal tender. Historians disagreed about whether Grant intended to pack the Court or whether it was merely a coincidence that he nominated the two additional justices—for the seats that Congress had taken away while Andrew Johnson lived in the White House—just hours after the Court acted against his wishes. But nobody denied that the stratagem succeeded. The Court took less than fifteen months to reverse itself.

Fourteen presidencies later, FDR and his attorney general were intrigued. They undertook a process of elimination. A constitutional amendment would be too easy to block and, in any event, could probably never be ratified "up to and through the 1940 national election," the president explained to Felix Frankfurter, while legislation to require more than a simple majority of justices for declaring a law unconstitutional was "in all probability, unconstitutional per se." A bill to narrow the Court's jurisdiction looked chancy at best. That left the justices themselves as the problem—and increasing their number as the solution. However, both the president and the attorney general "recognized that the proposition violated a taboo," a historian ventured, "and that some principle would have to be found to legitimate it."

Cummings had been exchanging letters with Edward Corwin, who was a special assistant to the attorney general, and the Princeton scholar had an idea. A friend of his, a Harvard government professor named Arthur Holcombe, had made "an ingenious suggestion," Corwin wrote—that the president be authorized to nominate additional justices if a majority of the sitting justices reached seventy or older, requiring only an act of Congress. Soon after receiving Corwin's letter, the attorney general had a sly recollection. With the help of a staff assistant, he had written a tome about his department's history, called *Federal Justice*, that was about to be published. In it, there was a mention of age. On page 531, it quoted a legislative recommendation in 1914 by one of his predecessors, which was meant to apply to all federal judges except the nine on the highest bench: if any judge declined to retire at age seventy, the president could appoint an additional one, to "insure at all times the presence of a judge sufficiently active to discharge promptly and adequately the duties of the court." The same contrivance, Cummings realized, could be applied to the Supreme Court. The idea gained even more appeal considering the identity of its author, the former attorney general who was now properly addressed as Mr. Justice McReynolds, the orneriest of the Four Horsemen.

THE PERSON WHO had contributed the most to Franklin D. Roosevelt's astonishing political ascent—at least of anyone whose name was not Roosevelt—had died the previous spring. Small and stoop-shouldered—"I resemble a medieval gnome," he once said—Louis Howe had served as FDR's oracle and alter ego. He had been the *New York Herald*'s man in Albany in 1911 when he latched on to the rebellious young state senator with the celebrity name and foresaw the presidency in his future. Even after Roosevelt was stricken with polio in 1921, Howe persuaded him that the presidency remained a possibility, though at no time in recorded history had there been a national leader who was unable to walk. It never would have happened for Roosevelt—this was a certainty—without the loyalty and labors of Louis Howe, and Roosevelt knew it.

Howe had revered the man he never stopped calling "Franklin," who possessed everything in abundance—breeding, wealth, looks, charm—that Howe lacked. Louis Howe knew in his bones which political tactics would work and which would backfire, and he was willing to say so. As the president's chief of staff, living in the Lincoln Bedroom, he would argue the loudest and the longest among FDR's advisers if he believed that his strong-minded master was about to make a mistake. And the president would listen. Other than Missy LeHand and occasionally Eleanor, nobody else but Howe could tell him "no" in a way that he would hear and heed. "After

Louis' death," Eleanor noticed, "Franklin frequently made his decisions without canvassing all sides of a question."

Three days before Christmas, in his spidery handwriting, Homer Cummings jotted a note to the president: "I am 'bursting' with ideas about our constitutional problems; and have a plan (of substance & approach)." On December 26, a Saturday, he arrived at the White House, a sheaf of papers in hand. For two hours, the pair of old political warriors engaged in what Cummings described as "one of the longest and most interesting conferences I have had with him in a long time." They chatted about the president's postelection trip to South America and about the autographed copy of FDR's speech at Chautauqua, New York, that the president had given Cummings for Christmas—"a very attractive volume," Cummings gushed, one of only fifty and therefore "priceless." Turning at last to the Supreme Court, the attorney general said he had one request to make—that the president not laugh at him for saying he had found a solution. Both men laughed.

Cummings acknowledged the drawbacks in every suggestion made to date and proposed that they return to the fundamentals, to understand the problem they faced. Had the Court's recent dissents been the majority opinions instead, the problem would disappear. The real difficulty lay not with the Constitution, he argued, but with how the justices had interpreted—or misinterpreted—it.

"Go on, you are going good," the president urged. "I wish I had a stenographer present."

The attorney general lamented the delays in litigation and cited the criticism leveled at the Court for accepting so few appeals. He recalled that William Howard Taft had argued for a constitutional amendment requiring judges to retire at age seventy, and he described a federal judge's recent plea for additional judges in the lower courts, to speed up their work.

Extending this to the Supreme Court, Cummings proposed adding six new justices—one for each of the sitting justices over seventy. Aligned with the three predictable liberals, the administration could then count on nine votes on a fifteen-member Court in favor of decisions that upheld the New Deal. The president's enthusiasm grew as the discussion went on. Cummings cautioned that President Grant had been accused of "packing the Court" in the year of the attorney general's birth, but he told Roosevelt that they were probably unduly terrified by a phrase. The entire task, he assured the president, could be completed within sixty days.

"The answer to a maiden's prayer," the president reportedly said.

The president summoned journalist George Creel to the White House. He often used Creel for trial balloons, for the writer-cum-politician—he had lost to novelist Upton Sinclair in California's Democratic gubernatorial primary in 1934—allowed the president's advisers a veto over his prose. In an article for *Collier's* before the New Year on Roosevelt's second-term plans, Creel reported that if other solutions proved ineffective, "Congress *can enlarge the Supreme Court*, increasing the number of justices from nine to twelve or fifteen." Despite Creel's italics, the public's reaction was nil.

Night after night during the following weeks, Homer Cummings used a secluded entrance into the White House to confer with the president and then slip away unseen. Wanting to maintain his own central role in the historical initiative meant excluding Tommy Corcoran from the policy-making process—which the aggressive young aide would likely have taken over—until the substance of the decisions had been made. "Once again," as Sam Rosenman recounted, "the president was willing to go to great wasteful lengths to keep conflicting personalities apart while the work was going on."

The plan went through a dozen drafts or more. Cummings cast it as a comprehensive program intended to unclog a backlogged judiciary by in-stituting a variety of procedural reforms, including hiring a "proctor" to monitor court calendars, assuring immediate appeals to the Supreme Court on constitutional issues, and almost incidentally, appointing new judges at every level to supplement the septuagenarians who refused to step down. And once the size of the Court had expanded, whether to fif-teen justices or something less, the larger number would never fall back to nine, even after the elderly justices retired.

Tommy Corcoran did not learn of the plan until just a few days before it was publicly announced, but three other presidential advisers did, and all of them pleaded with the president to forgo the deceptive arguments about a judicial backlog—the Justice Department's own reports disproved it—and offer the real reason instead, to aim his case directly at the Court's conservative course. The president refused, then refused again, and when he grew angry, they acceded.

FDR was an old hand at indirection. At age nine, he had conspired with his mother to keep any unnerving news away from his ill and aged father. Over the years, whether to sidestep his mother's strong will or to engage in his extramarital excursions or to keep his political opponents off-stride, he had raised obliqueness almost to an art form. The gamesmanship seemed to amuse him, and it enabled him to get his way while avoiding the personal confrontations he abhorred.

Homer Cummings offered another piece of strategic advice, beyond disingenuousness—that the president keep any advance word of the plan away from congressional leaders, lest they try to dissuade him, and also to preserve the element of surprise. Throughout his first term, the president had worked closely and successfully with his party's kingpins on Capitol Hill, but that was before the election. An overflow of Democrats had swept into the Seventy-fifth Congress, and many of them owed their good fortune to him. Overconfident and cocky after his smashing reelection, he felt certain that he could work his will on Capitol Hill and with the public alike. Sophistry and secrecy—these were the attorney general's recommendations on how to proceed, and on both counts the president agreed.

Louis Howe would never have allowed it.

# CHAPTER SEVEN

# An Ideal New Dealer

TOMMY CORCORAN HAD every pretext to invite Burton K. Wheeler, a tempestuous senator from Montana, to lunch. The two men had worked and sweated together before, in saving the administration's bill to regulate utility holding companies—Corcoran's co-handiwork, along with his sidekick Ben Cohen's—from a legislative sepulcher in 1935. As the Senate Interstate Commerce Committee's chairman, Wheeler ordered hearings at the critical moment that exposed the industry's persuasive lies, and then he pressed the bill through to enactment. Despite the eighteen-year difference in their ages, the two men had become friends.

On a cold and sunny February day in 1937, the week after Roosevelt unloosed his thunderbolt on the Supreme Court, Wheeler strolled the three blocks along North Capitol Street from the Senate Office Building to meet Corcoran. He turned left at E Street and entered the Dodge Hotel. The square and squat building, without artifice, had been constructed in 1921 as the Grace Dodge Hotel for women, named for a daughter-in-law in the automobile-manufacturing family. The row of high windows in the ground-floor restaurant evoked a gloom in the winter's light, and the wide spacing of the tables encouraged the powerful men of Washington to lean toward one another to swap confidences.

The son of the leading attorney in Pawtucket, Rhode Island, Tommy Corcoran had been earning money since age twelve, as a newsboy, a sales clerk, a farmhand, a lumberjack, a telephone lineman, an instructor in sports. He was short, barrel-chested, and increasingly stout, and his shock of wavy black hair had begun to gray. Many of his peers found him overbearing; to his elders he could be overly deferential. He seemed to understand in his bones what comforted or unnerved people and how to move them in whichever direction he wished, through charm or brusqueness, politeness or profanity.

His showmanship—and his musicianship—had first endeared Tommy Corcoran to the president one summer night in 1935. At the time, Joseph P. Kennedy was running the Securities and Exchange Commission, and Tommy had entertained at one of his parties, playing an accordion he had found in a Washington shop window. There he met Missy LeHand, and Kennedy took him over to the White House to play for FDR. The president loved sea chanteys, and Tommy knew them all. On the piano he could play anything—Gilbert and Sullivan or Beethoven and Brahms. He had played the accordion in Hyde Park on Election Night as the president and his family sang along.

The valedictorian at Brown, first in his class at Harvard Law, Tommy the Cork had plenty more to offer than musicianship. He had earned the president's confidence with his wit and his brains, along with his "passion for anonymity"—he had coined the phrase describing the virtue of a president's adviser—and, most of all, with his political cunning. He and Ben Cohen had coauthored several of the New Deal's most beloved bills, plotting all night above a shop on K Street in an apartment they shared that was almost bare of furniture except for the grand piano in each of the two parlors. They were truly a team—Ben Cohen, the shy and dreamy intellectual, the craftier draftsman, and Tommy Corcoran, the shrewd salesman, brilliant at making the case to lawmakers and at luring them to the president's side.

At lunch with Wheeler, Corcoran opened the conversation by relaying an invitation from the president for a personal briefing on the crisis in the Supreme Court. "He doesn't care about those Tories being against it," Corcoran said, "but he doesn't want you to be against it." Wheeler had genuine leverage—he knew it, and the White House did, too. The president and his advisers expected opposition from the Senate's surviving Republicans and from a smattering of Democrats, the probusiness conservatives and the states' righters who disliked the New Deal. Still, as long as FDR could keep the New Dealers on his side, the Court plan looked certain to pass. Some of the New Dealers felt philosophically squeamish about such a concentration of power in the president's hands, however, and others were politically shaky at home. A defection by Wheeler, the White House knew, might encourage weak-kneed New Dealers to follow.

Wheeler's credentials as a New Dealer were impeccable. Almost fifty-five years old, he even looked the part of the president's reverently invoked "forgotten man." His rimless octagonal glasses and his rumpled dress gave him a look of perpetual surprise, and his dainty hands moved at the wrist whenever he talked. If he looked like the common man, he spoke for him, too, and his skill at legislative infighting and willingness to win by any means necessary had made him an adversary to be feared.

Potentially more dangerous for the White House, Wheeler's credentials as a supporter of the president were equally potent. In the spring of 1930, at the Jefferson Day dinner in New York City, broadcast by radio over most of the nation, Wheeler waited until the then first-term governor had left the banquet hall before becoming the first nationally prominent politician to endorse FDR for the presidency—creating "a sensation," as a Roosevelt biographer wrote. Wheeler had been a New Dealer at heart long before there was a New Deal. While Roosevelt was still professing his faith in balanced budgets and states' rights, the progressive from the Great Plains was pleading for the federal government to fight the big corporations and Wall Street on the common man's behalf.

Wheeler had said nothing yet in public about the president's plan to expand the Supreme Court. He had been in New York City ("not visiting economic royalists," he noted, "although I was over there to investigate some of them") when he picked up a newspaper and read of the proposal. Beyond his ideological disgust at its succession of conservative decisions, he had a personal reason to resent the Court: his son-in-law had lost his job as an economist when the Court abolished the AAA. Still, he considered FDR's proposal a presidential grab for power and a risky one, not only constitutionally but politically, too. As Robert M. La Follette's vice presidential running mate on the Progressive Party ticket in 1924, Wheeler had seen how the party's call for a constitutional amendment to allow Congress to overrule the Supreme Court proved disastrous at the polls. "The Court," he had concluded, "was like a religion to the American people."

Upon returning from New York he had told his wife, Lulu, that he intended to oppose the president's plan, though it might mean the end of his political career. She kept on darning socks in their sprawling white-shingled house in the northwestern quadrant of Washington.

"Do you think that you are right?" she said.

He replied that he had never been more right in his life.

"If you feel that way, you should go ahead." Lulu had never succumbed to the president's charms, for she thought she had glimpsed a hunger for power underneath.

For six days after the president's announcement and for most of the seventh, Wheeler had kept silent in public. Press accounts listed him among the uncommitted. He was preparing a statement to the press—a strong one, denouncing "the concentration of power in any one branch"—when Corcoran had asked him to lunch.

Wheeler assumed that Tommy Corcoran had written the Court proposal, and Corcoran let him think so. It resembled the speech that Corcoran had written, calling for the addition of three justices to the Court, that he had twice urged Wheeler to deliver the year before. Wheeler had declined, and he showed no greater enthusiasm this time for the prospect of adding twice as many justices.

Tommy Corcoran had learned the phrase "an instinct for the jugular" from Oliver Wendell Holmes, and it was an attribute he admired. He offered a deal: if Wheeler would announce his support for the president's plan, he would be given a say in naming two or three of the new justices. Later, when Wheeler told his wife of the offer, Lulu would reply, "It isn't a knowing kind of cattle that's caught with moldy corn."

Corcoran pressed the senator about his desire to see a liberal Court, and Wheeler acknowledged it. He had detested the Court's decisions that blocked Congress from trying to soothe the Depression. Then Corcoran squeezed, warning Wheeler that if he declined to go along, the president would cut a deal with Tammany Hall and the southerners instead—"and he'll put their people on the Court."

Wheeler admitted that Corcoran was probably right. But he had made up his mind. They kept arguing, and still the stiff-necked senator refused. A writer in *Harper's* later described the confrontation as "a fearful row." At last Tommy Corcoran slammed his fist on the table and shouted, "It's going to pass!"

"I tell you it isn't going to pass. And what's more, I'm going to fight it with everything I've got."

The president's young emissary, however, did not leave the Dodge Hotel empty-handed. Wheeler agreed not to announce his opposition right away, a pledge that lasted until the following afternoon. Only after he had released his statement to the press—"there is nothing democratic, progressive or fundamentally sound in the proposal"—did he allow Democratic publicist Charlie Michelson to visit. Michelson asked if he should seek to arrange an invitation for Wheeler to dine with the president.

"Save the plate," Wheeler replied, "for someone easier to persuade."


BURTON K. WHEELER had never easily submitted to authority. His father's people were Quakers who had fled English persecution in 1635 and, with other Wheelers, founded a hamlet in Massachusetts they named Concord. His mother's forebears, no less severe in their morality, were Puritans who had arrived on the *Mayflower*.

His father had been a hardscrabble farmer and a shoemaker outside of Hudson, a shoe-manufacturing town a dozen miles west of Concord. Born in 1882, the youngest of ten children, B. K., as his friends called him, was raised to believe that right was right and wrong was wrong and that the greatest sin was to lie. He left his father's Republican fold, becoming a Democrat, after William Jennings Bryan and the populist gospel—corporate greed was to blame for the nation's ills—captivated him in 1896 and 1900. At the University of Michigan, studying law, he led the campus campaign that ended the fraternities' control over student politics; to work his way through law school, he waited on tables, washed dishes in a Negro restaurant, cut lawns, tended furnaces, and peddled books door to door. While selling Dr. Chase's recipe books (in English, Norwegian, and German editions) in the summertime, he knocked at an Illinois farmhouse and met Lola White. Lulu, as she was called, had a shyness that concealed a lively mind. He made no sale but secured an invitation to dinner. They were married after Wheeler finished law school and had settled himself out West.

Even as a boy, he had dreamed of leaving the "stultifying" East. Gaunt and asthmatic, prone to tuberculosis, Wheeler found that the freedom of the West—its clear air, its openness to opportunity—captivated his imagination. He went looking for a lawyer's job in the high, dry country of the Rocky Mountains and beyond, around Colorado, Arizona, California, Oregon, Utah, and Idaho. On a fall day in 1905, in Butte, Montana, he turned down an offer to work as a stenographer for an unpleasant lawyer and waited for the train to Spokane.

Standing nearby, in front of a saloon, two well-dressed men invited him in for a drink; then, after he told them he was a teetotaler, he settled for a cigar. They drew him into a poker game with two other men and soon fleeced him of everything he had. When he caught them divvying up the winnings, he flew into a young man's outrage and forced them to give some of it back, plus $11 for his ticket to Spokane. Their orders that he leave town only provoked him to track down the difficult lawyer and take the job. Soon he was accepting the court's appointment to represent penniless defendants, and then he hung a shingle of his own. Before long, a well-established law firm in Butte invited him in.

Butte was a rowdy city and an ugly one. Crammed on top of the "Richest Hill on Earth," named for the veins of copper beneath and all around, the city was pockmarked by smelters and copper refineries, crisscrossed with railroad tracks and transmission lines, slathered with brothels and saloons. Butte had no trees, no greenery at all, because of the arsenic that the smokestacks spewed. Indeed, Montana was becoming "scarred, charred and gutted" (in a journalist's description) by cattlemen who stripped the prairie of its grass, by railroaders who snapped up its land, and by the copper kings who ripped up the earth. Those last were the most dangerous to democracy, for across the immense and sparsely populated state, a single company, Anaconda Copper, had come to dominate the economy and, by flaunting its money and power, the political life as well. The Company, as it was called, bullied its miners, bought off the state legislators—paying as much as $30,000 for an ordinary lawmaker, more for a committee chairman—and controlled all but three of Montana's newspapers.

Once Wheeler had built up his practice as a trial lawyer, he was nominated for the legislature in 1910 on the Company's slate. The lingering traces of his Yankee accent posed no problem around Butte, where the natives were few, for he had learned to cuss, it was noted, "in pure Montanese." His value as a candidate on the Irish-dominated slate was his

English heritage, for its appeal to the miners of Welsh descent. Soon, however, his opposition to Anaconda began to emerge, in his unwillingness to block a Democrat from running for city alderman in his district, which allowed a socialist to sneak through to victory, and by his vote in the legislature to send populist Thomas J. Walsh to the U.S. Senate.

The more the Company tried to bring him to heel, the harder Wheeler fought back. At the Democratic state convention in 1912, he fell three votes short of the nomination for attorney general; the following year, at age thirty-one, Walsh helped him land an appointment as the U.S. attorney for Montana. Anaconda used the suspicions and paranoia unleashed by the Great War—toward German spies or foreigners of any description, toward anything that breathed of sedition—to bully the miners and their labor unions, casting them as radicals, which many were, and as traitors, which they were not. Wheeler made a name for himself, not so much by his prosecutions but by his refusals to prosecute the Company's enemies without evidence. The war munitions had sent copper prices soaring while wages lagged, driving the miners out on strike, at times violently. The Company and its Pinkertons fought the miners, while the radical Industrial Workers of the World, the Wobblies, competed for workers' loyalties with militant trade unions. The Company's newspapers whipped up sentiment for using the sedition laws to indict foreign-accented unions, while Wheeler pursued the war profiteers but left the unions alone. He refused to arrest a Wobbly organizer whose allegedly treasonous comments were, by Wheeler's reckoning, permitted under the law. After the organizer was found hanging from a trestle in Butte, a note of warning pinned to his clothes, the legislature came within a single vote of censuring Wheeler for his unwillingness to hunt targets of public enmity if he thought them innocent. In eastern Montana, he was nearly lynched.

Wheeler also bucked the pressure from Washington to go after the Wobblies, standing in the way of Attorney General A. Mitchell Palmer and his Red hunt. Thus began Wheeler's scorn for the Department of Justice as well as his reverence for the Supreme Court—"in large measure because I recalled how the local state judges, elected to office, were carried away by the World War I hysteria in their own communities," he explained many years later. Once the war ended, and the soldiers and war-industry workers lost their jobs, a series of anarchist bombings accompanied by militant strikes, especially in the Northwest, created a panic that confused foreigners with subversives and free speech with sedition. Fearful voters pressed their elected judges to wield the instruments of justice for the majority's protection, as soldiers patrolled the streets of Butte. "It was the federal courts—particularly the Supreme Court—which in most instances upheld the right to freedom of speech," Wheeler recounted. This was the judiciary's gravest duty, to protect the rights of the individual against the impassioned masses.

Wheeler quit as the U.S. attorney at last, so that his unpopularity would not ruin the political future of his mentor Tom Walsh, and soon Wheeler tried politics again on his own. The state's Democrats nominated him for governor in 1920, over the party regulars' objections, and the campaign against his Republican opponent, former senator J. M. Dixon, was the dirtiest in Montana's history. Wheeler was almost tarred and feathered not more than fifty miles from Butte. Posters accused him of loyalty to Lenin and the Kaiser—"Bolshevik Burt," the Company-owned newspapers called him—and it was whispered that he favored free love and marriage between the races. In the Harding presidential landslide, he was buried alive. In 1937 he would have occasion to tell a table of senators, "I have suffered for my liberalism as few of you have suffered."

In 1922, the partisans of the Non-Partisan League, whose name belied its socialist views, visited Wheeler at his cabin in Glacier Park and urged him to run for the U.S. Senate so he could join Tom Walsh in Washington. Wheeler was agreeable but set one condition: that the league not endorse him. The Democrats united behind him, and the Company was willing to dispatch Wheeler thousands of miles away, where by fighting for Montana's interests in Washington he would necessarily be fighting, at least on occasion, for Anaconda Copper's.

In the Capitol, first-year senators were expected to be seen but not heard. Wheeler sat in the rear row for less than a week before he stood at his desk and raised an objection to letting the president pro tempore of the Senate continue also to serve as the chairman of the Interstate Commerce Committee. The fight this touched off over the concentration of senatorial power and over the chairman's championing of the railroads ended in a spectacle. In the Republican-run Senate, progressive Republicans joined in electing a Democrat as the committee's new chairman. Wheeler felt

loyal to the Senate's progressives of both political parties and quickly proclaimed his reluctance to follow his own party's leadership or to let its
caucus bind him.

From the beginning of his tenure in Washington, Wheeler had a
knack for drawing attention to himself. Just three and a half months after the
new Senate convened, his face appeared on the cover of the sixteenth issue
of a new weekly magazine called *Time*. The occasion was his tour of the
young Soviet Union, where he concluded that its Communist leaders were
sincere, its peasants more prosperous than under the czars, and its government worthy of diplomatic recognition. Below his portrait lay this caption:
*He made friends with Trotzky.*

Less than a year after he took office, Wheeler rose again on the Senate floor and tackled his most formidable target yet: the attorney general of
the United States. Harry Daugherty, formerly the Republican Party boss in
Ohio, had commanded the smoke-filled room that turned a distinguished-
looking but shallow senator, Warren G. Harding, into a president—and
himself into the fox that was to guard a henhouse of corrupt cronies.
Wheeler had no hard evidence that Daugherty had accepted bribes from
the crooked oilmen who had profited from the government's Teapot Dome
fields in Wyoming, adjacent to Montana, but he felt sure that the proof existed. Even the absence of proof, in Wheeler's mind, seemed suspect, for if
Daugherty's brother and friends had accepted the money on his behalf,
Wheeler said, "he is a bigger fool than the people of the United States give
him credit for being." He called for an investigation, then offended the
Senate's traditionalists by suggesting the membership of a special committee that included himself. That he was doing to Daugherty what A. Mitchell Palmer had pressed Wheeler to do unto the Wobblies seemed not to
have crossed his mind.

Reporters in Washington who were bored by the capital's yearning for
normalcy in an age of flappers and bootleggers admired Wheeler for the
chances he took. "There is something soft in many reformers. There is
nothing soft in Wheeler," the liberal correspondent for the *Nation* gushed.
"Personally he is hard-boiled, hard-bitten, hard-headed, hard-fisted . . . a
soldier of fortune animated and dominated by a 'social conscience.'" The
*New York Times* described his diatribe against Daugherty as "the most
sensational of the present Congress."

Wheeler's boyish smile masked a willingness to play rough. "When you've been fighting the big copper companies for fifteen years, taking your chances with mine guards and private detectives," he said after a dustup in Washington, "this is pie." Just days before the Daugherty hearings began, Wheeler located in Columbus, Ohio, the most compelling—and exciting—of witnesses. Roxy Stinson was the divorced wife of Daugherty's intimate aide who had killed himself the year before in Daugherty's apartment. Her testimony broke open the case. Wheeler's questioning brought notoriety to the "little green house on K Street," where Daugherty and the other Harding cronies had played poker, dispensed patronage, and cut deals. Two weeks later, the attorney general resigned.

Daugherty soon had his revenge, thanks to Justice Department loyalists who had remained in their jobs. Investigators were dispatched to Montana to pore over Wheeler's records, and in Washington, Lulu reported G-men skulking outside in the shrubbery. Within days, a federal grand jury in Montana indicted Wheeler on the charge of discussing a client's federal oil leases with the Interior Department's solicitor, an old friend, after Wheeler had won his Senate seat but before he was sworn in. The grand jury had taken seven or eight ballots, then several hours of a recess, and a final haranguing from the prosecutor before it agreed. Wheeler scorned the indictment to reporters as "a pure and unadulterated frame-up," and to his colleagues he denounced "one of the most damnable conspiracies that have ever been started in the United States." His contempt for the Justice Department's understanding of justice had been fully confirmed. He had reason to be suspicious. "If I don't get them," became his motto, "they'll get me." Whether from a desire for revenge or from a nobler principle, or both, Wheeler found himself part of an honored—though often dishonored—American tradition, of idealists who loathed injustice to their core. Tom Paine, Patrick Henry, John Brown, the young William Jennings Bryan—now the uncompromising senator, the nervy Quaker, had joined their ranks.

Among those who admired his fearlessness was Robert La Follette. The shaggy-haired Wisconsin senator was an original in American political life. Nominally a Republican, he was a champion of progressive causes, an enemy of corporate power, a defender of the common man. When the GOP convention spurned the platform that La Follette wanted in 1924, he broke away and formed the Progressive Party and accepted its nomination for president. Then he approached Wheeler with a tantalizing offer: would the freshman senator with a flair for publicity serve as La Follette's running mate? Wheeler said no. He felt ill-equipped to campaign in the cities, and he lacked La Follette's faith that a third party could cause an electoral deadlock that might catapult at least one of its nominees into national office.

At the summer's Democratic national convention, when Wheeler's name was mentioned as a possible vice president, the Republicans spread the word that he would be indicted again, this time in Washington. Wheeler asked a friend to investigate and learned that there was no reason to worry—unless he accepted La Follette's offer. Immediately, he motored to the Capitol, found La Follette in his office, and announced he had changed his mind.

The novice nominee proved to be a whirlwind as he stumped the cities in the East. Alone among the three parties' six nominees, Wheeler also reached the Pacific Coast. He was unpolished as an orator but always entertaining—a fighting campaigner, forceful on the stump. He hardly ever raised his voice or spoke in a stampede or invoked the personal pronoun. Instead, he told the dramatic story of Harry Daugherty's investigation and detailed, quietly though passionately, the wrongs the corporations had wreaked upon ordinary people. His raw and reedy tenor sounded sincere. Subtlety was a stranger. Crowds filled the halls, and they loved it when he fired sardonic questions at an empty chair onstage and waited for "Silent Cal" Coolidge, the incumbent president, to reply. "I am a Democrat," he declared, "but not a Wall Street Democrat," distinguishing himself from the Democrats' presidential nominee, John W. Davis, a lawyer intimate with the House of Morgan. To an audience at Cooper Union in Manhattan, where Lincoln had declared his "faith that right makes might," Wheeler said he had no quarrel with being labeled a radical, for "Christ was the greatest radical of all time."

After Coolidge's landslide, the Republicans were as good as their word: a federal grand jury in Washington indicted Wheeler for a second time, for the same conversation with the Interior Department solicitor, on a charge of defrauding the public. His trial in Montana, stalled by the presidential campaign, began and lasted a week, with the state's senior senator, Tom Walsh, appearing as the junior senator's chief counsel. The jury took an hour for dinner, ten minutes to deliberate, and voted for acquittal. Though the indictment in Washington was quashed by the courts, Wheeler was left with an ever deeper distrust of a politically motivated judiciary.

His political faith, however he described it, had grown out of his own experience. It was ardent, even principled, but devoid of theory. "I have always pointedly avoided kowtowing to people of wealth, social position, or power," he said. He hated bullies, revered the individual, despised monopolies, believed that nature's resources belonged to everyone, and considered it society's obligation to help the poor and the aged. Whenever the gap grew too wide between what the consumer paid and what the workers and the farmers received, he was apt to see injustice. He believed these things before the economy collapsed, and afterward he believed them even more, but all the while "believing that capitalism can be saved," as *News-Week* said of him, "if it is sensibly managed."

This explained what had first drawn him to FDR—that, and an intuition that the New York governor could win the presidency. Wheeler and Roosevelt were only a month apart in age and similarly progressive and undoctrinaire in their views, though their temperaments contrasted like fireworks and a morning pond. Wheeler, for once, was being practical, however, when he pushed then governor Roosevelt for the presidency two and a half years before the 1932 election. In 1928, Al Smith had been an electoral fiasco as the Democratic presidential nominee, too much a nasal, big-city Catholic for prairie Protestants' taste. Smith, too, had been the governor of New York, but Roosevelt's aristocratic accent, his unself-consciously superior air, was less threatening to the western ear, for it suggested that he had no need to pretend. Wheeler stumped the West for FDR and labored for him at the Democratic convention. Rumors had persisted of a Roosevelt-Wheeler ticket until political necessity dictated the choice of a rival candidate, John Nance Garner—and Wheeler, or so a Roosevelt partisan charged a dozen years later, "has been grouchy ever since."

Lulu already had her doubts about FDR. "She thought him an opportunist of the worst kind," their eldest daughter wrote, "one who would flatter anyone as long as he could use him to his advantage, then crush him when he voiced opposition." But the senator found little to dislike. In 1934, the Associated Press described his support for the president's programs as "unwavering." Wheeler cruised for a weekend on the president's yacht, and he spent evenings at the White House in the company of other Senate progressives, even as their host did most of the talking. To the president, Wheeler was an ideal New Dealer, a paragon of what the Democratic Party ought to become.

On occasion they had parted ways. When Wheeler proposed instituting silver as a backing for dollars, in a throwback to William Jennings Bryan's populist crusades—not to mention that Montana produced silver as a by-product of copper—the threat of a presidential veto defeated him. Wheeler also voted against the NRA, out of his distaste for cartels and for too powerful a central government, having been a victim of both. "You can't fix prices without fixing profits and wages," he had cautioned, "and you can't fix those without government regulation of all business. That is dictatorship." He also worried about the flow of power to the White House. For a senator who wanted a dam or a post office built back home, a congressional committee was no longer in control. Instead, through the government's Reconstruction Finance Corporation, expanded since Hoover's day, the president held the power of the purse. "Wheeler's liberalism is the truest kind," wrote a syndicated columnist who had watched him for years, "based on the controlling principle of more power for the legislative representatives of the people and less for the executive. It is not a policy with him, but a principle."

In Wheeler's closest collaboration with the White House, in 1935 on the utility holding company bill, he was preparing to introduce legislation to protect customers from utility monopolies' greed when he acceded to the president's request that he sponsor the administration's bill instead. That included a "death sentence," to shut any holding company that owned utilities in disparate places. When the president whispered to senators that the controversial provision had been Wheeler's idea, the Montana senator marched into the White House alone and found the president propped up in bed, smoking a cigarette, the ashes spilling on the bedspread. "I discovered that the only way to deal with Roosevelt," Wheeler recounted, "was to stand up to him."

He had left the White House with a pencil-scrawled note—*Dear Bert*, misspelled—that verified that the "death sentence" was the president's position. During the Senate's debate, Wheeler pulled the paper from his pocket, and by a single vote, the "death sentence"—and the legislation—survived. But it was clear to a newspaperman who was close to Wheeler, "This working relationship could not last."

# CHAPTER EIGHT

# Leader of the Opposition

HERBERT HOOVER WAS the first, at least in public, to heave the age-old charge. The day his successor announced his plan to expand the Supreme Court, the former president was closeted at the Waldorf-Astoria in New York City, and he issued a statement to the newspaper reporters waiting outside his door. It accused the current occupant of the White House of ignoring the honorable way of negating the Court's hostility to the New Deal—by means of a constitutional amendment—and of proposing instead "to make changes by 'packing' the Supreme Court." Others took up the cry, in the newspapers and in the lawmakers' press statements, mainly though not exclusively by Republicans. Senator Warren Austin, a taciturn Republican Vermonter, was the tersest: "It is an ostentatious request for power to pack the courts." In the congressional cloakrooms, conservative Democrats had uttered the four-letter word—*pack*—but forbade reporters to publish what they heard.

The accusation had been hurled at President Grant in 1870 when he named the two additional justices who reversed the precedent he cared about most. But nearly every president had tried to pack the Court, in the sense of nominating justices whose presumed views on constitutional questions coincided, more or less, with his own—though not always successfully. Woodrow Wilson had surely been unpleasantly surprised when James McReynolds became a curmudgeonly conservative, and Herbert Hoover had reason to worry about Charles Evans Hughes. But John Adams's appointment of John Marshall had maintained a Federalist court long after his presidency ended—until Andrew Jackson appointed political loyalists and states' righters who turned the Court his way. Naturally, Lincoln had preferred staunch Unionists to anyone his hapless predecessor, James Buchanan, might have named. Unashamedly, William Howard Taft stacked the Court with conservatives, first as the president and then as the chief justice with the president's ear.

But FDR's proposal was by far the most audacious. He had labeled it a "judicial reorganization," but its opponents preferred the pejorative term—*pack the Court*—as "primarily a device to paralyze thinking," a professor at George Washington University pointed out. And everyone understood the unacknowledged motivation, to move the Court in the president's—and the public's—desired direction.

Opposition developed quickly in the predictable places. Investors greeted the prospect of a pro–New Deal judiciary by selling off stocks and bonds alike. The newspaper publishers who loathed Roosevelt spilled their ink in most lawmakers' districts. Lawyers took offense at the aspersions cast upon the highest in their profession. The president could count on opposition from his usual adversaries—the states' rights advocates, the rich and the well-born, the aspiring monopolists, anyone who had counted on the Court to protect the strong against the weak.

But another source of opposition was harder to measure, an abstraction—a sense of sacredness about the Court, now in its palace of white, the justices cloaked in their robes and remoteness. There was something hallowed in the only institution of government unblemished by the people. A 1936 opinion poll had found that nearly twice as many Americans believed that the Supreme Court protected them against rash legislation than worried that it was blocking the popular will. Felix Frankfurter warned the president of "the great mystery with which the work of the Court is enveloped . . . The easy, emotional slogans are mostly the other way." Politically and strategically, defending an object of worship was simpler than waging an assault.

The president, however, had his own sources of legislative strength. The dozen senators who allowed the newspapers to quote their opposition found themselves outnumbered by the twenty-six senators who quickly committed themselves to his side—the ardent New Dealers and the other Democrats beholden to the president's popularity. A Congress dominated by the president's party was only the beginning of his advantages. A greater one lay in the Court itself—in its decisions striking down New Deal legislation, which deprived millions of Americans of tangible dollars and self-respect, starting with three million farmers who received checks from the AAA, the women in New York and elsewhere who received the minimum wage, and potentially anyone who hoped for a hand from the Wagner Act, the Social Security program—the federal government.

This was FDR's boldest step since shuttering the nation's banks on his second day in office, yet it seemed obvious to everyone that he would prevail, and probably within weeks. Since entering the White House, he had lost only a single fight on Capitol Hill, in January 1935, over whether the United States should join the World Court. Rarely had he even seen the need to compromise. "The people are with me," he told his advisers, as he would tell them again and again. "The people are with me. I know it."

BURTON K. WHEELER's high-ceilinged office on the fourth floor of the Senate Office Building was spacious enough for an oversized desk, a couch, and enough chairs for an extended family. The walls held cartoons from his 1924 campaign and numerous photographs of the senator, several of them in cheerful tandem with the president. In a corner, a copy of the Declaration of Independence was attached to an easel, a flag drooped down across the top of it. The windows behind Wheeler's shoulder offered a panoramic view of the capital's holy places—the soaring simplicity of the Washington Monument, the dignity of the Lincoln Memorial, the hillside in Arlington that was a resting place for heroes. After a century and a third, the national Mall was in the process of being restored to the long, clean sight lines that Pierre L'Enfant had imagined. Gone and unlamented were the serpentine carriage paths through the clusters of trees, the heating plant with its smokestacks, and the barrackslike temporary buildings that had outlasted the Great War.

Sidney Hillman sat facing Wheeler across the desk. The president of the Amalgamated Clothing Workers Union was in the forefront of labor's militancy, a leader in the Committee for Industrial Organization, which had recently been suspended by the American Federation of Labor. He was a favorite of the president because he practiced what he preached about labor's strategic imperative to cooperate with the government. At President Roosevelt's request, he had invited himself into Wheeler's presence, to deliver a threat. If Wheeler insisted on opposing the president's plans for the Court, Hillman vowed, the labor unions would withdraw their support in 1940—in Montana, the unions were strong—when the senator presumably intended to seek a fourth term.

"Go ahead," Wheeler replied.

Then he lectured the labor leader about his experiences as a prosecutor in Montana during the war. "Another hysteria might sweep this country," he said, "and it might be against your people or some other group"—Hillman was a Lithuanian-born Jew—"and when that time comes they will all be looking to the Supreme Court to preserve their rights and uphold the Constitution."

The president was counting on organized labor to make its opinion felt on Capitol Hill. Labor had everything to lose from a conservative Court, which was soon to consider the constitutionality of the Wagner Act, the Magna Carta of the workingman, and he had been currying the unions' favor. Two weeks before apprising his cabinet of his plans, before Tommy Corcoran had been told, the president had taken John L. Lewis into his confidence and been assured of his support. Lewis, the force behind the CIO, was a deep-chested, combative, thundering bull of a man. When the AFL's executive committee endorsed the Court plan on February 17, the two labor federations had taken the same side for the first time in months. With their ample treasuries, their manpower, and their votes, no single interest wielded more influence over the Democrats on Capitol Hill. But Lewis's affection for the president was already fading. The $750,000 that the CIO had donated to FDR's reelection campaign had failed to elicit, in Lewis's mind, enough appreciation from the president.

Labor's lobbyists and the farmers' lobbyists—the White House was relying on both—were far from the only voices that lawmakers heard. Members of Congress had never seen such a torrent of mail. The volume was amazing. One senator received six thousand letters in the first week; another got five thousand in a day. In the wake of the president's announcement, more than a thousand telegrams arrived daily at the Capitol. The Senate's clerks pigeonholed the letters and telegrams in any of the ninety-six wooden squares on the mailroom wall. According to a newsreel shown in movie theaters all over the country, "The senators rival movie stars in the flood of letters that come pouring in."

The deluge listed to one side. The senator who received six thousand letters found that only seven of them favored the president's plan; the five thousand letters ran nine to one against. Millard Tydings, a conservative Democrat from Maryland, received five hundred messages, fifty to one against. And their tone was extraordinary. Maury Maverick, a representative from Texas—his grandfather, a rancher, had added a noun of defiance to the English language by refusing to brand his cattle—had never seen an issue arouse such vehemence. "Asinine . . . liar . . . treason . . . rubber stamp"—such were the sentiments delivered to a U.S. senator.

Yet there was something dubious about the influx of mail. A syndicated columnist who examined several senators' mail found that lawyers, educators, and students accounted for three fourths of it, overwhelmingly opposed to the president's plan; the other letters were mainly in favor. Elmer Wene, a Democratic farmer-turned-congressman from southern New Jersey, reported "a lot of letters on crisp legal stationery and a lot of letters with expensive engraved work on them piling up on my desk," all of them hostile to the president's plan. But the New Dealer felt sure that he understood what his constituents wanted: "The chicken farmers of Vineland and the hotel workers of Atlantic City must think they can depend on me"—to expand the Supreme Court in their interests—"without writing me letters about it."

The opposition was peculiarly well placed to make its position known—in the press, for instance. Barely one in seven of the nation's newspapers had editorially endorsed the president's reelection, and more than two thirds of those—including the *New York Times*—deserted him now. Frank Gannett, an ambitious and conservative publisher in Rochester, New York, prowled the corridors on Capitol Hill, organizing an opposition and raising money to support it. Bar associations, resentful at the assault on the judiciary, passed resolutions by the briefcaseful and articulated their misgivings in language that the lawmakers understood. Chambers of commerce, long thankful for the Court's devotion to laissez-faire, made their opinions clear to any and all lawmakers. Henry Ford, in a rare interview, announced that he opposed the Court plan because it would give one man—and he was in a position to know—"too much power." Most embarrassingly, Raymond Moley, the organizer of the president's famed brain trust—he had since broken with the White

House—said it "comes perilously near to a proposal to abandon constitutional government."

On the other hand, the White House was receiving hundreds of letters a day, running two to one in favor of the Court plan, reinforcing the support from the common man that FDR felt was his. "Our family is with you 100%," husband-and-wife farmers in Nebraska wrote. From Sullivan, Indiana: "Any thing you do for the Poor or Laboring Class man will be apreated. I don't no what people would off done if it had not been for Franklin D. Roosevelt." A family in Sacramento: "I believe that if we the common people of the United States had a chance to vote on this issue, the plan would go over overwhelmingly." A father in Minnesota: "It is high time that changes were made in that branch of our government." A telegram from Dallas: "PLEASE ACCEPT MY ENLISTMENT UNTIL DEATH FOR YOUR PRINCIPLES." Day after day, the messages mounted.

Only recently had a mathematically reputable means of learning the truths of public opinion emerged. Since the presidential election of 1916, the *Literary Digest* had been mailing surveys to millions of people, and through 1932, its predictions had always been right. Its reliance on listings of telephones, automobile registrations, and magazine subscriptions, however, limited its respondents to middle- or upper-class homes, unrepresentative of the entire electorate, and had prompted the weekly magazine to prepare the nation for the coming of President Alf Landon. But the era of scientific polling had already begun. George Gallup started conducting national polls on political questions near the end of 1933 and publishing a weekly presentation in scores of newspapers by the fall of 1935; a few months earlier, *Fortune* had inaugurated a quarterly survey by Elmo Roper as "a new technique in journalism." Both pollsters' method was to survey many fewer Americans than the *Literary Digest*—numbering in the thousands, not the millions—but they were chosen "with mathematical care," Roper wrote, to form a cross section of society by age, locale, gender, and economic condition. Gallup added to the available lists by dispatching a hundred interviewers to round out the sample, knocking on doors and stopping people on the street, taking pains to include unskilled laborers and people on the dole. Roper dispensed with the lists entirely and hired "mature people of proved integrity" to interview forty-five hundred Americans every three months, to capture the opinions not only of people with telephones but also of those who relied on the corner drugstore to make a call. This was how both pollsters foretold the outcome of the 1936 election. (Roper's forecast of Roosevelt's share of the popular vote fell short by just a percentage point and a third.) Their accuracy made their reputations and that of their "infant science," as Gallup described it.

George Gallup, in particular, had lofty ambitions for the importance of polling, as a scientific gauge of the people's opinion that would deepen the responsiveness—the effectiveness—of American democracy. He aligned himself with Thomas Jefferson's faith in the judgment of the masses and against Hamilton's mistrust. "Unless the ordinary citizen can find channels of self-expression, the common man may become the forgotten man," Gallup fretted. "In a democratic society, the views of the majority must be regarded as the ultimate tribunal for social and political issues." He predicted that the newspapers of the future would have departments of public opinion.

But, he had never polled before on an issue as volatile as the proposal to enlarge the Supreme Court, and his results showed the public in a muddle. Soon after the president had announced his plan, Gallup's surveyors found 53 percent of their respondents in opposition and 47 percent in support. Given more nuanced choices, almost equal proportions approved and disliked the president's plan, and nearly a quarter of the public—the balance of opinion—wanted it modified in some unspecified way.

For a practicing politician, such ambiguity was dangerous. The president could assure himself that he could secure the public's support, once he pursued it, while nervous lawmakers were bound to foresee political trouble no matter what. Their most vivid fear was not the proportions of opinion but its intensity. Newspapers were publishing a multitude of letters from readers, a full page or two at a time. The issue provoked arguments in the unlikeliest of venues. Ladies at the capital's exclusive Sulgrave Club listened to a lecture on the Court proposal. At the Women's City Club in Los Angeles, the discussion of the Court plan continued long after the closing hour. In Lancaster, Kentucky, the Negro women in the Earnest Workers Club listened to a talk on poultry raising, points on beauty culture, and then a professor's thoughts on the Supreme Court. The citizens of New Canaan, Connecticut, a Republican stronghold, called a town meeting to denounce the president's plan, which prompted local Democrats to circulate a petition of support. The Arlington, Virginia, chapter of the Daughters of the American Revolution overwhelmingly passed a resolution in opposition, and soon the national organization followed. (The next morning, Mrs. Charles Evans Hughes sat next to Eleanor Roosevelt at a DAR-attended breakfast at a Washington hotel.) In New York, the Women Investors in America, Inc., created the National Women's National Committee for "Hands Off the Supreme Court" that sent a sound truck around Manhattan, entreating passersby to wire or write their senators or U.S. representatives and to persuade ten friends to do the same. Jim Farley discussed the Court bill (while sidestepping a question about the president's intentions for a third term) in front of the national convention of Elks in Denver. State legislatures offered their opinions unbidden—endorsing the president's plan in Colorado, Delaware, and Indiana, and opposing it in Connecticut, Kansas, Maine, New Hampshire, and Texas.

The nation had seen nothing like this in years, not since the political bloodletting in 1919 and 1920 over whether America ought to enter the League of Nations. That monumental battle, reflecting the anxieties of a newly imperial nation's expanding role in the world, had transfixed the capital and destroyed Woodrow Wilson's health. Yet the Supreme Court and its fate seemed to stir something deeper still, and among ordinary citizens as well as the elites—the need for a rock, perhaps, in a turbulent world. Feelings were running high and seemed to be rising. Week by week, the avalanche of mail that landed on Capitol Hill grew heavier and angrier.


FIFTY THOUSAND PEOPLE, many times as numerous as Elmo Roper needed to peer into the American soul, gathered on a Saturday afternoon in February 1937 at the Santa Anita racetrack in Southern California. It was the largest attendance ever at a Pacific Coast track, to see the world's richest race. The Santa Anita Handicap awarded $100,000 to the winner, at a time when the average factory worker was earning $1,250 a year. The splendid Rosemont, beloved in the East, had defeated Omaha, the Triple Crown winner of 1935, and was the favorite. Lightly regarded by the eastern racing establishment was an undersized, homely local long shot named Seabiscuit.

For a citizenry struggling to emerge from the Depression, Seabiscuit would soon capture the imagination as a Horatio Alger on four fast legs, a down-and-outer lacking size and respect—everything but an unquenchable heart. His jockey, Red Pollard, who was blind in one eye, liked to quote Shakespeare on the uses of adversity. Seabiscuit overtook the leader and was running three lengths ahead of the field when, on the homestretch, for fifteen strides, Red Pollard froze at the reins, unable to see that Rosemont was gaining. It was a photo finish, but for democracy's champion, fame and fortune would have to wait.

The theme ran through the culture, of the underdog versus the fortunate, the haves against the have-nots. *Little Orphan Annie*, its character homely but with an inner grace, was the most popular comic strip (edging out *Popeye* and *Dick Tracy*). In the movie theaters, which more than a third of all Americans patronized at least once a week, the Marx Brothers outfoxed the stuffed shirts or drove them to distraction. Errol Flynn swashbuckled his way to victory over the powers-that-be, and W. C. Fields's everyman and his family stopped to picnic on a rich man's lawn and left it covered in trash.

The movies also were obsessed with money and class. Other than gangsters and an occasional hobo, nearly everyone's home had a marble foyer and a butler. "Money is our god here," Katharine Hepburn would declare in *Holiday*. The stories dwelled on rich people who feared losing everything, on poor people striking it rich, on rich people who pretended to be poor, on poor people who showed more class than the rich.

It was the have-nots who bought the bulk of the eighty million movie tickets, typically for twenty-five cents apiece, that a depressed nation of 130 million people purchased each week. There they watched not only the escapist comedies and melodramas but also glimpses of the real world, through the newsreels. The public had never had the chance before to watch and listen to Hitler or Albert Einstein or George Bernard Shaw, who unwittingly betrayed themselves as ordinary men. Americans could witness events that previously they could only have read about or imagined— the sack of Addis Ababa, the courtroom testimony of Bruno Hauptmann, John Dillinger on a mortician's slab (prompting a lawsuit by a woman who claimed that the sight had caused a miscarriage). Already, the battle over the Supreme Court was becoming a popular subject for the newsreels, entertaining theatergoers who had every reason to care. Both sides in the controversy claimed to represent the little guy, and both had a case. For the president, the demands of the time required that the entire government, including the Court, serve the people's needs; there was no other point to a government except to keep its citizenry safe and secure. His opponents had the longer term in mind.

MILLARD TYDINGS COULD never have afforded to buy the gray stucco mansion on Massachusetts Avenue, at the edge of Rock Creek Park, on his senatorial salary of $10,000 a year. The second-term senator had risen from a modest farm in backwater Maryland, a war hero who found he excelled at politics. Tall and slender, he had a strong will and a sharp mind, as well as well-born tastes in opera, art, and fashion. (He had recently joined the president on the annual list of best-dressed American men, along with Fred Astaire, William Paley, and Angier Biddle Duke.) Fourteen months earlier, at the advanced age of forty-five, he had been married for the first time, to the stepdaughter of cereal heiress Marjorie Merriweather Post, whose generosity to the president's recent campaign had secured her third husband, Joseph Davies, his present posting as the ambassador to Moscow. This had left their stately house in Washington, with its Greek pillars flanking the front door, available for Millard Tydings's use, and he had grown comfortable as the host.

The Maryland senator said nothing immediate in public about the Court after the president's announcement, though he had made up his mind. He was a Democrat but a conservative, who had first broken with Roosevelt over deficit spending and had opposed the AAA, the NRA, and even the TVA. Because of his standoffish manner, as well as his conservative votes, the New Dealers loathed him. Since his marriage into American aristocracy, it amused them to mispronounce Millard Tydings's first name as "Mi-Lord."

One evening in mid-February 1937, he invited seventeen other senators, all Democrats, to join him for a meal. The dining room in his house was beautiful in an old-fashioned way, with high windows, exquisite furniture, candelabra, and a painting of Marjorie Merriweather Post's redheaded Aunt Polly. Seated around the table, as they broke bread, the southerners, the midwesterners, the New Englander, the Marylander, the westerner, and the senator from Tammany Hall all had one thing in common besides their party: opposition to the president's Court plan. Seventeen of them could be counted as conservatives. The eighteenth was Burt Wheeler. Without dissent, they chose Wheeler, with his perfect political credentials, as their leader.

"Burt, we can't lick it," Harry Byrd of Virginia piped up, "but we'll fight it."

Asked why he was against the president's proposal, Byrd called it wrong in principle. The principle that Byrd undoubtedly cared about the most was states' rights, the underpinning of white supremacy, and one that a liberal Court might well dispel. Wheeler did not bother to point out that, in Montana, states' rights helped put the Company in control.

The Montana progressive stood at his seat and addressed the senators around the table. He had disagreed with them about almost everything—on the role of government, on the value of the New Deal, on the personal and political honor of the president. The Court fight had put him in strange company, he conceded, but if he was going to lead, they must promise to follow. Senators were not accustomed to toeing the line, but the conservatives at Millard Tydings's table recognized their own best interests and agreed. Only if some of the Senate's liberals broke with the president did the opponents stand a chance to succeed.

Wheeler sought out William Borah, an Idaho Republican, to determine a bipartisan strategy. Though they belonged to rival political parties, neither was much of a party man. They represented neighboring states and, on policy issues, agreed on almost everything. Wheeler admired Borah, as almost everyone did. When Wheeler first arrived in the Senate, Borah had invited him to lunch and advised him how to make his reputation—"if you're honest and you're willing to work . . . So damn few of them want to work." They had grown close, politically and personally, to the extent that Wheeler had even volunteered to campaign for the Republican's reelection the previous fall. In discussing strategy for fighting the Court plan, they agreed that Republicans should stay in the background. This would prevent the president from framing the issue in partisan terms, as a loyalty test for Democrats. The Senate's Republican leaders had already acceded to the need for silence, but the party's past two standard-bearers were aghast. Alf Landon flew into a fit before he agreed to skip his attack on the president's Court plan at a Lincoln Day dinner in New York. When Herbert Hoover learned of the Republican senators' decision, he demanded, "Who's trying to muzzle me?" Only with difficulty was his craving for a public campaign put aside. Thus the Republicans found themselves "outsphinxing the sphinx," as a columnist noted, and they asked Wheeler to lead the bipartisan opposition.

Wheeler and his dinner companions named a steering committee of nine senators who met daily in one or another of their Capitol hideaways. Each senator was assigned to keep tabs on particular colleagues and to identify any who wavered. Their early head counts were as muddled as the public opinion polls. Roughly a third of the senators stood in the president's corner, a third were opposed, and the rest of them were frightened for their political lives.


A FEUD WAS brewing between Jack Benny and Fred Allen, as the rival comedians traded thinly veiled insults on their national radio broadcasts, an hour apart on Sunday nights (with Charlie McCarthy in between). "Toothpaste peddler!"—this was Benny's sneer at Allen, late of *The Sal Hepatica Revue*. "Gelatin hawker!" came the retort. Year after year, pollsters had named Jack Benny, the violin-playing skinflint, as the nation's favorite radio personality and his Jell-O show as the most popular program. Soon he would sign a contract that assured him $1 million a year, and there was every reason to suspect that the on-air "feud" was simply a press agent's ploy that might culminate in a joint movie. Twentieth Century-Fox currently had in production a film called *Wake Up and Live*, a spoof of the well-publicized squabble between Broadway columnist Walter Winchell and bandleader Ben Bernie.

Americans had taken to radio with a vengeance. More than two thirds of American homes, twenty-six million households, owned one, and they switched it on for an average of five hours a day—*Amos and Andy*, Fred Astaire's variety hour, *The Guiding Light*, Guy Lombardo's orchestra, Ozzie Nelson, Nelson Eddy, Eddie Cantor, Cantor Shapiro, the Mormon Tabernacle Choir, and so much more. Radio offered more than entertainment. It was a balm for the lonely; for anyone on a remote farm, it was a connection to the outside world. For immigrants, it was a teacher of English and a means to learn about the country they now called home. The *Church of the Air* brought solace to the wretched, Jack Benny's deadpan made people laugh, and Lowell Thomas or H. V. Kaltenborn delivered the news. More than what anyone on the radio said, what mattered was that millions of Americans all over the country, whether in a tenement, a mansion, or a farmhouse, could hear it directly and at the same time. Not until recently had a person been able to address an entire nation at once. In Germany, a mesmerizing chancellor was broadcasting his rallies to meld an Aryan people into one. The powerful medium was becoming an instrument of American politics—and of political division—but it also was bringing an interconnected nation together as never before.

On the evening of February 19, 1937, a Friday, George Gallup spent three minutes on the NBC Red Network describing his polling on the Supreme Court. That was at six thirty-five in the East. At ten o'clock in New York City, the nation's largest radio market, Eugene Ormandy conducted the Philadelphia Orchestra on the CBS station, a radio skit called "Witch's Tale" played on the Mutual network, and NBC's Red Network offered a half-hour drama, "The Preacher." On NBC's Blue Network, Senator Wheeler addressed the nation on the topic "Reform of the Federal Judiciary."

Wheeler had demanded the airtime after Homer Cummings, five nights earlier, had spoken on all of the major networks. In his haughty tenor, the attorney general had used successions of polysyllabic words in attesting to the congested judicial dockets and the need for new blood in federal courts. By all accounts other than his own, he had persuaded no one. But it gave Wheeler an opening, and NBC, with its two radio networks, could hardly refuse the chairman of the Senate committee with jurisdiction over the airwaves, who had drafted legislation to block newspapers from owning radio stations to prevent monopolies over the public's channels of information.

"Hello, folks. On February fifth of this year the president of the United States sent a message." Over the radio, Wheeler's rough-edged voice lacked the warmth of his live speeches, yet with his simple words, unhurried pace, and matter-of-fact tone, he was easy to listen to. "On last Sunday evening," he went on, "the attorney general, speaking with the pride of authorship, presented to the country the administration's arguments for the proposal.

He told us that in nine short days since the president sent his recommendations to Congress, 'unfriendly voices have filled the air with lamentations.'"
Wheeler's plain delivery underscored the sarcasm. "This indicates that the
people lost no time in letting the White House know that there were limits
to their confidence!" The pitch of his voice rose in derision. "We differ with
him and therefore he says we are unfriendly. Are we to understand that only
those who agree are to be called friends? What an attitude, my countrymen,
that is to the exercise of the constitutional right of petition by Americans!
What unrealized arrogance that reveals."

For thirty-three minutes, Wheeler refrained from berating the president of his own party, whose popularity had grown to a staggering 65 percent since his landslide reelection. But Homer Cummings was an enticing
target. Any listener could sense the rage beneath the patience, but none of
them knew the deeper reasons why. These began with Wheeler's loathing
of long standing for attorneys general as a class, bequeathed by A. Mitchell
Palmer, then by Harry Daugherty and the henchmen he left behind, and
sharpened by the circumstances of Homer Cummings's appointment in
the wake of Tom Walsh's death. Wheeler found reason to refer to his mentor that night: "Walsh was a true progressive, not a political progressive. He
was a real liberal, not an official liberal. He would never have advised his
president to *pack*"—he spat the word—"the Supreme Court. And if his
president had advised Congress to do so, he would have had to look for a
new attorney general."

His scorn only hinted at his personal animus. Wheeler divided the
world between honest men and scoundrels, and he had no doubt on which
side of the fence Cummings belonged. In Wheeler's eyes, his worst sin was
not his history as a political conniver, nor the fluidity in his philosophy of
government, but rather the company he kept—one friend in particular.
J. Bruce Kremer, a lawyer from Butte and Anaconda Copper's lobbyist in
Washington, was Wheeler's mortal political enemy. As the longtime Democratic national committeeman from Montana and as the party's vice chairman, Kremer (pronounced *Kramer*) and Homer Cummings had become
pals. They and their wives socialized often—on New Year's Eve, in a European jaunt, twice at dinner parties in recent weeks—and Kremer was suspected of financing the attorney general's own lavish trips. The Justice
Department's lands division had hired Kremer's son Alf as a special attor-

ney at a higher salary, $5,500 a year, than any of his peers. For Wheeler, the political and the personal had merged.

"Let us examine the attorney general's proposal." Wheeler proceeded to skewer Cummings's arguments, starting with the premise of age—for age, he argued, had little to do with competence or a modern outlook. "The oldest man in the Supreme Court is the greatest living liberal, Mr. Justice Brandeis, aged eighty years and going strong." The newspapers had been listing the notables whose best work had continued into their seventies and beyond—Michelangelo, Isaac Newton, Voltaire, Handel, Immanuel Kant, Herbert Spencer, Henry Ford, even Thomas Jefferson. "And next to Mr. Justice Brandeis," Wheeler pointed out, "which justice was the greatest liberal of our time on the Court? Do I have to call the name of Oliver Wendell Holmes?"

"I speak to you tonight as a lifelong liberal," Wheeler declared. "A liberal cause was never won by stacking a deck of cards, nor by stuffing a ballot box, nor by packing a court." The president had framed his proposal as a means of furthering democracy's rule, by forcing the Court to follow the people's will, but Wheeler feared a different threat to democracy, in a concentration of power. "Every labor leader, every farmer, and every progressive-minded citizen in the United States would have been shocked and protested from the housetops if President Harding, President Coolidge, or President Hoover had ever intimated that they wanted to increase the Supreme Court so as to make it subservient to their wishes." The precedent for danger lay across the Atlantic. "Hitler and Stalin talk of their democracies. Every despot has usurped the power of the legislative and judicial branches of the government in the name of the necessity for haste to promote the general welfare of the masses—and then proceeded to reduce them to servitude. I do not believe that President Roosevelt has any such thing in mind, but such has been the course of events throughout the world . . .

"If there must be a dictator in the United States of America," he finished, "I nominate the American people as dictator."

# CHAPTER NINE

# King Franklin

JUST THREE DAYS after he had shaken the capital and the nation with his proposal, the president had invited the chairmen of both chambers' judiciary committees over for lunch, along with a last-minute addition, Senator Robert F. Wagner of New York, a devoted New Dealer who had remained worryingly silent about enlarging the Court. The food arrived on trays in an electrically heated oven, and FDR carved the baked pheasant for his guests and passed around the plates and the cutlery.

President Roosevelt talked while his guests ate. He had always known instinctively how to bring someone around to his way of thinking. A gymnast in conversation, he could pirouette between topics without ever boring his listeners or running out of facts. For the wheelchair-bound president, the act of talking was strenuous; his hands and arms were in motion, and his face kept changing expression. His verbal circumlocutions allowed him to control the conversation, by fending off a subject with long digressions or by meeting it head-on. He could sidle or he could pounce, always affable and yet always, in essence, remote.

His monologue lasted most of an hour as he made his best case for the judicial reorganization. He had received a handwritten note from Speaker Bankhead: "I think it quite important for you to ask Hatton Sumners, Chrm. of Judiciary to see you <u>alone</u> at as early a moment as possible." That day, in an off-the-record conversation with reporters, Congressman Sumners had described the Court plan as "infamous," and it appeared that a majority of his committee would see things his way.

The White House was ready to concede that the Senate would have to act first, because Sumners's opposition had created an obstacle in his committee that only legislative momentum might overcome. Indeed, it served the president's purposes to include Sumners's counterpart. Henry Fountain Ashurst of Arizona, the Senate Judiciary Committee chairman, was almost a caricature of a senator. Tall and courtly, he had been born in a covered wagon in Nevada, on the old California trail. By age twelve he was inscribing in his schoolbook, *Henry Fountain Ashurst, United States Senator from Arizona*. That was twenty-six years before Arizona became a state, and he had been serving as its senator ever since. The covered wagon was long gone, but something anachronistic about Ashurst remained. He favored pince-nez with a black ribbon, pinstriped trousers, and a cutaway coat past its prime, and he proffered an elaborate politeness and a florid oratorical style—"acidly eloquent," by Wheeler's account—that was often a parody of itself.

"My faults are obvious," Ashurst would soon acknowledge to his colleagues. "I suffer from *cacoëthes loquendi*, a mania or itch for talking, and from vanity, if you please, and morbidity"—the senators would laugh—"and, as is obvious to everyone who knows me, an inborn, an inveterate, flair for histrionics. But there never has been superadded to these vices of mine the withering and embalming vice of consistency." For Ashurst, principle sometimes yielded to a higher good. "I may be driven from my opinions," he wisecracked, "but never from my seat."

Even Ashurst's devotion to inconsistency, however, was feeling the strain. During the 1936 campaign, when Republicans hinted that the president might wish to pack the Court, Ashurst had sprung to the president's defense, publicly ridiculing any such notion as a "prelude to tyranny." When the president announced his plan, without bothering to forewarn any lawmakers, Ashurst had fallen uncharacteristically silent at first; only later in the day had he stated for publication that he favored it. Soon he would tell the Senate, without evident embarrassment, that he marveled at the "moderation" of the president's plan—"the mildest of all the bills that could have been introduced." Later, when a constituent applauded him on his stand on the president's Court bill, he replied, "Which stand?"

The president could only hope that Ashurst's old-fashioned habit of deference would rub off on Hatton Sumners. Over the pheasant, Ashurst suggested that the president announce his support for Sumners's bill to guarantee Supreme Court justices that they could retire at full pay once they turned seventy and had served ten years on the bench. Its purpose was to persuade the elderly justices to retire—one or more of the Four Horsemen, according to rumors, wished to leave the bench—by correcting the wrong done to Oliver Wendell Holmes Jr. a year after he had stepped down, when Congress halved his pension as a budget-cutting measure. The president took Ashurst's counsel, and the House passed the bill on February 10. Soon the Senate followed suit, and it was signed into law. Yet none of the justices resigned.

Acceding to his advisers, the president set out to persuade the lawmakers who would decide his proposal's fate. His plan was to meet with senators one by one "and take down what they suggest as alternate proposals," as his son Jimmy reported, "and then show the hopelessness of such proposals." Day after day, clusters of ambivalent senators and an occasional House member were ushered into the calm of the president's presence as he sought to ease their resentment at not being consulted in advance. Hatton Sumners came back for seventy minutes alone with the president, upstairs in the residence, and for another fifteen minutes four days later. The president tried making his case that the public had already consented to his plan by reelecting him in a landslide.

But his efforts showed limited success. None of the lawmakers left the White House and announced a conversion. That included George Norris of Nebraska, the father of the Tennessee Valley Authority and an ardent New Dealer, who had just been reelected to a fifth term, as an independent—no longer a Republican—anointed with the Democratic president's open support. Norris loathed the Supreme Court for legislating in Congress's place, but he offered nothing more to the reporters who ambushed the president's visitors as they left than a willingness to vote for the bill if no other remedy emerged. He was silent about his annoyance at having to wait an hour before the president saw him, though it was not the sort of slight a U.S. senator overlooked. "It is things like that which may seem unimportant," Jimmy Roosevelt fretted to himself, "but often make the difference between the warm-hearted and luke-warm supporter."

Late on the afternoon of February 20, the president hosted half a dozen Democratic pillars of the Senate, all of them administration loyalists committed to his plan for the Court. Jack Garner led them in—Joe Robinson, his top lieutenants, and Henry Fountain Ashurst. They had requested the audience for a specific purpose: to urge him to accept a compromise of two or three additional justices instead of six. Their argument was political. They feared that a breach was opening among the Democrats and that nothing else would repair it. The president laughed at the idea, so loudly that some of the senators promised themselves never again to offer him their counsel unless he asked.

SIDNEY'S MAYFLOWER ORCHESTRA finished "Hail to the Chief" and, as the applause of the thirteen hundred Democrats swept to a crescendo, launched into "Happy Days Are Here Again," the party's theme song. Using a cane and leaning on the arm of an aide, the fifty-five-year-old president made his way into the grand ballroom of the stately Mayflower Hotel on Connecticut Avenue for the Democratic Victory Dinner, on the evening of March 4, 1937, four years to the day since Roosevelt had entered the White House.

For two long minutes the ovation went on. The southerners let loose with rebel yells. The president crossed to the center of the head table, then seated himself in an armchair with flowered upholstery. The marble pillars and the vaulted ceiling with a golden sheen sheltered the eight cabinet officers, the dozens of lawmakers, the bureaucrats galore, the presidents of Chrysler and of the AF of L, and the rank-and-file partisans who had paid $100 apiece—$5 for the food and the rest for the party treasury, which after the recent election stood $430,000 in debt. This explained why the dinner jackets far outnumbered the gowns. "Would you bring your wife," a guest said with a sigh, "at a hundred dollars a throw?"

The president sipped the diamondback terrapin soup, a favorite of his, out of a dainty, twin-handled bowl, but he waved away the breast of capon on the Smithfield ham. He rarely ate meat at night, and even after so many years in politics, he was often nervous before delivering a speech. He lit a fresh cigarette and bantered with Jim Farley, who sat to his right. The big, bald party chairman had served at FDR's side since 1928, when as a Democratic county chairman not far from Hyde Park's Dutchess County, he had helped to engineer Roosevelt's candidacy for governor. First as an eminence in the Elks Club, with its far-flung chapters, and then as the most energetic of political hobnobbers, Jim Farley probably knew more people across forty-eight states, in every county and ward, than any other person in political life. Now he told anyone who would listen that the Court plan was "in the bag."

Farley introduced the president at ten thirty, just as the broadcast was scheduled to begin. Half a million Democrats in forty-three states were seated at more than a thousand dinners (at prices ranging from $1.25 a plate in Alexandria, Virginia, to $50 in New York) to hear the president on a nationwide radio hookup.

The president grasped the podium with two strong hands. His courage, physical and political, was matter-of-fact. ("The simple job of getting up and sitting down several times was almost as much exercise as the ordinary man takes during an entire day," Sam Rosenman noted.) At the microphone, the president looked out over the crowd. Seldom, judged a veteran reporter, had he seemed so earnest.

Originally, he had intended to stay clear of the subject that was on everyone's mind, to save his rhetorical fire on the Court until after he returned from his two weeks in Warm Springs, Georgia, for his first visit since 1935 to the rehabilitation center for polio victims he had founded and financed. His advisers had persuaded him otherwise. Seven of the administration's best and brightest had begun to meet every day, early in the morning or in the late afternoon, as a working group° on the Court fight, to plot their strategy on Capitol Hill and to plan radio speeches by supporters of the plan. All of them had seen the danger if the president waited too long to make his case to the public, and he agreed to address the subject head-on at the Victory Dinner and again, five nights later, in a fireside chat.

Homer Cummings had argued that FDR should stick to the original rationale for expanding the Court, of dockets congested and justice delayed. But the attorney general had gone to Florida for two weeks of golf

---

°Jimmy Roosevelt represented his father, and Tommy Corcoran guided the overall strategy. Corcoran and Joe Keenan, an assistant to the attorney general, took on the hardest job, bringing the Senate into line. Charlie West, the undersecretary of the interior, handled the House of Representatives, in which he had once served. The other participants were Robert M. Jackson, by now the assistant attorney general for the tax division; Democratic Party publicity man Charles Michelson; and Michelson's assistant, Edward L. Roddan.

and "the usual number of inevitable dinners," as he described it in his diary—startling his colleagues with what one of them derided as an "unfortunately timed" vacation. This left Tommy Corcoran and his allies with the president's ear. They pressed him to tell the truth about why he wanted to expand the Court—to assure a majority that would accept the New Deal. No matter how much he relished obliqueness, the strength of his presidency had been his willingness to confront the hard realities that his listeners already understood. Action was the secret to his success at reinvigorating a nation in pain, and the source of the intractable optimism that had inspired the voters to elect him twice. Already, the murmurings had started about an unprecedented third term, though he had been coy.

The Victory Dinner speech had gone through twenty-one drafts, the product of late nights in the Cabinet Room, where Tommy Corcoran, Ben Cohen, Sam Rosenman, and Jimmy Roosevelt haggled over words and tone. From draft to draft, the president himself, in his bold, angular handwriting, had penned in phrases of his own. The words "Supreme Court" were never to cross his lips, nor any explicit mention of his proposal, yet his meaning would never be in doubt.

Roosevelt started by acknowledging the reason for the celebration. "The Democratic Party, once a minority party, is today the majority party by the greatest majority any party ever had," he declared. He reveled in the rhythm, and he articulated every syllable. "And it will remain the majority party so long as it continues to justify the faith of millions who had almost *lost* faith"—those last nine words were the president's own, in the twenty-first draft—"so long as it continues to make modern democracy succeed, so long and no longer."

He thrust his broad jaw into the air to emphasize his points, for he needed his hands to keep himself upright. No president had ever taken on the judiciary so publicly. Lincoln had been muted about his defiance, and Teddy Roosevelt had been an ex-president when he called for letting the people overrule the Court. This president was specific in his criticisms of the unmentioned institution. The Agricultural Adjustment Act, meant to help the farmers in distress—"You know who assumed the power to veto, and did veto, that program," he intoned again and again as he cataloged the legislation that had been overturned. The attempts to raise wages and reduce hours to help the jobless—"You know who assumed the power to veto, and did veto that program . . . The Railroad Retirement Act, the National Recovery Act." There was nary a word about geriatric jurists or the passed-over appeals, as his sonorous voice shaped a reality of its own. "And I defy anyone to read the opinions concerning the Triple-A, the Railroad Retirement Act, the National Recovery Act, the Guffey coal act, the New York minimum wage law, and tell us exactly what, if anything, we can do for the industrial worker in *this* session of Congress with any reasonable certainty that what we do will not be nullified as unconstitutional."

The president cast himself as democracy's savior, not as its foe. "After the World War, there arose everywhere insistent demands upon government that human needs be met. The unthinking, or those who dwell in the past, have tried to block them . . . Democracy in many lands has failed for the time being to meet human needs. People have become so fed up with futile debate and party bickerings over methods that they have been willing to surrender democratic process and principles to get things done. They have forgotten the lessons of history that the ultimate failures of dictatorships"—the president had scrawled this sentence himself in the margins of the fourth draft—"cost humanity far more than any temporary failures of democracy." Like his opponents, he raised the specter of dictatorship, but he drew the opposite lesson, that a democracy must meet the people's needs if it hoped to survive.

Roosevelt had a gift for simple words and homely metaphors, and now he offered one to characterize the three branches of the government: "If three well-matched horses are put to the task of plowing up a field where the going is heavy, and the team of three pull as one, the *field . . . will . . . be . . . plowed.*" His powerful face bobbed in time with the words. "If one horse lies down in the traces or plunges off in another direction, the *field . . . will . . . not . . . be . . . plowed.*" The audience erupted in whistles and cheers.

He had been searching for a dramatic conclusion to underscore a sense of urgency, and he borrowed a sentence from his recent inaugural address and turned it into an incantation.

"Here is one-third of a nation ill-nourished, ill-clad, ill-housed," and then he added ever so softly—"now!

"Here are thousands upon thousands of farmers wondering whether next year's prices will meet their mortgage interest"—softer still—"now!

"Here are thousands upon thousands of men and women laboring for long hours in factories for inadequate pay—now!" He was appealing over the lawmakers' heads to the constituents who had never failed him, the families huddled around their radios in a farmhouse or a row house or a tenement, listening to a president they knew was on their side. "Here are thousands upon thousands of children who should be at school, working in mines and mills—now! Here are strikes more far-reaching than we have ever known, costing millions of dollars—now! Here are spring floods threatening to roll again down our river valleys—now! Here is the dust bowl beginning to blow again—now!" The decibels had climbed and his pitch rose to a peak and twice he thrust his arm out at the dinner guests. "If we would keep faith with those who had faith in us, if we would make democracy succeed, I say we must act—now!"

LONG BEFORE EITHER man's presidency, the young Franklin had always idolized "Cousin Theodore," as he had originally known his glamorous fifth cousin, twenty-three years his senior. There was probably no one he admired more. As a boy, he had wanted to stuff the birds that he shot after learning that Cousin Theodore had done the same. His schoolmates at Harvard, while his cousin was president, had snickered when he shouted "Bully!" When he married Theodore's favorite niece, the then president gave Eleanor away, displacing the bride and the groom as the center of attention.

Franklin's desire to follow in Teddy's footsteps took him from Harvard College to Columbia Law School and then into the New York legislature. ("I'm not Teddy," he declared on the stump.) Then they occupied the same spacious, high-ceilinged, wood-paneled office in the State, War, and Navy Building, reserved for the assistant secretary of the navy, which looked out over the White House. Franklin could gaze down upon the West Wing, which his cousin had built as a refuge from his six rowdy children. Later they worked in the same State House office in Albany and slept in the same governor's mansion.

The defining event in FDR's life occurred on an August afternoon in 1921. At his family's summer retreat on Canada's Campobello Island, near the Maine coast, at first he developed a fever, and by the next day he was unable to stand, stricken by infantile paralysis—polio—at the unlikely age of thirty-nine. Doctors suspected he had been exposed in Washington or at a Boy Scout camp in New York to a virus that someone with a less sheltered upbringing and stronger immune system might have squelched.

He never openly discussed his disease, so far as anyone recorded, though occasionally he acknowledged its reality. "Burt, when you get mad," he once said wistfully to Senator Wheeler, "you can walk around the room," meaning that he could not. But his facility at ignoring the obvious was also, in its way, a means of exerting control. If he seemed not to notice, maybe nobody else would, and remarkably, that proved to be the case. For anyone who saw him often, the wheelchair soon went unnoticed. As for ordinary citizens, they knew but did not know, in a sort of willful and collective amnesia. He was never photographed in a wheelchair—the news photographers who covered the president enforced the courtesy in case a newcomer tried—and the extent of his disability was not mentioned in print. Yet the public usually saw him seated, and when he stood, he looked propped up; that he had polio was commonly known, but the seriousness of his affliction was not.

His illness made every trait in his personality more intense. If his paralysis showed the limits of his power, it also increased the power of his will. Polio made him tougher and, at the same time, more serene—more patient, according to Eleanor. A man could sling him over a shoulder and carry him up the stairs, and then FDR would straighten his tie and proceed with dignity intact. Nothing about being president could be harder.

On entering the White House, he emulated his cousin yet again by finishing the transformation of the modern presidency that Teddy had begun. By challenging the boxer John L. Sullivan to a match, by sparing a mama bear from his shotgun—and seeing "Teddy bears" sweep the nation—Theodore Roosevelt had been the first president to build a cult of personality, one that he exploited to bolster his political power. He had mounted the bully pulpit, having invented it, in appealing to the public to get his way on Capitol Hill. He furthered the goals of the progressives against the "malefactors of great wealth," the fathers of FDR's economic royalists. Teddy had never accepted the givens of political life, nor would Franklin. Unintimidated by convention, both of them understood the value of the grand gesture, the bold move.

The New Deal was in many ways the culmination of the Square Deal, the embodiment of Teddy's progressive agenda. And both presidents had to confront a conservative Supreme Court. During TR's presidency, the Court's *Lochner* decision locked the nation into supporting laissez-faire policies. In 1912, Teddy had sought to regain the presidency on a third-party ticket, and he proposed the popular recall of judicial decisions and also of judges—another lesson his fifth cousin absorbed.

BEFORE HER HUSBAND rose to speak at the Mayflower Hotel, Eleanor Roosevelt had slipped away. She was driven the few blocks to the Willard Hotel, on Pennsylvania Avenue, where she was the guest of honor at the $10-a-plate Junior Victory Dinner attended by fifteen hundred allegedly Young Democrats, many with gray hair. She did not disappoint them. After her husband's remarks had been piped in, she stepped to the podium in a blue velvet gown, an orchid corsage, and two long strands of pearls.

"No one could be a dictator in a land as peaceful as ours in spirit," she trilled. "For as long as you think and act on your real convictions, you will be the government. The minute you leave it to a small group of people, it ceases to be a democracy."

Her listeners loved her; they always did. Her sincerity and good heart were obvious to everyone. People had placed such trust in Eleanor Roosevelt Roosevelt that she had recently been forced to spike rumors that she might run for president herself in 1940. She toured factories and mines, Indian reservations and CCC camps and squatters' camps, anywhere that Americans were struggling and falling short. Even before her six-day-a-week column, *My Day*, found a home in as many as ninety newspapers, her role was celebrated in the outside world as the president's eyes, ears, and legs. Immediately after the banquet, she was leaving for a lecture tour of the Southwest.

This was Eleanor's second visit in four days to the famed Willard Hotel, which had hosted every president since Franklin Pierce. It was where Lincoln had slept before his inauguration, where President Grant had supposedly coined the term "lobbyist" to describe the men who kept bothering him in the lobby, and where Coolidge had lived during his two and a third years as vice president. Earlier in the week she had attended the

Women's National Press Club's annual evening of skits, as the guest of honor but also as a butt of satire. The curtains had swung open to reveal a picket line outside the White House. *Sit-down Strike*, said the signs, and Mrs. Roosevelt, it turned out, was the one on strike.

Four nights after Eleanor addressed the Junior Victory Dinner, a real sit-down strike broke out at the Willard Hotel. It started when a coffee-shop waitress was fired for her efforts to organize a union, minutes after her supervisor had praised her work. At six o'clock on the evening of March 8, in the cellar kitchen, the twenty-two cooks in their immaculately white uniforms sat down on the benches and in the chairs. The waiters in the cocktail lounge took the seats along the bar, and in the main dining room, the staff waited until the few customers finished their meals, then locked the doors and extinguished the lights. In the lush marble lobby, the bellhops sank into the armchairs and read their newspapers, never deigning to glance up when a mink-draped dowager stalked through and cried, "If Landon had been elected, such an outrage would never have occurred!" Outside, in the chilly drizzle, busboys and waiters and cooks marched in ovals along Pennsylvania Avenue and Fourteenth Street. *WILLARD HO-TEL IS NOW ON STRIKE*, the placards announced, along with the hotel's slogan, *THE RESIDENCE OF PRESIDENTS*. More than a hundred workers had stopped working, and sixty of them were sitting down.

Labor's latest tactic in its long-running war against capital had reached the nation's seat of government at last, and a mere two blocks from the White House. With its paucity of industry, Washington's local economy was out of sync with the rest of the nation's. It bore little resemblance to the economy of Flint, Michigan, where the sit-down strike as an instrument of coercion, copied from France, had burst across American front pages the previous December. When members of the United Auto Workers had sat down at their workstations in a General Motors plant and refused to leave, the company was reluctant to attack its own machinery, and the judicial precedents that the strike was even unlawful were few. In Flint, the stand-off had continued for weeks, until February 2, when the company sent in its private policemen wielding blackjacks, bayonets, and tear gas bombs along with National Guard troops and their machine guns; eight days later, GM's representatives sought out John L. Lewis in his hotel room and agreed to bargain exclusively with the UAW.

The tactic had started at the Goodyear factory in Akron and spread to the Bendix plant in South Bend, the Midland Steel mill in Detroit, a Fisher Body assembly line in Cleveland, a battery plant in Philadelphia, a Tennessee shirt manufacturer, the American Trouser Company in Pittsburgh, a coffinmaker in Ohio, even Woolworth five-and-dimes in New York City. Workers sat down on the job to demand bargaining rights or higher pay. More often than not, they succeeded in getting at least part of what they wanted, though sometimes they wound up bloodied or unemployed—and always with at least a temporary loss of income. But they understood who their enemies were. Day after day, the striking autoworkers in Detroit took up the chant "Nine old men! Nine old men!"

The sit-down strikes had presented the president a dilemma. They offended many people, if not yet as a crime in the laggard technicalities of the law, then as a sin against private property, in a way that even the propertyless could understand. Opinion polls showed that three fourths of Americans—and three out of five factory workers—opposed the sit-down strikes. Even within the administration, the president's more conservative advisers urged him to publicly assail the sit-down strikes for what Vice President Garner called their "mass lawlessness, which, to me, is intolerable." At a cabinet meeting, Garner grew so irate at the president and at Secretary of Labor Frances Perkins that she started to cry, and the meeting ended. Yet the president could hardly risk offending the unions. He needed the support of organized labor, not only for its campaign dollars and its presence at the polls but—more than ever, in the Court fight—for its muscle on Capitol Hill.

If the administration kept away from the labor unrest in the heartland, it wasted no time in settling the sit-down strike on the president's doorstep. Ed McGrady, an assistant secretary of labor, the department's ace in mediation, involved himself in the hotel's strike as if it were a major industrial disruption, spending hours on the telephone with the hotel's managers and the union's representatives, then summoning the strike leaders to his office. Twenty-six hours after the strike began, he strolled into the hotel and told the picketers they could lay down their signs: the management had agreed to bargain with Local 781 of the Hotel and Restaurant Workers' Union, affiliated with the AF of L. In the main dining room, the candelabra were relit, the joyous waiters draped the napkins over their forearms, and a three-piece orchestra struck up "The Star-Spangled Banner."

For the administration, this victory came at a cost, albeit a modest one. When the strike began, John L. Lewis happened to find himself in the lobby of the Hotel Washington down the block, preparing to champion the president's Court plan to labor's Nonpartisan League that evening in the Willard's tenth-floor ballroom. He was unwilling, though, to cross a picket line, and even when the strikers volunteered to desist for a couple of hours, he refused. Labor peace returned to the capital, at the price of a lost opportunity for the president's Court proposal.


ON HIS NBC variety show, sponsored by the Packard Motor Car Company, Fred Astaire introduced a couple of new Gershwin tunes from his forthcoming movie *Shall We Dance*. On the Mutual network, George Jessel cracked one-liners, and his fourteen-year-old protégée, Judy Garland (only three years removed from being Frances Gumm) burst through her songs. At ten thirty in the East on Tuesday night, the ninth of March, all four radio stations in the capital and more than two hundred of them around the country carried this nasal announcement: "Ladies and gentlemen, the president of the United States." Thus began the half hour "upon which much of our hopes are based," as Jimmy Roosevelt acknowledged in his diary. Then, through the static, came the most famous salutation in America, one that the president had borrowed from a Poughkeepsie newspaper editor and occasional political candidate: "My friends . . ."

This was the president's eighth fireside chat, his first since his reelection. He was seated as usual in the Diplomatic Reception Room, behind a desk littered with microphones, facing the wallpaper painting of West Point, on the Hudson River, so near to his home. The still photographers had finished snapping and the five newsreel cameras had started to roll, for the excerpts that would be rushed into theaters and viewed by more than twenty million people apiece. The president was dressed immaculately, as usual, in a soft collar and a bow tie, but he had made no attempt to conceal the darkness of fatigue under his eyes. A few family members sat across the desk and looked on as he leaned toward the microphones that connected him to the American people.

Since Warren Harding's day, from time to time, presidents had spoken to their constituents over the radio. "Silent Cal" Coolidge had tried it thirty-seven times in his seven years; and Herbert Hoover, in just four years, more than a hundred. But those had been remarks delivered to a particular audience. No previous president had spoken directly to the American people, as if one on one. He had started his fireside chats during his first term as governor, aiming them especially at upstate New Yorkers who otherwise learned of the world by reading Republican newspapers. As president, he was preparing his first fireside chat on his ninth night in the White House when he glanced out at a workman who was disassembling the inaugural grandstand and resolved to talk so that the workman could understand. But he never talked down to his listeners; it was to the best in the workman, to his wisest and most responsible self, that the president spoke. The secret to the success of his fireside chats, and to the connection he had forged with the public, was addressing his fellow Americans with a tone of respect. He had also taken pains not to speak too often, for fear of putting the presidency "on the same appeal-level as toothpaste and patent medicines," as the radio critic for the *Washington Post* warned in the fall of 1933, on the eve of FDR's fourth fireside chat.

This eighth presentation required nine drafts to fashion the simplicity of language that allowed the president to create the effect of a friend who was visiting in listeners' homes. Tommy Corcoran, Ben Cohen, Don Richberg, Sam Rosenman, and Jimmy Roosevelt had all had a hand, and the president had canceled his engagements for the day (other than lunch with Secretary of State Cordell Hull) when he remained dissatisfied with the latest draft.

"Last Thursday," he began, "I described in detail certain economic problems which everyone admits now face the nation." After his partisan call to arms at the Democratic Victory Dinner, this was to be reasonable in tone, quieter—more persuasive, his advisers hoped. "For the many messages which have come to me after that speech, and which it is physically impossible to answer individually, I take this means of saying 'Thank you.'"

FDR spoke gravely and rapidly, if a little less sonorously than usual. Seated at the desk, his hands moved naturally, as if he could see his listeners, creating a world and inviting everyone in. He preferred Anglo-Saxon words, informal and concrete, to Latinate abstractions. As many as 80 percent of the words in his fireside chats ranked among the thousand most commonly used, his English almost as plain as Lincoln's in the Gettysburg Address.

"I hope that you have reread the Constitution of the United States. Like the Bible, it ought to be read again and again." He explained how the original Articles of Confederation among the thirteen states had proved too weak to handle national problems, which was why the Constitution's framers had given Congress the power to levy taxes to promote the general welfare—"having in mind that in succeeding generations, many other problems then undreamed of would become national problems." He described why he had ruled out a constitutional amendment to broaden the interpretation of crucial phrases, then cited the precedents for increasing the number of justices. He criticized the Court for acting like a third house of Congress, "reading into the Constitution words and implications which are not there and which were never intended to be there. We have, therefore, reached the point as a nation where we must take action to save the Constitution from the Court and the Court from itself."

Scrubbed from the various drafts was any trace of his original arguments about judicial congestion. Instead, the president confronted his critics head-on. "What do they mean," he said, "by the words 'packing the Court'? Let me answer this question with a bluntness that will end all honest misunderstanding of my purposes." He glanced up at the newsreel cameras, suspicion covering his face. "If by that phrase, 'packing the Court,' it is charged that I wish to place on the bench spineless puppets who would disregard the law and would decide specific cases as I wished them to be decided, I make this answer: that no president fit for his office would appoint, and no Senate of honorable men fit for their office would confirm, that kind of appointee to the Supreme Court." He spoke each word with a ringing tone and pronounced every patrician *r* as an *h*. "But, if by that phrase the charge is made that I would appoint and the Senate would confirm justices . . . who understand these modern conditions, that I will appoint justices who will not undertake to override the judgment of the Congress on legislative policy, that I will appoint justices who will act as justices and not as legislators, if the appointment of such justices can be called 'packing the courts,' then I say that I, and with me the vast majority of the American people, favor doing just that thing—now."

Even a conservative columnist concluded that opponents and law-makers had found the president's arguments "plausible." But the *Chicago Daily Tribune* suggested that the president, in his roundabout way, had admitted his true intention when he called on Congress to apply its own interpretation of the Constitution and on the Supreme Court to defer. And the president, as everyone knew, controlled Congress.

*WHEREAS, FRANKLIN DELANO Roosevelt controls the executive and legislative and is soon to control the judiciary, and has provided a succession of heirs unto the third generation . . .*

As Great Britain was preparing for the coronation of King George VI as the successor to Edward VIII, who had abdicated for the love of a Baltimore divorcee, a group of Yale undergraduates announced the formation of a "Roosevelt for King" club. The *Yale Daily News* published a manifesto for the coronation of King Franklin I, "by the Grace of God and the Democratic organization." The Supreme Court was to be stuffed and placed behind glass at the Smithsonian, leaving the shiny new building available for use as a palace. The press was to be abolished "and the people informed only of what is good for them through fireside chats with his Imperial Majesty." The king would be compelled to retire at age seventy—in fifteen years, after his fifth quadrennium.

The movement swept through the nation's swankiest campuses, where sympathy for the progressive-minded president was in shortest supply. Students with enough time on their hands to establish satirical clubs were the ones whose parents could afford the tuition and, thus, were the most inclined to regard the president as a traitor to his class. The day after Yale, it was Princeton, the birthplace of the Veterans of Future Wars, where the student body had favored Landon by three to one. At Harvard, the president's alma mater, undergraduates Cleveland Amory and Nathaniel Benchley, humorist Robert Benchley's son, launched a chapter of the "Roosevelt for King" club and proposed a royal seal that featured a donkey—"or better yet, a jackass"—swallowing the Constitution. The idea spread as far as the University of Virginia, the home of Thomas Jefferson's antimonarchical soul, where Franklin D. Roosevelt Jr. was to enroll at law school in the fall. The law students who founded the club proclaimed the president's son as

the Duke of Virginia and proposed that he be granted quarters at Monticello, Jefferson's residence nearby.

The notion of a dynasty was not entirely a joke. There were rumors
that the president aspired to have Jimmy Roosevelt take his place—
far-fetched, of course, not the least because the Constitution would require
the twenty-nine-year-old to wait until the 1944 election. Nor could the eldest son hope to match his father's judgment or depth of character; it was
becoming clear that he was in over his head. (In 1938, he admitted in a
national magazine that he had used his name to solicit insurance business
during his father's first term.) When a Kentucky newspaper editorial dis-
missed a father-to-son succession as "silly, idle talk," an admirer sent it to
the White House and scribbled across the top: "He could not <u>wish</u> to have
a better successor."

It was not the specter of a king that worried anyone, of course, but
that of a dictator. According to Frances Perkins, who had worked for FDR
since Albany, "He was totally incapable of comprehending what a dictator
is, how he operates, how he thinks, how he gets anything done." Yet the
fear, while exaggerated, was not outlandish. "Dictator" was not quite a profanity. For a decade, Studebaker had called one of its automobile models
the Dictator, though this would be its final year. Walter Lippmann, the
voice of the Establishment on the editorial pages, had told Roosevelt as the
president-elect that he "may have no alternative but to assume dictatorial
powers," and later he called for "a mild species of dictatorship." Lincoln
had assumed dictatorial powers to save the Union, and history absolved
him. The day after FDR had entered the White House in 1933, elections
in Germany brought Hitler enough parliamentary support to force the legislators who feared his popularity, his storm troopers, and his unrelenting
will to turn over their powers to him, and the judiciary's powers as well. In
America, too, the public felt a measure of desperation and a willingness to
take the necessary steps. Still, the experiences in Europe suggested that
granting one man control of every branch of government presented temp-
tations that no leader who believed in himself could easily resist.

# CHAPTER TEN

# The Voice from Olympus

THE SENATE JUDICIARY Committee was to launch its hearings at ten thirty A.M. on March 10, which gave Henry Ashurst, the committee's baroque-mannered chairman, time to bake in a Turkish bath. The night before, at the Mayflower Hotel, the banquet for Manuel Quezon, the president of the U.S.-controlled Philippines, had lasted almost until midnight, and as the designated toastmaster, Ashurst needed to stay. The opening day of the hearings promised to be grueling.

At first, President Roosevelt had complained to him about the Senate's slow work on his Court bill, which Ashurst as a courtesy had introduced. And then the White House had asked him for a delay until after the fireside chat—the morning after, Ashurst decreed. Jimmy Roosevelt had advised his father that it was "absolutely important that Ashurst be given real orders" to limit the hearings to two or three weeks. But the chairman had no intention of hurrying them along.

The morning's session had initially been slated for the committee's small corner room on the ground floor of the Capitol. But the intensity of the public's attention prompted Ashurst to move the proceedings to the most commodious location possible, the ornate and high-ceilinged Senate Caucus Room, on the third floor of the Senate Office Building. Its marble walls and gray-swirled Corinthian pillars had been witness to drama before, notably in the 1912 hearings on the sinking of the *Titanic* and during Tom Walsh's Teapot Dome interrogations of 1923–24. At least four hundred spectators jammed the seats or stood along the sides. Reporters filled the eighty seats at the small tables near the front, and dozens of photographers roamed. Flashbulbs popped as Ashurst led the procession of eighteen senators in from the anteroom.

The Judiciary chairman looked natty in a stiff collar, his cutaway, and a vest with white piping. Ashurst saw his task in these hearings as soothing the tensions that had built up in the Senate over the Court plan. Even on such a dignified committee, he confided to his diary, the feelings were running high.

Feeling the importance of the occasion and loving the limelight, Ashurst stood to announce that "the committee is here to consider S. 1392, a bill to reorganize the judicial branch of the government. The committee observes the presence here of the attorney general of the United States." The senators sat behind the long, rectangular table and along both ends, as Homer Cummings shook hands with the chairman and seated himself across the table, all the while chewing his gum. A retinue of assistants carried armfuls of his prepared statement. Back from Florida, Cummings had labored over his statement all the previous day and until four o'clock that morning.

An amplifying system had been installed at Ashurst's request, because of what he called the Caucus Room's "damnable acoustics," but the voices still echoed off the marble walls and occasionally the loudspeaker stopped working. For almost an hour, the attorney general droned on through his statement of five thousand legalistic words. In place of the frankness of the president's fireside chat the night before, Cummings reiterated the original arguments for the Court plan, as a response to congested dockets and doddering jurists. For a Supreme Court justice to examine all of the briefs and records for every Supreme Court proceeding, Cummings said, "would be like reading *Gone with the Wind* before breakfast every morning." He voiced his distaste for the justices' narrowly divided decisions, and he mocked the notion that a single person could pack the Court. "That would require," he said, "the concurrence of the president, forty-nine senators, and the appointee himself—fifty-one prominent men. A preposterous suggestion."

William Borah, the committee's senior Republican, broke in to ask a question out of turn. "Suppose after the six additional members of the Supreme Court are appointed, the Court should divide seven to eight, this entire plan would fall, would it not?"

"It would depend upon which side the seven were on," Cummings replied with a grin, "and upon which side the eight were on."

"But you would still have the divided decision, the same as you now have it."

"I do not complain of divided opinions," Cummings said.

"Then I misunderstood you."

"Let me not mislead you. I do complain of split decisions which declare void an act of Congress."

Borah was not to be deflected by sleight of word. "In that event," he persisted, "we would be right back where we are now, would we not? We would still have the split Court."

"I do not think it is apt to happen," Cummings answered, "if we have upon the bench forward-looking judges."

For an hour and a half, the senators chased him around, while the attorney general dodged and escaped. He had grown practiced at his weekly press conferences in using wisecracks to turn aside questions he preferred to ignore. But it was one thing to spar with reporters and quite another to annoy the senators he was hoping to convince. Some of the senators he enlisted in a game of cat and mouse lay beyond any power of persuasion, but others did not. Joe O'Mahoney, a slightly built young Democrat from Wyoming, was a reliable New Dealer who was assumed to be in the president's camp. Yet he wondered aloud if Cummings would help him to draft a constitutional amendment as an alternative to enlarging the Court.

"I have so much confidence in your ability, senator, to draft legislation and to secure its enactment—" Cummings replied.

O'Mahoney interrupted, "I take it that you would accept anything I drafted."

"I am not so sure of that."

"The confidence you expressed did not last very long."

Homer Cummings failed to change any minds, at least not in the direction he wanted.


ALICE BRANDEIS FELT even angrier about the Court plan than her husband did. She was his second cousin as well as his wife, a slim and attractive woman whose long dark hair, usually wrapped in a bun, had turned white decades before. Despite her own frail health, she organized and managed her husband's life and took pains to protect him. The justice's vigor at age eighty was partly her doing, for they were partners in every way, and the insult he took from the president's attack on old age had moved her to fury. They had lived in Washington for nearly twenty-one years, and Alice had learned a thing or two about the capital's back channels. And so on the eighteenth of March, she drove south along Connecticut Avenue and through the city, then crossed the Potomac into Virginia.

Alexandria had originally been part of the District of Columbia until Virginia repossessed it in 1846, fearing—presciently, as it turned out—that Congress would outlaw the slave trade in the District and thereby end Alexandria's lucrative slave market. As the federal workforce almost doubled in the 1930s, Washington's population grew by more than a third. The pressures on housing and real estate prices drove young families out to Maryland or across the river to Virginia, in search of homes they could afford. Northern Virginia was fast becoming a suburb, with its $8,000 brick colonials and its $50-a-month garden apartments to house the civil servants, lawyers, journalists, and file clerks flocking to the capital. Alice Brandeis was heading to a house on Quaker Lane, which was almost rural and therefore affordable for a young couple with a newborn. Her visit was a mission of state.

Six-week-old Tommy Colman's mother had helped Mrs. Brandeis in 1934 to obtain the appointment of a woman as a juvenile court judge, and despite their four-decade difference in age, they had become friends. Elizabeth Colman's ability to do a kindness had had nothing to do with her husband's influence at the Agricultural Adjustment Administration or her own Federal Housing Administration publicist's post or her past position as the Young Democrats' national vice president. She had been able to satisfy Mrs. Brandeis's request simply because she was Senator Burt Wheeler's daughter. It would have been inappropriate for a justice's wife to request a favor directly from a senator, in case it nicked the Constitution's careful structure of checks and balances. But a back channel—this was how Washington worked. Wheeler's daughter, a slim-faced, earnest young mother, resembled her father in looks but even more in political temperament. Her résumé included stints at the Women's International League for Peace and Freedom and later at the League of Women Shoppers, where she had caused a splash the previous year by picketing a pants factory to press for higher wages.

She was flattered by the visit from the justice's wife, who seldom paid social calls. But something else seemed to be on the visitor's mind. Only as Mrs. Brandeis was leaving did she make herself clear.

"Tell your father," she said, "the justice is in favor of his fight against the Court bill."

Alice Brandeis's automobile had not left the driveway before Elizabeth telephoned her father. The senator, as it happened, had already tried an indirect approach of his own to Justice Brandeis. Marquis Childs, a young newspaperman in the capital for the *St. Louis Post-Dispatch*, had grown friendly with Wheeler and also with Brandeis, who was partial to reporters, especially from St. Louis, where he had started his career. Wheeler had asked Childs to query the justice on what he thought of the Court plan, and Childs had obliged. "A very destructive blow," one that "impugned the integrity of the Court," Brandeis had told the newspaperman in confidence.

Two days after Mrs. Brandeis's visit, on Saturday, March 20, the Montana senator telephoned Justice Brandeis at home and was invited over. The two men had known each other since 1923, shortly after Wheeler's arrival in Washington. The liberal justice sought out the young senator, who had quickly carved a progressive reputation. Wheeler accepted the second spot on the Progressive Party's national ticket in 1924 only after Brandeis had turned it down, and invariably they saw eye to eye on political philosophy. Both of them despised bigness, whether practiced by the Company or the industrial trusts. They exalted the individual and championed the underdog against corporate interests.

Louis Brandeis lived as he preached. He and his wife had agreed early in their marriage not to accumulate material goods, because they distracted people from the important things in life—family, justice, truth. They invested their money instead and had become millionaires, though nobody could tell, for they lived unpretentiously, even ascetically, in the sunny apartment they rented in a slightly run-down building on California Street.

In a slanting light, Louis Brandeis bore a startling resemblance to an Old Testament prophet or, especially in Alice's eyes, to Lincoln himself. There was something ethereal about him, in his chiseled features, in his soft but penetrating gray-blue eyes, in the tousle of hair that was silkily white with a purplish tinge. Unlike Benjamin Cardozo, who was warm to everyone,

Brandeis seemed somehow aloof. He was a jurist of unquestioned—indeed, intimidating—integrity, a man of humility who listened well but in whose presence it was hard to relax. As the last important person in Washington to trade in a horse and buggy for an automobile, in many ways Brandeis was a conservative at heart, a nineteenth-century man, a Jeffersonian nostalgic for a simpler economy and a more graceful time.

The justice ushered Wheeler upstairs into his cramped study stacked with legal papers and lined with bookshelves floor to ceiling. Wheeler got right to the point. He asked if the justice—or perhaps the chief justice—might be willing to appear before the Senate committee to refute the administration's charges that the judiciary was lagging behind in its work. Wheeler was slated as the first witness on Monday morning, when the opposition was to start presenting its case.

Brandeis firmly declined. Allowing a lawmaker to question a justice, he observed, would violate the Court's independence and the sanctity of its decision making. A justice ought not write or speak in public about the Court, he explained, except in a judicial opinion. Then he surprised Wheeler by adding, "You call up the chief justice and he'll give you a letter."

Wheeler demurred until Brandeis went to the telephone himself—he used one only under duress—and dialed the chief justice's number at home. When he told Hughes that Wheeler wanted to see him, the invitation was immediate.

Wheeler had in fact called on the chief justice just two days earlier, accompanied by the top Republican and the second-ranked Democrat on the Senate Judiciary Committee, to ask if he would testify in person on the Court plan. At first Hughes had been inclined to agree. But when he invited Brandeis to sit beside him, he received a quick and unambiguous "no," and Hughes turned the senators down.

Wheeler now returned to the chief justice's door, four blocks south of Brandeis's. It was after five o'clock on Saturday, the Hugheses' night to socialize, but the chief justice was gracious in his greeting. The senator said Brandeis had told him that the chief justice would give him a letter.

"Did Brandeis tell you that?" If he was surprised, he must have been pleased that Brandeis had thought of an acceptable means of making the Court's opinion known.

Wheeler confirmed it, and Hughes said, "When do you want it?"

"Monday morning." The rumor had spread—surely the work of the Court bill's proponents—that Wheeler might not testify on Monday, or at all.

Hughes glanced at his wristwatch and said that the library was closed and his secretary had gone. He would also have to phone some of the other justices. "Can you come by early Monday morning?"

"Certainly."

The chief justice then inquired about Wheeler's plans for Sunday afternoon and learned he had none.

PROBABLY BETTER THAN anyone alive, Charles Evans Hughes understood that the Supreme Court had been a political institution from the first. George Washington had mainly appointed ideological soul mates to the Court. John Jay, the first chief justice, campaigned twice for political office before quitting the Court, while another of Washington's appointees, Samuel Chase, campaigned for John Adams's reelection in 1800. After Adams lost, he named John Marshall as the chief justice (who stayed on for a month as also the secretary of state) to keep a Federalist eye on President Jefferson, who pursued his own judicial politicking in pressing the House of Representatives to impeach Justice Chase, though the Senate refused to convict. The early justices wrote unsolicited letters of advice to presidents and lawmakers, and later several justices corresponded secretly with James Buchanan while he was the president-elect to tell him of the decision they were drafting in the *Dred Scott* case. William Howard Taft, as the chief justice, represented President Coolidge in persuading Harry Daugherty to resign as the attorney general in the Teapot Dome scandal; on the bench, Taft was unabashed in taking property's side.

In Hughes's mind, because the Court had taken sides against the people, it had sunk to its low standing in the public's eye—self-inflicted wounds, as he liked to say. If he hoped to restore the Court's reputation, and thereby to protect it from further harm, he felt it had to do the people's bidding—to follow, at least in a rough way, the election returns. Otherwise the president would surely succeed in expanding the Court, and forever after the justices would have reason to worry about the president and the election returns.

Since the days of Reconstruction, the justices had maintained a resolute public silence about anything political. But that tradition was giving way. Just four nights earlier, James McReynolds had spoken extemporaneously, and not for the first time, to the annual banquet of his college fraternity, at the Carlton Hotel, just south of K Street. But this time he strayed beyond the subject of Phi Delta Theta. "We're in a troublesome world," he told a few score of his brethren from an earlier day. "There is a strange restlessness, a strange desire to break away from that which is proved—to rule or ruin." His objective was equal justice, for rich and poor alike, he explained, "to protect the poorest darky in the Georgia backwoods as well as the man of wealth in a mansion on Fifth Avenue. And I have the same obligation to the man in the mansion on Fifth Avenue as to the humblest man in any walk of life." Then he deplored the tendency by attorneys on the losing side of a case to whine about the unfairness of the result. "The evidence of good sportsmanship," he said, "is that a man who has had a chance to present a fair case to a fair tribunal must be a good sport and accept the outcome." Everyone understood the accusation he was leveling at the man in the White House.

HUGHES HIMSELF HAD benefited from the connection between politics and the Court. He had stepped down from the Court to run for president in 1916, after the Republican bigwigs appealed to him as the only figure of national repute who was acceptable to both wings of a fractured GOP, to its Old Guard as well as to the Bull Moose progressives the party needed to lure back in the fold.

Hughes had always been a political creature in a nonpolitical guise. He had first burst into public notice in 1905 as a precocious young lawyer who led the New York legislature's investigation into monopoly practices of the natural gas industry and the life insurance business, among the great commercial scandals of the age. His grasp of the intricacies of how both industries worked, his pitiless cross-examinations, and the subsequent reforms propelled him into the State House in Albany. "He did not seek the Governorship; it sought him," a writer in *Everybody's* magazine noted.

Hughes enjoyed a tug from Teddy Roosevelt, a former governor of New York himself. The muckrakers lionized him as a true public servant who had no price. "In private life he is a buoyant, joyful person," Ida Tarbell rhapsodized in 1908, "fond of books of all sorts, stories of adventure—Mr. Dooley, Ibsen, Henry James—a most catholic taste—fond of music, a golf player, a mountain climber—he has been over most of Switzerland on foot—fond of his friends and his family, his college and his church." He was a paragon of self-discipline who worked from nine in the morning until midnight, and he dominated the legislature without making deals. His father, a Baptist preacher, had once told a writer for *McClure's*, "At an early age I taught my son that a straight line was the shortest distance between two points."

As a politician, it turned out, Hughes was mediocre. Stiff in public, he was not the sort of man whom others slapped on the back. In 1916 he had lost the presidency to Woodrow Wilson, the equally unsociable incumbent, because of a failure—inadvertent, he insisted—to shake hands with Hiram Johnson, who was then the progressive Republican governor of California. Hughes was campaigning in the state, ushered around by the stand-pat Republicans, and only after leaving a reception in Long Beach had he learned that Hiram Johnson had been elsewhere in the hotel. He had missed a chance to bridge the bitterness between the state party's warring halves; on Election Night, after a delayed count, California came within 3,775 votes of making Hughes the president. Instead, he was out of a job.

Yet he had always had an eye for opportunity. As a young lawyer in New York City, he had courted his senior partner's daughter and married her. After losing the presidency, he established himself as the nation's leading trial lawyer, who probably argued more cases before the Supreme Court than any litigator in the country. The most spectacular allegation of his ambition surrounded his return in 1930 to the Court. As the story emerged five years later, President Hoover had wanted to nominate Harlan Fiske Stone, who was already an associate justice and a member of Hoover's "medicine ball" cabinet. But an adviser persuaded him that Hughes's stature required that he be offered the position first, though he was certain to turn it down; accepting it, after all, would force Charles Evans Hughes Jr. to step down from his position as the solicitor general, since he could hardly argue the administration's cases before a Court that his father would lead. So Hoover made the hollow offer, and without a moment's pause—or so the tale went—the man with the golden résumé accepted. Both principals had denied the story, but everyone else was prone to believe it. To President Roosevelt and his advisers, it only added to their grudging respect for Hughes's shrewdness and assertions of will.

From the beginning, Hughes's political skills had been rooted in his mastery of the facts, his skill in analyzing them, and his guile in putting them to use. Never had these skills been so useful as in resisting President Roosevelt's assault on the size—and the independence—of his Court. With an instinct for recognizing his opponent's vulnerabilities and an ingenuity in framing his strongest argument, Hughes considered his best tactic for the letter that was beginning to take form in his mind. He bored in on the president's strategic blunder, ignoring the president's real motive—to move the Court to the left—and instead targeting the president's first, disingenuous argument about an inefficient judiciary. He quickly collected the statistics he needed and drafted his argument, one that protected the institution he loved while leaving the Court's own disingenuous fiction—that it was an apolitical institution—intact.

Satisfied with his handiwork, he showed it to Brandeis and to Willis Van Devanter, the longest-serving associate justices in their respective philosophical camps, who both lived in apartments a few blocks away. "Each went over it carefully," Hughes recounted, "and approved it." On Sunday afternoon, the chief justice telephoned Wheeler and asked if he could drop by. As the senator passed through the door on R Street, Hughes handed him a letter and said portentously, "The baby is born."

Wheeler read through the seven pages of well-ordered facts and noted Van Devanter's and Brandeis's concurrence. "They are the Court," Hughes told him. At the bottom, *Charles Evans Hughes* was scrawled in blue.

Wheeler was delighted. When he started to leave, Hughes invited him to sit. Wheeler took it as an order.

"I think I am as disinterested in this matter, from a political standpoint, as anyone in the United States," Hughes said. "I am interested in the Court as an institution. And this proposed bill would destroy the Court as an institution."

As the senator left, the chief justice said, "I hope you'll see that this gets wide publicity."

Wheeler was tempted to laugh, but he stopped himself and assured the chief justice he had no need for concern.


ALICE ROOSEVELT LONGWORTH arrived early at the Senate Caucus Room on Monday, March 22, to assure herself a good seat. "Princess Alice" was the nearest that America knew to royalty. She was suitably eccentric, with her dangling cigarette and her brash opinions. She had attended several of the Judiciary hearings during the preceding two weeks, and this morning's session, in which the Court bill opponents were to open their arguments, was not to be missed. It drew the largest crowd yet. Would-be spectators lined up outside the room and grew short-tempered with the police once they realized that the hearing would start without them. Inside, every seat was filled, and people squeezed into crevices along the marble walls. In the front row, Lulu Wheeler sat among the senators' wives, knitting.

The administration's witnesses had been testifying for two weeks, and though the witness list was only half finished, Tommy Corcoran had decided to end it. At least a couple of the witnesses had helped the president's cause. Robert Jackson, as an assistant attorney general, had followed Homer Cummings to the witness chair and detailed the accelerating pace of judicial activism by the conservative Court. The Supreme Court had acted as "a super-government," Jackson said, in striking down a dozen federal laws during the past three years alone, versus nineteen during all of the 1920s and never more than nine during any earlier decade. Princeton's constitutional scholar Edward Corwin had urged senators to "unpack" the Court from its prevailing "economic bias." Still, Corcoran decided, presumably with the president's assent, that continuing the testimony in favor of the president's plan would constitute a filibuster of sorts that would play into opponents' hands. It was an impulsive judgment, one he was soon to regret.

"Senators, we are signally honored this morning," Henry Ashurst began. "We have before us one of the most, if not the most, distinguished member of the United States Senate." Necks craned as Burton K. Wheeler of Montana, seated across the table from Ashurst, started to speak. In the course of the next hour or more, he would leave cigar ashes and wads of scrap paper on the plum-red carpet around his feet. "I want it to be understood at the outset," Wheeler said, "that anything I may say is not said because of the fact that I have any unfriendly feeling toward the president. On the contrary . . ."

Wheeler spoke in low, earnest tones as he leaned across the table. He detailed his seven years of political support for a president who had only recently entered his fifth year in office, and he acknowledged their occasional disagreements on policy. When he raised the issue posed by the Court bill, he framed it exactly as the president had at first—as a remedy for judicial inefficiency—and as the attorney general had repeated in opening the Senate hearings. "It was only after the attorney general of the United States came before this committee . . . that I went to the only source in this country that could know exactly what the facts were." He paused. "And I have here now a letter by the chief justice of the United States, Mr. Charles Evans Hughes." Excitement rippled through the crowd as Wheeler started to read slowly, emphasizing the sentences that mattered the most. "'Dear Senator Wheeler,'" he began, "'In response to your inquiries, I have the honor to present the following statement with respect to the work of the Supreme Court:

"'One. The Supreme Court is fully abreast of its work . . .'"

The letter was dry and methodical, replete with statistical tables and legalese. It made a show of ignoring the president's case against the Court's conservatism as a matter of "policy" that lay beyond the chief justice's proper reach. But it demolished every argument on which the administration had originally rested its case. The Court's docket was up-to-date, and only 20 percent of the petitions for the Court's review had any merit. Because most appeals turned on questions of law, not of fact, the justices need not examine the evidence by reading thousands of pages before breakfast. Far from smoothing the Court's procedural pace, Hughes declared, expanding the number of justices "would impair that efficiency so long as the Court acts as a unit," which the Constitution requires. It was this argument that clinched his case.

"'On account of the shortness of time'"—Wheeler continued reading the chief justice's words—"'I have not been able to consult with the members of the Court generally with respect to the foregoing statement, but I am confident that it is in accord with the views of the justices. I should say, however, that I have been able to consult with Mr. Justice Van Devanter and Mr. Justice Brandeis, and I am at liberty to say that the statement is approved by them.'"

There was a hush when Wheeler stopped reading, as if something had happened that could never be undone. "You could have heard a comma drop," Wheeler said later. The letter had been a shock that needed to sink in. No chief justice since John Marshall had played so public a role on a controversial issue. The endorsement by Brandeis was a particular embarrassment to the White House—"the most powerful weapon that has yet come into [opponents'] hands," the *Wall Street Journal* judged the next morning. The senators who disliked the president's plan had broken into smiles, as supporters scribbled possible lines of rebuttal.

"Mr. Chairman, will the witness yield?" William Dieterich, a first-term Democrat from Illinois, had been elected on President Roosevelt's coattails. He had rested his support for expanding the Court on the supposition of a clogged judiciary.

"I am glad to," Wheeler said.

Dieterich recalled that at the previous session, the committee had refused to place a letter into evidence because the writer was unavailable for cross-examination. Here, too, he objected, "notwithstanding the high character of the gentleman who writes the letter."

"Anybody can cross-examine *me*," Wheeler broke in. Only two of the senators bothered to try.

The chief justice, working at home, sent word to the reporters who had gathered outside that he had no copies of his letter to distribute—they should ask Senator Wheeler instead. In Warm Springs, the president was taking his daily swim when the word reached him. In public, he was serene. That afternoon, when members of Phi Beta Kappa from the University of Georgia arrived at his cottage to make him an honorary member—joining the likes of James Buchanan and Jefferson Davis—he showed his customary cheer. In private, however, he was bitter, especially at Louis Brandeis's apostasy. Roosevelt was angry at Hughes, and presumably also at Wheeler, but he might have expected nothing better. In Roosevelt's moral code, however, a man did not turn on an old friend in public, even on a matter of principle. The president was irate, or so senators heard. "I never thought old Isaiah would do that to me," he told Tommy Corcoran.

The president eventually forgave Brandeis, but Tommy Corcoran never did. He blamed Alice Brandeis for treating her husband with such a deference that he had come to see himself as something of a Messiah. In June, after the Court's session ended, Corcoran stopped by the justice's apartment as a courtesy, but he never visited his old friend again.

# CHAPTER ELEVEN

# A Switch in Time

"DO I EAT IT?" Five-year-old Bill Roosevelt had been handed an Easter egg on the South Lawn of the White House. He wore a brown snowsuit and a blue beret and carried a fuzzy elephant, the symbol of the wrong political party.

"Not just now," Eleanor Roosevelt, his grandmother, replied. In the chilly morning sun of Easter Monday, she was squiring the boy around on his first Easter egg roll. He was one of more than twenty thousand children and adults who had crowded inside the White House fence to unearth the hidden eggs, then to roll them down the hillocks that Andrew Jackson had raised on the flat lawn to remind him of his native Tennessee. When the children tired of rolling the eggs, they pelted one another.

"Good morning, everybody, both here and on the air," Mrs. Roosevelt said into a microphone and to the nation. "It is a beautiful day in Washington."

The president was to make an appearance on the South Portico at three o'clock that afternoon, after meeting with two of his cabinet officers and then lunching with a third. He had returned on Saturday from Warm Springs, sporting a tan. His wife and his attorney general had met his train at Union Station. Homer Cummings had been wondering how to regain the political high ground against a chief justice so cowardly that he would issue a pronouncement and then refuse to make himself available, even privately, to respond to counterevidence.

The morning's most gratifying news for the Roosevelts emerged in Wilmington, Delaware, where Mr. and Mrs. Eugene du Pont announced a wedding date for their daughter, Ethel, and the president's third son,

155

Franklin Jr. The groom's family considered the marriage a godsend for the most foul-tempered of the Roosevelt boys, a Harvard senior who was living lavishly at school, much like his father had. But the president had another reason for feeling a frisson of delight at the marital alliance with the wealthy family of industrial chemists. He could only savor the provocation of his presence at the wedding reception on June 30, when the du Ponts would have no choice but to welcome a traitor to their class into their home.

"OYEZ, OYEZ, OYEZ."

Precisely at noon on Easter Monday, the twenty-ninth of March, the vast velvet drapes parted and Charles Evans Hughes stepped into the courtroom, his eight brethren following. The courtroom's high ceiling and indirect lighting evoked the feel of a church, as did the rules of decorum, which barred spectators from squirming or chewing gum or reading a newspaper or taking notes.

The courtroom had been packed each decision day, in anticipation of verdicts in the five Wagner Act cases pending since February and in another minimum wage case, from Washington State, which had been argued in December. By eleven o'clock, as many as four thousand people had entered the building, though the courtroom itself seated no more than three hundred. Every seat was occupied, and a double line of spectators waited to get in. The presence of senators and especially of most of the justices' wives foretold an event of consequence. As the gavel fell, the justices took their seats, and then the lawyers, reporters, VIPs, social hostesses, and throngs of Easter tourists did the same.

The announcement of the second case brought spectators to the edge of their seats. *West Coast Hotel Co. v. Parrish* was a challenge to the pre–World War statute in Washington State that prescribed a minimum wage for women of thirty cents an hour. It was strikingly similar to the New York law that the Court had struck down, to such public disgust, just ten months earlier. The very fact that the justices had accepted the *Parrish* case at all, and on the same day in October that they refused a rehearing of the New York case, had aroused competing conjectures among lawyers in the know. Did the Court intend to change its mind or—this was considered more likely—did it mean to bury the issue by striking yet another conservative blow?

Elsie Parrish was a forty-six-year-old grandmother and a chambermaid at the Cascadian Hotel in Wenatchee, Washington, at the base of the Cascades. She was paid $12.00 for a forty-eight-hour week, short of the $14.40 the state law required, so she and her husband sued for $216.19 in back pay. The state's own supreme court had found in their favor, which prompted the hotel's appeal to the highest court in the land. The attorneys for Elsie Parrish and for Washington State had specifically asked the Court to uphold the state law by overturning its fourteen-year-old judicial precedent, in the *Adkins* case, which had struck down a minimum wage for women in Washington, D.C.

Charles Evans Hughes himself was delivering the majority opinion. He had voted with the minority in the New York case, against the five conservative justices who had overturned the minimum wage on the grounds that it deprived employers of their right of due process to bargain freely with workers. If Hughes was presenting the majority opinion, either he had switched to the conservative side to assign the opinion to himself—a chief justice's prerogative—or the Court was reversing itself. The answer became evident just before Hughes started to read, when Justice McReynolds, an unbending conservative, rose from his high-backed chair and, with a swish of the curtains, vanished from view.

"This case presents the question of the constitutional validity of the minimum wage law of the State of Washington," Hughes began, and he left no one in suspense for long. "We are of the opinion," he declared, "that this ruling of the state court demands on our part a reexamination of the *Adkins* case." To reexamine, everyone understood, was to overturn. He specified three reasons for such a step: the narrow margin, five to four, by which the Court had decided *Adkins*; the potent—indeed, poignant—fact that eighteen states had passed minimum wage laws, mainly for women and children; and the economic conditions that had arisen since the *Adkins* decision in 1923. In Hughes's mind, apparently, the case did not involve legal principles or even the intent of the Constitution, but matters more temporal—the thinness of a long-ago majority, and the political and economic developments in the fourteen years since.

This case, like the earlier minimum wage cases, hinged on the liberty of contract that the conservative jurists had discerned in the due process clauses in the Fifth and Fourteenth amendments, which guaranteed that neither the federal nor a state government, respectively, could deprive a "person" of property without a legal proceeding. Hughes cared deeply about the stability of the law, as a bulwark of the judiciary's standing with the people, and he had no wish to scuttle the liberty of contract. But he had every intention of limiting it. Any such liberty is not "absolute and uncontrollable," he declared in a tone of triumph. Instead, it is "liberty in a social organization which requires the protection of law against the evils which menace the health, safety, morals and welfare of the people." The devoted husband and father of three daughters wanted to know, "What can be closer to the public interest than the health of women and their protection from unscrupulous and overreaching employers?"

And even if a policy was unwise, the chief justice decreed, "still the legislature is entitled to its judgment." This was the doctrine, invoked more often than obeyed, of judicial self-restraint. As long as the regulation was reasonably related to its goal and was adopted in the community's interest, Hughes reasoned, the requirements of due process had been met. The Constitution, in short, was a living document, and its meaning depended upon lawmakers' assessments of society's needs.

This was not the first time the Court's majority had accorded such a deference to legislators' judgment. If the chief justice's reasoning sounded familiar, it was meant to. It echoed Justice Roberts's reasoning in the *Nebbia* case, three years before, the far-reaching liberal opinion that had allowed New York regulators to control the retail price of milk. Hughes persisted in quoting from Roberts's ruling—three times—in making his case, and at last the Court's judgment was plain. "Our conclusion," the chief justice boomed, his eyes flashing, "is that the case of *Adkins v. Children's Hospital* should be, and it is, overruled."

The reversal was blunt and unembarrassed—and a shock. The Court had frequently overturned its own precedents. Justice Brandeis had once listed fifty such occasions in a footnote. But never before had it happened so quickly. In the most famous instance, after President Grant had filled his two vacancies, fifteen months passed before the Supreme Court reversed its decision on legal tender—its swiftness a serious mistake, by Hughes's reckoning, one that had shaken popular respect for the Court.

This time the Court had taken less than ten months since it had ruled the other way in the *Tipaldo* case involving an almost identical law in New York. And unlike in Grant's day, the very same set of justices had changed its collective mind.

The size of the reversing majority remained a mystery, however, until Hughes finished and Justice Sutherland began. Even his ideological antagonists admired the cultured Utahan with the Vandyke beard—"for whatever you may say of him," Brandeis had once remarked, "he has character and conscience." Just the previous Thursday he had turned seventy-five, and from the bench he viewed the world in black and white, as if the nineteenth century still lived and the frontier had never died. A friend of Warren G. Harding and a devotee of Herbert Spencer and his social Darwinism, Sutherland had once proclaimed that the natural law of supply and demand ought to be ranked with the multiplication tables, the Constitution, and the Sermon on the Mount as fundamental truths. He had voted to overturn every New Deal law that had come before the Court other than the TVA.

From his seat to the right of Justice McReynolds's vacant chair, Sutherland began to read his dissent in a voice that could hardly be heard. "Mr. Justice Van Devanter, Mr. Justice McReynolds, Mr. Justice Butler and I think the judgment of the court . . ." In an instant, everything was clear: Owen Roberts had switched sides. It had been Roberts and nobody else. On a five-to-four vote, the Court was reversing its five-to-four vote in the *Tipaldo* case of the previous June.

Justice Sutherland took a sip of water, and suddenly in place of the mild-mannered justice sprang a man unwilling to shrink from a fight. He had watched his black-and-white world corrode into grays, and he meant to deliver a eulogy of sorts, a defense of his fourteen and a half years on the Court.

"The meaning of the Constitution does not change with the ebb and flow of economic events," the most eloquent of the Four Horsemen proclaimed, rapping his knuckles on the bench. He quoted a legal scholar that "the meaning of the Constitution is fixed when it is adopted, and it is not different at any subsequent time." To Sutherland, the proper conclusion could not have been more obvious. To the extent that a minimum wage for women "exceeds the fair value of the services rendered," he deduced, "it amounts to a compulsory exaction from the employer for the support of a partially indigent person, for whose condition there rests upon him no peculiar responsibility, and therefore, in effect, arbitrarily shifts to his shoulders a burden which, if it belongs to anybody, belongs to society as a whole." Time and again, he noted, the Court had recognized a liberty of contract, "and we do not understand" what has changed.

Justice Roberts sat in his swivel chair at the left end of the bench and pressed a handkerchief to his lips. While the chief justice presented the majority opinion, Roberts had leaned back in his seat, his eyes shut, but as Sutherland delivered the dissent, Roberts sat up and kept glancing along the bench at his erstwhile ally with a look of annoyance. Sutherland was demanding that he explain himself, and Roberts had no such intention.

He alone had switched sides and everything had changed. "Here, truly, was another Saul at another Tarsus," Professor Corwin wrote. Roberts had voted with the conservatives in striking down New York's minimum wage for women, and now he sided with the liberals to uphold a minimum wage for women in Washington State. Suddenly, the "no-man's-land" the president had scorned, where neither the state nor the federal government could intervene, had disappeared. At last, it seemed, state legislatures possessed the authority to regulate business to help society's needy, and presumably the federal government could do the same.

Before the day's session ended, the justices had announced four other decisions that allowed the government to protect the weak against the strong. White Monday, the New Dealers called March 29, 1937, in contrast to Black Monday, the day in 1935 when the NRA had been struck down and the liberals' accomplishments were slipping away. The *Christian Science Monitor* trumpeted the gist of the news that afternoon, in a subheadline reporting that the nation's High Court

"Opens the Way
to Liberal Era."

Unless, of course, the Court decided to reverse itself once again. Of the day's five rulings, one had been unanimous but the other four were decided by the narrowest of margins—in each case, the same five justices prevailing over the Four Horsemen. Every time, Owen Roberts lined up with the liberals, without once explaining why. At least in regard to the minimum wage for women, Arthur Krock pointed out the next morning in the *New York Times*, "the Constitution . . . is today what Justice Roberts says it is." Justice was a seesaw, on the fulcrum of a single justice's scale.

Owen Roberts's paternal grandparents had named his father Josephus, because of its biblical sound, and Josephus Roberts had bestowed it as a middle name upon his only son. Neighbors had tried to persuade Owen's mother that it was a Jewish historian's name, but she did not believe them. As it happened, they were correct, and it offered an omen for the justice-to-be. In A.D. 70, a general for the Jews during their revolt against the Romans abandoned his troops in the midst of battle, changed his name from Joseph ben Matthias to Flavius Josephus, moved to Rome, and served as the emperor's court historian. "The traitor of Jerusalem," he was called—quick to betray his people, too willing to switch sides.

"Roberts' somersault"—such was Felix Frankfurter's epithet, in a letter to Harlan Stone, the day after the Court reversed itself on the minimum wage. "Everything that he now subscribes to he rejected . . . and everything that he rejected in your dissenting opinion of last June, especially the significance of his own opinion in the *Nebbia* case, he now subscribes to. What kind of respect for the institution can be aroused in informed and able young minds?"

"A sad chapter in our judicial history," a disheartened Stone replied, though Roberts's switch had given the liberals a victory, alluding darkly to "explanations which do not explain."


PEOPLE IN WASHINGTON, by and large, were finicky in their humor. They shunned slapstick or farce or anything off-color. Irony was a hard sell, and Hollywood's favorite comedies, about the careless rich and the virtuous poor, left many in Washington unamused. The thriving city was not a dour place, but it was not a frivolous one either. People took themselves seriously; power was not only an aphrodisiac but a depressant as well. Humor in the capital assumed a certain level of knowledge.

This was the case for the witticism that swept the capital in the spring of 1937, a twist on one of Benjamin Franklin's famous maxims that had made such a commercial success of *Poor Richard's Almanack*: *Early to bed and early to rise, makes a man healthy, wealthy, and wise. A stitch in time saves nine.*

It was the latter that supplied the basis for the quip that described Justice Roberts's reversal, and a polite competition broke out over the proper credit. The best guess, according to scholars, was Edward Corwin of Princeton. Six weeks after the Court's reversal on the minimum wage, the eminent political scientist joked in a letter to Homer Cummings that "a switch in time saved nine." Three weeks later, the *New York Times* quoted a Yale Law School professor, Abe Fortas, at a meeting of labor activists in New Jersey. They applauded the future justice when he cracked, "Mr. Justice Roberts's theory must be a switch in time serves nine." Others credited the jest to Harvard's legal heavyweight Thomas Reed Powell.

It was witty because it was more than a joke. While the fate of the Court plan remained unresolved, nobody could know for sure whether Roberts's reversal would, indeed, save the Supreme Court as a nine-member body. That might depend, in turn, on whether Roberts had truly switched. If the Supreme Court had genuinely reversed its course, if it continued to act as the New Dealers—and the public—might wish, the rationale for adding justices would erode.

No one could be certain, of course, except perhaps for Owen Roberts. "The liberal margin of advantage is the margin of Justice Roberts's very changeable mind," cautioned the *Nation*, a champion of the president and the New Deal. Another witticism, in the *New Yorker*, described the Court building's "soundproof room, to which justices may retire to change their minds." A justice who had changed his mind could easily change it again.

# CHAPTER TWELVE

# The Heat of Democracy

"IT IS THE economic royalists who go to the Supreme Court for certiorari." Senator Burton K. Wheeler made the Latin term, for a request of judicial review, sound like a curse word. In the early afternoon of March 29, he held the floor in the Senate during a heated discussion over the chief justice's week-old letter defending the Court's performance. Kenneth McKellar, a long-haired New Dealer from Tennessee, had instigated the debate by trying to refute the points the chief justice had made in his letter "filled with excuses." McKellar was the archetype of a southern senator, with his frock coat, his black bow tie, and his talent for indignation. He stormed at the Court for rejecting 87 percent of the petitions for appeal and for its "un-American" secrecy in never saying why. Twice, Wheeler asked him to yield the floor, and both times he refused. McKellar was pressing Wheeler for an answer on whether the Court had ruled correctly or incorrectly on the AAA when Joe Robinson rose at his front desk on the center aisle.

"Before the senator from Montana passes to that point—" the majority leader broke in. A messenger had rushed from the Supreme Court into the Senate chamber. Wheeler yielded, and the burly majority leader announced that the Supreme Court had reversed itself and upheld the minimum wage law in Washington State.

Joseph T. Robinson, then sixty-four, had been born in a country cabin near Little Rock, the ninth of eleven children. Strong and scrappy even as a youth, his emotions often spilled out in public. Once, in an angry debate, he stalked along an empty row, roaring as he went, until he hovered over Huey Long and shook a fist under the Louisianan's chin; another time, he almost started a fistfight with "Fightin' Bob" La Follette the elder. One day on the golf course at Chevy Chase Country Club, he had punched a surgeon who wanted to play through, and the club expelled him. "Scrappy Joe," the press called him. "Senator Robinson's wrath was fearful to behold, and it contributed greatly to his success as a battering-ram of a leader in the Senate," a newspaperman wrote.

But his temper was not the source of his colleagues' respect; rather, they appreciated his quiet, unrelenting sense of honor. Everyone in Washington—in the Senate, certainly—knew that he was a man of his word. In his life, it was said, he had never broken a promise. He had sacrificed the oil company fees at his law firm in Little Rock for a cramped two-room apartment on Capitol Hill, because he and his wife were unable to buy a house within their means in the capital, the most expensive city in the country. Yet when a tobacco merchant had arrived in his office, offering $1,000 if he would endorse Lucky Strikes, he ordered the man off the premises. His incorruptibility extended to his legislative labors. As the president's strong-arm man in the Senate, Joe Robinson devoted his tireless energy on behalf of New Deal proposals, many of which he disliked. He continued to do so even after the White House enraged him by ignoring his patronage requests for postmasterships and the like back home. ("There is something in what he says," Jimmy Roosevelt conceded.) Other politicians admired him, and his fellow senators, almost without exception, loved him.

His occasional shows of emotion sustained his air of authority. "I have never been able to understand the legal theory," he stormed, "on which the Supreme Court of the United States held unconstitutional the New York minimum-wage law." He waggled his finger at conservative senators. "Today, the Court has completely reversed itself and directly and explicitly overruled the case on which the decisions against the New York statute was based—namely, the *Adkins* case."

"Fine!" Wheeler interjected.

"Yes, fine. But what happens to the thousands of women and children in the great state of New York who"—that state's law already struck from the books—"are compelled to work unlimited hours in sweatshops and in factories on the basis of the *Adkins* case?" Robinson shouted. "I was made miserable when the Supreme Court decided that Congress could not fix minimum wages for women and children workers in the District of Columbia. I was made more unhappy when, following that precedent, the Supreme Court said that the New York State lawmaking power could not do it in the state of New York." The majority leader slammed his brown and freckled fists down on the mahogany desks nearby. "I am glad that the Supreme Court has completely faced about and recognized the necessity of overruling its former decision."

"I entirely agree with everything the senator from Arkansas said," Wheeler replied. But not really: they disagreed on the lesson that each man deduced. In Wheeler's mind, if the Supreme Court had changed its mind on the minimum wage—and possibly other economic quandaries as well—it reduced the problem that the president's plan was trying to fix. But to Joe Robinson, the Court's reversal showed the truth of something that Charles Evans Hughes had said thirty years earlier and had regretted ever since. Addressing an audience in Elmira, New York, the then governor had observed, "We are under a Constitution, but the Constitution is what the judges say it is." Hughes had presumably meant to suggest that the Constitution was a broadly worded document that needed jurists to interpret its principles for specific circumstances, but his statement had often been invoked—and recently, more than ever—in defense of the quest to appoint justices who were likely to rule in a particular way.

"From 1922 until a few hours ago," Robinson railed, "it was unconstitutional for a state to have a minimum-wage law for the protection of women and children from oppressive conditions pertaining to their employment. Now, within the last few hours, it has become entirely constitutional to have such a law, and yet the Constitution has not been touched. So that what Mr. Justice Hughes said is in a sense correct." There was still every reason, in other words, to insist on bringing new blood to the bench, though Joe Robinson made sure not to mention that he already knew whose new blood that would be.

AS A PASSIONATE man himself, Joe Robinson was alarmed at the emotions that the Court fight was stirring up, even among people who had long separated themselves from the soiled world of politics. He had complained on the Senate floor about a letter that an evangelist in Wichita,

Kansas, had mailed to half a million people. "Dear Christian friend," it began, then warned of "the end of Christian Americanism" and denounced "Mr. Roosevelt's shocking demand that he be allowed to pack the United States Supreme Court with radicals who would serve as his personal puppets." Each letter included three slips of paper—*Hands Off the Supreme Court*—for recipients to send to members of Congress and another three to pass along to friends. He could "easily increase the number of petitions to a few million if necessary," the Reverend Gerald Winrod boasted to a reporter for the *New York Times*.

The Christian fundamentalists had kept away from the public arena since the Scopes "monkey" trial, of a teacher in Tennessee who taught evolution, had brought them such ridicule a dozen years past. Rev. Winrod was hardly alone, however, in feeling compelled to exert the influence of the church upon the state. A front-page editorial in the *Baltimore Catholic Review*, which also circulated in Washington, carried the headline "Hands Off the Supreme Court." Some of the ten Jewish congressmen had reminded their colleagues of the consequences in Germany—at least ninety anti-Jewish laws—after the central authority had suspended constitutional guarantees of civil liberties. In the Marble Reformed Collegiate Church in New York, at Fifth Avenue and Twenty-ninth Street, the Reverend Norman Vincent Peale warned, "Fascism, in essence, is established in America the minute this Supreme Court bill passes, for it places dictatorial power in the president. That means that slowly but surely civil liberties will tend to go." The precedent of adding justices to the Court suggested the alarming possibility that a president could pack the Court with justices likely to reinterpret the Bill of Rights in whatever manner he wished.

The supporters of the president's Court plan encountered other pockets of resistance, most of them expected. The president's men insisted that the opposition to his Court plan sprang mainly from the "economic royalists" and the reactionaries who had fought his reelection, and to an extent this was true. The U.S. Chamber of Commerce, the National Association of Manufacturers, and other business groups lambasted any attempt to subvert a Court that had served for decades as property's friend. Nor was anyone surprised that most of the law school deans and legal eminences scorned the president's plan as an attack on a judiciary that was the epitome of their profession.

To counter the forces of commerce, the men of God, and the conservatives who could never be convinced, the president's political strategists were counting mainly on two groups of his strongest supporters, the farmers and organized labor, to mobilize pressure on the lawmakers from back home. This made the farmers' ambivalence especially worrying to the White House. After decades of industrialization, urban dwellers now constituted a majority of the U.S. population, but only barely. Forty-four percent of Americans still lived outside of cities and towns. Nationally, the thirty million farming households held the balance of political power, in pollster Elmo Roper's judgment. By all rights, they should have flocked to the president's side. Most of their troubles, it was true, lay beyond any mortal's control. The worldwide overproduction of the 1920s had ruined their foreign markets and cast them into a depression a decade earlier than their countrymen. Then everyone else's depression, plus the almost biblical drought across the Great Plains, brought debt, foreclosures, and destitution to America's rich soil, along with an urgency for progressive reforms. But the farmers also could trace a part of their plight directly to the nine old men seated on the highest bench in the land, or at least to the majority who had struck down the Agricultural Adjustment Act and ended, at least temporarily, the government's largesse. "The farmer . . . knows the Supreme Court has been inconsistent and unfair with him," an agricultural lobbyist in Washington declared in a statement to the press, in urging "direct action to unpack the Court."

The administration went to work. Secretary of Agriculture Henry Wallace conferred with farm leaders one by one. The most liberal member of the cabinet described the Court bill as a "conservative" measure— "intended to make livable the capitalistic system." The attempts at persuasion took various forms. "No threats exactly," reported the man from the National Grange, but the message had been made clear: "In return for big things the New Deal has done for agriculture in the past four years, you owe it to us." The Grange and the American Farm Bureau, both dominated by the larger commercial farmers, had been deeply involved in conceiving and enacting the AAA. The Farm Bureau was the largest of the farmers' groups, with half a million members; Roosevelt invited its president in for a chat, but to little avail. The Farm Bureau bucked the pressure and decided to stay neutral. The Grange, the nation's oldest farm organization, had been expected to endorse the Court bill, but after its directors voted twenty-nine to nine against, it declined. An official would say only that the organization "doubts the wisdom of giving to any president of the United States at any time the right to change the size of the Court because of the age of its members."

The administration had no better luck with the National Farmers Union, the most radical group, which spoke for small farmers on less fertile land. "Personally," the organization's president said, "I am no more in favor of making or attempting to make the Supreme Court of the United States a rubber stamp than I am in favor of making Congress a rubber stamp for the executive." The farmers were close-mouthed about the reasons for their reluctance, but they were conservative by nature, apt to put their faith in the whims of nature and in their own strong backs. They had reason to fear the aggregation of power, the prospect of monopoly, such as they had endured from the middlemen and the railroads.

Organized labor felt differently. The unions had learned to confront power with power, whether exercised by the strikers who seized factories or by a government willing to grant workers the instruments—such as in the Wagner Act—that they needed to stand their ground. Power, political and otherwise, was the only language the employers understood. Comfortable with politics, and especially with the Democrats in control, labor had learned to parlay their millions of votes and the millions of dollars they had spent on election campaigns into getting their way around Washington— everywhere, that is, except at the Supreme Court. This was the unions' chance to change that. They had lost the NRA, with its mandate on employers to bargain with the unions, and the Court would soon rule on the resurrected provisions in the Wagner Act. The lobbyists for labor prowled the corridors on Capitol Hill, merciless in singling out their enemies, even those who had recently been friends. For decades, Burt Wheeler had ranked as the workingman's advocate, an ally in tangling with the industrial trusts. Even now, he was investigating how the railroads were financed, earning the House of Morgan's wrath. None of this meant a thing, however, in the unions' eyes. The mildest epithet they hurled at the Montana progressive was "traitor."

The unions' leverage on Capitol Hill had been undercut, however, by their aggressiveness on the factory floor. The number of sit-down strikes had doubled between January and February, then almost quadrupled in March, to 170 nationwide, involving 160,000 workers in industries of every description. "Sitting down," said the *Detroit News*, "has replaced baseball as a national pastime."* The reason was simple: the tactic worked. Strikers had brought General Motors to its knees, then Chrysler. Now, Ford was next. At an auto plant in Kansas City, workers unscrolled a sign from the top floor: "Lincoln freed the slaves. Ford brought them back." When chocolate workers sat at their machinery in Hershey, Pennsylvania, the dairy farmers who were losing business marched into the factory wielding clubs and sticks; then the strikers emerged with their faces bleeding and their arms in the air. If the violence of the strikes repelled the public, the workers' audacity in seizing control of the factories—"the revolutionary quality," as a conservative commentator thundered—upset people more.

The epidemic of sit-down strikes, inevitably, had become a preoccupation on Capitol Hill, though in terms of constructive action, there was surprisingly little that Congress could do. Hugo Black, an ardent New Dealer from Alabama, had a villain to blame for the sit-down strikes: the Supreme Court, as "an insuperable, impossible obstacle" to laws that might ease the conditions that had caused the workers' woes. The Senate, hoping to offend neither side, condemned the sit-down strikes and also the employers' unwillingness to bargain with the unions, with only three dissenting votes.

Thus, organized labor had more pressing matters before Congress than to help the president lobby for his Court plan. The unions had reason to worry about the Wagner Act's constitutional fate, but there was nothing they could do about it now. The AFL's mild-mannered president, William Green, had buttonholed a few senators and testified before the Judiciary Committee in support of the Court bill. But otherwise he and his lobbyists did little, leaving the White House more reliant than ever on the Committee for Industrial Organization (CIO), which stood behind the sit-down strikes.

Unfortunately for the president, the AFL and the CIO, with their entangled histories, loathed each other like Abel and Cain. The half-century-old AFL was a confederation of craft unions that organized the

---

* There was a report that John L. Lewis intended to organize a baseball players' union.

skilled workers in each craft—the electricians, the railroad engineers, and such—while keeping the unskilled workers out. This was partly a matter of economic shrewdness—the fewer craftsmen, the higher the wages—but it also reflected the tradesmen's Caucasian contempt for teaching the swarthier immigrants and the Negroes the necessary skills. John L. Lewis, the leader of the mineworkers' union, had formed the CIO in 1935 inside of the AFL, in a national campaign to organize, industry by industry, the assembly line workers, the unskilled laborers—the masses. Frustrated by its stodgier parent, the CIO broke away in the fall of 1936, taking ten of the AFL's constituent unions and adopting a militancy that contradicted the craftsmen's nature. The auto workers and the steelworkers conducted the fiercest of the sit-down strikes, despite the increasingly transparent opposition of the AFL, which further widened the breach over temperament and tactics between labor's backbiting siblings.

The sit-down strikes, so unpopular with the public, had put the president on the defensive. The New Deal's labor policies—notably, the assurance of collective bargaining—had been intended to empower the labor unions to bring economic democracy to industrial capitalism as long as the government remained too weak or unwilling to step in directly on the workers' behalf. Labor already had what it wanted from the New Deal, unless the Court struck down the Wagner Act, too, and so for the moment, at least, in the Court fight, the president needed labor—its lobbyists, its letter writers, its money, its political embrace—more than labor needed him. In the marriage of convenience between the president and John L. Lewis, the strains had started to show. Sidney Hillman had appealed over the radio for the workingman's support in enlarging the Court, but for the most part, labor's enthusiasm for the president's plan had cooled. Whether it would heat up again depended, more or less entirely, on whether the justices upheld the Wagner Act—a decision was expected any day now—or struck it down.

The lawmakers on Capitol Hill felt badgered from all sides, making for hectic days and sleepless nights. The deluge of mail had continued, on both sides. The Nebraska Federation of Labor told George Norris, who was still on the fence, "There is no doubt but ninety percent of Nebraskans would vote to support our President," before a small-town Nebraskan wrote to him, "This must be defeated. And no compromise." The administration exerted pressure wherever it could, in its opponents' backyards. Agriculture Department officials went from state to state to enlist the farm groups to confront the Democratic senators skeptical about the Court bill. Wheeler complained to Postmaster General Jim Farley, the party chairman, that it "was extremely unfair for men who are on the payroll of the Government to go into my state and line up the labor organizations." Twice in a single week, dozens of congressmen convened "indignation meetings" to commiserate about the burdens of public service. Any position they took on the Court bill was bound to cause them problems back home, and taking no position was perhaps the riskiest position of all.

HOURS AFTER THE Supreme Court reversed itself on the minimum wage, Senator Carter Glass of Virginia took to the airwaves coast to coast for only the second time in his thirty-eight years in politics. The first time had occurred late in the 1932 presidential campaign, when he delivered the most effective speech given by anyone—the acclaim was universal—in support of Franklin D. Roosevelt's candidacy. The president-elect then invited him to serve as his treasury secretary, as Glass had once served President Wilson, but the senator distrusted FDR's monetary views and turned it down. This was fortunate, as things developed, for Roosevelt's accommodation to an unbalanced budget and his ventures in centralized government had driven Carter Glass into increasingly open opposition to the New Deal. His unwillingness to deliver another radio address on the president's behalf during the 1936 campaign had only increased the anticipation around the capital about the hour he had scheduled on the Columbia Broadcasting System, starting at ten P.M. in the East (preempting the Wayne King Orchestra), to discuss the Supreme Court.

He had been writing and rewriting the speech for more than two weeks as he convalesced from a long illness in his rooms at the Mayflower Hotel. At age seventy-nine, he was the oldest senator and probably the shortest—at five foot four—but still the most combative. His father, as a matter of honor, had supposedly shot a man to death on a Lynchburg street, and the son's quick temper had earned him a nickname in the Senate cloakroom: the "Bantam Cock." On the Senate floor, during an argument over branch banking, he had once shoved Wheeler, a six-footer, and invited him into the Democratic cloakroom to settle their disagreement like men. By now he was a decade crankier, and a month's absence from his beloved Senate had not improved his mood. "An unreconstructed rebel," the president had called him, referring not only to his temperament but also to his enduring devotion to the shibboleths of the South—Jim Crow, states' rights, nineteenth-century ideals.

The venerable senator with the Roman nose and a Phi Beta Kappa key—though he had quit school at age twelve—spoke to the nation from his rooms at the Mayflower. It was vintage Carter Glass, fiery but also high-minded. No one could doubt for a moment what he thought of the president's plan. "Repugnant scheme . . . utterly destitute of moral sensibility . . . six judicial wet-nurses." In his syrupy twang, he unleashed his invective in volleys, like arrows on a sticky summer's noon—"an executive's puppet . . . ventriloquisms of the White House . . . evil portents." He weaved in references to John Marshall, Andrew Jackson, Woodrow Wilson, and, again and again, Thomas Jefferson. Glass lived fifty miles from Monticello and thought of himself as the original Democrat's political heir. "I am, and always will be, a Jeffersonian Democrat," he had said. And so he assailed Homer Cummings for an "indefensible libel" in suggesting that George Washington and Thomas Jefferson had tried to pack the Court—in Jefferson's case, by the addition of a seventh justice in 1807 to meet an expanding nation's needs. Though Jefferson had hated John Marshall and suspected him of trying to undermine his presidency, even "with overwhelmingly supporting Congresses," Glass said, "he never then or at any time in all his life would have done such an abominable thing."

Glass was wise to tread carefully, however, in cloaking himself in Jefferson's view of the Court. From the first, Jefferson had sought to minimize the Court's authority, despite the power of judicial review that Marshall claimed in 1803. In *Marbury v. Madison*, Marshall outmaneuvered his cousin in the White House by ostensibly granting Jefferson a victory in the minor issue involved, but using a line of reasoning that established a principle—the Court could kill a law by finding it unconstitutional—that would forever secure the judiciary's leverage at the elected branches' expense. Jefferson had feared a strong Court as antidemocratic, as a hindrance to the people's will. This was precisely what appealed to Carter Glass and other white southerners about a strong and independent judiciary, that it was antidemocratic. To the South, the conservative Court served as a shield against the nation's emerging urban and ethnic majority, as a means of holding the power in the states instead of sending it to Washington, as an instrument for keeping the future at bay. Letting a liberal president name a passel of new justices, and thereby dominate the Court, could mean the end of states' rights and of white supremacy—this was the southern Democrats' not unreasonable fear.

The Solid South, by and large, had accepted the New Deal, at least at first. Especially when the federal spigot opened, the poorest and most backward region of the country stood to gain more than it lost. But by 1935 or thereabouts, conservatives in the South and elsewhere had begun to feel that the New Deal "had gone far enough—or too far," as a historian recounted—and they worried that an expanded Court would make everything worse, by ridding the New Deal of its last constraint.

Conservatives, however, accounted for less than a fourth of the Senate's seventy-five Democrats, and to the dinners they shared around Millard Tydings's table, they invited some unlikely guests: Republicans. After the 1936 election, their presence in Congress had collapsed. The number of Republican senators had dwindled to sixteen, and on most issues they stood disunited—conservatives, mainly from New England and the Midwest, versus the handful of noisy progressives from the West. As a political force, they had perished, at least on their own, and they needed an instrument outside of themselves if they were to reunite and to restore their soul. The president's plan for the Court had supplied it.

Within weeks, the bipartisan dinners to chew over the Court bill led to bipartisan meetings and joint discussions of strategy. Soon a tactical collaboration began to jell into a heartfelt alliance. Historians would detect in the battle over the Supreme Court the birth of a congressional coalition between Republicans and conservative Democrats that would dominate the political dynamics in Washington for decades to follow. For the president, this raised the political stakes, but in a way that he welcomed. If he pushed his Court plan too forcefully, as a matter of party loyalty, it could provoke a realignment of the political parties into conservative and progressive groupings, possibly as early as 1940. The president had already confided to Harold Ickes, his interior secretary, that this was a prospect he savored.


EVERY WEEKDAY MORNING, at too early an hour, Lulu Wheeler coaxed her husband from their white-shingled house on Jocelyn Street, in

Northwest Washington, and out past the Maryland line. In the clean air and rolling fairways at Congressional Country Club, they puttered through seven holes of golf. This was her response to the stresses of the Court fight, to help keep her husband in shape. She made sure that "Burton," as she called him, ate well and got enough sleep, to prepare him for each day of battle.

People in Washington, at first, usually thought of Mrs. Wheeler as quiet and meek, because of her delicate features, her slender frame, her bright hazel eyes, and the politeness of her native Midwest. Most of them soon changed their minds. Members of her family saw her as bossy and austere, humorless but shy, with her dark, no-nonsense hair swept back—"frightening, in a way," said one. "You wouldn't argue with her. She ruled . . . the family with an iron hand." Though a teetotaler, other than an occasional mint julep later in life, she was modern in her ambitions and outlook. Twice she enrolled at George Washington University with her sons. She held strong opinions about politics and politicians, many of them unflattering to Franklin D. Roosevelt. Three years earlier, she had ridden in his limousine—just the two of them—to the presidential yacht on the Potomac. Several times he tried to engage her in conversation, but failed. She considered him a self-seeker who lusted for power, and it was not long before the contempt was mutual. Joseph Kennedy, a friend of FDR and the senator, too, reported to Mrs. Wheeler of the president's remark, "Wheeler's all right, but that wife of his is Lady Macbeth." When she heard this, she bowed and replied, "I'm glad that he thinks I'm up to something." The next day, Sam Rosenman phoned Wheeler and told him the president had heatedly denied saying any such thing.

For Wheeler, the Court fight was getting personal. Their middle daughter, Frances, a senior at Connecticut College, had been moving left-ward in her political views amid the campus fervor aroused by the Spanish Civil War. At home for spring vacation, she told her parents that she wanted to issue a statement to the press declaring her support for expand-ing the Court. "Frances, there is only one senator in this family," Lulu scolded. But the senator was not the only outspoken Wheeler. Once she returned to school, Frances told an Associated Press reporter that she fa-vored adding justices with a modern spirit to the Court. "There is more than one political viewpoint in the family," she said. Her father blamed her leftist professors. Soon Frances married a young man the family considered almost a Communist, and her communication with her family would cease.

The tensions grew personal in unpredictable places. In a medieval-looking mansion out along New Hampshire Avenue, north of the White House, the Woman's National Democratic Club was ordinarily a refuge for harried congressional wives. But now it became a snake pit of scowls and slurs, directed at the spouses of lawmakers who opposed the president's plan. Lulu Wheeler spoke her piece and resigned from the club. In Kansas, the state's board of censors snipped sixty-six of Wheeler's words from a *March of Time* newsreel that showed the president delivering his fireside chat followed by Wheeler and Carter Glass preaching their objections. Deemed unfit for Kansans' ears—as "partisan and biased," the censors' chairman said—was Wheeler's accusation that Montana would lose federal projects because he was fighting a plan he considered "morally unsound." Wheeler blamed Jim Farley for ordering the censorship from Washington, but the political maestro took offense. "I thought you knew me better," he wrote to Wheeler.

The president's men suspected Wheeler of low motives—of being miffed at having been passed over for the vice presidency in 1932, of imagining himself as the president's worthiest successor, of having a wife who foresaw the same. They may have been right on all three suspicions, but they saw him through a prism of their own, in terms of motives they understood. The president's lack of principle had been the secret to his success, both in his policymaking and in his politicking, and he had gathered men around him who felt the same. They were incapable of understanding a man like Wheeler who had never been a pragmatist. It was not like him to consider the alternatives or to weigh the consequences of every action; that was not the source of joy he gained from politics. Instead, he considered the world in terms of good and evil, of right and wrong, of black and white. Lost causes were as precious to him as victories.

THE HEAD TABLE for the semiannual dinner of the Gridiron Club seated seventy-nine of the capital's VIPs, and the club's mischiefmakers had placed Homer Cummings next to Harlan Fiske Stone. The dinner got under way at seven-twenty on Saturday evening, the tenth of April, and lasted almost until midnight. This gave the attorney general and the justice plenty of time for (as Cummings boasted to his diary) "a long and very intimate conversation."

The five hundred men in white tie and tails in the Willard Hotel's ballroom included the forty-eight distinguished Washington journalists who belonged to the Gridiron Club and their guests, among them the president, the vice president, the chief justice, a quarter of the Senate, a caucus of congressmen, numerous ambassadors, William Green and John L. Lewis, Tommy Corcoran, and two thirds of the cabinet. Only the labor secretary, Frances Perkins, had not been invited to the male-only event, but instead to the counter-Gridiron dinner at the White House, the costume ball for female journalists and the wives of Gridiron guests that Eleanor Roosevelt had hosted since 1933.

The incoming president of the Gridiron Club, G. Gould Lincoln, a reporter for the capital's *Evening Star*, sat at the center of the immensely long head table. Seven seats to his left, Homer Cummings took advantage of an opportunity, as he had done so many times in his career. He leaned to his right, toward Justice Stone, and wondered aloud how Justice Roberts had come to reverse himself on the minimum wage. Stone, with his bluff manner and open face, said he did not have the remotest idea—he could not understand it. Cummings supposed that Chief Justice Hughes, in his majority opinion in the Washington State case, had built a bridge for Roberts to walk across. Stone concurred, while observing that it would have been better for the Court in the long run had Roberts written his own concurring opinion, even a short one of four or five lines, that simply acknowledged his earlier mistake.

Their colloquy continued after the terrapin course, between the servings of rare wines, before and after the evening's nine or ten skits. The musical sketches were the point of the evening, their satire intended—like a gridiron—to singe but not burn. The club members who wrote and performed in the skits affected to ridicule the nation's leaders, but in truth they were showing their pride in belonging to the small circle at the top. Most of the men who ruled Washington, and the nation, could fit into a single room, and on this spring evening in the capital, most of them did. Gathering for dinner could only deepen their admiration for a system of democracy that had seen fit to bring them to the fore.

The newsmen and the newsmakers laughed at the skit about a fireside chat delivered by "a prince of privilege," then at another that featured a sit-down strike at the White House on Inauguration Day in 1941 by out-of-work Republicans. "These sit-down strikes strike at the very vitals of the, er, er, Constitution we all revere, ahem, in a manner of speaking," stuttered an attorney general in a bald wig and a long frock coat. ("There were some sketches that many people considered in rather bad taste," the real attorney general told his diary that night, while assuring himself, "I did not seem to feel that way about it.") The theatrical climax took place after the salad course and before the ice cream. As the U.S. Marine Band played "March of the Toys," journalists who portrayed the chief justice and fourteen brethren marched onto the stage, each costumed in a blond wig, a drooping mustache, and a miniature straw hat—a Caspar Milquetoast in a judicial robe—and carrying a giant rubber stamp. They crooned,

*Nobody knows the opinions I sign,*
*Nobody knows but Franklin . . .*

"The court is far too crowded," one of the faux justices complained.

"What do you expect in a packed court," a colleague rebuked—"a private room and a bath?"

The fifteen "justices" paused in their rubber-stamping the New Deal laws to hold their noses and echo Cole Porter in describing the president's Court bill:

*It's delib'rate, it's deceptive,*
*It's deplorable, it's delirious . . .*
*It's de novo, it's de-limit,*
*It's de bunk, it's de-lousy . . .*

The real chief justice was laughing in his seat.

President Roosevelt's speech capped the evening, and he was in excellent form. Part of his charm was a talent for self-deprecation. By the rules of the dinner, his remarks were not to be reported, and so he poked fun at his fear that "Dictator Gould Lincoln will find it hard to restrain his iron impulses in directing the affairs of the Gridiron Club. Members, guard well your liberties against executive usurpation. Do not hitch your Gridiron horse and buggy to the *Star.*" His drollness in mocking himself sent the assembled into a rapture. One of the club's newly inducted members, Erwin Canham of the *Christian Science Monitor,* marveled in print that the president's willingness to expose himself "to four hours of pretty steady joshing is quite plainly one of the most important facts in American government today."

Once the president had finished his talk, and Saturday had nearly passed into Sunday, something unscheduled took place. Gould Lincoln stood and offered a salute to the lushly bearded man three seats to his left. Charles Evans Hughes was minutes away from turning seventy-five. A chorus of club members led the audience in "Happy Birthday." The chief justice rose, bowed deeply, listened to the cheers and applause, but kept silent. He would save what he wanted to say until Monday at noon.

# CHAPTER THIRTEEN

# No Compromise

WITH HIS CAUSTIC conservatism, Justice James McReynolds was a natural villain to New Dealers. Thus, his vow, recently overheard at a party, that no matter how dramatic the president's threats, the Four Horsemen would never allow the New Deal to survive, caused concern throughout Washington, and nowhere more than at the White House.

Possibly nothing mattered more to the New Deal's success than the 1935 law devised by New York's Democratic senator Robert F. Wagner that had created the National Labor Relations Board and assured workers the right to organize into unions and to bargain collectively with employers. The Supreme Court had heard the five Wagner Act cases the week after the president announced his judicial reorganization plan, and the government's lawyers worried that the justices' about-face on the minimum wage might have given them the political cover to butcher the Wagner Act. Henry Ford had simply ignored the law, in refusing to bargain with the United Automobile Workers—"or any other union," the industrialist declared after a short-lived sit-down strike at his company's St. Louis assembly plant—and he had not been alone. If the Court struck down the Wagner Act, blood was bound to flow in the factories and—literally, perhaps—in the streets. Prospects for labor peace rested on the Court's decision, which was presumed to rest, yet again, in Owen Roberts's hands. During the oral arguments, Justice Roberts had not even glanced at the government attorney, and recently he had seemed sulky on the bench. If the New Dealers won even two out of the five cases, filed by sundry sorts of companies with varying degrees of participation in an interstate economy, they would be relieved.

On Monday, April 12, the capital was crowded with tourists drawn by the cherry blossoms. People had waited since dawn outside the Supreme Court Building in hopes of a seat. Inside the courtroom, the air was electric. The attorney general had arrived, along with some of the justices' law clerks and—tipping off the drama to come—the chief justice's wife, who had watched as her husband divulged the Court's reversal on the minimum wage fourteen days earlier. The courtroom was hushed, as if nothing from the outside world was allowed to intrude, save for what the justices let in.

Justice Roberts was the first to deliver a majority opinion—two of them. He swiveled slightly in his leather chair, and his nasal baritone was strong and clear as he spoke mainly from memory. The first case involved the Associated Press, which had fired one of its news editors in New York City for trying to organize the wire service's workers into a union. The issue was whether the New York office was engaged in interstate commerce and therefore subject to the edicts of Congress. The AP had pleaded freedom of the press as a reason to be left alone, but Roberts would have none of it. "The New York office receives and dispatches news from and to all parts of the world," Roberts ruled. "The Associated Press is engaged in interstate commerce," and thus the Wagner Act applied. So decreed five justices, everyone but the Four Horsemen. His second opinion was unanimous: the Greyhound bus line, even more obviously involved in interstate commerce, must also submit to the law and refrain from firing drivers and mechanics for union activity. But these two cases were the easiest and the least consequential of the five; neither decision expanded the meaning of "interstate commerce." Charles Evans Hughes had evidently honored Roberts by assigning him the opinions, which left the shrewder minds to wonder if this had been in exchange for Roberts's vote on other cases.

Then Hughes himself started to read. "Seldom has the Supreme Court chamber been more evidently charged with suspense," the *New York Herald Tribune* noted the next morning, "for on this decision hung not only an extremely important act of Congress but perhaps the fate of the Court itself." This was the case involving Jones & Laughlin Steel—the most crucial of the five. In detail, Hughes described how the nation's fourth largest steelmaker shipped three fourths of its metal across state lines. It conducted its operations not only in Pennsylvania but also owned or controlled coal mines in Michigan and Minnesota; limestone quarries in West Virginia; four ore steamships on the Great Lakes; a fleet of towboats and barges; steel fabricating shops in New Orleans and in the New York City borough of Queens; and warehouses in Chicago, Detroit, Cincinnati, and Memphis. It was, he determined, "a completely integrated enterprise." Still, when the company fired ten workers for union activity at a steel operation near Pittsburgh, its lawyers had invoked a tried-and-true constitutional argument—that the plant was a local enterprise, only indirectly connected to the commerce that transpired when the steel was sold in another state. Since 1895, as the industrial trusts created a national economy—and over and over again in the decades since, in striking down a succession of progressive laws—the Court had consistently protected the burgeoning businesses by distinguishing between a "direct" and an "indirect" role in interstate commerce, excluding the latter from Congress's potentially heavy hand.

But, the chief justice continued, those precedents "are not controlling here." Why, he did not say. Instead, he applied an ingenious, convoluted argument: even if a steelmaking plant was not itself directly involved in interstate commerce, imagine the "most serious" impact on the movement of goods across state lines should the plant's operations suddenly cease because of a sit-down strike or other interruption. "It is idle to say the effect would be indirect or remote," Hughes reasoned. "It is obvious that it would be immediate and might be catastrophic. We are asked to shut our eyes to the plainest facts of our national life and to deal with direct and indirect effects in an intellectual vacuum." He was speaking faster than usual. "We have often said that interstate commerce itself is a practical conception. It is equally true that interferences with that commerce must be appraised by a judgment that does not ignore actual experience."

Four other justices, for a bare majority, agreed, but the impact was momentous. The Court had expanded its understanding of interstate commerce to take account of the world as it was. It had not erased the distinction between the national and the local economy, or between the degrees of involvement in interstate commerce. Rather, the Court had aligned its definitions with reality. A steel plant *was* a part of interstate commerce, even if it was rooted on a single parcel of land. In legal terms, the Court had abandoned its precedent in substance, though keeping the form of it intact—evidence, again, of Hughes's legal canniness and his political guile. Smiles swept across the faces of the New Dealers in the pews, remaining

fixed as Hughes read the next two opinions, which defined local manufacturers (of men's clothes in Virginia and of trailers in Michigan) as participants in interstate commerce and therefore subject to the Wagner Act's
strictures. In all five Wagner Act cases, the law had been upheld, in four of
them by the identical five-to-four lineup.

The audience sat stunned, the lawyers most of all. Nothing like this
had happened in more than a century, since 1835, upon the conclusion of
John Marshall's long tenure. His expansive understanding of interstate
commerce, and thus of the federal government's reach, had done more to
knit together the nation than anything but war. But ever since Marshall's
death, the definition of interstate commerce had been narrowing. First the
southerners who were desperate to preserve slavery had deified the notion
of states' rights, and then the corporations intent on keeping the federal
government out of their affairs clung to the Court's distinction between
the "direct" and "indirect" effects on interstate commerce, to minimize
Washington's reach. Now, in a trice, these interpretations had crumbled.
*Jones & Laughlin* would prove to be a pivotal case in erecting a new constitutional order. The federal government was to be permitted a potent role
in the economy, in regulating any business that conducted commerce on a
national scale. It was a presence—an ambition—that Washington would
never give up.

Minutes after Hughes had finished his majestic opinion, a lawyer in
the audience turned to his neighbor and said, "Chief Justice Hughes has
saved the Supreme Court."

"I think he has saved the United States as well," his New Dealer com-
panion replied.

It was not the chief justice's accomplishment alone, of course. Again
he had provided a bridge for Owen Roberts to cross. In his majority opinion, Hughes had de-emphasized any mention of the precedents on interstate commerce to spare Roberts the embarrassment, for Justice Roberts's
vote the previous May against coal regulation had last sustained the precedent just shattered. Now, once again, he had switched sides.


"OFF THE RECORD, and really off the record and just in the family,
I have been chortling all morning, ever since I picked up the papers," the

president said. The day after the Supreme Court upheld the Wagner Act, the White House correspondents had gathered around his desk. "I have been having a perfectly grand time and when I picked up one of the papers, the dear old *Herald Tribune*, and saw the editorial entitled 'A Great Decision,' I harked back"—and sure enough, Steve Early had found an editorial in the elegant, establishmentarian New York daily written in 1935, when the Wagner Act was passed, that denounced it as unconstitutional.

"This is all off the record," FDR interrupted himself. "What are you taking this stuff down for?" The reporters laughed.

"You may change your mind," one of them said to more laughter.

"No, I won't change my mind."

He was asked about Jim Farley's comment the previous night in Philadelphia, that the margin of a single vote was no guarantee of a liberal Supreme Court. He had known nothing about it beforehand, the president replied, but he quoted a Democratic Party publicity man's remark upon learning that the no-man's-land of regulation was gone: "Well, in the last two days the no-man's-land has been eliminated, but see what we have in place of it: we are now in Roberts' Land."

The president's mood had been darker the afternoon before. On hearing of the Court's decision, he had burst out in "an old-fashioned fit of temper," journalists Joseph Alsop and Turner Catledge recounted. He had banked on the Court to strike down the Wagner Act, as a means of galvanizing his prospects for increasing the number of justices, and he suspected Hughes of playing politics yet again. Even before the attorney general had returned to his office following the rulings, the president had been trying to reach him. By the time Homer Cummings arrived at the White House, carrying copies of the Court's opinions, the president had regained his composure. They were lucky the Court had waited a week, he joked to the attorney general, or it would have ruined the Gridiron Club skit. As for whether to keep pushing the Court bill, the president had not changed his mind.

The reporters had ambushed Homer Cummings as he passed through the West Wing lobby and asked him about the rumors on Capitol Hill that the president would withdraw his Court plan if two justices stepped down.

"Hooey," Cummings replied. That night, he assured his diary that the Court's decisions had actually bolstered the bill's prospects. If Congress were to pass legislation on child labor or the minimum wage, he argued to himself, "nobody can tell how Justice Roberts would stand."

Joe Robinson, the Senate majority leader, summoned Joe Keenan to his dimly lit office in the Capitol basement. The attorney general's ruddy-faced aide was a shrewd ex-prosecutor who had made his name in Washington in 1933 by securing the conviction of "Machine Gun" Kelly. "Joe the Key," as the president called him, was short and plump, friendly and unpretentious, and carried a whiff of the smoke-filled room. Lawmakers liked him.

"The thing to do, Joe," the majority leader said, "is to settle this thing right now. This bill's raising hell in the Senate. Now it's going to be worse than ever, but if the president wants to compromise, I can get him a couple of extra justices tomorrow. What he ought to do is say he's won, which he has, agree to compromise to make the thing sure, and wind the whole business up."

When this message was conveyed to the president, he would hear none of it.

He had reason to think the public would support him. The White House mail continued to show a thumping approval for enlarging the Court. The scientific opinion polls, on the other hand, still showed a public almost evenly divided—tilting against the president's plan, according to Gallup's measurements, but by no more than half a dozen percentage points. The president, not yet six months beyond his landslide reelection, felt that he understood the American people's wishes and needs better than any interviewer carrying a clipboard.

If he entertained doubts that a majority of the public was on his side, the results of the April 10 special election in central Texas had put those to rest. A congressman died in his thirteenth term, and among the eight Democrats who competed to take his place was an ambitious twenty-nine-year-old who had served the New Deal as the Texas director of the National Youth Administration. Reared in poverty, Lyndon B. Johnson had seen no way forward in life other than through politics. He understood how his strapped neighbors in the Hill Country of Texas loved the New Deal for its largesse, and in hopes of standing out from the crowded field, he wrapped himself in the president's popularity and placed the Court plan at the center of his campaign. "Now, Lyndon," Alvin Wirtz, his political

President Franklin Roosevelt addressing the Senate in 1935.
(LIBRARY OF CONGRESS: PRINTS AND PHOTOGRAPHS DIVISION)

FDR giving his second inaugural address, Wednesday, January 20, 1937.
(LIBRARY OF CONGRESS: PRINTS AND PHOTOGRAPHS DIVISION)

Joseph Parrish,
*Chicago Tribune*
(NEWSPAPERARCHIVE.COM)

FDR giving one of his famed "fireside chats" to the nation.
(LIBRARY OF CONGRESS: PRINTS AND PHOTOGRAPHS DIVISION)

The Supreme Court in 1936. (Top row, l to r): Owen Roberts, Pierce Butler, Harlan Fiske Stone, Benjamin Cardozo. (Bottom row, l to r): Louis Brandeis, Willis Van Devanter, Charles Evans Hughes, James McReynolds, George Sutherland.

Louis Brandeis

Willis Van Devanter
(LIBRARY OF CONGRESS: PRINTS AND PHOTOGRAPHS DIVISION)

James McReynolds  (LIBRARY OF CONGRESS: PRINTS AND PHOTOGRAPHS DIVISION)

Charles Evans Hughes (LIBRARY OF CONGRESS: PRINTS AND PHOTOGRAPHS DIVISION)

Harlan Fiske Stone (LIBRARY OF CONGRESS: PRINTS AND PHOTOGRAPHS DIVISION)

Benjamin Cardozo and
Charles Evans Hughes
(LIBRARY OF CONGRESS: PRINTS
AND PHOTOGRAPHS DIVISION)

Owen Roberts (LIBRARY OF CONGRESS: PRINTS AND PHOTOGRAPHS DIVISION)

The Old Supreme Court Chamber, home of the Supreme Court from 1819 to 1860, in the United States Capitol. (LIBRARY OF CONGRESS: PRINTS AND PHOTOGRAPHS DIVISION)

The hearing room in the Supreme Court's new building.
(LIBRARY OF CONGRESS: PRINTS AND PHOTOGRAPHS DIVISION)

Vice President John
Nance Garner
(LIBRARY OF CONGRESS: PRINTS
AND PHOTOGRAPHS DIVISION)

Senator Henry
Fountain Ashurst
(LIBRARY OF
CONGRESS: PRINTS AND
PHOTOGRAPHS DIVISION)

Attorney General Homer Cummings
(LIBRARY OF CONGRESS: PRINTS AND PHOTOGRAPHS DIVISION)

Senator Burton K. Wheeler from Montana

Tommy "the Cork" Corcoran
(NEWSPAPERARCHIVE.COM)

James Roosevelt (LIBRARY OF CONGRESS: PRINTS AND PHOTOGRAPHS DIVISION)

Senate Majority Leader Joe Robinson
(LIBRARY OF CONGRESS: PRINTS AND PHOTOGRAPHS DIVISION)

Clifford Kennedy
Berryman,
*Washington Star*
(US NATIONAL
ARCHIVES
AND RECORDS
ADMINISTRATION/
NARA)

Clifford Kennedy Berryman, *Washington Star*
(US NATIONAL ARCHIVES AND RECORDS ADMINISTRATION/NARA)

The Supreme Court at the end of 1937. (Top row, l to r): Benjamin Cardozo, Harlan Fiske Stone, Owen Roberts, Hugo Black. (Bottom row, l to r): George Sutherland, James McReynolds, Charles Evans Hughes, Louis Brandeis, Pierce Butler.
(LIBRARY OF CONGRESS: PRINTS AND PHOTOGRAPHS DIVISION)

Hugo Black
(LIBRARY OF CONGRESS: PRINTS AND
PHOTOGRAPHS DIVISION)

Felix Frankfurter
(LIBRARY OF CONGRESS: PRINTS
AND PHOTOGRAPHS DIVISION)

# THE BEST HE CAN HOPE FOR NOW

Vaughn Shoemaker, *Chicago Daily News* (NEWSPAPERARCHIVE.COM)

mentor and campaign manager, had counseled, "of course it's a bunch of bullshit, this plan, but if you'll flow with it, Roosevelt's friends will support you." From his hospital bed, where he was recovering from an appendectomy, the congressman-elect heralded his victory as a vote of confidence in President Roosevelt and his program.

In Washington, the president was only too pleased to agree, for it confirmed what he wanted to believe. He did not believe, as Woodrow Wilson had, that God was guiding his decisions or that he was a divine instrument on Earth. But everything he had accomplished in life—the presidency, most of all—had happened because of his refusal to give up on himself. "In nearly every major enterprise," Arthur Krock had occasion to observe in the *New York Times*, "he has been as stubborn as any of his Dutch ancestors in their resistance to Philip and the Duke of Alba." He had once asserted in a speech that he would be the first to acknowledge when he made a mistake, but more often, he was the last.

Nor did his advisers see any point to a compromise. Tommy Corcoran and Joe Keenan scoffed at Joe Robinson's gloom and deemed him a defeatist. Corcoran felt confident that only twenty-two senators would oppose the president in the end—that the rest would return to the fold—overlooking the fact that Joe Robinson carried the truest head count, replete with senators' secrets, around in his head. One evening, during a long discussion at the White House, in the untidy study upstairs, Robert Jackson advised the president not to accept a compromise of two justices. Recently named the assistant attorney general for antitrust, admired for his frank manner and organized mind, Jackson had helped to draft the president's plan to enlarge the Court.* "If you're going to pack a court at all," he said, "you've got to really pack it." The president would become responsible, his advisers understood, for everything a packed Court did.

Then the president confided something to Jackson that very few people knew, the real reason that two more justices would not be enough: the president had already promised the first Supreme Court vacancy to Joe Robinson. During the president's opening term, at the end of a wildly productive congressional session, Jim Farley invited the Senate majority leader to lunch, and as the bearer of political favors and the dispenser of presidential

---

*In four years, Jackson himself would sit on the Court.

patronage, praised the heavy-handed Arkansan for his legislative legerde-main and asked what he might want in return. Robinson told him that ever since boyhood, he had yearned for a seat on the Supreme Court. Farley listened and later reported to Robinson that he had taken up the matter with the "proper party" and that the first available seat would be his. The president had never spoken directly to Robinson about it, but it was a pledge that FDR could violate only at his peril. Yet, while the president had no better friend in the Senate than Joe Robinson, the White House suspected he was a conservative at his core and that once beyond the electorate's—and the president's—political reach, he would vote his heart. Nominating Joe Robinson along with a reliable liberal could well leave the Court's ideological balance where it already teetered, subject to the whim of Justice Roberts.

ONE OF THE most desirable of the Capitol's hideaways, well lit, on the main floor of the Capitol, steps from the Senate chamber, belonged to Burt Wheeler. It was behind a stairwell, adjacent to the hearing room of the Interstate and Foreign Commerce Committee, which he chaired. The high-ceilinged room with a chandelier was crowded with filing cabinets and heavy walnut furniture, including a table that seated six. Its two tall windows looked out across the Mall, west along the vista recently cleared, all the way to the Washington Monument.

The nine senators on Wheeler's committee gathered here almost every weekday, unless they rendezvoused elsewhere to keep their adversaries and the reporters at bay. Wheeler met on the sly with Bill Borah, to keep the Republicans' profile low, and every night the Lion of Idaho phoned the man from Montana. Wheeler had also unearthed a source in the opposition camp, and he received a nightly telephone call from the secretary of the Senate majority, Leslie Biffle, who told him which of the president's supporters were wobbling. Senator Peter Gerry of Rhode Island—the great-grandson of Elbridge Gerry, famed for his spidery skill at redrawing the boundaries of legislative districts to maximize the electoral might of the party in power—assigned his colleagues to seek out their wavering friends and to report back to him daily. Since the Court had upheld the Wagner Act, those reports had grown optimistic. "It looks like the Supreme Court has reformed," said freshman senator Harry Truman of Missouri, a dependable New Dealer who seemed to be cooling toward the president's bill. If, as reported, two uncommitted members on the Judiciary Committee were edging away from the president, this would tip the panel into opposition, by a margin of ten to eight. "You don't run so fast for a train once you have caught up with it," explained a senator who had not budged from his support for the president. "The only real argument left is this: Is Judge Roberts going to stay put where he is?"

Organized labor remained in the president's corner. "Apparently, the destiny of our Republic and the well-being of its population," John L. Lewis said, "depend upon the legalistic whims and caprices of one man." Still, labor had won most of what it wanted from the Court—only the Social Security Act still awaited a judicial decree—and any urgency that the unions might have felt was bound to fade. They worried more about the legislation that would turn a sit-down strike into a federal crime.

Surveys of the senators suggested that fifteen of them, mainly moderate Democrats, held the outcome in their hands. Wheeler kept busy buttonholing his friends, needling opponents, and assuring any reporter willing to listen that his side would win. He plotted with Frank Gannett and his National Committee to Uphold Constitutional Government, which mailed seven hundred thousand copies of Carter Glass's recent radio diatribe to newspapers, civic organizations, business groups, and community leaders. Wheeler also went on the road to tongue-lash the Court bill, first to Baltimore ("Why does the administration still cry for the gray-haired scalps of those nine old men?"), to a mass meeting in Rochester, New York, and then to Tulsa, Oklahoma, where he debated Joe Keenan before fifteen hundred delegates from women's clubs in the forty-eight states and Alaska. If necessary, Wheeler threatened, opponents of the Court's expansion would filibuster all summer to block the addition of even two justices. "We've got it licked," he assured reporters, exuding more confidence than he felt.

LAWYERS MOBBED THE ballroom at the Mayflower Hotel on the first Thursday in May, for the annual meeting of the American Law Institute. The scholarly organization's self-appointed mission was to restate the nation's law in light of the latest Supreme Court decisions. But this high-minded, if tedious, purpose was not what had lured a thousand attorneys to the Mayflower. George Wharton Pepper, who was now the institute's president, introduced the day's main attraction. Only once a year did Charles Evans Hughes deliver a speech outside of the courtroom, and it was in front of the organization that he himself had headed until he occupied the Court's center seat. The chief justice had asked the Mayflower's management to make sure that no one photographed him inside the hotel, for he felt undignified when he wore nothing more than a business suit. As he strode into the ballroom, the attorneys erupted into an ovation that lasted for several minutes. In the American Bar Association's nationwide survey of more than seventy thousand lawyers, those opposed to the president's Court plan outnumbered the supporters by four to one.

Hughes's speech, for the most part, was dull. It centered on the exploits of Elihu Root, Theodore Roosevelt's brainy secretary of state and, not incidentally, a founder of the American Law Institute. Yet Hughes understood that this was not what his audience had hoped to hear, and with the most innocuous of segues, he did not disappoint. "For several years I have been able to report at these meetings that the Court is fully up with its work," he announced. "I am happy to say that this is true of the current term." Laughter erupted, then applause. He reiterated the arguments about the Court's work ethic that Senator Wheeler had read in public—"There are no inordinate or unjustified delays in the Supreme Court"—but this time he did it in person.

He had mastered the ability, so crucial in diplomacy and in politics, of making his point without stating it. "The success of democratic institutions lies in the success of the processes of reason as opposed to tyranny of force," he said. "Between these, society must choose. If society chooses the processes of reason, it must maintain the institutions which embody those processes." This was his lawyerly way of telling the lawyers that democracy's fate depended on the Court's. The chief justice had, in his veiled way, declared war.

As he left the Mayflower, accompanied by Justice Cardozo, they acceded to the photographers' requests and agreed to pose on the Connecticut Avenue sidewalk. "Go ahead," Hughes told them, "but not too close."

TWO HUNDRED MILES to the north, at Ebbets Field in Brooklyn, the Dodgers were playing the Pittsburgh Pirates when the 5,847 fans suddenly lost interest in the ball game. They gazed skyward as the *Hindenburg*, the world's largest dirigible, nearly as long as the *Titanic*, floated past at the end of its transatlantic voyage.

Soon it reached Manhattan, where thousands of people along the narrow downtown streets, on rooftops and on fire escapes, heard the roar of the airship's motors and craned their necks higher than at any skyscraper. Automobiles tooted their horns, and chauffeurs abandoned their limousines to watch. Above the six-year-old Empire State Building, originally designed with a mooring mast for dirigibles, the *Hindenburg* turned south toward its terminus in Lakehurst, New Jersey.

This was the *Hindenburg*'s first ocean crossing of 1937. It had established regular passenger service the year before, with ten flights of sixty-some hours from Germany to central New Jersey (though only fifty-one hours flying east). Ninety-seven passengers were aboard, at a fare of $400 each, four months' wages for a breadwinner on an assembly line. Sixty-five passengers waited to board the return flight, many with tickets for the coronation of King George VI in London on May 12. At twilight, after a thunderstorm had passed, the *Hindenburg* was making its third approach for a landing when the dirigible's nose plunged, then its tail dropped, and its rudder smacked the ground, before it bounced up and burst into flames. Within barely half a minute, only a skeleton of the *Hindenburg* remained. Miraculously, only thirty-five people on the airship and one on the ground perished.

Eleanor Roosevelt was changing airplanes in Chicago the next morning when a reporter sought her reaction. "There is not much to say," she answered. "Everyone involved has my sympathy." Then with a smile she added that she had not lost her "flying nerve." But many Americans had. Pollsters found that 62 percent of the public would turn down a free airplane trip to Europe.

The president dispatched a message to the German chancellor, Adolf Hitler, extending "you and the German people my deepest sympathy for the tragic loss of life." The precise cause of the conflagration would never be known, but the president mentioned nothing about his own role in the tragedy. The *Hindenburg* had been designed to run on helium, which only the United States produced. The president had leaned on Harold Ickes to stall the export of helium to Germany, to annoy the Nazi regime, and the *Hindenburg* was buoyed with highly flammable hydrogen instead. The federal government's constitutional authority over international commerce had never been in doubt.


WHEN THREE OF the Senate's titans invited young Jimmy Roosevelt to lunch, he did not realize that he was to be the entrée. Tall, lean, and prematurely balding—his hair in "a Garbo bob," as a newspaperwoman described it—he looked startlingly like his father, with the same blue eyes and broad smile. He also shared his father's even temper and much of his charm. With an office across the West Wing lobby, thirty feet from the president's door, he had quickly become a VIP around the capital, the man with his father's ear.

He ambled into the office that belonged to Colonel Edward Halsey, the secretary of the Senate, just off the Senate floor. This was where a Democrat in need of a whiskey or a cigar—or cash for his campaign—might find succor, or where Joe Robinson could speak privately on a direct line to the White House. This time, the majority leader had brought along his two ablest lieutenants, Pat Harrison of Mississippi and Alben Barkley of Kentucky, to lend weight to the information he wished to convey. Earlier, Robinson had promised the White House that he had fifty-four votes for the president's plan, but now that number had slipped. If the president insisted on adding six justices to the Supreme Court, Robinson said he would lose. The president was deep-sea fishing off the Texas coast, so Robinson sent the message by way of his son that the choice was compromise or defeat. "Mr. Roosevelt," he told Jimmy, "you tell your poppa that he'd better leave this whole thing to us to get what we can out of it. We'll do our best for him."

The next day, Jimmy Roosevelt described the senators' pessimism to Tommy Corcoran, Joe Keenan, Steve Early, and the rest of the strategy board, and to Homer Cummings. To a man, they felt relieved. Corcoran had been hoping to persuade the president to suspend the Court bill for the rest of the congressional session, so that the antagonism might dissipate and some bills of substance might be passed in the meantime. Regulations on wages and hours, subsidies for tenant farmers, the creation of other TVAs—these would inspire gratitude among farm organizations and labor unions that might, in turn, invigorate the Court bill. Even the attorney general agreed that the president ought to hear Joe Robinson's message before returning to Washington.

The president had started toward home and was visiting with Lyndon Johnson, the congressman-elect, who assured him of the Court bill's popular appeal. Jimmy Roosevelt caught up with his father in Fort Worth and delivered Joe Robinson's message, which the president rejected out of hand. He was certain that the senators were simply defeatists. Then Jim Farley tried. He joined the president's train in Indianapolis and argued that the Senate was so evenly divided that the vice president might have to break a tie. "Let him do it," the president snapped. When Farley pleaded that the Court bill could cause the Democratic Party to split apart, the reply startled him: "And good riddance, too."

Eleanor Roosevelt, the vice president, and two thirds of the cabinet braved the cloudbursts on the morning of May 14 to meet the president's train at Union Station. As a welcoming party, it paled beside the thirty senators and two hundred congressmen who had greeted him home from a fishing trip two years before. The president continued on to the White House and met with his cabinet, making it clear that the fight would go on. Afterward, Jim Farley bantered with the newspaper correspondents who were waiting.

"Why compromise?" he said with a laugh. "The bill is going through."

A reporter asked about the two Judiciary Committee senators, Joseph O'Mahoney of Wyoming and Pat McCarran of Nevada, both Democrats who had been uncommitted until recently on the Court bill but now were shifting into outright opposition. O'Mahoney, in particular, was a down-the-line New Dealer who had worked for Farley as the top assistant postmaster general until he was appointed to the Senate in late 1933. Later, Farley claimed that his reply had been off the record, and he may well have been right, because only the *Washington Post* reported it. "Well, when Senator O'Mahoney comes down here wanting help on a sugar bill, his conscience won't be bothering him, will it?" Farley said with a sneer. "Or when Pat McCarran wants aid for his state. It's all in the viewpoint."

It was the brazenness of Farley's calculations about the tit-for-tats, hardly unknown in Washington but ordinarily kept concealed, that upset the lawmakers so. "The whole mess smells of Machiavelli," O'Mahoney had said in March about the administration's means of persuasion, "and

Machiavelli stinks." The New Deal offered goodies galore—the WPA jobs, the post offices and courthouses, the dollars dispensed to constituents in need. These gave the president and his minions more carrots at their command, and more leverage over the legislators, than any administration before. "They are getting desperate now," Burt Wheeler charged, "and apparently are threatening people."

The issue had come up a few weeks earlier, pointedly and publicly, when the youngest member of the upper chamber had risen on the Senate floor. Rush Holt, a Democrat from West Virginia, had been unable to take his seat for six months into 1935, until he reached a senator's constitutional minimum age of thirty. "For fourteen months, I was not even consulted about any appointment in my state," Holt flared. "Immediately after the president submitted his proposal, I was called by a high official—"

"Who?" Hugo Black of Alabama broke in.

It was Joe Keenan who had solicited Holt's suggestions for a federal judgeship in West Virginia. "He did not say, 'I am going to give you a judge for your vote,'" Holt said. "I hope he did not think I was that dumb, but I knew what he meant and *he* knew what he meant."

Hugo Black was visibly furious. "I would be ashamed to rise on the floor of the Senate," he exclaimed, "and admit that I had a reputation that would justify anybody in thinking I could be bribed with a federal judgeship."

The senators laughed, but they were shocked at Holt's accusation. Even the virginal West Virginian was not naïve about the brutalities of politics; everyone knew the facts of patronage. But openly exchanging a judgeship for a legislative vote blatantly violated the traditional fiction that governed the relationship between the constitutionally coequal branches of government.

Just as "Big Jim" Farley's acknowledgment was complicating Joe Robinson's task, the president was welcoming the majority leader into the Oval Office. Half an hour later, the dispirited senator sank into a sofa outside the president's door and dictated a statement for the press. He predicted a close vote on the Court bill and "a fair prospect" of success. "I see no prospect at this stage of compromise or settlement," Robinson composed. Then he deleted "at this stage" and downgraded "settlement" to "adjustment."

Three nights later, his low expectation was met. Reporters had been tipped off about a secret meeting of the bill's leading opponents, but they failed to find it until one of them remembered seeing Burt Wheeler whisper to colleague after colleague on the Senate floor as the afternoon session waned. Two newspapermen glimpsed several senators entering Wheeler's office, but when they reached the door, the transom slammed shut. For two hours, the committee of fifteen senators who led the campaign against expanding the Court conferred inside. Carl Hatch of New Mexico proposed a compromise of his own devising, to add a justice for every sitting justice older than seventy-five, instead of seventy, and no more than one in any calendar year. The fourteen others would brook no compromise at all. Pat McCarran had gone home and found Nevadans overwhelmingly opposed to packing the Court. He and Joe O'Mahoney, both of Irish blood, had been amenable to compromise until Farley insulted them. Liberals such as O'Mahoney, and moderate Democrats—Frederick Van Nuys of Indiana, for instance—were breaking away from the president. Wheeler's defection had made it easier for them to jump ship.

When the senators emerged, Wheeler spoke to the waiting correspondents. "We're all taking the president at his word," he told them. "He said, 'No compromise.' *We* will not accept any compromise. We will vote against any and all amendments and against the bill."

# CHAPTER FOURTEEN

# Out of the Impasse

JOHN SUTER'S TELEPHONE rang at eight o'clock on Tuesday morning, the eighteenth of May, and a voice asked him to stop by Justice Willis Van Devanter's apartment on his way to the office.

The seventy-one-year-old reporter for the Associated Press rose from his sickbed. He had been covering the Supreme Court for forty-five years, which was nearly two decades longer than Van Devanter, the longest-serving justice, had sat on the bench. In the taxi he could think of only one reason for the summons.

The seventy-eight-year-old justice met him at the door, dressed for work and smoking a pipe. The fourth-floor apartment, comfortable but somber, was in a gracious old building on the stateliest stretch of Connecticut Avenue. The justice's angular face and thin lips gave him a stern look on the bench. But in private, he was the most genial of men. John Suter was his favorite reporter, and for fifteen minutes the justice inquired after his health and offered unsolicited advice. Then he said, "What I really wanted to see you about is that I'm going to notify the president of my retirement."

At the carved mahogany desk in his old-fashioned parlor, the eldest of the Four Horsemen had composed a dry and legalistic note to the president, no easy task for a justice who had been so bedeviled in recent years by arthritis and writer's block that he had drafted just a handful of opinions each term. Shortly before John Suter arrived, Van Devanter had dispatched his letter to the White House, announcing his retirement from active service once the Court finished its 1936–37 term.

He had been thinking of retiring at least since 1934, when his wife suffered a fatal heart attack during their annual summer's sojourn, taking the waters in Wiesbaden, Germany. He had already bought more than seven hundred acres of rolling farmland in Maryland, two miles from a paved road, and had fixed up the old house, meaning to live in it someday. He had long played a critical role on the Court. His close friendship since Cincinnati Law School with William Howard Taft had catapulted him in 1910, while Taft was president, from a federal appeals court onto the highest bench. When Taft himself joined the Court in 1921, he relied on Van Devanter as his "lord chancellor," as he liked to say, for his mastery of judicial principles and procedure. In his early years on the Court, Van Devanter had written some liberal opinions, and he had shown compassion for the Scottsboro Boys in 1932; siding with the majority in ordering a new trial for the black youngsters in Alabama sentenced to death for rape, he invoked the Fourteenth Amendment as originally intended, to protect due process of law for the freed slaves and their descendants.

But his values were largely rooted in the past, faithful to a frontiersman's laissez-faire, a jurist "who doesn't like to permit abrogation of freedom of contract," *Fortune* noted, "even when it is a matter of local experiment." Of the forty-one laws the Court had struck down during Van Devanter's twenty six and a half years on the Court, he had voted with the majority on all forty-one—"The Great Assenter," according to a wag in the press. All the while, relying upon an unyielding jurisprudence, he had kept his brethren's respect. The chief justice admired his "perspicacity and common sense," and Felix Frankfurter considered him "the brains of the Court." He showed a certain integrity, such as in returning his farm's benefit checks to the Agricultural Adjustment Administration after he helped end the agency's life. He had continued to make his presence felt in the Court's Saturday conferences, where he could listen to the competing arguments and find grounds for a compromise. When he had thought of retiring because of illness in 1935, Justice Brandeis helped to dissuade him. "My dear Van," he had written. "The Court never needed you more. L.D.B."

The president's assault on the Court had given him pause about retiring—as "undignified," he told his son—but the recent enactment of the judicial retirement bill assured his full salary as a pension. At last he told Brandeis that he was ready to step down, hoping not to leave alone.

But Brandeis, his only older colleague, refused to quit while the Court was under siege. Brandeis prevailed on the newspaperman Marquis Childs to pass the word about Van Devanter's intentions to Burt Wheeler, knowing that Wheeler's friend and confidant Senator William Borah lived three floors above Van Devanter on Connecticut Avenue. (Justice Cardozo shared the same building.) Borah had hinted to Van Devanter about timing his retirement to maximize the damage to the president's Court plan. The justice acceded to the suggestion, publicizing his intentions the same morning that the Senate Judiciary Committee was to vote on the president's bill.

At the White House, the president's valet delivered the justice's letter on a tray at a quarter to ten, while FDR, as was his custom, still occupied his narrow iron bed. With its old dark furniture, the marble Victorian mantelpiece, and the tail of his father's favorite horse over the doorway, his bedroom was "a little too large to be cozy," as Frances Perkins recounted, but "not large enough to be impressive." The president cast his newspapers aside and read the letter, then reached for a pencil and a tablet. *My Dear Mr. Justice Van Devanter*, he scribbled—not *Dear Willis*, as the press would delight to point out. Along with his best wishes he asked the justice to "come in to see me" before the summer started, confident that the invitation would be refused. The note was typed and delivered to the ex-justice-to-be.

Steve Early tried to put the best face on things to the press. "One up and five to go!" he said, supposedly quoting the president. Nobody was fooled. The first of the Nine Old Men was on his way out, without the necessity of expanding the Court. At long last, the president could now name a justice of his own choosing, but that would raise a new set of complications.

IN WASHINGTON, THE Depression had really ended in 1934, and the recovery was already under way. Indeed, in some neighborhoods in the capital, the Depression had never taken place. Out along Wisconsin Avenue, at her mansion, "Friendship," the mining heiress Evalyn Walsh McLean had worn her Hope Diamond *and* her Star of the East (plus six diamond bracelets) in hosting something like a thousand celebrants at a

$50,000 party on New Year's Eve. The city's bank deposits had reached an all-time high, the Christmas trade in some stores had been the strongest in eight years, and the construction of houses and apartments in the metropolitan area during 1937 was expected to set a record. Wages were rising, and job placements in the capital's private companies shot up by two fifths during the first quarter of 1937 versus a year earlier. The head bellhop at a downtown hotel saw more customers than the year before, "and what's more, they tip with quarters instead of dimes."

Nationally, too, the economy had been showing signs of reviving. "Business recovery is here," the *New Republic* declared near the beginning of 1937. Industrial production had surpassed the levels of 1929. Steel production was nearing capacity, automobile output was heading for record levels, and textiles were prosperous. The outlook was bright for electrical equipment, furniture, machinery, plastics, and air conditioning. Many big companies had moved into the black for 1936, including U.S. Steel, Bethlehem Steel, the Baltimore & Ohio Railroad, Mack Trucks, and Lehigh Portland Cement. Farm prices had risen by a fourth, wages were rising, and unemployment had fallen by 10 percentage points since 1933, soon to dip below 15 percent. Five million to six million additional Americans now held jobs, compared to the Depression's nadir in 1933. Tens of millions more children slept with their bellies calm, as their parents regained self-respect and a manageable fear of the future.

The public was mindful of the improvement. An opinion survey published in *Fortune* in January 1937 found that a quarter of Americans believed that the Depression was already over, and another third thought that the end was in sight; fewer than a third answered point-blank, "Not over." And only a third of the respondents had lost hope that a youth with thrift, ability, and ambition still had the opportunity to own a home and to rise in the world. Slowly, fitfully, as the world showed signs of returning to normal, the sense of emergency—including anxiety about the Supreme Court—was on the wane.

THE SENATORS ON the Judiciary Committee learned of Justice Van Devanter's resignation as they filed in for their executive session at ten o'clock. In their seven arduous weeks of hearings, they had heard an estimated 1,150,000 words. The past five weeks had offered a stage for the opponents of the president's Court bill, as an unremitting parade of law school deans, business leaders, and newspaper columnists played to the dwindling audiences. Tommy Corcoran tried to persuade Chairman Ashurst to truncate the hearings, to no avail. More and more, the loquacious senator's witticisms were getting on Corcoran's and Keenan's nerves. They suspected him of leading a filibuster without admitting it, and indeed Ashurst had promised before the hearings started that they would continue for as long as any "coherent citizen" wished. Only a few days earlier, he had said, "The show must go on," though it ended soon thereafter.

For two hours, the Judiciary Committee debated and voted on half a dozen proposals for a compromise. One required that two thirds of the justices would have to agree for the Court to declare a law unconstitutional. Another added two more justices, to create an eleven-member Court, the chief justice plus an associate justice for each circuit court of appeals. The most serious proposal was put forward by Marvel Logan of Kentucky, a former chief justice of his state's court of appeals, and one of the senators friendliest to the president's plan. He proposed to add an extra justice for each of the four incumbents, other than Van Devanter, who had turned seventy-five, but no more than one a year. His plan was the same as Carl Hatch's, but it was politically more affecting for a reason that did not reside in the text: it carried Joe Robinson's endorsement. The majority leader was not to be found—nobody knew quite where he was—but he had authorized Logan to disclose his support.

The committee members discussed six possible compromises, all of them proposed by the president's supporters, but none of them attracted enough votes to pass. Logan's formulation came the closest to attracting a majority, for it drew one of the Court bill's opponents into support—its originator, Carl Hatch of New Mexico. But otherwise, the lines remained firm: eight of the committee's senators supported the president's Court plan, and ten of them opposed it. Joe O'Mahoney and Pat McCarran, still seething at Jim Farley, insisted on taking the president's political avenger at his word: no compromise. The vote on Marvel Logan's compromise was a nine-to-nine tie.

The committee's eighth and final ballot was a foregone conclusion. The seven Democratic regulars and the Senate's only independent, George

Norris of Nebraska, voted in favor of the Court bill. The three Republicans joined the other seven Democrats, all but one of them from the West, in voting to recommend that the full Senate not pass the bill. The vote was ten to eight; the president had lost. The opponents named four of their number, including O'Mahoney and McCarran, to write an adverse report.

Reporters huddled in the cul-de-sac outside of the committee room heard a roar of laughter from inside: Tom Connally of Texas, an opponent of the Court bill, had joked that the ten-to-eight decision counted as "another five-to-four" blow to the administration. That night, Burt Wheeler said with a snort to reporters, "They are begging for a compromise, but they ought to know it's too late to talk of compromise." The president's last hope lay in the Court itself, in the possibility that it would strike down the Social Security Act. Nothing else was likely to coax the public or the recalcitrant lawmakers to his side.

THAT AFTERNOON, AS the Senate convened, most of the senators gathered around Joe Robinson's desk. They squeezed his hand, pounded his back, and called him "Mr. Justice." The majority leader looked happy for the first time in months, drained of the stress that had ruled his life since the Court battle began. Whether from exultation or simply as a tactic to discourage the president from changing his mind, he had confided in friends about the promised vacancy, and word had spread until most senators were in on the secret; even colleagues across the aisle showed their excitement. The Republican leader, Charles McNary of Oregon, said, "I will personally move that he be confirmed unanimously," without even bothering to assign the nomination to a committee. All over the capital, the tension seemed to relax. "Each side in the controversy has the feeling of gaining something," the *Christian Science Monitor* reported the next afternoon, "while the emergence of Mr. Robinson's name has had a somewhat mollifying influence on senatorial antagonists."

Indeed, the surge of senatorial passions on Robinson's behalf hinted at motives beyond their affection for the majority leader. For some senators, it was a matter of ambition; a line of senior Democrats was already forming to claim his front-row desk on the aisle. For others it was undoubtedly a sublimation of hostility toward Roosevelt for so often forcing them to his will, for a political predominance he did not always conceal. Honoring their leader was the least he could do; nominating anyone else would be an affront.

The president, however, was not to be rushed. At his desk, a reporter asked, "Do you intend to confirm the Senate nomination of Senator Robinson to the Supreme Court?" Everyone laughed.

"I'm afraid I will have to tell you the truth," the president replied. "I have not considered the Supreme Court vacancy at all. Really, not at all." This was only the appointment he had craved more than any other—for more than four years.

Even Joe Robinson's admirers conceded that he was hardly the ideal for a Supreme Court justice. His volatile demeanor was anything but judicial, and when it came to legal brainwork, he was no Benjamin Cardozo. Rather, it was his ordinary mind that had always comforted his colleagues. He had been a trial lawyer in rural Arkansas and then a partner in a Little Rock law firm with blue-ribbon clients, none of whom were his. He "did not know enough corporate law to draw the simplest corporate papers, and had never advised a Big Business client on Big Business matters in his life," *Fortune* had recently pointed out.

For the president, trapped in a box of his own making, Joe Robinson posed other problems, too. One was age. The presidential message that had accompanied the judicial reorganization bill prescribed a policy of appointing justices who were younger than sixty. Robinson was almost sixty-five; in another five years, he would be expected to retire. He also suffered from a bad heart, but even more worrying to the president was the question of what Robinson truly believed. The fifth-term senator was more progressive, surely, than the northern liberals around the president liked to think. He loathed the industrial trusts, and he favored labor. Earlier in his career, he had led the Senate battles to create the Federal Trade Commission and to outlaw child labor, he supported women's suffrage and the regulation of food and drugs, and he opposed the Ku Klux Klan. In 1928 the Arkansan had showed no small measure of political courage in castigating the Alabama senator Tom Heflin for bigotry against Catholics, which propelled Robinson onto the Democratic national ticket that year as Al Smith's running mate. "I don't know why they call me a conservative," he complained.

Still, the president and his advisers had their reasons to think he was, beyond Robinson's horror at deficit spending and his southern attitude toward race. Even while he served as the president's indispensable man in the Senate, privately he was growing disaffected with the New Deal—with the growth of government expenditures and the additional powers that accrued to the president. Harold Ickes was not alone in concluding, "He isn't anything but a conservative at heart." Should the quest for new blood on the Supreme Court wind up naming a fifth-term senator holding yesterday's views, "it really is an occasion for sardonic laughter," the interior secretary wrote in his diary. "I don't relish the position that the president is in."

President Roosevelt said nothing. Robinson had enraged him, by Tommy Corcoran's account, when he dispatched messengers to the White House to ask that his appointment be announced at once. The president could hardly count on Robinson alone to assure the about-face in the Court's direction. Rumors of other retirements ran rampant—of Brandeis, of conservatives Sutherland and McReynolds, even of Hughes. But Brandeis was staying put, Hughes and McReynolds made their denials known, and Sutherland kept quiet. Even so, the speculation about another vacancy gave the president an excuse to delay any nomination, in the hope that he could name a reliable liberal along with Joe Robinson.

When Henry Morgenthau, the secretary of the Treasury took a Saturday night cruise with the president in the cutter *Potomac* along the Potomac, he ventured, "What are you going to do about Joe Robinson?"

"I cannot appoint him," his Hudson Valley neighbor replied.

"Why not?"

"Because he is not sufficiently liberal," the president said. "However, if I had three vacancies I might be able to sandwich in Joe Robinson."

The president hated to deliver bad news, and a man of Robinson's temper might well explode. He hesitated to invite Robinson to the White House for fear that the meeting would be interpreted correctly as bait to keep the majority leader doing his damnedest on the Court bill. Instead, it fell to Farley to telephone Robinson the next morning at his apartment on Capitol Hill with an assurance. "Think no more about it," he said—the seat on the Court would be his.

For Joe Robinson, that did not suffice. He distrusted the polish of words and the glib men who delivered them. After all that he had done for the president, he wanted a public acknowledgment of his nomination, and he vowed to say nothing to the president until the president said something to him. For two long weeks, a mutual silence reigned between the two protagonists who needed one another the most.

THE SPECTATORS STRAINED to glimpse Joe Robinson, who was seated in the front section of the courtroom. He had shown up on May 24, the next-to-last decision day of the Supreme Court's already historic 1936–37 term, to introduce a lawyer as a candidate for admission to the Supreme Court bar. The five other senators in the crowded courtroom, including Henry Fountain Ashurst and William Borah, had made their way across First Street for a loftier reason: to witness history being made.

After the justices stepped through the curtains and took their seats along the bench, Charles Evans Hughes nodded toward the justice farthest to his left. Benjamin Cardozo was the frailest of the nine, especially seated next to the hearty Harlan Fiske Stone. Cardozo was a wisp of a man, lit from within, with graceful hands, a keen but gentle face, a shock of silvery white hair, and a weak heart. The lifelong bachelor was a man without pretense. He often answered his own telephone ("This is the justice speaking. Is there anything I can do for you?"), and he would rescue a lawyer befuddled in an oral argument. But the meekness of his demeanor did not conceal the directness of his gaze, the determination in his chin, or the beauty and force of his intellect. His erudition was unparalleled. At Columbia Law School, his pen was said to produce the most potent English of any student since Alexander Hamilton, and he was still inclined to read Greek and Latin for pleasure. During his years on New York's highest court, lawyers wondered why he always wrote the opinions in the most interesting cases. The reason, by Felix Frankfurter's account: whatever Cardozo wrote, he made interesting.

May 24 was Justice Cardozo's sixty-seventh birthday, and he celebrated by doing what he loved more than anything. "I have here number eight hundred thirty-seven, the case of the Charles Steward Machine Company . . ." A rustle passed through the courtroom as the spectators leaned toward the bench. If the renowned liberal was reading the Court's opinion on the unemployment insurance in the Social Security Act, the outcome was ordained.

Three years earlier, while the president's advisers were struggling to design a system to provide for the citizenry's social security, Frances Perkins had found herself at a reception with Justice Stone. The labor secretary confessed her perplexity at how to structure a grant of power to the federal government so it passed constitutional muster—because "your Court tells us what the Constitution permits," she had said with a laugh.

"The taxing power of the federal government, my dear," Stone had whispered back, with his customary candor. "The taxing power is sufficient for everything you want and need." He meant Congress's constitutional power to levy taxes to "provide for the common Defence and general Welfare of the United States."

The administration had taken his advice and had relied on a payroll tax in drafting the landmark Social Security Act in 1935, which the president would always regard as his grandest achievement in domestic policy. The legislation sought to salve the Depression in two ways—most immediately, by making payments to the unemployed and, in the longer run, by arranging a system of pensions for the elderly (though levying a payroll tax for later disbursal weakened the economy in the short run). Nearly three million employers and twenty-six million industrial workers had reason to care about the fate of unemployment insurance, along with the nearly seven million Americans aged sixty-five or more—and everyone else who hoped to be old someday—who had been rescued from the fear of pauperism because of a federally arranged pension. Never had an instrument of government touched so many Americans' lives.

An Alabama company that manufactured coal mining machinery had challenged the mechanism for reducing the pain of unemployment, to recover $46.14 in payroll taxes that it had contributed against its will to insure its workers against losing their jobs. Cardozo's voice, stronger than usual, carried across the courtroom. Point by point, he explained why Congress had responded to society's needs that lay beyond the capacity of the forty-eight states to handle on their own. For one thing, because the states competed with one another to attract business and investors, any state that insured the jobless by levying a payment on employers would put itself at a disadvantage. And the magnitude of the problem was simply too overwhelming. "There is need to remind ourselves of facts as to the problem of unemployment that are now matters of common knowledge," he advised, citing the millions of Americans out of work and the tens of millions of their dependents. "The problem had become national in area and dimensions," he said. "There was need of help from the nation if the people were not to starve." He outlined the hard realities of the everyday world, as a matter of the "general" welfare—quite literally—that was beyond the capacity of the individual states to handle, and was therefore a constitutionally suitable subject for Congress to take up.

The interpretive history of the general welfare clause in the U.S. Constitution had always depended, in part, on a problem of grammar. The section in Article I that enumerated the powers of Congress began:

*The Congress shall have Power To lay and collect Taxes, Duties, Imposts and Excises, to pay the Debts and provide for the common Defence and general Welfare of the United States.*

Jefferson and Madison insisted that it ought be read as if no comma existed after "excises," which would cast the provision as nothing more than a limit on the purposes for which Congress could levy taxes, and confine Congress to the powers listed below. But Hamilton discerned in the thirty-one words a separate bestowal of power, one that allowed Congress not only to collect taxes but also to enhance the "general Welfare" as it saw fit. Some historians even posited a lost semicolon that had somehow vanished from the constitutional text following the word "Debts," which would prove Hamilton's case.

Wisely, Justice Cardozo sidestepped the grammatical thicket by invoking the authority of the justice at the far end of the bench. This was in Cardozo's second opinion of the day, on the other portion of the Social Security Act, its system of old-age pensions. Never before had the Court applied the general welfare clause directly to a case. He quoted Justice Roberts's reasoning in the Court's AAA decision, which accepted Hamilton's contention about Congress's expansive power to promote the general welfare. "Nor is the concept of the general welfare static," Cardozo read to the hushed courtroom. "Needs that were narrow or parochial a century ago may be interwoven in our day with the well-being of the nation. What is critical or urgent changes with the times."

"More like economic and sociological treatises than legal decisions," a spectator murmured insightfully. The government had crammed its legal briefs with pages of statistics on population trends, economic performance, the effects of unemployment, and the troubles of the elderly in an industrial age. Justice Brandeis, while he was still practicing law, had been the first to drag the real world into the courtroom, through the briefs he had filed with the Supreme Court rife with sociological and economic facts. He had tried to persuade Oliver Wendell Holmes, without success, to spend his lengthy summer breaks reading tomes on the workings of industry or the causes of social woe. Nonetheless, Holmes stood in the forefront of the movement known as legal realism, which had emerged in the leading law schools and in rarefied legal circles during the 1920s. It recognized that judges were humans and that their interpretation of the law was bound to be influenced by their own experiences—even, in a famous formulation, by what they had eaten for breakfast. Legal realism also connected the purposes of the law to society's needs of the times, and in this sense it reached an apotheosis of sorts in Cardozo's opinions on the Social Security Act. "The hope behind this statute is to save men and women from the rigors of the poor house as well as from the haunting fear that such a lot awaits them when journey's end is near." To a reporter, Cardozo once made his feelings clear: "The final cause of law is the welfare of society."

Justice McReynolds could hardly contain himself. The instant that Cardozo had finished delivering his first opinion, McReynolds leaned forward, smiled, and then grew stern as he denounced the majority's views. The two justices were hardly on speaking terms. The syllables *McReynolds* were not to be uttered in Cardozo's apartment. During Cardozo's swearing-in in 1932, as the Court's second Jew, McReynolds had ostentatiously ignored the proceedings, and when McReynolds circulated an opinion to his brethren, the newcomer had the audacity to suggest an improvement or two in the wording. Soon McReynolds took aim at Cardozo's most vulnerable spot. Cardozo's father, a New York City judge enmeshed in the Tweed Ring, had resigned in 1885 to avoid being impeached for selling justice at a price, and his son had spent his career trying to restore the reputation of a family that had arrived on American shores in the 1600s, as McReynolds's had. One day, Cardozo passed by as McReynolds was chatting in a corridor with Justice Stone, who counted as Cardozo's best friend on the Court. "Strange that they could not find in New York,"

McReynolds remarked, loudly enough to be overheard, "someone whose father was not a thief."

McReynolds reached beyond his written dissent in detailing his disgust from the bench, using a tone that his own law clerk, John Knox, described as one of "contempt and alarm." Cardozo showed no expression and sat stock-still in his seat as his nemesis on the Court cut to the core of their constitutional dispute. "We should keep in mind that we are living under a written Constitution," McReynolds cried out. "No volume of words, no citation of irrelevant statistics or appeals to the feelings of humanity, can expand the powers granted to Congress. Neither can we, by attempts to paint a white rose red, view that situation differently from that seen by the fathers of the Constitution." That the meaning of the Constitution was immutable, its definitions fixed by its authors and their original intent, was McReynolds's sacred belief. Cardozo argued that the proper understanding of its words and its wording evolved with the times.

For the third time in eight weeks, a majority of the Supreme Court had invoked the realities of modern life to trump the precedent and purity of legal reasoning. First, the *Lochner*-era understanding of the due process clause, as a godsend to employers, had expired in the minimum-wage case from Washington State. Then the Court, in upholding the Wagner Act, had expanded the scope of interstate commerce to reflect the changes in the economy since 1787, as it swept from a local to a national scale. Now the Court's majority had stretched the interpretation of "general welfare" even beyond what the government's lawyers had imagined. In effect, the Court had granted Congress, whenever it deemed wise, the power to ease Americans' suffering. These were three distinct constitutional clauses, each with its own interpretive history and abstruse arguments. Strictly speaking, none of them had anything to do with the others. Yet surely it was more than coincidence that all three long-standing premises of constitutional theory had been abandoned almost simultaneously. It signified more than merely a change in interpretation, but a reversal of attitude about the Constitution—about its purpose in American life, about the duty of the law in achieving justice. The Court's changes of heart in the spring of 1937 became known to legal scholars as a constitutional revolution.

Though his fingerprints were hidden at the time, Charles Evans Hughes had laid the groundwork. Not until three years later did Roberts drop a hint to Felix Frankfurter of Hughes's spadework. Cardozo had died, and Frankfurter had taken his place. The short, brilliant, ingratiating Jew had grown close to the husky, unpretentious, Protestant, Anglo-Saxon Owen Roberts. Frankfurter asked Roberts if he had realized the door he had opened in the AAA case in 1936 when he endorsed Hamilton's expansive view of Congress's power to promote the general welfare, thereby conceding the federal government broad authority to improve the citizenry's lives. "I do realize it," Roberts replied, "and often wonder why the hell I did it just to please the Chief."

At last, the outlines of a judicial deal had become apparent. Ever since the Court had struck down the AAA in January 1936 by a six-to-three vote, the rumor had persisted that Hughes had jumped sides at the last minute, granting the conservatives a comfortable majority and the prestige of having lured the chief justice to their side. Now it was evident what Hughes would have traded for his vote. In the majority opinion that abolished a New Deal agency, Roberts had included a passage that seemed to point to the opposite conclusion, specifically endorsing Hamilton's vision of the Constitution as the template for a strong and active central government. That language had surely been Hughes's doing. At the time, it had seemed an odd sidelight to the AAA's death, but just sixteen months later, it came to the fore. The chief justice, playing a game of judicial chess, had evidently been thinking a few moves ahead. His earlier maneuver had now placed the king—the president and his judicial ambitions—into check.

Yet once again, while Hughes had created the opportunity, Owen Roberts had controlled the outcome. By yet another vote of five to four, he had joined the liberals in upholding the federal system of unemployment compensation. (In sustaining the old-age pensions, two of the Four Horsemen had switched sides.) Justice Cardozo was unworldly by temperament, but he had been wily enough to rest his decision on Justice Roberts's own Hamiltonian handiwork, and he succeeded. "It gives me chills today to realize what might have happened if Justice Roberts had cast his vote with the four archconservatives in this case," John Knox, McReynolds's law clerk, wrote years later. In all three dramatic departures from the Court's long-constricted interpretations of the Constitution, Roberts had delivered the decisive vote. "It was, in fact, Roberts's Court and not Hughes's," Knox concluded. "Charles Evans Hughes merely presided as chief justice, but it was Owen J. Roberts who decided in which direction the Court would go."

Justice Roberts, far from the most brilliant man on the Court, had developed no original conception of the Constitution or even a consistent view of the law. He was known, above all, for inconsistency. He was an ordinary man, at best, among the justices. Yet he had managed to accomplish the most consequential shift in the century-and-a-half history of the Court, exerting an impact on the nation for decades beyond. Unless the Court changed its mind again, the government had been granted the right to take the side of the people.

# CHAPTER FIFTEEN

# A Good Man's Mind

NOT UNTIL EIGHTEEN years later, after his own death, did Owen Roberts try to explain clearly why he had switched sides on the Court. He was a private man, and before he died he had burned all of his personal and judicial papers—"because he did not want them subject to interpretation which he would not approve or correct," a friend explained. But after he stepped down from the bench, in 1945, at Felix Frankfurter's behest, he drafted a memorandum of explanation and gave it to Frankfurter, who, by then, as a justice himself, had become Roberts's best friend on the bench and his judicial executor. "I had to wheedle, if indeed not to extort, the memorandum out of him," Frankfurter said later. "I do not believe there ever was a man on this Court who was less concerned 'to be understood' about his judicial conduct than was Roberts." Another decade passed, until Roberts's death, before Frankfurter made it public.

In the memorandum, Roberts attributed his change of heart not to the substance of the constitutional issues but rather to a legal technicality. In the *Tipaldo* case, as Roberts recalled it, the lawyers defending the New York State law had argued that the Court need not reverse its earlier precedent, in the 1923 *Adkins* case, in order to uphold New York's minimum wage because the circumstances of the two cases could be distinguished—an argument, Roberts said, that was "disingenuous and born of timidity." The lawyers for Washington State, he noted, did not repeat that mistake.

There was a problem, however, with Roberts's explanation: it was inaccurate. The lawyers for New York had in fact asked the Court to rethink its precedent in *Adkins*. In their original plea that the Court hear the case, they argued that the economic troubles that had moved the legislature to enact a minimum wage for women "call for a reconsideration of the *Adkins* case." Later, in its petition for a rehearing, the state claimed it had "assumed" that the Court would, in fact, reexamine the 1923 precedent. If Roberts had wanted to take up the *Adkins* precedent, he had ample grounds without being accused of judicial activism.

He had indeed switched—and not once, but twice, first when he abandoned the liberal interpretation he had proclaimed in his 1934 *Nebbia* decision to join the Court's conservatives, then again in forsaking the conservatives by reversing himself on the minimum wage. Neither time did he explain himself, even to colleagues, for he possessed what Frankfurter described as "a hidden rather than an obvious nature." Roberts's reason—or reasons—for switching sides on the minimum wage for women was to become a historical mystery, one destined never to be unambiguously resolved.

President Roosevelt, however, thought he knew, and Homer Cummings did, too. In their minds, the threat to enlarge the Court had had its desired, daunting effect. The Court bill itself was "the major cause in reversing an unfortunate trend of decisions," Cummings told his diary. Yet it was indisputable, as a simple matter of timing, that the Court-packing plan had made no impact at all on Roberts's reversal on the minimum wage. His conversion, though announced in March 1937, had already occurred by December 1936. The *Parrish* case had been argued before the Court on the sixteenth and seventeenth of December, and the justices, in their customary practice, took a tentative vote on the following Saturday, the nineteenth. Harlan Stone was home in bed, stricken with dysentery, and in his absence they split four to four, the Four Horsemen against Roberts and the liberals. Stone's opinion on the minimum wage was already known, for he had voted to uphold the New York statute, so it made sense to await his return and produce a five-to-four vote, to set a new precedent. Hughes waited a while after Stone returned to work in February, precisely to ward off the perception that the Court had bowed to the president's threat.

That Roberts had switched sides on the minimum wage no later than mid-December, only six and a half weeks after the president's landslide reelection, suggested another motive for his—and the Court's—about-face. In his *Parrish* dissent, Justice Sutherland had practically accused the majority of kowtowing to the popular will, and administration officials suspected the same. "It may be wrong to talk about the president and a stick," said Charles Wyzanski, a special assistant to Homer Cummings, "but it is not wrong to talk about the president and twenty-six million sticks," each from a voter who wished to keep FDR in the White House. As literary bartender Mr. Dooley had prophesied, the Supreme Court followed the election returns.

Roberts, however, may have changed his mind even earlier, before the election. On October 10, 1936, the justices had agreed to hear the appeal on the minimum wage in Washington State. Harlan Stone had not yet fallen ill, so the three liberals and Hughes could have supplied the four votes required to accept the appeal. But Roberts added a fifth vote, by his own account to Frankfurter. One of the Four Horsemen asked another, "What is the matter with Roberts?" But no one, including Roberts, answered.

One explanation in particular for Justice Roberts's switch bounced around the power centers and salons of Washington. It bore three names: Charles Evans Hughes. "Hughes is the best politician in the country," the president told a future justice, William Douglas. FDR's advisers felt so bitter that they checked the Constitution and the statutes to determine if another chief justice might be named in his place if the Court plan passed. On the Senate floor, Sherman Minton of Indiana suggested that Roberts "was just listening to the wee small voice of the chief justice that was talking politics to him. There is no other explanation for such an unprecedented, unknown about-face on the part of a justice of the Supreme Court."

Indeed, the two justices were close. Arriving at the Court only fourteen weeks apart in 1930, they had hit it off from the start. Roberts grew to adore the chief justice, who was thirteen years his senior. He felt like a son or a younger brother to him. "In most ways, he was the greatest man I have ever known," Roberts said later. In 1931, after Roberts broke his shoulder in a fall from his favorite horse, the chief justice visited him every weekday for three weeks. In a tribute to Roberts in 1935 for his fortieth college reunion, Hughes extolled "his amiability and talent for cooperation." They exchanged birthday notes and socialized together. Most intriguingly, Hughes and his wife motored from Washington to the Robertses' beloved farm near Philadelphia. What the two justices discussed, and when, was never made known. But it was plausible, certainly, that they conferred about the institution that both of them cared for—its lowly stature and the possible means of repair.

Still, it seemed unlikely that Hughes had openly coerced his younger brother on the bench. For one thing, the Baptist preacher's son made a point of never discussing the outcome of cases beyond the Court's conference room. "Chief Justice Hughes was a stickler for proprieties," Roberts said later. "He neither leaned on anyone else for advice nor did he proffer advice or assistance to any of us, but left each of us to form his own conclusions." When Roberts disclosed his decision to switch sides on the minimum wage, in a private conversation a few weeks after the election, Hughes was so surprised that he almost hugged him.

There was every reason to think that Roberts had changed his mind on his own. Since joining the Court, he had been his own man, as he had promised his friends in Philadelphia. He showed no reluctance to write a dissent, far more often than Hughes did. He also might have been embarrassed by the derision he took in the law journals, including the University of Pennsylvania's, for his convoluted reasoning in striking down the AAA and also for providing the fifth and decisive vote in striking down New York's minimum wage for women. A scholar who surveyed law journals found that eight of the nine that ventured an opinion on the *Tipaldo* decision jeered, criticizing the conservative majority for ignoring the fact that the Court had carved other exceptions into the sacred liberty of contract by upholding laws on fraud, usury, Sunday closings, and a ban on paying sailors while still in port.

Another factor may have been Roberts's political ambitions—or the end of them. As the 1936 election approached, he had "a bad dose of presidentialitis," as the gossipy columnists Drew Pearson and Robert S. Allen reported. The Young Republicans had given him a few votes in a New York straw poll, and he had been expected to serve as Pennsylvania's favorite son at the GOP national convention. But that was before his wife's discouragement—and political reality—restored him to his senses. "It is a matter of common knowledge," he admitted all too knowingly to a congressional committee in 1954, "that ambition to go from the Court to the chief executive of the government has hurt the work of a number of men on the Court." In June, he might have been hoping for the support of Republicans; by the fall, any such need had passed.

How any justice made up his mind was, of course, a mystery. A judge typically had precedent to rely on, yet that was only the beginning of the path toward a decision. As Cardozo had once explained, a judge's initial choice was whether to invoke precedent or to ignore it, if departing from precedent was necessary to satisfy society's needs. Then, a judge who determined to follow precedent often faced a choice of precedents, each credible on its face, requiring decisions about which to apply and which to pass by. The outcome was ordinarily far from obvious, as the frequency of the Court's split decisions suggested.

Jurists often took a short cut by hewing to a philosophy—an ideology, really—of the law. The Four Horsemen, for example, trusted in laissez-faire and perceived it as woven into the Constitution. Oliver Wendell Holmes had placed his faith in elected legislatures as embodying the people's will—"I try to remember that I am not God," he had once remarked. Yet this only begged the question as to why a particular justice favored one philosophy over another.

Over the years, introspective jurists have reached a strikingly similar conclusion describing a process that has little to do with the intellect. "There is nothing on which to draw to decide constitutional cases of any novelty other than discretionary judgment," an eminent conservative judge explained decades later, marveling at "the essentially personal, subjective, and indeed arbitrary character of most [justices'] constitutional decisions." Typically, it is life experience that has seemed to shape a justice's philosophy of the law. John Marshall's presence at Valley Forge in the desperate winter of 1777–78, as General Washington begged the states to rescue his ragged army because the Continental Congress lacked the authority to compel them, made him a believer in a strong central government. Living on the frontier shaped the Four Horsemen's faith in laissez-faire. "The words of the Constitution are so unrestricted by their intrinsic meaning or by their history or by tradition or by prior decisions," Frankfurter explained, "that they leave the individual justice free, if indeed, they do not compel him, to gather meaning not from reading the Constitution but from reading life."

Owen Roberts's life had dictated no overarching philosophy of the law. He had a prosecutor's mind. In the lurid detective stories that Elsie brought home for him, he invariably guessed the solution by the end of chapter one. He was a problem solver by nature, captivated more by a pattern of facts than by a conceptual framework—"untheoretical," as a scholar described it. "Roberts was not a man who had an organic constitutional philosophy comparable, say, to Holmes's or Brandeis's," Frankfurter conceded. Indeed, his theoretical inconsistency was the essence of who he was. The denizen of Rittenhouse Square who liked to think of himself as a farmer had seen different sides of life, and he had liked them all. As a lawyer, he had represented big corporations, and he had fought against them. He believed in property rights and in human rights—"a conservative with liberal tendencies," it had been written as he arrived on the bench. Dogma contradicted his nature; he had learned to see life from vantage points other than his own. It was no surprise that as a jurist he displayed what an admirer, the famed Harvard Law School dean Erwin Griswold, described later, with a trace of derision, as "a very considerable flexibility of mind."

He was modest about his legal brilliance, and rightfully so. "He did not have an original or innovating mind," Griswold wrote, and Roberts would not have disagreed. "I have no illusions about my judicial career," he wrote after it ended. "But one can only do what one can. Who am I to revile the good God that he did not make me a Marshall, a Taney, a Bradley, a Holmes, a Brandeis, or a Cardozo."

Yet something about him was refreshingly naïve. He was intellectually honest, personally tolerant, essentially a simple man—a good man. "His beliefs were not of a complicated sort," according to his old friend and mentor George Wharton Pepper. "He accepted unquestioningly the teachings of his Church." He was a conventional man who believed in the conventional things, though perhaps to an unconventional extent. He served as a vestryman at St. John's Church, across Lafayette Park from the White House, and after leaving the Court, he became the first layman in the national Episcopal Church ever elected as president of its House of Delegates. He had an idealism that emerged even while he was serving on the bench. During the world war already on the horizon, he spoke publicly about the need to avoid "world crises begotten by race pride, by the lust for national aggrandizement, and by national selfishness." Only in retirement, however, did the depth of his idealism become evident. In the wake of World War II, he championed an Atlantic Union, a super-government of democracies, as "the way to stop World War III," and devoted himself to the ideal of world federalism. ("I am George Washington in disguise," he

jested.) He also led the United Negro College Fund's campaign in Philadelphia, chaired the National Mental Health Foundation, and oversaw a
nationwide campaign for Planned Parenthood. His grandson recalled "a
man searching for a higher ideal."

Yet his idealism had a practical cast. The justice who rode the trolley
to work had never separated himself from the reality around him. On his
farm he favored a khaki shirt, breeches, and a battered straw hat. As he
scythed along the fence one day, wearing a sweat rag beneath his hat,
someone stopped and asked for Justice Roberts; he directed them to the
farmhouse but suggested that they stay away. Roberts was a man who went
to church, donated to charity, and involved himself in the community,
working for the Boy Scouts though he had no son. His neighbors in Pennsylvania thought of him as "a humble, calm, everyday person." In Washington, he was too thrifty ever to take a taxi or to let the electric lights burn
unnecessarily at home, yet he gave the most generous tip of any
justice—twenty-five cents—to the Supreme Court barber. Clumsy on the
tennis court, when he drove his automobile he tended to straddle the center line. But he felt comfortable in the twentieth century, rooted in the real
world. By temperament, he was willing to accept the changes that the new
century, and its hard times, required.

He had evidently reached this conclusion sometime during the summer or fall of 1936, and there may have been no single event that changed
his mind. Everywhere, democracies were on the run. Civil war erupted in
Spain, as the fascists of Generalissimo Franco turned their guns on the
republican government. In Nicaragua, military strongman Anastasio So-
moza had ousted the democratically elected president. At Yankee Stadium,
in a boxing ring, Max Schmeling knocked out Joe Louis, the Brown
Bomber, and then as Hitler's luncheon guest was heralded by the Nazi
press as proof of white supremacy. At Madison Square Garden, U.S. Olym-
pic chairman Avery Brundage brought an audience to its feet with his
homage to Hitler. "We can learn much from Germany," he cried, "if we
wish to preserve our institutions."

A nation's stability was not to be assumed. John Maynard Keynes
preached that an economic depression could be sidestepped. Yet across the
land, amid the foreclosures, the bankruptcies, the persistent unemployment—
the social fabric continued to unravel. For Roberts, a week before he voted

to accept the minimum wage appeal from Washington State, a tragedy hit close to home, no more than a dozen miles from his farm in Pennsylvania. As the customers arrived at Pratt Dutton's Chester County farm for an auction of his possessions—to satisfy his $75 debt to the bank—the elderly farmer opened fire from his barn, killing a neighbor and wounding three others. The anguish of the Depression on deadly display was front-page news in Philadelphia and New York. Had Roberts not voted to abolish the AAA's agricultural subsidies, farmer Dutton might have been $75 richer, and his neighbor Atlee Jackson might not have died.

The economy had changed—the world had changed—in ways that the Founding Fathers could never have fathomed. Yet they had been wise enough, Roberts had begun to believe, to have provided for that. "We live today under a very different system from that contemplated by those who drafted our Constitution," he explained in a law review article after retiring from the Court. "A great virtue of the Constitution is the breadth and generality of its language. Its phrases left latitude of action and room for interpretation to meet changing conditions." He was persuading himself in 1936 and 1937 of the need for a living Constitution. In his seventh year on the Court, a lawyer's lawyer was becoming a justice.

The political circumstances had obviously changed by the time the justices heard oral arguments on the Wagner Act the week after President Roosevelt announced his plan to enlarge the Court. No one in Washington could plead ignorance of the president's slap with his glove. Roberts himself admitted after leaving the Court, in testifying before the Senate Judiciary Committee in 1954, that he had been "fully conscious" at the time of "the tremendous strain and threat to the existing Court." The previous May, he had voted with the Four Horsemen to strike down the law that regulated prices and wages in the coal mining industry, on the grounds that when coal is brought out of the ground, its entry into interstate commerce has not yet begun. Less than a year later, in judging the interstate nature of steel and four other industries, Roberts had switched.

Fourteen years would pass before Roberts explained his reasoning in the Wagner Act cases. It was almost an aside, toward the end of a ponderous lecture, "Conflicts of Police Power," the second of three that the ex-justice delivered at Harvard Law School in 1951 as a memorial to Oliver Wendell Holmes Jr., who for eighteen months had been his brother on the

Court. Roberts was discussing the declining autonomy of state governments when he noted: "The continual expansion of federal power with
consequent contraction of state powers probably has been inevitable. The
founders of the Republic envisaged no such economic and other expansion
as the nation has experienced. Looking back, it is difficult to see how the
Court could have resisted the popular urge for uniform standards throughout the country—for what in effect was a unified economy."

That last, passively constructed sentence explained his U-turn. Two
factors had moved him in 1937. One was reality—*what in effect was a unified economy*. The other was democracy—*the popular urge*, the people's
will. He said not a word about the law.

Roberts's explanation for his actions did not end there. He acknowledged that relying on the commerce clause, say, or the general welfare
clause "to reach a result never contemplated when the Constitution was
adopted, was a subterfuge." But he had accepted such a sophistry to avert a
deeper danger to the American system of government. "An insistence by
the Court on holding federal power to what seemed its appropriate orbit
when the Constitution was adopted," he said, "might have resulted in even
more radical changes in our dual structure than those which have been
gradually accomplished through the extension of the limited jurisdiction
conferred on the federal government." He had switched sides, that is, to
save the American system of federalism, to prevent the central government
from assuming full power, as in Europe. By giving a little, he could avert
something worse. Justice Roberts had intended to assure a working democracy, safe from the desperation of its people and the ambitions of its leaders. And, in fact, he had done just that. The truly conservative position was
to bend with the times.

# CHAPTER SIXTEEN

# Jefferson's Last Stand

TEN DAYS AFTER the Supreme Court had foiled the president by sparing his beloved Social Security law, the president's advisers, at last and possibly too late, saw the stupidity in cold-shouldering the man they needed more than anyone on Capitol Hill. And so Jimmy Roosevelt called on Joe Robinson about a forgotten matter of patronage. Nothing was so precious to the fifth-term senator as putting Arkansans on the federal payroll. Once the appointment had been settled to the majority leader's satisfaction, the president's son said, with a practiced casualness, that his father had been wishing Robinson would visit. "In fact, he's rather hurt that you've stayed away so long."

Jimmy dialed the White House and handed the black telephone receiver to the majority leader. As arranged, the president came on the line and invited him to stop by that night. At half past eight, as the president was finishing dinner, Robinson arrived. For two hours, they conferred about the fate of the Court bill, which, since Willis Van Devanter was over seventy, would now expand the Court by five justices, not six, upon his departure. Robinson made clear it was dead. The president's choices were stark: compromise or defeat. Tommy Corcoran and other aides were pressing for a principled defeat, but finally accepting the inevitable, the president hoped to avoid an erosion in the perceptions of his power. Now that Robinson was pleading to let him negotiate in the Senate, to strike the best compromise he could muster, Roosevelt found himself willing to give it a try.

Neither man said a word about the vacancy on the Court until the meeting was about to end. Even then it was opaque. "If there is to be a bride," the president was reported to have said, "there must be brides-maids, at least four of them." Robinson took this to mean that he would receive his reward once he had delivered an acceptable compromise on the Court bill. That night the Senate majority leader emerged, grinning, and spoke to the reporters who had waited for two hours in the rain. No, he was not a candidate for the Court vacancy, he said, and yes, the Court bill would go ahead. He spoke vaguely of possible amendments; he was even thinking of proposing one himself.

"Mr. Justice," Jim Farley greeted him when he telephoned the next morning, to assure Robinson again that the seat would be his. Launching his search for a compromise, Robinson summoned his senatorial confidants to the Capitol basement to contemplate the options. One was to create a Supreme Court of eleven justices, one from each of the ten appeals court circuits plus the chief. But for Robinson, that posed a problem, and not only because of the president's confidential, hardly comprehensible memorandum calling the proposal "clearly unconstitutional, as the Supreme Court is a constitutional office and not a legislative office except as to numbers." Worse from Robinson's vantage point was that Justice Pierce Butler, from Minnesota, already represented the judicial circuit that included Arkansas, leaving Robinson without an available seat. Worst of all, the number of bridesmaids fell short of the president's expressed wish. The most plausible alternative was Carl Hatch's compromise, to add an extra justice to the Supreme Court for every incumbent who turned seventy-five years old but still refused to retire, and no more than one a year, with the added assurance that the Court would revert to nine justices once the old men were gone.

Clearly nothing involving the Court would be easy to pass. The public's support for the president's Court bill was deteriorating; having remained steady at just below 50 percent from February through April, it slipped after the Court upheld the Wagner Act, then the Social Security Act, and Van Devanter announced his departure. By the end of May, opinion polls found that fewer than two of five Americans favored the president's plan—"the first time since Mr. Roosevelt took office," Elmo Roper pointed out in *Fortune*, "that an issue had proved to weigh more in the public mind than the President's personal popularity." Among the prosperous and the professional, with their disproportionate influence on many members of Congress, opposition to the president's plan exceeded three quarters. Yet Robinson could find reason for hope in the public's muddled mix of opinion: of those opposed to Roosevelt's plan in Roper's poll, one of three respondents still wanted the Supreme Court reformed in some other, unspecified way. This meant that three of five Americans wanted a change.

The majority leader's hopes for a compromise that the president could accept suffered another setback on the fourteenth of June. The Senate Judiciary Committee's adverse report on the Court bill was to have been written within a week but took a month. Tommy Corcoran and Joe Keenan had tried to persuade Chairman Ashurst to publish a minority report—they had written one for him—but, as Corcoran complained, he "wriggled out of doing anything about it." The adverse report was twenty-three pages of invective. It described the Court bill "as an invasion of judicial power such as has never before been attempted in this country . . . as a needless, futile and utterly dangerous abandonment of constitutional principle . . . which should be so emphatically rejected that its parallel will never again be presented to the free representatives of the free people of America." Its tone of contempt toward the president, so recently and easily reelected, stunned the capital. "Let us, of the Seventy-fifth Congress, in words that will never be disregarded by any succeeding Congress," wrote a majority on the Democratic-controlled committee, "declare that we would rather have an independent Court, a fearless Court, a Court that will dare to announce its honest opinions in what it believes to be the defense of the liberties of the people, than a Court that, out of fear or sense of obligation to the appointing power, or factional passion, approves any measure we may enact."

In the following days, Robinson doggedly canvassed his colleagues, listened and talked, argued and reargued, then canvassed again. At last his count of votes willing to accept one or another compromise reached fifty-one, a majority of the ninety-six-member Senate, though insufficient to stop a filibuster in case Wheeler followed through on his threats. That would take sixty-four votes, for which the majority leader would need the support of several senators who opposed the Court bill. Robinson knew he needed the president's help, and offered a suggestion. Before they unveiled a compromise bill on the Court, the president could host a getaway for

Democratic lawmakers, a long weekend of eating and drinking and carousing. And Robinson had just the place in mind.

NINETY-THREE FEET BELOWGROUND, the drillers reached rock at last, though whether it was bedrock or just plain rock remained to be seen. They had had an easier time finding bedrock, at forty feet, in excavating for the Lincoln Memorial, less than a mile to the northwest along the Potomac shore. But the memorial to Thomas Jefferson was to be built next to the Tidal Basin, fashioned in the 1880s to keep sediment out of the harbor, and his statue was to stand in what had been midriver while he lived in the White House. The location would complete the fifth and final cardinal point in the cross that Pierre L'Enfant had envisioned when, with Jefferson's help, he designed the new nation's capital. Jefferson's memorial was to stand at the southern tip of the north–south axis extending to the White House, which crossed—at the Washington Monument—the east–west line from the Capitol to the Lincoln Memorial.

Only in April had the president settled the argument over the form the memorial should take. After the rains had nearly washed out FDR's second inaugural ceremony, Harold Ickes, among others, proposed construction of an auditorium as a tribute to Jefferson's devotion to free speech. There was no doubt that the city needed a first-class gathering hall, but the president preferred a classic memorial, similar in structure and spirit to Lincoln's. After ten minutes' deliberation, he chose the design, rejecting the Greek-cross shape in favor of a round, domed, marble monument modeled on the Pantheon in Rome, resembling Monticello as well as the last building that Jefferson ever designed, the Rotunda at the University of Virginia.

The controversy was immediate—and precedented. One of the leading proposals to honor Lincoln had been a parkway from Washington to Gettysburg, Pennsylvania, until the venture was exposed as a real estate scheme. The disputes over Jefferson's memorial involved both the location and the design. The Senate's Republican leader, who sat on the memorial commission, preferred to honor the Democratic Party's founder on the Mall itself or in Anacostia, far from the city's monumental core. ("[T]he 'Great Republican' has already appropriated a very fine position," a letter writer noted in the *Washington Post*.) The Washington Board of Trade and the Daughters of the American Revolution denounced the prospective loss of cherry trees ringing the Tidal Basin, a tourist-luring gift from the Japanese government; when the excavations began the following year, women threatened to chain themselves to the trees, until a compromise was reached to plant more of them. The preeminent architectural modernist Frank Lloyd Wright despised the imperial Roman design. "It is the greatest insult yet," he railed to federal architects at the Mayflower Hotel, grieving that government buildings in Washington "are not built to serve the people, but to satisfy a kind of grandomania utterly obsolete."

The memorial had been Roosevelt's idea, for like all Democratic presidents, he labored to identify himself politically with his party's founders. The party's latest chairman, Jim Farley, had recently touted Jefferson as the "real inventor of the New Deal," though everyone knew this was bunk. Jefferson had favored a weak central government and a Congress that dominated the presidency—that is, until he became president and exercised powers (notably, in purchasing the vast wilderness stretching from Louisiana to what became Montana) that the Constitution had not thought to mention. The New Deal presupposed a strong central government ruled by bureaucracies and run by a president with the executive capacity to meet a crisis or to solve a problem. The government that FDR created was much more Hamilton's aspiration, which may have explained the president's compulsion to cloak himself in the symbolism of Jefferson.

Roosevelt agreed with Jefferson, however, on one particular: in their antipathy for the third branch of government, its unelected justices with lifetime tenure standing in democracy's—in the people's—way. As president, Jefferson had been outfoxed by his kinsman John Marshall. Roosevelt still hoped to prevail.

"HELLO, BURT!" the smiling president, seated beneath the spreading boughs of a shade tree, hailed his senatorial foe. On the last Sunday in June, they were on a tiny island in the Chesapeake Bay, four miles from Maryland's Eastern Shore.

"Hello, Mr. President," Burt Wheeler cheerily called back. That was the extent of their conversation until they exchanged farewells.

It was the third and final day of the Democrats' picnicking on the Jefferson Islands. Before the Depression, the Senate Democratic caucus had acquired the Poplar Islands, three islets that had been a hideout for bootleggers, and had turned them into a retreat that Maryland's Democratic-controlled legislature had obligingly renamed for the new owners' Founding Father. Invitations to the "harmony meeting" had gone to every Democrat in Congress—to the men, that is. The six Democratic women at least pretended to understand. Senator Hattie Caraway of Arkansas said she would welcome the extra day at home. Congresswoman Caroline O'Day of New York, who was a friend of Mrs. Roosevelt's, empathized, "The men might feel hesitancy about letting down their hair—taking off their coats and perhaps their shirts, I don't know—with us along." Of the more than four hundred lawmakers invited to spend one of the three days at the woodsy retreat, all but forty accepted. Thirteen senators declined, most of them opponents of the Court bill, though only one of them was candid enough not to plead a previous engagement. "You know, there's an old Roman custom—first feast them and then acquire them," the West Virginia youngster Rush Holt had told a reporter. "And I don't want to be acquired."

The most notable man missing was the vice president. During John Nance Garner's thirty years in the House of Representatives and his past four and a third years as the president of the Senate, he had never abandoned the capital for more than a few days while Congress was in session. But a week earlier, he had stolen out of Washington, despite the efforts of Sam Rayburn of Texas, the House majority leader, to persuade him to stay. Garner headed for the modest frame house with a shady back porch that overlooked a pecan grove in Uvalde, Texas, supposedly for a vacation. "The Mystery of Jack Garner: Fisherman or Rebel"—that was a columnist's title for the poser that tantalized Capitol Hill, though it was not much of a mystery. His departure had followed a great row with the president, according to a White House confidant. The president's "'no' man," as he was known, was already disgusted with FDR for doing nothing about the sit-down strikes and for unbalancing the federal budget. On the Court fight, Garner had urged the president to declare victory in light of Justice Roberts's about-face and to end his quest for an obedient Court; the reply drove the vice president away from Washington. "This is a fine time to jump ship," the president grumbled to Farley.

Candor was a daydream on the Jefferson Islands. The lawmakers had been led to expect time with the president, one on one, for many of them had never met him before. Some of them had stepped off the Naval Academy training boats carrying briefcases with typewritten points of view. The arithmetic, however, limited each lawmaker to two minutes with the president, so instead he greeted each member and then chatted with small groups in the summertime shade. The president wore old linen slacks, having left his jacket and necktie aside, and (as Homer Cummings observed) "dispensed wisdom like Buddha under the banyan tree" while skillfully avoiding any issue of substance.

Diversion, not substance, filled each hot day. The lawmakers fished, swam in the nude, tossed horseshoes, shot skeet, hog-called, roasted wieners, and played cards—bridge, pinochle, and poker, with the president showing his usual phenomenal luck. The Senate challenged the House to a game of baseball and was crushed, 13 to 2, even with eleven men on its team. To the president's delight, a New York congressman crooned "When Broadway Was a Pasture."

The president had gone so far in his efforts to reestablish harmony among the Democrats as to invite Lulu Wheeler to motor with him from Washington to Annapolis. Lulu disapproved of gossip and jokes, which the president adored, and she was not a person to let her indignation go unnoticed. The ride to Annapolis "only reinforced her belief that he was an egotist who had to win and wanted everyone around him to tell him how great and infallible he was," her eldest daughter recounted. "He should have saved it for someone more susceptible."

He had more luck with the men. The Senate's Republican leader had mocked the weekend as a charm school, and clearly bonhomie alone could not overcome the deep differences on the Court, on the sit-down strikes, on the proper balances in a workable democracy. Newspaper correspondents, stranded in Annapolis, buttonholed the lawmakers each evening as they climbed back onto the Naval Academy dock. No opinions had changed, they found, but the antipathy had eased. And on Capitol Hill, the mood mattered.

As Joe Robinson stepped ashore in Annapolis on Sunday night, he insisted to reporters that the weekend had been strictly a social affair, though he had an announcement to make. The congressional leaders had conferred with the president and among themselves, and the Senate planned to start debate on a Court bill just after the Fourth of July. The majority leader was cagey about its precise form, but he let the correspondents conclude that it would entail one extra justice a year and possibly, in total, no more than two. Maybe a compromise was possible: Burton K. Wheeler had been quoted as saying he was certain the Senate would defeat a bill for six new justices, was fairly confident about four, but he was not so sure about two.

ON THE MORNING of July 6, not long before the Senate was to open its debate on enlarging the Supreme Court, Wheeler received a telephone call from Homer Bone. The first-term senator from Washington State, a slightly built but zealous New Dealer and a friend of Wheeler, was calling from the president's office. He asked if Wheeler could stop by the White House at noon. No, the Montanan said. That was the hour at which the Senate was set to convene, and after Joe Robinson took the floor, Wheeler intended to offer a response.

"Well, can you jump in a cab and come right now?"

Wheeler did, and at eleven o'clock he was ushered into the Oval Office. "Burt, I just want to give you a little background on the Court matter," the president began. He launched into a long story about a British judge who had quashed a conviction because of a procedural injustice—"the sort of thing we ought to have over here," he said.

"That's what we've got here," Wheeler replied.

The president bemoaned the delays in the criminal dockets, and he questioned the chief justice's unwillingness to step into the tax evasion case that the administration had pursued against Andrew Mellon. The Treasury secretary for the past three Republican presidents, the epitome of an economic royalist, Mellon had been charged with trying to cheat the government in 1931 by prematurely deducting $3 million from his income taxes for art work that was to be donated to the nation along with a gallery on the national Mall. The president pleaded that he wanted nothing more than a judicial system responsive to reason.

He was careful not to insult Wheeler by asking him to back off from his opposition to expanding the Court, but he appealed to him as a Democrat to let the Republicans take the lead. When the senator declined, President Roosevelt hoped at least to keep bitterness out of the debate.

"The Supreme Court and the Constitution are a religion with a great many people in this country," Wheeler retorted, "and you can't keep bitterness out of a religious fight." He then advised the president that enacting a Court bill would kill his popularity. "It is the difference between your coming out as a great president or as a bad one. I don't want that to happen." Wheeler said he could support enlarging the Court if he were the president's enemy, but not as his friend. When Roosevelt mentioned the liberals who were on his side, Wheeler countered with the cruelty done to Justice Brandeis, who had been a liberal longer than any of them.

Then the senator from Montana offered a compromise of his own. William Borah had authorized him to promise the resignation of two more justices if the president withdrew his Court bill.

The president seemed interested. "How can I be sure?" he said.

"You can be just as sure," Wheeler replied, "as Senator Borah and I giving our word."

But to Roosevelt, that was not sure enough.

# CHAPTER SEVENTEEN

# Death Knell

BURT WHEELER EXITED the White House at twenty minutes before noon without a solution in hand and arrived just as the Senate chamber was springing to life. Boy Scouts wearing khaki, in Washington for their national jamboree, crowded into one corner of the gallery, while diplomats, reporters, lawmakers' relatives, tourists, and civic-minded Washingtonians of leisure filled the rest. Wheeler stopped by the majority leader's desk.

"How did you get along down there?" Joe Robinson inquired.

"Not very well."

As soon as the routine business ended, Robinson rose at his desk and said, "I move that the Senate proceed to the consideration of the bill to reorganize the judicial branch of the government." The capital's most momentous debate since the League of Nations had begun. The majority leader proposed Carl Hatch's compromise as a substitute bill, setting a justice's age of presumed incompetence at seventy-five years old and limiting the appointment of additional justices to one per calendar year. This would authorize the president to name two justices right away—Van Devanter's successor plus a new one—and then another justice in each of the next three years, four additional justices overall.

"It is not that all men who reach seventy-five lose their powers of reasoning or of judgment," the sixty-four-year-old senator said, "but it is that by common acceptance those who have passed beyond seventy-five usually are in a state of mental and physical decline."

Senators did not ordinarily interrupt the majority leader, but this time

227

the opponents peppered him with questions. Warren Austin, a tart-tongued Republican from Vermont, wondered if this contradicted, at least morally, the Constitution's dictate of life tenure for Supreme Court justices. "Men are not always conscious of the time," Robinson answered, "when they have passed the climax of their usefulness." In politics, too, he noted, "one who has served long and well is seldom, if ever, conscious of his failing powers, and he keeps on running for office, running and running and running, until everyone gets tired of him and until some man whom he considers his inferior defeats him for office—"

"Even at the risk of making somewhat of a nuisance of myself." Ed Burke, a stolid anti–New Deal Democrat from Nebraska, interrupted him.

"The senator never makes a nuisance of himself," came Robinson's riposte. "Whenever he is a nuisance, nature does it for him." Robinson basked in the applause from the galleries that violated the Senate's rules and ended with a warning about the threatened filibuster. He would keep the Senate in session for long days and nights, he said, "in a test of physical endurance. Much as it might surprise the members of the Senate, I would probably come out of that kind of a test better than those who are in the opposition, at least some of them. I think I could endure it longer than could the senator from Montana." Laughter swept the chamber.

Wheeler, not to be outdone, stood tall and svelte in his white linen suit. Lulu still had him on a regimen of morning golf, nutritious meals, and an early bedtime. "I am in very good physical condition," he said. "I have been training for it."

Ed Burke broke in to ask if Robinson intended to vote on the president's original bill.

"No," Robinson said. "I am not going to take a vote on the original bill at all."

"Of course not," Wheeler jumped in, "and the reason why you are not going to take a vote on the original bill is that—"

Robinson beat him to it. "We do not have the votes to pass it."

The senators roared at the rare show of frankness.

Joe Robinson showed an exaggerated patience as he tried to explain the proposed compromise, while Ed Burke kept firing questions. Was the compromise a substitute for a constitutional amendment? "There are fifty pending," Robinson replied, "and I have never been able to find two sena-

tors in favor of any one of them. Each senator is in favor of his own constitutional amendment." That brought a knowing laughter.

Suddenly the majority leader clutched his chest and gasped for air.
He turned pale; his eyes looked glassy. Senators gaped as he pulled out a
cigar and lit a match, for he had always obeyed the chamber's prohibition
against smoking. He held the match until his fingers burned, which brought
him back to his senses.

Burke, in the back row, kept on. "I would like to ask the senator another question."

"No," Robinson stated. "I am through."

"No more questions?"

"No more questions today. The senator may reserve them until next
week." With a feeble smile and a flourish of his arm, he added, "Good-bye."
There was light laughter at the word that seemed so out of place.

Once he stopped speaking, Royal Copeland rushed to his side. The
senior senator from New York was a physician. "Joe, take it easy," Copeland
begged, "or you'll die on the floor. This isn't worth your death."

JOE ROBINSON REFUSED to cancel the second day of debate on
the Court bill, on July 7, merely to let the senators go to a ball game. In his
absence, a perfunctory session convened at ten o'clock instead of at noon,
so the senators could make it to Griffith Stadium, twenty blocks to the
north, in time to watch Lefty Gomez hurl the opening pitch of the 1937
All-Star Game.

This was the fifth annual All-Star Game for the national pastime, but
the first to be played in the nation's capital. So many autograph hounds had
mobbed the Shoreham Hotel lobby that Babe Ruth, in his second season of
retirement, took ten full minutes to cross from the entrance to the registra-
tion desk. Scalpers charged as much as $20 a ticket for box seats that cost
$1.65. This was to be the first All-Star Game at which a president threw
out the first pitch. (Clark Griffith, the impresario-minded owner of the
lowly Washington Nationals, had arranged it.) President Roosevelt had
done the honors at the Nats' opening game, in April, during which a silver
monoplane buzzed over the stadium, pulling a red pennant that said, "Play
the game. Don't pack the court." This time the president arrived a few

minutes late, and standing erect in the bunting-bedecked box by the first-base dugout, wearing a double-breasted white suit, he arched the ball into the crowd of players, who scrambled for it as if it were a bride's bouquet. When Luke Sewell, the Chicago White Sox catcher, muffed it, the Cubs' wiry shortstop, Bill Jurges, picked it up and shoved it into his pocket.

The hottest day of the summer so far sent four people in Washington to the hospital with heat prostration and would drive thousands of others that night to a riverbank or into a park to sleep (though only the capital's federally administered parks admitted residents of any race). The president, seated next to Jimmy, kept smoking his Camels and mopping his face. They watched the greats, young and old, Lou Gehrig and Carl Hubbell, who were both thirty-four, and twenty-two-year-old Joe DiMaggio, and twenty-seven-year-old Dizzy Dean, who had already racked up four straight seasons with twenty wins or more.

Scattered boos greeted Dean as he took the mound for the National League, and not only because Washington was an American League city. Now that Babe Ruth had hung up his spikes, the right-hander for the St. Louis Cardinals was baseball's most magnetic player. But he was also an eccentric, a tad too eager for the limelight. In his latest publicity stunt, he had first refused to play in the All-Star Game ("I am tired of having people tell me what to do") and then, at the last minute, he changed his mind, so tardily that he had no choice but to travel from St. Louis by airplane. Washington-Hoover Airport, in Virginia, directly across the Potomac from the proposed site for the Jefferson Memorial, was known to be unsafe—covering a mere fifth of a square mile and bordered by power and telephone lines, with a heavily trafficked road that bisected the longest of its too-short runways. (Congress was arguing over the location of a replacement.) But the air station was only a ten-minute ride from downtown, and the Boy Scouts who had gathered in Washington poured across the river to see him in, swarming around the celebrated pitcher before he sped off to a radio station to announce his arrival.

On the mound, Dean shut out the American League All-Stars for the first two innings, but in the third, Gehrig followed DiMaggio's single with a home run. Then with two men out, Cleveland center fielder Earl Averill smashed a line drive at Dean's feet. Only after the lean right-hander returned to the dugout did anyone realize that the ball had caromed off his left big toe—and fractured it. ("Fractured, hell, the damn thing's broken!" he said.) Barely two weeks later, he returned to the mound too soon, and the pain affected his delivery, which ruined his arm, ending his storybook career.

The American League ran away with the game, 8–3, but its success was due to more than the superiority of its roster. The younger and cockier league had won three of the four previous All-Star contests because it had cared more about winning the game than about using as many players as possible to please the fans. This time, the league's All-Star manager, Joe McCarthy of the New York Yankees, left ten of the ballplayers on the bench, including sluggers Jimmie Foxx and Hank Greenberg, while he maximized his own powerful Yankees, who were heading for their second of four consecutive world championships. As Franklin Roosevelt looked on "perhaps wistfully," sportswriter Shirley Povich noted in the *Washington Post*, "McCarthy packed the All-Star lineup with five of his own Yankees, thus gaining a 5-to-4 majority."


MASTERY OF THE Senate's proceedings lay in the mastery of its parliamentary rules, and nobody knew the rules more thoroughly than Joe Robinson did. On the president's Court bill, his head counts still showed sufficient votes to approve a compromise, but nothing like the two thirds required to block a filibuster. The rat-a-tat-tat of opponents' questions on the opening day of debate had thrown Robinson's troops off stride, and he saw no choice but to apply the rules as a bludgeon. Upon his return to the Senate on July 8, shortly after it convened, he made his move.

Long lines had formed outside the Senate gallery door; an hour's wait earned a few minutes of debate. Part of the allure on the sizzling day was the air conditioning inside the chamber. (Installation of an air conditioning plant to cool the rest of the Capitol and the House and Senate office buildings was soon to begin.) Yet the tourists and the others in line were drawn not only by creature comforts but also by the affairs of state. Everyone had an opinion about the Court fight, sometimes two or three.

"Let me say to the senator from Montana that I have great respect for his ability"—jowly Marvel Logan of Kentucky was arguing in favor of the compromise—"and there is no one more sorry than myself to see the company he is with at this time, when apparently he has turned his back on everything he has ever stood for since he has been in the Senate, and is lending aid and comfort to those who, he knows, would destroy the government if—"

When Wheeler rose to disagree, Joe Robinson broke in, "I rise to a point of order." An administration stalwart, Key Pittman of Nevada, the Senate's president pro tempore, sat in the presiding officer's chair. Robinson had prepared him, and Pittman explained Rule XIX, which stated that a senator who had the floor could yield it to a colleague only for a question—not for a statement or a speech—or else risked losing the right to keep talking.

Wheeler shouted, "I do not know anybody on this floor who violates that rule more than does the senator from Arkansas!"

"I never violate any rule when I am required to conform to it," the majority leader replied, "and am now seeking to require my good friend the senator from Montana to conform to the rule."

"From now on," Wheeler retorted, "we shall require the senator from Arkansas, as well as every other senator, to conform to that rule."

"I shall be very glad to do so," Robinson said. "The rule of the Senate is well defined, however, and it is my intention to invoke it."

This was not the only parliamentary restriction that Robinson meant to enforce. Another Senate rule, also usually ignored, limited each senator to two speeches on a given topic in any single day, which Pittman vowed to define as a "legislative day." Robinson squeezed further by announcing that he would continue the same "legislative day" for the duration of the debate, by ordering a recess instead of an adjournment when the session ended each evening. As a result, no senator would be allowed to speak about the Court bill more than twice, no matter how many days—or weeks—the debate went on. And if these measures failed to defeat a filibuster, Robinson threatened to keep the Senate in session around the clock.

In retaliation, Wheeler pledged to block all other business on the Senate floor. He had already refused to yield the floor when a colleague asked to introduce a new farm bill. But there was little else he could do. The next two hours were a slugfest of parliamentary arguments, rhetorical barrages and counter barrages, long-winded questions that resembled speeches, unceasing interruptions, then inevitable squabbles over who held the floor.

In the galleries, the Boy Scouts in their summer uniforms and the tourists in linen jackets or summery frocks stared down in silence at the unsightly spectacle of the legislative process. Veteran reporters had seen nothing so ugly in years. "[N]ot the 'great national debate' which had been forecast," Arthur Krock tut-tutted, "but a fusillade of 'dead cats.'"

At noon the next day, the chamber showed a nervous excitement. Knowing that Wheeler was about to take the floor, ninety-one of the ninety-six senators answered to their names. Lulu and their eldest daughter, Elizabeth, sat in the gallery, as they had every day, as Wheeler rose at his desk just behind Joe Robinson's left shoulder. Wheeler still believed that oratory could change a senator's mind, and it was clear that the parliamentary rules he had assailed meant he could keep on speaking almost without interruption. Three hours would pass before he sat down.

He began, as he often did, on the low road. He used an epithet of his native New England—the broad vowels and intrusive r's still flattened his speech—in denouncing the other side's tactics. "It was *cheap* for the secretary to the president of the United States to say, 'One down and five to go.' It was cheap"—his voice was low and harsh—"for the postmaster general to say, 'We have it in the bag.'" Wheeler turned beet red as he spoke, and his linen suit was limp with perspiration. "It was cheap, I say, to appeal to members here and say, 'You rode in on the president's coattails, and now you owe it to him to vote as he wants you to vote.' It was cheap to say, 'You are going to break the president's heart unless you vote for this bill.'"

But then Wheeler rose to the moment. Daniel Webster and Henry Clay belonged to a distant age, and their classical, cultivated style of rhetoric had given way to plainer speaking. "There is not a Patrick Henry among them," an observer of the Seventy-fifth Congress had lamented. However, Wheeler harkened back to the past and invoked the Founding Fathers, applying the weight of history to the issue at hand. He cited Jefferson's dictum that "the judicial power ought to be distinct from both the legislative and executive, and independent of both." From George Washington, he borrowed the curse of "usurpation." The people could change the constitutional balance, if they liked, through the mechanism of an amendment ratified by the state legislatures, with their presumed proximity to the popular will. This Wheeler could accept as a means to enlarge the Court—but not by allowing two of the government's branches to impose their will on the third. "'For though this in one instance may be the instrument of good,'" Wheeler quoted George Washington, "'it is a customary weapon by which free governments are destroyed.'"

He acknowledged that Congress possessed the constitutional power to expand the Supreme Court, or even to withhold the justices' salaries—or the president's. These were within the letter of the Constitution, but not its spirit. "Why have a written Constitution at all?" he said. "We have one, my friends, because my forefathers, like the forefathers of most of the senators, had left foreign shores, where they had seen the tyranny of one-man government in Europe." In safeguarding the liberties won by blood and treasure, the framers of the Constitution had in mind the fate of Mary, Queen of Scots, who was denied the right to confront her accusers before her beheading in 1587; and of the six farm laborers banished from England in 1834 because they had petitioned for higher pay; and of the European armies that quartered troops in citizens' homes. "Oh, but it is said, 'What has that to do with the Court-packing bill?' If four men can be put upon the supreme bench to override the Constitution of the United States in one particular, they can say as to every other provision of the Constitution of the United States that it shall be inoperative. They can say whatever they choose to say, and make the Bill of Rights become as nothing to the people of this country."

This was more than a lesson in history. To Wheeler, the danger was present and clear. "Why should we be zealous about this cause? When we look at world affairs we realize that in Germany there is a dictator, under whose iron heel are seventy million people. How did he come into power?" Wheeler's relentlessness was mesmerizing. "He came in under the constitution of Germany. Every step that was taken by him at first was taken in a constitutional way. Mr. Hitler acted to meet the needs of the times. Mussolini came into office upon the plea that he would improve economic conditions and he assumed the power of a dictator and abolished the legislative body of Italy and set up his own court, in order that he might meet the needs of the times in that country. In every place where a dictatorship has been set up, it has been done in order to meet the needs of the times."

THROUGH THE OPENING week of debate, despite ample provocation, Joe Robinson had remained cool and imperturbable. Every time he rose at his desk and claimed a point of order, Wheeler or one of his followers made sure to ask if the majority leader was obeying his own unmerciful rules. Wheeler had spoken on Friday, and the Senate met again on Saturday, but on Sunday, Joe Robinson rested, or tried to. His wife, Billie, had gone to Arkansas to tend to her ill brother, the first time in ages that she and her husband had been apart. Ordinarily she was always at his side, counseling him on the Senate's best course, planning their weekend jaunts by automobile.

The heat wave in Washington had continued. Every day, two or three Washingtonians died because of the mercury climbing into the midnineties—a total of ten in recent days, hundreds nationwide. "People in Washington are committing suicide to escape the heat," a congressman wrote to a friend. Robinson's tiny apartment, without cross-ventilation, felt like an oven. His energy had always been legendary, but now he was exhausted and dejected. He had scarcely eaten anything solid since Thursday, subsisting mostly on buttermilk. The tensions of debate and the legislative labyrinth had ruined his digestion.

Joe Robinson stood at the fulcrum of the U.S. Senate. Its members confided things in him that they told no one else, and they were willing to do favors for him alone; in turn, he was careful not to share everything he knew. "You could never tell a president of the United States the truth," he complained to an intimate in the White House. The majority leader had passed the word that he counted fifty-one votes in favor of a compromise to add as many as four justices over four years' time. But he had not mentioned that three or four of those votes were personal pledges to him. (Publicly, the administration had claimed fifty-four votes.) The survey that Robinson shared with Joe Keenan—and nobody else—listed only forty-five senators as "Pretty Sure Pro," which was four votes short of a majority, now that the vice president was unavailable to break a tie. Thirty-nine senators were labeled "Pretty Sure No!" This ran surprisingly close to Wheeler's own survey, which showed forty-two senators opposed to the compromise he had maligned as "slow packing." That was too few senators to defeat it but more than enough to continue a filibuster without having to say so. Then Wheeler could ask the Senate to send the compromise back to the Judiciary Committee, supposedly to be reworked—an easier vote for a nervous senator than having to kill the bill outright.

In his four and a half years as the majority leader, Robinson had rarely lost a showdown on the Senate floor; if he lost this one, he knew that his boyhood ambition, the justice's seat so tantalizingly within his reach, would doubtlessly fall forever beyond his grasp.

When he returned to the Capitol on Monday, the majority leader felt refreshed. Outside the Senate chamber, the corridors held the largest crowds yet; inside, members of the House of Representatives had gathered along the back wall, having heard that Joe O'Mahoney planned to speak his piece. The first-term Democrat from Wyoming abandoned his desk in the next-to-last row and stood in the front, near the majority leader's desk, and faced his colleagues. With his flattened skull and his deeply set and serious eyes, O'Mahoney made up in earnestness and spunk what he lacked in physical command. Like Wheeler, he was a Massachusetts native who had found his true home in the West, as a fierce New Dealer with a booming voice. Having worked for Jim Farley as the party's vice chairman and then as the top assistant postmaster general until late 1933, O'Mahoney had been considered an administration loyalist, not the least because—as Farley had thoughtlessly reminded him—of the federal subsidies for the sugar beet crop back home. His straying to the opposition had hurt.

He delivered the first cogent analysis of the proposed compromise that the Senate had heard. It would centralize the judiciary to an unprecedented extent, he maintained, because of the provision authorizing the chief justice to dispatch judges into districts with congested dockets. He questioned the discretionary language that said the president "may"—not "shall"—name an additional justice for every incumbent who turned seventy-five. Could a president, whether for reason of strategy or political extortion, allow the nominations to accumulate? And O'Mahoney wondered about the wisdom of granting such power to future presidents less to New Dealers' liking. Joe Robinson kept interrupting with questions, though he seemed to wilt by the end.

"Certainly not since the League of Nations fight has the *Congressional Record* been enriched with greater eloquence and logic than fell from the lips of Senators Wheeler, McCarran, O'Mahoney and Bailey," a columnist wrote. "Their speeches are likely to be bracketed with those of the Webster-Calhoun-Clay era." Bailey was Josiah Bailey of North Carolina, whose peroration had followed O'Mahoney's. A bony, bespectacled, priggish-looking former editor of the *Biblical Recorder*, he had supported FDR in 1932 and in 1936 but had recently soured on the New Deal, mainly because of its trespasses against states' rights. He had been preparing this speech for weeks, and as he rose to begin, senators summoned their colleagues from the cloakroom. Bailey held forth with his customary melodramatics, shouting his points, banging his desk, shaking a preacher's finger. The southerner was offering an argument that was calculated to appeal to his colleagues from the North—that "the Negroes in the South feel secure tonight because they know there is a Constitution and an independent Court"—when Joe Robinson slipped away.

He was feeling ill, and not only physically. He retreated across a corridor from the Senate chamber to the senators' reception room, which was meant as a meeting place for the lawmakers and their constituents, its décor so baroque and lushly colored as to impress the supplicants of their representatives' worth. He telephoned Joe Keenan, the attorney general's aide, who had finished an early lunch with Robinson in the Senate secretary's office, troubled that the majority leader was taking on too much. "Bailey's in there and he's making a great speech," Robinson despaired. "He's impressing a lot of people, and I tell you I'm worried." Then Henry Fountain Ashurst happened in, and Robinson complained of a sharp pain in his breast. The Judiciary chairman dispatched two youngsters to bring hot water and bicarbonate of soda—"which appeared to relieve him," Ashurst said later.

Joe Robinson moved next door to the small but flamboyant Vice President's Room, ornately painted and luxuriantly tiled, and then he ventured out onto the veranda that faced north toward Union Station in hopes of finding some fresh air and shade. But when he left the air conditioning and stepped outside, "the hot air hit me," he told a senator the next day. "I had terrible pains in my chest." In the heavy heat, he curled his massive torso into a wicker rocking chair, then called for a page and asked him to fetch Sherman Minton from the Senate floor. The headstrong Indiana senator, only two years in office but already one of the majority leader's lieutenants, had delivered an effective response ("I am unwilling to have the balance of power reside thus in the hands of Mr. Justice Roberts") to Wheeler's opening oration. What Minton saw on the veranda scared him: Robinson's face had darkened, and he was gasping for breath. "I've got a terrible pain here," Robinson said, pounding his chest. "Go in and tell Alben Barkley to take over for the rest of the day. I've got to go to my room." Barkley, a folksy Kentuckian, was the assistant majority leader, comfortable in the rough-and-tumble on the Senate floor. When he hurried out to the porch, Robinson told him he had "had a little flurry" in his chest and was going home for a rest.

Robinson wondered whether he ought to see a physician, and Barkley urged him to. The Capitol had had a physician of its own since the 1920s, when twenty congressmen died in a single year, but the quality of the medical care was uneven at best. Robinson contacted his own doctor, a colonel in the Army Medical Corps and a personal friend, and went home to rest.

Home for Robinson was a fourth-floor apartment hardly a hundred yards away from the Capitol, situated directly between the Senate Office Building and the Supreme Court's marble palace. The bland beige Methodist Building, named for the denomination whose politically minded members had paid for it, appealed to lawmakers who cared more for convenience than for ostentation. Robinson's apartment looked down on the roof of the Court, and as he entered, its hot, lifeless air felt like a blow to his brain. That evening he went to an air-cooled movie house with an old friend who was visiting from Little Rock. Afterward, Robinson still felt unwell, and his Arkansas friend stayed at the apartment overnight.

Robinson felt better the next morning and returned to work, meeting with an illustrator for the *New York Times*, who noticed nothing out of the ordinary as he sketched the majority leader smoking a big black cigar and leaning back in his vast leather chair. As he posed, Robinson discoursed on the leading issue of the day. "I would hate to think that when the founders of this country got together to give us a Constitution, they were so blind to the future that they did not foresee that great changes would come over this country," he said. "I am sure that when the Supreme Court was created by the framers of the Constitution, they intended that it should in no way attempt to thwart the will of the people." Afterward he met with thirty Democratic senators who backed the compromise bill, even as three more were showing signs of slipping away; his latest count put forty-three senators in favor, forty-four opposed, and nine who were anyone's guess. He asked each of the steadfast senators to speak in favor of the compromise now that the opposition was "cutting [it] to pieces." He turned to Ashurst and said, "Henry, when will you speak?"

"My physician will tell you when I may speak," the silver-tongued senator replied, "and you, Joe, should not speak unless your physician permits." Ashurst added, "Joe, I wish you'd go to see my doctor."

Robinson went home and spent most of the afternoon in bed. The elevator boy looked in and offered to stay, but the senator said he was "quite all right." His secretary, Joseph Brewer, stopped by at about six o'clock and left assured. The heat had eased a little, into the midseventies overnight, though a summer's night in Washington could feel heavier than the daytime. The majority leader put on pajamas and crawled back into bed, the latest *Congressional Record* in his hands. The bedroom was no larger than ten feet by fifteen, and its two narrow windows overlooked the building that housed his lifelong desire. At maybe an hour past midnight, he swiveled out of bed, got to his feet, and headed for the bathroom, carrying the *Congressional Record*. His eyeglasses lay on the bed.

He took a single step.

The next morning, the maid arrived at her usual early hour, brewed the senator's coffee, prepared his breakfast, and waited for him to emerge. He was always punctual, and she wondered if he had overslept. She went to his bedroom to waken him. The lamp was on, but no one was in sight. She could see that the bathroom was empty. She rushed for the elevator boy and asked him if the senator had gone out. Together, they returned to the apartment. On the far side of the bed, the president's last hope of victory lay crumpled on the floor.

# CHAPTER EIGHTEEN

# Burial

"IT IS WITH deep grief that I rise to announce the death of my late colleague and the majority leader of this body."

The woman who was now the senior senator from Arkansas stood at her desk in the back row on the Senate floor. Hattie Caraway had succeeded her late husband, and her relationship with Joe Robinson had been strained, in part because of disputes over patronage, publicity, and policy—she was far more progressive than he—but mainly because Huey Long, Robinson's party rival, had been instrumental in her being reelected to the Senate in 1932. She usually dressed in black, and at noon on July 14 she had reason to. The chamber was crowded with senators, and it was customary on such occasions for the Senate to adjourn immediately and to offer its eulogies later, at a memorial session. This time the senators could not stop themselves.

Alben Barkley of Kentucky, who hoped to take Robinson's place, prayed aloud, "May God rest his militant soul," and Joe O'Mahoney of Wyoming extolled, "He was a brave man, he was a simple man, he was a loyal man, he was an able man." To the senators in mourning, the most affecting tribute was undoubtedly the opening one, because the subject was them. Royal Copeland, the physician-politician from Tammany Hall, recalled warning Joe Robinson that the Angel of Death was touching his elbow—"and I say in all seriousness to my brethren that the menace is here in this chamber today." Every senator was aware that ten of their number had died since 1933, five of them in the past year alone, two in automobile accidents, another in a plane crash, and Huey Long by an assassin's bullet. In Robinson's case, Copeland suggested that the Capitol's irregular air conditioning was also to blame. "We come to this chamber, which seems cold as we come into it," he said, "and the first impression is a shock to the system. We go from it into the heated air, with another shock. All the conditions of our lives make for the possibility of physical disaster. Then when are added the mental conditions incident to argument and dissension, as well as the combat of discussion . . ."

William Borah's wife offered a simpler explanation to the society writer for the *Washington Daily News*: Joe Robinson had died of a broken heart, physically if not metaphorically. He had suffered intermittent heart afflictions for nearly four years, and the recent pressures on him had been obvious to all. The consensus was that the impassioned battle over the Court had claimed its first death.

Burt Wheeler, so proud of his reputation for telling hard truths, went too far, stating the obvious in a manner too crude for anyone's good, especially his own, in a press statement issued later in the day. "Joe Robinson was both a political and personal friend of mine," it said. "Had it not been for the Court Bill he would be alive today. I beseech the President to drop the fight lest he appear to fight against God"—this last, an allusion to the Pharisees' self-admonition in the Book of Acts. His adversaries were aghast—"positively ghoulish," Harold Ickes decried—and even Wheeler's allies cold-shouldered him on the Senate floor for the next two or three days. "I was so emotionally upset" was all that he could explain in later years, but his rashness gave the White House an opening.

The president had learned of the Senate leader's death when Steve Early telephoned him at eight fifteen that morning. Still clad in pajamas, he immediately wrote a note to Mrs. Robinson in his thick, slashing strokes. "I am shocked and distressed beyond words—my old friend and associate of these many years—I just can't believe . . ." He wrote of Robinson's "conscience that knew no compromise," then crossed it out.

But in regard to the Court bill, he saw no reason to change his mind. Instead, he determined to take command himself. The next morning, he summoned Homer Cummings and Tommy Corcoran to his bedside and, unprompted, offered his own explanation for Joe Robinson's untimely demise. The always charming and genial president, famed for his first-rate temperament, placed the blame on Joe Robinson's anxious disposition. "He suggested that it was this very inability to take things calmly," the attorney general told his diary, "that proved the undoing of so many men."

If the president had not yet realized what he had lost, he was about to.

Cummings and Corcoran left, still holding tight to their mutual disdain, and half an hour later the facts started to make themselves clear. Four senators showed up at the White House, apparently without an invitation or a scheduled meeting, and asked to see the president. They were freshly elected Democrats, sent to Washington on the president's coattails, who had been souring on the Court bill. They were ushered into the upstairs study, where the shirt-sleeved president sat at his desk. As he often did when he saw a confrontation in the offing, he seized control of the conversation. For half an hour he related an incident during the 1928 presidential campaign, one that showcased Joe Robinson's fealty to the party and its leader. At last, Prentiss Brown of Michigan broke in.

"Mr. President, it's the hardest thing in the world to tell you something you don't want to hear," he said, "but we're here to tell you that we can't go along on the Hatch bill." They pleaded with the president to withdraw Carl Hatch's compromise and suggested others in its stead, but he resisted. Congress knew what he wanted, he replied, and it could deliver legislation to him in whatever form it wished. They took this to mean that they could act as they liked.

Without the majority leader's beloved and dominating presence, the number of senators committed to a compromise on the Court had slipped below fifty—and possibly below the forty-eight needed to win, now that the number of senators had declined to ninety-five. Sliding away, it appeared, were the three or four senators who had personally promised Robinson a "sort of last-minute help," in Cummings's words. After Alben Barkley thumbed through Robinson's papers and found mention of the personal pledges, he telephoned the president in alarm. The result was the letter that the president released to the press early that evening.

*My dear Alben* . . . As long as FDR lived in the White House, the avuncular Kentuckian would be known around Washington as "dear Alben." The president told him that villains he chose not to name (on the draft, he had scratched out "a few members of the legislative branch of the Government and on the part of some of the Press") had taken advantage "of what, in all decency, should be a period of mourning." Therefore, Roosevelt maintained, he must do the same, to clarify his position on judicial reform. He had already set forth his objectives, he wrote, ones that "the overwhelming majority" of Americans endorsed, but he had never insisted that his proposal was "sacred or final." Nonetheless, the courts needed younger judges, not only to help the aged ones but also—here, he merged the disingenuous reason with the true one—to keep "the social viewpoints of the courts abreast of changing conditions." Now Wheeler accused the White House of ghoulishness. "I cannot believe President Roosevelt could make political capital," he told a reporter, "out of tragedy such as this."

The political truce was over, and the battle had been joined once again. Four of the friendliest senators, including Barkley and Sherman Minton, visited the president at the White House to report in person on the dwindling Senate support. "It may have been at this meeting that the president ceased to rebel against reality," according to Joseph Alsop and Turner Catledge, journalists who interviewed everyone involved except the president, "and began to move towards his second attitude, that some means, any means must be found to make it seem he was not beaten."

A second battle had emerged over the Democratic senators' choice of their next majority leader. The campaign had been under way on the sly for two months, ever since Justice Van Devanter announced his resignation and Joe Robinson was expected to take his place. The president's "dear Alben" letter and its reference to Barkley as "the acting majority leader" suggested to the suggestible that the president had taken sides, as indeed he had, though he denied it. Barkley's main rival for the post, Pat Harrison of Mississippi, was a sarcastic old-timer whose support for the Court bill came with a wink; there was probably no more popular senator still living, but the White House had reason to worry that he would be his own man. Barkley, ever the good soldier, believed in party rule, and his supporters included the Senate's newcomers, its truest New Dealers, and anyone in the president's debt. So far the race was a standoff, and the president's advisers kept busy twisting senators' arms, ever reminded of how much had been lost with Joe Robinson's death. He had served as a bridge between the New Dealers and the southern conservatives, probably the only senator whom all of the party's factions—indeed, all of the parties—held in esteem. Robinson and Wheeler had always, to each other, been "Joe" and "Burt," no matter how high the decibels of their confrontations. The senators' affection for Joe Robinson had run deep, and their need for him even deeper.

This made the irony all the more pungent when Hattie Caraway

finished the sad forty-five-minute eulogy session by declaring, "As a further mark of respect to the memory of the deceased senator, I move that
the Senate do now adjourn." Without objection, the Senate agreed. The
adjournment, instead of a recess, ended the legislative day of July 6, which
had continued—because of Robinson's parliamentary wizardry—for eight
long days. And so the clock began again, in the rule that restricted a senator from addressing a particular topic more than twice in a day. The final
accomplishment of Joe Robinson's truncated life had been undone.

THE PRESIDENT WAS the last person to enter the Senate chamber,
on the arm of his military escort. Everyone remained standing until he
took his seat directly in front of the majority leader's desk. He looked gray
and drawn in his morning suit and silk top hat. To his left, the silvery casket occupied the spot in the green-carpeted well of the Senate where Joe
Robinson had delivered his last remarks. It was covered so completely with
gladioli, orchids, snapdragons, carnations, tiger lilies, and roses that it was
possible to forget for a moment what rested beneath.

This was only the fifteenth state funeral in the Senate chamber since
the Civil War, the first since Thomas Walsh, the Montana senator and attorney general–designate, died in 1933. The cabinet members sat behind
the president, and Pierce Butler, the only Supreme Court justice vacation-
ing near Washington—his brethren had scattered after the Court's term
ended in June—sat across the casket from the representatives of the executive branch. Robinson's heavily veiled widow carried a black fan and wept
silently nearby. Every senator's seat was filled, other than Joe Robinson's
red-leather chair, and scores of House members squeezed in along the
back wall. In the gallery, where admission required a ticket, Joseph P. Kennedy, the Maritime Commission chairman, sat in the front row of the section reserved for family and friends. Eugene Meyer, who had acquired a
mediocre daily, the *Washington Post*, at a bankruptcy auction four years
earlier, was behind him. (The *Post*'s own account misspelled his name as
"Myer.") Most of the men had left their formal dress in the closet in favor
of a linen summer suit. Mrs. Roosevelt sat in the members' gallery.

The funeral, like the decedent, eschewed all flourishes. No eulogy
was delivered. The soprano from the National Presbyterian Church on

Connecticut Avenue sang sweet hymns, and the Senate chaplain recited passages from Scripture—"*For I reckon that the sufferings of the present time are not worthy to be compared with the glory which shall be revealed in us*"—and offered Episcopal prayers for a Methodist. The president bowed his head and shielded his eyes with his hands. Afterward, he greeted the senators in the President's Room, near the Senate floor.

That evening, the casket was taken to Union Station and loaded onto the last car of the special twelve-car train, for the overnight cortege to Little Rock. Thirty-eight senators boarded, including Alben Barkley and Pat Harrison, along with twenty-three House members and a dozen reporters. At the last minute, Jim Farley and Joe Keenan decided to join them, but one man was conspicuous by his absence. The president's advisers had begged him to go, knowing how resentful the senators would feel if he stayed behind in Washington. But he refused to be persuaded—missing, yet again, the correcting presence of Louis Howe. First he cited the crisis in the Far East, where Japan had landed troops in northern China and threatened to march on the city gates of Peiping, the capital. Then he objected that the trip would set a precedent, requiring a president's attendance at any lawmaker's grave. His advisers took his disingenuous refusals as a measure of his antipathy toward Congress. The lawmakers did the same.

The powerful diesel locomotive arrived in Little Rock by seven thirty the next morning. Talk of politics filled the Pullman compartments, and murmurs of "Is it Harrison?" and "Is it Barkley?" got muffled in the carpeted aisles. Wheeler conferred with most of his steering committee and decided to provoke a showdown once they returned to Washington, by proposing to send the compromise Court bill back to the Judiciary Committee, as a means of burying it. Joe Keenan conversed with as many senators as possible and hinted at changes in the compromise, even to the extent of exempting the septuagenarians already on the bench from having new justices appointed alongside them—nullifying, in effect, the Court plan's very purpose. Yet his presence seemed to annoy his targets of persuasion, mindful as they were of his additional role at the Justice Department involved in selecting judicial nominees, a subject dear to every senator's heart. Keenan would return to Washington by airplane.

In Little Rock, Joe Robinson's mortal remains were delivered first to his own home, a many-gabled house on Broadway, where Hattie Caraway greeted callers at the door. Thousands of people lined the route to the State House. For three hours the casket lay open in the rotunda, and John Nance Garner led the members of Congress past. The vice president had motored from Texas and planned to return to Washington on the special train, one thing he could still do for his friend. As he approached the casket, he averted his head, for he preferred to remember the laughing and jovial Joe.

The church funeral was simple and informal, and then nature intruded. As the hearse entered the cemetery, the sizzling sun gave way to clouds, then to thunder and flashes of lightning and, just as the casket reached the gravesite, a torrent of rain. The family and the pallbearers crowded under a cover, and most of the two thousand mourners rushed to their cars, while Jack Garner and a few others stood their ground. With a sun-baked hand, Cactus Jack brushed away the water that teemed down his weathered face.

The vice president was a small-town ex-banker and pecan grower, by instinct an antimonopolist and a skeptic of overbearing capitalism, yet suspicious toward the New Deal and its centralizing instincts—"a labor-baiting, poker-playing, whisky-drinking, evil old man," as John L. Lewis would famously describe him, to the president's delight. Garner's father had insisted that he always tell the truth, and he prided himself on doing just that. His capacity for honesty, like Robinson's, in a city that valued half-truths, had made him the shrewdest of politicians, formerly as the House Speaker and now as the Senate president. The president's advisers blamed him for sabotaging the Court bill, and the distaste was reciprocal.

After the funeral, for the journey back to Washington, Garner took up residence in the rear car of the train, in place of Joe Robinson's remains. He shed his coat and his soaked-through shirt and called to a porter, "Boy, bring me some branch water." Senator after senator stopped in, and Garner probed and prodded the men he had understood so well for so long. Similar conversations about the Court bill—whether to add two justices instead of four, to abandon any limit on age, to leave the current justices untouched—were going on all over the train, with Jim Farley at the center or Alben Barkley or Pat Harrison.

When the train paused in southern Ohio, at Chillicothe, the news of a defection on the Court bill raced through the cars. Herbert Lehman was more than the governor of New York. He had been the lieutenant governor to Roosevelt and was still a friend and ally of the man he had succeeded, an impeccable liberal, a stalwart of the New Deal. But his brother, a judge on New York's highest court, had kept telling him that he had a responsibility to speak up if he could prevent a miscarriage of justice. At last, the governor sent a letter to Senator Robert Wagner, denouncing the Court bill as a "greatly dangerous precedent," and released it to the press. "Roosevelt was very much incensed and hurt," Sam Rosenman said. His supporters aboard the train of mourning tried to hide their disappointment, but by the time the Capitol-on-wheels rolled into Union Station just before midnight, Garner understood where his duty lay.

AT A QUARTER past nine the next morning, the twentieth of July, the vice president returned to the White House. During his five and a half weeks away, his disrespect for the president's constitutional judgment had become the capital's common wisdom. The front-page headline in the *Washington Post* reported, "Gov. Lehman's Attack on Court Bill Spurs New Fight in Senate." Garner hoped to prevent it.

The president saw him right away. Franklin Delano Roosevelt and John Nance Garner disapproved of each other, and they had every good reason. Their backgrounds could not have differed more. One was the son of landed gentry in New York, educated at Groton and Harvard; the other, a Confederate cavalryman's son, born in a log cabin in the Red River Valley, whose hazy boyhood education had proved no impediment to becoming a lawyer and a country banker. The lush woods along the Hudson had produced a sophisticate who reveled in conversation and excelled at it; the arid ranchlands of South Texas had molded "that sphinx of sphinxes," as a newspaper called Garner, who understood the uses of silence. Roosevelt would plot his path, though more by instinct than by planning, in the belief that artful deception could offer the straightest line to an objective; he played the protagonist and expected other people to react to him. Garner relied on his knowledge of his fellow men, of their longings and vulnerabilities, to intuit how to get his way with them. As the Senate president, he had begun to convene a Board of Education, like the one he had hosted as the House Speaker, inviting convivial senators in for a whiskey or two and some educational conversation (though these had ceased in 1936, after Garner opposed the president's election-year desire for deficit spending). He was a man without pretense, a tightwad with common tastes. As vice president, he and his wife took three rooms in the moderately priced Hotel Washington, barely a block from the White House, and ate their breakfasts and dinners in the coffee shop.

The Roosevelt-Garner ticket had been a marriage of convenience. Garner, conservative and isolationist, had run for president in 1932 as publisher William Randolph Hearst's fondest hope. Roosevelt's drive for the presidential nomination, which required two thirds of the convention delegates, had been stymied by the doubts of the South, and his chances of escaping a deadlock after the third ballot lay in luring Garner's supporters. As vice president, he operated on Capitol Hill as a "fifth wheel," by his own description, in steering the New Deal's social legislation through the Senate. Except possibly for Joe Robinson's, Garner's influence with the senators was considered to be unmatched. Inside the White House, his presence at cabinet meetings eventually ended once the president became convinced that Garner had "told a few cronies, then others" about what had happened inside. His influence, however, with the "Boss" was about to reach its peak.

The president greeted him warmly, and Garner's statement that he wished to talk about the Court bill prompted a nod.

"Do you want it with the bark on or the bark off?" Garner said. The president did not understand what he meant, and Garner explained the Texas colloquialism that distinguished between shades of candor.

"The rough way," Roosevelt said with a laugh.

Garner told the president that he lacked the votes in the Senate, that he was beaten. Roosevelt still believed the public was on his side, that an obstreperous Senate was his antagonist, just as it had been to Woodrow Wilson in his crusade for a reorganization of the international order, through the League of Nations. But Garner told the president all that he had learned on the train from Little Rock, that Wheeler had rejected any talk of compromise, that too many senators were queasy. After an hour's conversation, the president authorized Garner to explore yet another compromise on Capitol Hill.

The vice president had returned to his office on the second floor in the Senate Office Building when Prentiss Brown of Michigan, a serious-minded ex-prosecutor, telephoned. Eight freshman Democrats, first elected in 1932 or since—and thus in the president's political debt—were meeting in Brown's office across the corridor. All of them were publicly uncommitted on the Court bill, and as they thrashed out their ambivalence, seven of them realized that they had made up their minds: they would vote to kill the compromise by sending it back to the Judiciary Committee, unless the president accepted a bill that added no justices at all. Only Richard Russell of Georgia, a thirty-nine-year-old with promise, had pledged his vote to the White House and was unwilling to renege without the president's okay.

Their visit was "the *coup de grace*," in Harold Ickes's telling. The vice president went back to the White House at four thirty, with Alben Barkley and Pat Harrison in tow, to strengthen the message. They were pleasantly surprised at the president's willingness to take reality, at last, into account. For an hour and twenty minutes, Garner, the two senators, and the president talked over tactics for a face-saving escape. They reserved a decision until after a new majority leader was elected the next morning, but word sped around the capital that the president had abandoned his ambitions for the Supreme Court.

At ten o'clock on the morning of July 21, all seventy-five Democratic senators gathered in the Senate Caucus Room to choose their next leader. The morning's front pages deemed the Court bill to be the day's biggest news. (The *New York Times* announced, "Court Change to Be Shelved for Present, Capital Hears . . ." and the *Washington Post*, "Swing of 7 Senators Dooms Court Bill; Caucus to Pick Leader Today.") The senators deposited their ballots for majority leader into Carter Glass's battered panama hat. When the count reached thirty-seven for Alben Barkley and thirty-seven for Pat Harrison, the Senate clerk fumbled to unfold the final ballot. "I bit my pipe stem in two," Barkley told a friend later in the day, after he had learned that the seventy-fifth ballot bore his name. Tommy Corcoran claimed to have procured the decisive votes.

As soon as the word reached Garner that the caucus had finished its work, he rode the elevator to the fourth floor of the Senate Office Building, strode down the long, dimly lit corridor, and turned into Wheeler's

office. He had already shown his affection for the president's leading opponent at a March luncheon in Joe Robinson's office, when he had clapped
Wheeler on the back and cried, "Burt, you're a real patriot. The day is
coming where we'll have to go down to the White House and tell the
president so."

The vice president stared across Wheeler's paper-strewn desk and
asked the Montanan if he would agree to two additional justices.

"Jack, I won't give you two," Wheeler said. "I won't give you one." The
senator had no reason not to press his advantage.

"Well, that's out. What about this idea of a roving judge?" The compromise bill would authorize the chief justice to assign lower-court judges
to preside over particular cases in judicially congested circuits.

"You don't want a roving judge, Jack." Wheeler argued that a vindic-
tive attorney general—such as Harding's man, Harry Daugherty—could
arrange for a politically dependable judge to pursue anyone the authorities
considered a threat.

"That's out," the vice president said. "What about a proctor?" Wheeler
was equally dismissive. The compromise, like the president's original bill,
adopted the notion from old English law of an administrator to prescreen
cases before the Supreme Court decided whether to hear the appeals—
placing too much power, Wheeler warned, in one person's hands.

Garner puffed on his cigar. "Well, go to it and God bless you," he said
at last. "Burt, write your own ticket."

This was the moment that the White House accepted defeat. Wheeler
smiled a genuine smile and said, "All right, Jack."

The president's men were furious at Garner. "The best bargain was
not made," the attorney general groused to his diary. "Some persons of a
cynical nature have remarked that [Garner's] idea of a compromise was to
surrender." The vice president was dropped from the list of intimates
privileged to lunch with the president at his desk.

Wheeler was so excited that he was almost trembling. He telephoned
one or two friends and then found Josiah Bailey of North Carolina, the
stern ex-preacher, in the Senate restaurant. Together they ventured to Garner's office in the Capitol for further discussion, then strolled back across
to Wheeler's office. They opened the door to room 421 and stood amazed.
Twenty-seven senators opposed to the president's Court bill had crowded

into the dreary anteroom, chattering, sprawling on chairs, and chewing on cigars. As Wheeler entered, they swarmed all over the man of the hour.

SINCE AIR CONDITIONING had been installed in the Senate and House chambers, important committee rooms, and parts of the Senate and the second House office buildings, it was no longer necessary in the summer to tie starched sheets of wrapping paper to the backs and seats of the chairs to keep the senators from sticking to the leather. All eighteen members of the Judiciary Committee met behind closed doors at ten o'clock the next morning, in their quarters on the ground floor of the Capitol. Against all precedent, the vice president joined them and, even more surprisingly, he delivered a speech. The topic was an odd one, given the presence of the four Republicans: the need for the Democrats to make peace. As the party's leader, the president had to be spared any unnecessary "kicks in the face," Garner lectured. "This thing has split the party and has the country turned upside down. We must have party harmony for the country's good."

"I think that's very important, too," Republican William Borah broke in, and the Democrats laughed.

The presence of two other visitors underscored the vice president's hopes. Alben Barkley, the new majority leader, was seated at the long dark table, along with Burt Wheeler. At Wheeler's urging, Garner outlined the settlement they had reached, while Joe O'Mahoney served as a scribe. In a loopy cursive penciled on a Senate notepad, the New Dealer from Wyoming jotted down the terms of the president's capitulation, a mirage of a judicial reorganization plan, hardly enough to save face:

*No change in S.C.*
*No proctor*
*No roving judge*
*Direct appeal to S.C.* [when constitutionality of a law was at stake]
*Intervention of A.G. in cases involving constitutionality of statutes*
*Assignment of judges by Senior Circuit Judge*
*New judges on basis of need not age*

Days later, a New York lawyer offered a hundred dollars for the page of notes, but O'Mahoney declined.

As the committee members pored over the details, Alben Barkley asserted his freshly acquired authority. He insisted that the earlier compromise remain on the legislative calendar until the new one was ready, which unleashed anger from around the table that reduced the new majority leader to silence. "You'll get the party harmony you are looking for," Pat McCarran of Nevada snapped, by keeping Jim Farley in the post office. He accused Farley of grooming a Democrat to run against him in Nevada in 1938, and he asked for a promise of no political reprisals. Garner agreed, and so did Barkley, as far as they could personally guarantee. Everyone understood how flimsy an assurance that was; the president and Jim Farley would decide.

The chaos of conversation prompted Ed Burke of Nebraska to propose that the committee ask the Senate to let it rewrite the Court bill in accord with the scribbled understanding. When Barkley strenuously objected, the ever-conciliatory chairman, Henry Ashurst, broke in, "Senators, senators, let the Chair state that we did not meet here today to take any action." Too many senators begged to differ. They brushed Barkley aside, and Ashurst, too. The respect for the legitimacy of hierarchy had collapsed. All but two of the committee's members agreed that the Supreme Court was to remain untouched—no additional justices, no word about new blood. The lower courts would add judges, but not on the basis of age and only in districts or circuits where the dockets had overflowed. Judicial reorganization would be confined, that is, to the problems that the president had originally cited but never intended—a sly humiliation. Yet he was to be spared humiliation of another sort. When the Senate debated the wisp of a compromise, it was agreed, no one was to utter the treacherous term "Supreme Court."


AFTER FINISHING THEIR work, the committee members ascended to the Senate floor in time to hear an Episcopal minister's opening prayer. *"Bestow upon us such a measure of His spirit that we may make no compromise with wrong,"* the minister intoned. A mood of anticipation filled the chamber. House members collected on the couches in the rear, while the senators gathered in clusters. All but five of them answered to the call of their names. The privileged order of business was a motion to override the president's veto of a bill to keep interest rates low on federal mortgages to farmers. The Senate was expected to join the House in overriding the veto, and it did, by a lopsided vote of seventy-one to nineteen, but it was the glee that the senators showed in jilting the president that surprised the spectators.

Alben Barkley kept his seat when Marvel Logan of Kentucky stood in the second row and addressed the vice president in the presiding officer's chair, asking unanimous consent to make a motion to send the Court bill back to the Judiciary Committee "with the understanding that it would be instructed to report a bill for the reform of the judiciary within ten days." Barkley had refused to perform the chore himself, after the morning's parliamentary mutiny, and Ashurst had, too, so the committee asked the junior senator, who had served as his state's chief justice.

Then silence fell as Hiram Johnson of California struggled to his feet on the Republican side of the aisle, in the front row. Short and squat, he was old and ill but still unbowed, a bulldozer of a senator, without subtlety or sense of humor. Maybe no senator boasted such a pedigree of progressivism. As Teddy Roosevelt's running mate in the Progressive Party in 1912, as the governor whose pique had denied Charles Evans Hughes the presidency in 1916, the old warrior believed that the deference he was owed had earned him the right to say what he liked in whatever manner he wished. He had loathed the Court bill from the first.

"I desire to know what the judicial reform refers to," he exclaimed. "Does it refer to the Supreme Court or to the inferior courts?"

A spell was broken. Marvel Logan waved around Joe O'Mahoney's scrawled list and muttered that the committee's understanding of judicial reform "did not refer to the Supreme Court."

"The Supreme Court is out of the way?" The square-faced Californian would not be stopped. A gentleman's agreement to which he had never been a party meant nothing to him.

Logan's answer was firm and clear. "The Supreme Court is out of the way."

"Glory be to God!" Hiram Johnson proclaimed and sank back into his seat. The galleries exploded into applause and cheering, and Garner let them continue.

Then he asked for a vote on Logan's motion to return the president's bill to the Judiciary Committee to be rewritten, in effect, with invisible ink. At five minutes before three o'clock, on the afternoon of July 22, 1937, at Republican leader Charles McNary's urging, the Senate's clerk called the roll. The vice president made clear he wanted loyal senators to vote "aye." He left the rostrum momentarily to persuade Sherman Minton, the volatile young Hoosier, to go along. Some of the senators who had championed the president's passion to remake the Supreme Court saw themselves as the last defenders of a glorious lost cause. "No!" the diehards shouted out, in defiance of the president's surrender, and many of the "ayes" sounded grudging, provoking giggles in the galleries. After Ashurst voted to recommit the bill that he had sponsored but had disliked from the start, Carter Glass of Virginia handed him two handkerchiefs and chuckled, "You'll need both to wipe away your tears."

"I wish some day I could have a victory," Ashurst retorted with equal insincerity, "so I could prove I am just as gracious in victory as I am in defeat."

By a vote of seventy to twenty, an exaggeration of the Senate's true sentiment, the president's plan to expand the Supreme Court was buried.

# CHAPTER NINETEEN

# Victory

"OH, I DON'T know that any comment is necessary. I think it goes back—just for background . . ." The president looked cheerful yet resigned as the crowd of reporters gathered around his desk the next morning. "There was a lot of feeling in T.R.'s time," he was saying about his beloved cousin, "about the need for judicial reform and it took the form, in the 1912 campaign, of the Progressive Party asking for all kinds of things like recall of judges and overriding of decisions by popular vote." Again in 1924, "the elder Senator La Follette and Senator Wheeler, the La Follette-Wheeler ticket, ran on a platform that demanded all kinds of drastic things." The sarcasm was unmistakable. "The courts listened and they legislated"—the reporters laughed—"I mean they decided"—they laughed again—"it is the same thing. They made their decisions more on judicial lines than on legislative lines." But the fear instilled had lasted only so long. "The same thing had to be done again this year," the president asserted.

His history lesson ignored the Supreme Court's unrelentingly conservative record in the 1920s, during William Howard Taft's tenure as chief justice. Taft's Court could not have extended the bounds of laissez-faire any further; its interpretations of the Constitution's vague but powerful words could hardly have been narrower. The precedent that prevailed had been as conservative as a minimally fair-minded Court could have managed.

That had changed, the president insisted. He referred to a memorandum the attorney general had sent over that concluded, "The President has attained the most difficulty [*sic*] of his <u>objectives</u>, e.g., the liberalization of the interpretation of the Constitution." The reporters had lost none of their affection for a president who treated them with respect, and he patiently explained his position. Since the fifth of February, when he had announced his plan to reorganize the judiciary, the Court had reversed itself on three momentous precedents—all three legs, really, of the laissez-faire stool. In the minimum-wage cases, FDR observed, the Court had overturned its indulgent understanding of the liberty of contract (as a manifestation of the due process of law) to bestow upon government the authority to help the otherwise powerless workers to earn a living wage. Then, in preserving the Wagner Act, the Court abandoned its long-standing definition of "interstate commerce" to allow Washington a potentially powerful role in regulating the national economy. As the climax, in upholding the Social Security Act, the Court had unleashed the power of the national government to tax and spend for the purpose of furthering the general welfare.

All three of the changes in constitutional interpretation flowed from the Court's willingness to accept reality as the basis of its jurisprudence. Did the liberty of contract truly apply to the employee as well as to the employer? Were the operations of a factory or a mine disconnected, in fact, from interstate commerce? The president could hardly have hoped for any better answers from the Court. Even as judicial changes of heart were shifting power from the states to the national government, the ubiquity of crisis and the need for quick and coherent decisions had already shifted the power and initiative to the west, along Pennsylvania Avenue, away from the inefficiencies of Congress and toward the nimble and single-minded executive.

"A good part of that objective"—a turnabout in the Court's constitutional interpretation—"has already been obtained, temporarily," the president declared, without specifying how much remained. "I say, 'temporarily,' but I hope permanently." The Court's course still depended, to be sure, on the whim of Justice Roberts, but once a successor to Willis Van Devanter was named, Roosevelt could expect that the margin of constitutional safety would expand to six to three. "We lost the battle," he said in private again and again, "but we won the war."

Who had won it, however, was less clear. Justice Roberts had switched his vote on the minimum wage even before the president had announced, or even settled on, his plan to expand the Court. But the justice's subsequent changes of heart took place after the president had launched his assault on the Court, after the constitutional stalemate had jeopardized any solution to an economic crisis, after the chief justice had begun to fear for the future of his beloved institution and had surely shared his worries with his friends. Owen Roberts could well have kept such things in mind.

For once, the president's exquisite sense of political timing had failed him. "The thing that killed it," according to Sam Rosenman, speaking of the president's wish to enlarge the Supreme Court, "was Roosevelt's refusal to compromise, when there was still time to compromise." He might still have won the battle, at least a compromise, had Joe Robinson lived. "We could have had an eleven-judge Court with all the rest of the bill," Homer Cummings told his diary, "but we sinned away the day of grace." After they had won, the opponents of the compromise bill, apparently including Wheeler, acknowledged that they had been bluffing in predicting defeat for it—until Joe Robinson died. His personal influence with his charges, their affection and their trust, had given the sturdy Arkansan the ability to affect the nation's course, whenever the last few senators made the difference.

But no rationalizing could disguise the plain and painful outcome: the battle, if not the war, had been lost. FDR was seething inside. "That this was a terrific defeat for the President cannot be denied," Harold Ickes conceded. The newspapers called it the worst drubbing for a president since Woodrow Wilson's on the League of Nations, and this one had played out in much the same way: the Senate had rebuked a president unwilling to bend.

The explanations for his defeat, beyond the troubling implications of placing so much power into one person's hands, read like a catalog of Roosevelt's personal weaknesses. "It was a bitter pill for him," Rosenman recounted, "so soon after the glorious victory of his re-election. That it came largely from his own party made it more difficult to swallow. I do not think he ever did completely swallow it. Many mistakes were made during this fight: the mistake of overconfidence, the mistake of refusing to discuss the measure in advance with Congressmen, the mistake of stubbornness, the mistake of not personally leading the fight, as he did other fights. I think he later realized all the mistakes he had made." Harry Truman suggested another reason, one he would come to know closer at hand—"that growing ego of his, which notably wasn't too minuscule to start with."

As a result of the defeat, FDR was no longer invincible either with Congress or the public. Though 60 percent of Americans—and a majority in every region—still told pollsters that they were "for" him, the proportion that favored an unprecedented third term had slipped by 10 percentage points, from a majority in April to only 42 percent by the fall. "[H]is prestige especially suffered from the defeat of his plan to enlarge the Supreme Court," the pollster Elmo Roper explained in *Fortune*. On Capitol Hill, the Court fight had fractured the majority party, and the man who could best reunite it was gone. Alben Barkley was rough-and-tumble on the Senate floor, permitting no attack on the administration to go unanswered, yet he lacked the undertone of force that had made Joe Robinson so effective.

Soon Congress began to go its own way. In August, as an anticlimax, Congress passed the ghost of a judicial reorganization bill that authorized direct appeals to the Supreme Court of cases challenging a law's constitutionality, allowed the attorney general to intervene, and allowed circuit courts to assign district judges to places of judicial congestion—and nothing more, not even an increase in lower-court judges. Five important pieces of legislation meant to further the New Deal had been pending when the Court plan perished—to regulate workers' wages and hours, to reorganize the executive branch, to make loans for low-cost housing, to create TVA-like authorities in seven other river basins, and to find a constitutional means to control farm production. These expansions of the New Deal had been considered sure bets to become law, but by the time Congress adjourned at summer's end, only the housing bill had passed, and that was credited more to Senator Robert Wagner's legislative touch than to the president's. A special session in November proved less productive still. After the wage-and-hours bill failed, Frances Perkins would recall, "Most of the congressmen swept into office in 1936 had relied heavily upon the magic of Roosevelt's name, but the clamor against the Court bill and the fact that no one expected him to be a candidate for re-election in 1940—and therefore that his influence and authority over appointments would not be operative—had caused numerous defections."

These were not the only factors. A fatigue with the New Deal had set in—"already ample signs of a movement against the New Deal as a whole," the *Nation* lamented. And it was unarguable that the economic recovery had more than stalled; by the fall of 1937, the nation had slipped into a recession. The stock market plunged after the federal government cut back on its spending, and the unemployment rate spurted in months, from 14 percent to almost 19 percent. That meant another two and a half million Americans had been put out of work—more than ten million, all told—in what the newspapers called the "Roosevelt recession." The end to the Great Depression would have to await the buildup in munitions and manufacturing to get ready for another world war. Eventually the farm bill passed, and by mid-1938, so did the wage-and-hours bill, setting a minimum wage of forty cents an hour and requiring that workers get paid time and a half beyond forty hours a week. But it was the last New Deal law of consequence. Roosevelt's activist use of government as a remedy for society's ills had embedded itself into the nation's expectations, but the forward motion of the New Deal had, in reality, ceased.

SHORTLY PAST NOON on the third Thursday after the Court-packing plan had perished, John Nance Garner rapped the ivory cylinder on the desktop to gain the Senate's attention. He had noticed the messenger from the White House arrive through the door at the rear of the chamber and summoned him forward. Before the vice president could tear open the envelope, Henry Fountain Ashurst shot to his feet from his third-row desk, on the aisle, and asked for unanimous consent to "consider a message from the president of the United States." The Judiciary Committee chairman was alone in the chamber in already knowing the message's contents, except for one other person—the slightly built senator in the white double-breasted linen suit who sat hunched over his desk in the second row, to Ashurst's left.

"The message of the president of the United States—" Garner betrayed his surprise as he announced it—"is the nomination of an associate justice of the Supreme Court." He handed the document to the Senate's chief clerk, John Crockett, who started to read, "I nominate Hugo L. Black . . ."

A gasp passed through the chamber. Hugo Black, the senior senator from Alabama, seemed to flinch. He looked shaken as his colleagues surrounded him. He had learned of the nomination only the evening before. The president had made up his mind during the afternoon and invited the fifty-one-year-old, second-term senator to stop by the White House after dinner. At nine o'clock, in the study upstairs, the president pulled the formal-looking document—to submit a nomination to the Senate—from the clutter on his desk. He had already written in his decisive hand, *Associate Justice of the Supreme Court of the United States.* "Hugo," the president said, pointing to the blank, "I'd like to write your name here."

After Joe Robinson died, and the Court plan died with him, the president's first thought had been to wait until Congress went home and then to make a "recess appointment," a temporary ordination meant to last through the next session of Congress, without any need for Senate approval. The Constitution had authorized such a procedure a century and a half before, when a congressional recess truly left the lawmakers out of reach, but it had never been used to appoint a Supreme Court justice. It would surely embitter the senators, which carried an appeal of its own. But Burt Wheeler and a couple of other untrusting souls suspected his stratagem and publicly questioned the constitutionality of a recess appointment in the case of the Court, which prompted the president to back down. Roosevelt summoned Homer Cummings, who compiled a list of sixty candidates and pared it to seven, then to three. The gentlemanly solicitor general, Stanley Reed, was a loyal and reliable New Dealer, though hardly as militant a liberal as the president had in mind. The two others were senators, and their advantage was obvious: the custom of senatorial courtesy, a kindness-cum-blindness toward the Senate's own, almost assured confirmation. Sherman Minton of Indiana was an ardent enough New Dealer but obviously too high-minded in the current circumstance. Because he had demonized the justices during the battle over the Court, he decided he would find it embarrassing to sit among them, and he withdrew his name.*

That left Hugo Black. He was a provocative choice, one that "will certainly stir up the dry bones," as Homer Cummings surmised. A shopkeeper's son, born in an Alabama country cabin, by background he was a southerner's southerner, but politically he had fallen out of step. This may have dated to his boyhood, when a jury had acquitted the white youth who had killed Hugo's Negro playmate, or possibly it was the result of his lifelong self-education in history, economics, political philosophy, poetry—a

---

*President Truman asked Minton again a dozen years later, and he accepted.

book a day—that inspired an intellectual journey that moved him to the ideological left. During the fight over the Court, late at night in the Library of Congress, he pored over Adam Smith's *The Wealth of Nations*, the complete works of Thomas Jefferson, and the chronicles of the Constitutional Convention. He was a rarity in the South, a genuine liberal, even a radical, on almost everything but matters of race. His voting record on New Deal legislation had been perfect, twenty-four for twenty-four, and he had zealously favored the president's Court plan. A product himself of Tobacco Road, he cared deeply about helping the poor. For years he had pushed a bill to limit the workweek to thirty hours, on the premise that capitalism had reached its peak and that technology would cast an increasing number of Americans out of work. There was no more aggressive New Dealer the Senate would confirm. And he had another virtue that any president intent on revenge would savor: in the clubby Senate, he was widely disliked. A loner by nature, he could be cutting and cruel in debate, in ways that his adversaries did not forget. He was prosecutorial and partisan rather than dispassionate, a stranger to judicial temperament.

The president had written *Hugo L. Black, of Alabama* in the blank, and then told no one in the White House and not a soul in the administration other than Homer Cummings. Roosevelt spoke with Farley the next morning for an hour, but for the first time since 1933 left him in the dark about an appointment. The president showed Homer Cummings the sealed envelope, and they laughed about the surprise they were about to spring on the capital. "Jesus Christ," Steve Early muttered when he learned of it. The *Washington Post* reported "a complete surprise in every part of the city." Yet the president was about to discover, again, the price of secrecy.

Ashurst had learned of the envelope's contents from the Senate clerk who had accompanied the White House messenger. "It is an immemorial usage of the Senate that whenever the Executive honors this body by nominating a member thereof, that nomination is confirmed without reference to a committee," he entreated his colleagues, "because if we do not know him after long service with him, no one will ever know him." All too soon, he would prove himself right.

Bursting onto the Senate floor, Hiram Johnson objected to taking up the nomination immediately, as Ashurst had proposed. Not in half a century had such a request been thwarted, since the Senate dawdled over

Grover Cleveland's nomination to the Court of Lucius Quintus Cincinnatus Lamar, the former Mississippi senator who in 1861 had drafted his state's ordinance of secession. Hugo Black sat ashen-faced, his shoulders slumped, twisting a sheaf of papers in his hands.

Within a day, the murmurings began. In the Senate offices and cloakrooms, senators with long memories gossiped about the Alabaman's reputed past ties to the Ku Klux Klan. They passed around copies of the *Daily News*, a tabloid in the capital sympathetic to the New Deal, in which an article credited the Klan's support for Black's original election to the U.S. Senate in 1926 and claimed that—"according to ex-Klansmen who are his friends"—he had been a member. The nominee said nothing in public, but in private, he implied to his colleagues without ever saying so that he had once belonged to the Klan.

The president had known nothing of this, of course, nor had Homer Cummings. But Charlie Michelson had; as a reporter for the *New York World* in 1926, the party's publicity director had written articles about Hugo Black and the Klan. But nobody had asked him, nor any of the veteran senators who might have remembered. In their two-hour conversation, the president had not asked about the Klan, and Black had not volunteered a word. A special subcommittee approved the nomination without a hearing, and the full Judicial Committee argued bitterly but did the same. Confirmation was considered a certainty when the nomination reached the Senate floor on August 17.

The debate went on for six uncomfortable hours, while Hugo Black closeted himself in the secretary of the Senate's office nearby. Royal Copeland, as Tammany Hall's candidate for mayor of New York City, was eager for votes from Negroes and Jews. He begged the president "to withdraw this name and send us another, that of a New Dealer if you must, but one free from the taint of religious and racial prejudice," and otherwise he implored the Senate to question the nominee directly about any untoward connections. Only once before had a Supreme Court nominee suffered the indignity of a personal appearance—Harlan Fiske Stone, in 1925, to explain why he had agreed as the attorney general to reindict the senator from Montana, Burton K. Wheeler. Hauling Hugo Black before a Senate committee, however, meant putting a *senator* on trial—a frightening precedent. Few senators had any stomach for another ruckus over the Supreme

Court, especially waged against one of their own. They would accept their colleague at his word that he was not a member of the Klan.

The final roll call was an anticlimax. Sixty-three senators voted to confirm Hugo Black, and sixteen senators, including six Democrats, opposed him. (Carter Glass's "no" was the loudest.) The most telling votes were the sixteen that went uncast, including Wheeler's. He had been seen on the Senate floor—indeed, he had asked two or three technical questions—but when the roll was called, he had disappeared.

Another month passed before the *Pittsburgh Post-Gazette* published half a dozen articles reporting that Black had, in fact, belonged to the Klan from 1923 to 1925 and had received a "gold card" lifetime membership in 1926, three weeks after he won the Democratic primary, which was tantamount to election. Later it was learned that he had campaigned more than a hundred times robed in Klan regalia. But by then, the newest and youngest justice, who was almost eleven years Owen Roberts's junior, had been secretly sworn in and had sailed with his wife to Europe. Upon his return in late September, a few days before the Court was to convene, he spoke for eleven somber minutes over NBC's Blue and Red radio networks. "I did join the Klan," Justice Black said in a soft drawl. "I later resigned." In lieu of apology or explanation, he mentioned friends who were Negroes, Catholics, and Jews, and cited a senatorial record free of intolerance. The conservatives gloried in the New Dealers' discomfiture at finding themselves "stuck with a Kluxer," as columnist Westbrook Pegler exulted. Three days later, on the first Monday in October 1937, the ex-Klansman and devout New Dealer took his place on the nation's highest bench, seated at the chief justice's far left. He had given up his white robe, the wags said, for a tasteful black, as he embarked upon a thirty-four-year judicial career that would make him the greatest civil libertarian in Supreme Court history.

The president was silent in public about the predicament of his first Court appointment, and he said little to reporters, either on the record or off, other than "Get out your pencils," then started to read, "I know only what I have read in the newspapers." He had responded to his defeat on his plan to expand the Court by making the same mistake again, placing his penchant for surprise ahead of collaboration with Congress. That he survived this misjudgment may have emboldened him yet again in trying to reshape the capital more to his liking—while exacting his revenge.

His opportunity was the congressional elections of 1938. The president decided to intervene in the Democratic primaries, in hopes of reducing the ranks of conservatives—the "purge," as it became known. "The purge had its birth in Roosevelt's personal resentment at the two major legislative defeats dealt him by members of his own party," Sam Rosenman recounted, alluding to the Court bill and the failed 1937 special session. No president since Andrew Johnson had involved himself in particular congressional races. Democrats held seventy-four of the ninety-five Senate seats, fifteen more than when he entered office. Of the twenty-seven Democrats facing reelection, Roosevelt settled on ten, all of them conservatives, along with three members of the House Rules Committee he hoped to defeat in their party primaries. He personally involved himself in the campaigns against four of these, most strenuously in Maryland. Over Labor Day weekend he traipsed across the state alongside Millard Tydings's Democratic opponent though never mentioning the incumbent by name. Yet Tydings survived, and the president's three other senatorial targets did as well. The president's sole success was in terminating the political career of the House Rules Committee chairman, John O'Connor of New York, a Tammany Hall man, which was credited largely to Tommy Corcoran's efforts to unseat his fellow Irish American graduate of Brown University and Harvard Law School. Nor did the purge help the president with the nation's rank-and-file Democrats, who told pollsters by more than a two-to-one margin that they disapproved.

Perhaps the failure of the purge brought the president to his senses at last. The Supreme Court fight and the unburying of Hugo Black's past had demonstrated the dangers of trying to lead the country, in Louis Howe's absence, without confiding in anyone but Homer Cummings. In the purge of 1938, he tried to lead but found, once again, that not enough people would follow. "It's a terrible thing to look over your shoulder when you are trying to lead—and find no one there," FDR told Sam Rosenman, reflecting on a speech he delivered in the fall of 1937 that marked the beginning of the nation's gradual shift from an isolationist foreign policy toward a reengagement with a world menaced by dictatorships. In the course of the next four years, Roosevelt prepared a reluctant citizenry a step at a time for another world war. The Great War had left Americans with a deep aversion to foreign entanglements, and the protective oceans made the nation feel safe. But as events in Europe and the Far East spiraled out of any democracy's control, the president seemed to understand what lay ahead. "Roosevelt saw leadership in public life," Rosenman explained, "as the ability to see what is coming around the corner, to devise the best means of meeting it, and to win the people's approval to meet it."

That third feat—persuading the public—he had found the hardest to master, but his brilliant half measure, the Lend-Lease program in 1941, showed that at last he had learned how. Great Britain was in desperate need of weaponry and matériel, yet the American public was unwilling to countenance any direct aid. By framing the transfer of military equipment to America's closest ally as nothing more than a loan ("Suppose my neighbor's home catches fire, and I have a length of garden hose," he famously explained), the president asked no more of a war-wary public than it was willing to give. His legislative campaign was shrewd from beginning to end. He let members of Congress take the lead, and he made none of the mistakes that had plagued him in the Court fight. And he had already taken steps to prepare the way. When the Nazis swept across western Europe in the spring of 1940, he allowed the public reaction to develop before he addressed a joint session of Congress and the American people. Clearly the lessons he had learned from his spectacular failure to pack the Supreme Court mattered the most when the stakes were the highest.

# EPILOGUE

TO THE PRESIDENT'S chagrin, Senator Burton K. Wheeler would not face Montana voters again until 1940. FDR detested him as he detested few others, so he tried to make his displeasure known in other ways. Federal patronage for Montana was no longer to be funneled through the state's senior U.S. senator but through its two House members and through Anaconda Copper lobbyist Bruce Kremer, Homer Cummings's pal and Wheeler's bitter enemy.

This hardly stopped Wheeler from getting his way, however. As chairman of the Senate's Commerce Committee and the second-ranking Democrat on the Agriculture Committee, the federal bureaucracies were apt to pay attention to his requests. According to the Agriculture Department's own records, Wheeler's preferred applicants received thirteen jobs in 1938. Members of his own family fared just as nicely. "I do not have a son who was in the insurance business," the senator sniped, alluding to Jimmy Roosevelt's earlier career,* "nor has one of my sons married a du Pont heiress." Still, Wheeler's eldest son worked as a lawyer at the Justice Department, and the two younger sons, students at Harvard and Dartmouth, found summer employment at Glacier National Park, in Montana, where the senator kept his cabin. His oldest daughter, Elizabeth, had given up her $3,600 post at the Federal Housing Administration, earning almost three times as much as the typical factory worker, and her husband earned

---

*Jimmy Roosevelt admitted in *Collier's* in 1938 that he had used his name to sell insurance during his father's first term; under political pressure he released his income tax returns, and within months he was gone from the White House.

$4,400 at the Securities and Exchange Commission. Wheeler had hired his sister as his congressional secretary for $3,900 a year, while her son held a $3,800 investigator's job at the Bituminous Coal Commission.

Any president, even an unprecedently powerful one, was bound to exercise less influence over an agency's hiring decisions than the congressional barons who controlled their budgets. But Roosevelt found his revenge where he could. In the fall of 1937, when he visited the Fort Peck Dam under construction in the dust bowl of northeastern Montana, he invited both of the state's U.S. representatives to join him but only its junior senator, James Murray. Wheeler, anticipating the snub, had arranged to conduct a trial in California at the time and wired his regrets, assuring the president that "all the people are grateful" for his accomplishments on their behalf.

For Wheeler, the rewards of having conquered a president surpassed any petty humiliations. The *Evening Star* reported that the Court fight "has transformed the raw-boned, rangy boy from Butte from an economic bomb-thrower, in the eyes of the socially and politically elite, into the darling of the Capital's most exclusive drawing rooms." He had always laughed at the thought of being invited into Alice Roosevelt Longworth's celebrated salon, but by 1938 he was boasting on the Senate floor—"I am proud of the fact that she asked me to go to lunch"—of his social success. In time he would be described as "an ornament" at hostess Evalyn Walsh McLean's soirees. The outsider had wangled his way inside, to his unfeigned delight, raising suspicions that this had been his desire all along.

The company that Wheeler kept was improving, and never more so than on an October evening in 1939, when he and Lulu found themselves sharing a box at Constitution Hall with the famed movie director Frank Capra. It was the largest concert space in the city, and only the Easter before, the Daughters of the American Revolution, which owned the hall, had refused to permit the Negro contralto Marian Anderson to perform there. (Eleanor Roosevelt and Charles Evans Hughes had arranged to move the concert to the Lincoln Memorial.) This occasion, the world premiere of Capra's latest film, promised to be cheerier, though it would be every bit as much a taunt to the capital's customs.

The handsome young Sicilian-born moviemaker had won three Oscars in the previous five years, for patriotic tearjerkers that lionized the little guy and exalted the possibilities of American life. This was his first film set in the nation's capital, and official Washington was enthralled. Most of the cabinet secretaries, two thirds of the senators, more than a hundred House members, and even a Supreme Court justice (Stanley Reed, who had joined the bench after George Sutherland's death) accepted the National Press Club's invitations. A block and a half southwest of the White House, the politicians passed between the giant searchlights, as if they were movie stars themselves, and entered the classically pillared building to witness a paean to democracy titled *Mr. Smith Goes to Washington*. The original name of the film had been *The Man from Montana*—vetoed by Will Hays, the Hollywood censor—and it was loosely based on the career of the tuxedoed senator who sat at Frank Capra's side. James Stewart played Jefferson Smith, an appointed senator from some state in the West. When the wide-eyed idealist arrives in Washington and learns of the corruption by his state's political machine—which "reached right into this sacred chamber," the guileless nonpolitician cries out in despair—he conducts a one-man filibuster and smites it.

The audience in Constitution Hall marveled at the perfect reproduction of the Senate chamber, three-quarters scale except for the senators' desks, built on a studio lot in Hollywood. It was accurate down to the snuff boxes on both sides of the presiding officer's dais and the twenty busts of former vice presidents in niches along the walls. Capra had hired the longtime superintendent of the Senate press gallery, Jim Preston, as his technical adviser, to oversee the construction of the set and to verify the script's parliamentary details. Preston had handpicked the actors to play the senators, using a statistical composite of the real ones (average age, 52; weight, 174 pounds; hair, graying); they included a grandson of Edmund Ross, the Kansas senator whose vote to save President Andrew Johnson from conviction on charges of impeachment became one of the entries in John F. Kennedy's *Profiles in Courage*. Preston himself, tall and gaunt, a dead-ringer for Neville Chamberlain, the British prime minister who had signed the Munich pact with Hitler in 1938, appeared in a cameo as one of the onlookers while Jefferson Smith is roughed up in the Press Club bar. Some of the shots had been filmed in the Senate Office Building's dim corridors.

The nation's capital had never before hosted a Hollywood premiere, and rarely since Shakespeare's day had the workings of government been treated as a subject of popular entertainment. The movie's emotional ending—Jimmy Stewart collapses on the Senate floor even as he topples the political machine—left the audience cheering, Jim Farley's applause among the loudest. But many in the audience demurred. The lawmakers were pained by the portrayal of the Senate as a tool of corruption. Alben Barkley, the majority leader, complained about the "grotesque distortion" in the film's portrayal of how the Senate conducted business—senators turning their backs on a colleague and leaving the chamber when he stands up to speak, a senator's taking direction from Jean Arthur as his aide in the gallery. "And it showed the Senate as the biggest aggregation of nincompoops on record!" Barkley complained. "I did not hear a single senator praise it. I speak for the whole body. The vote was ninety-six to nothing—and no filibuster." The critics, he said, included Wheeler. Capra alleged in later years that several senators sought to acquire the film rights, so that no one would ever view it again.

Many journalists, too, left the auditorium with a scowl, stung by the portrait of a Washington press corps too fond of malice, fisticuffs, and drink. "Exceedingly fraudulent," spat the *Washington Post*. In the *Christian Science Monitor*, Richard L. Strout sniped at "a fairyland like that of Oz." A columnist in the *Evening Star* was more menacing: "The Capra caper ought to go over big in Berlin, Rome and Moscow, because it shows up the democratic system and our vaunted free press in exactly the colors Hitler, Mussolini, and Stalin are fond of painting them."

The rest of the nation, however, did not share the capital's misgivings. Coast to coast, the film was a hit, trailing only *Gone with the Wind* at the box office in 1939. Moviegoers were willing to be reminded of the nation's shortcomings—President Roosevelt had already shown this—as long as virtue and hope ultimately carried the day. *Mr. Smith Goes to Washington* embraced the nation's oldest and noblest story line, of the common man, the principled individual, who takes on the powers-that-be and prevails. A nation scarred by economic calamity and sliding toward another world war, its people undone by impersonal forces beyond anyone's control, had never needed America's political fable more.


IN 1941, WHEN Charles Evans Hughes felt himself slowing down, he knew it was time to leave the Supreme Court. At age seventy-nine, he became the only chief justice since the first one, John Jay, to step down while he could still walk. His departure brought hosannas for his judicial statesmanship, for his political savvy in saving the Court, for his willingness to realign it with the citizenry's needs—that is, with the election returns.

Owen J. Roberts, the instrument of the chief justice's success, felt lonely on the Court after Hughes left. "To work under you was the greatest experience and the greatest satisfaction of my life," he wrote to the former chief justice after Roberts, too, stepped down, in 1945. "When you left the Court, the whole picture changed. For me it could never be the same." He took on outside jobs—notably, heading an investigation that cleared the president of any responsibility for Japan's surprise attack on Pearl Harbor. Roberts's only intimate remaining on the Court was Felix Frankfurter. The two drew close in part because of the shift that was under way on the Court. First, George Sutherland stepped down in January 1938, to take advantage of the retirement law, and was replaced by Stanley Reed, the solicitor general. (Sutherland had wanted to retire earlier but had deferred his departure because of the president's assault on the Court.) Then Louis Brandeis retired, in frail health, and a young, rambunctious liberal, William Douglas, took the old and disciplined liberal's place. Pierce Butler died in November 1939, and FDR named Frank Murphy, the reliably liberal ex-governor of Michigan who had spent a year as Homer Cummings's successor at the Justice Department. James McReynolds hung on until 1941, the last of the Four Horsemen to yield to Father Time. By early 1940, President Roosevelt had named five justices—a majority—of his own, and he would name three more during his third term.

As liberal justices replaced conservatives, the middle-of-the-road interpretations that had once seemed daringly liberal were now deemed mundane. More and more, Owen Roberts and Charles Evans Hughes, and then Roberts and Frankfurter, found themselves isolated as a conservative minority on divisive cases. By 1941, Justice Roberts was writing more dissents than anyone on the Court—fifty-three of them alone, increasingly bitter in tone, during the 1944–45 term. The justice who had twice switched sides became the chief defender of precedent, angry at his brethren for applying emotion in place of logic. His fiercest dissent, in 1944, argued that to force Japanese Americans into relocation camps was clearly unconstitutional, and that to suggest otherwise was "to shut our eyes to reality." Privately, he accused Black of making up his mind on any case once he learned which lawyers represented which side. He worried about the impact of Black's, William Douglas's, and Frank Murphy's ambitions for the presidency—something that Roberts could understand. Relations had turned bitter with Harlan Fiske Stone, Hughes's successor as the chief justice and the only other holdover from the pre-Roosevelt Court. "Stone dreaded conflict," another justice noted, and his willingness to accept the Roosevelt Court's scorn for precedent drove Roberts into paroxysms of uncustomary eloquence. He dissented in one case because Stone's majority opinion would leave the lower courts "on an uncharted sea of doubt and difficulty without any confidence that what was said yesterday will be good tomorrow."

The resignation of Justice Roberts in the summer of 1945, not long after President Roosevelt died, caught Washington by surprise. He announced it in a letter from his Pennsylvania farm, after the Court had finished its work for the term. He had recently turned seventy, the age that Roosevelt had deemed too old, which made him eligible to receive a pension at full salary. His departure left a Court composed of the seventy-two-year-old Stone and eight middle-aged men—an average age of fifty-seven, a decade and a half younger than in 1937. Roberts showed his indignation at Stone and the Court by resigning, not retiring, a technicality that left him unavailable for any temporary judicial assignment. "I will not come to the Capitol," he wrote Frankfurter a year later, "for fear of having to be polite to any former colleague I might meet."

Stone, nevertheless, practiced the customary courtesy and drafted a letter of regret to the departing justice. He sent it first to the longest-serving associate justice for his signature. That was Hugo Black—a measure of how completely the Court had changed in eight years. The former Alabama senator insisted on two deletions in a draft that was already (as another justice complained later) "formal and not too cordial." One was to blue-pencil the brethren's regret "that our association with you in the daily work of the Court must now come to an end." Even more telling was Black's objection to an innocuous compliment: "You have made fidelity to principle your guide to decision." Stone was amenable to the deletions, but when Frankfurter learned of Black's "derogatory excisions," he exploded.

He had already complained to Stone about the departing Justice Roberts's "serious intellectual limitations—above all, a lack of a more or less coherent juristic or social philosophy, except in a very few defined areas." But Roberts was always faithful to whatever he considered the governing principles in a particular case, Frankfurter pointed out. "If there's one thing true about Roberts, that's it!"

When the justices discussed the farewell letter to Roberts at their first Saturday conference in October, the discussion quickly grew heated. There had been talk of sending two letters or of sending a single letter that not all of the justices signed. Frankfurter announced that he would sign Stone's original letter but not with Black's deletions, with their implication of Roberts's intellectual dishonesty. As Stone floundered for a solution, Hugo Black, his eyes blazing, declared that he would sign no letter at all.

In the end, no letter was sent.

Hugo Black's stubborn objection was not misplaced, for it spoke directly to Owen Roberts's lack of belief in a set of jurisprudential principles. Frankfurter might have been correct about Roberts's fidelity to the governing principles in an individual case, but whenever a decision presented him with a choice of principles that he might follow, Roberts made up his mind between them on pragmatic grounds. He had begun his tenure on the bench trying to hew to the particulars of the law, but he learned to rely on his own evolving judgment of the realities of American life and of the citizenry's needs. He had started as a liberal, then joined the conservatives, before famously switching back to the liberals' side, and finally finished his tenure as the Court's archconservative.

Both Black and Frankfurter, however, had missed the point about Justice Roberts: his indifference to principle was his strength. Roberts was a conservative at heart, "but he did not vote his prejudices during one of the most crucial times in the history of the country," John Knox, the law clerk for Justice McReynolds, recounted. "Owen J. Roberts was impartial after he became aware of the need for social change . . . Roberts literally saved the Supreme Court of the United States from being wrecked by the four conservative justices. His contribution, therefore, was of immense significance, and his importance as a justice during the 1930s can scarcely be exaggerated."

He had come to believe, in effect, that the job of a Supreme Court justice was to administer justice, not the law. His evolving approach to the purpose of the law was a matter of character more than of jurisprudence. "He was, if not a great judge, a good man," Charles Wyzanski, later an eminence himself on the federal bench, wrote to Frankfurter after Roberts died in 1955. "That is how he would chuse [*sic*] to be remembered, as would we all."

"ALL IN ALL, the Court bill fight has been a wonderful thing," Burt Wheeler told a reporter soon after it ended. "The agitation brought the people to a study of the fundamentals of their government, gave them a veritable lesson in elemental civics. The fight has done the judiciary good, too. Courts had become arrogant, and sometimes disrespectful of the rights of the public." Wheeler rarely understated anything, but this time he had an excuse: he could scarcely have foreseen the far-reaching effects of the Constitutional Revolution of 1937.

The transformation happened swiftly, within a couple of years. Roosevelt's nominees, steadfast New Dealers, were young—not quite forty-eight years old, on average, when they were named to the Court—and nearly devoid of judicial experience. Hugo Black had spent eighteen months as a police judge in Alabama, and Wiley Rutledge, Roosevelt's final appointment, had sat for two years on a federal appeals court. "With the arrival of the new appointees," a scholar recounted, "the complexion of the Court completely changed, for the new judges were favorably disposed toward legislative experimentation to find solutions for the social and economic problems of the day." They let Congress weigh in on wages, hours, and working conditions, using its power over interstate commerce, to help people who could not compete in the marketplace on their own. The constitutionality of any legislation that Congress passed and the president signed was practically a sure thing. Judicial self-restraint became the Court's byword. Hardly two years in the grave when Owen Roberts switched sides, Oliver Wendell Holmes Jr. had emerged triumphant. His 1918 dissent in favor of banning child labor became the view of the unanimous Court in 1941. The Roosevelt Court, as it picked up steam, made a habit of turning Holmes's elegantly liberal dissents into the law of the land.

All told, the Roosevelt Court overturned thirty-two judicial precedents, in a variety of legal fields, well-known and obscure. In twenty-two of the discarded decisions, Holmes or Louis Brandeis or Harlan Fiske Stone had written a dissent. The Court's eagerness to depart from precedent provoked Justice Roberts to accuse his brethren of a contempt for the past. He lamented "an intolerance for what those who have composed this court in the past have conscientiously and deliberately concluded," evidently rooted in "an assumption that knowledge and wisdom reside in us which was denied to our predecessors." The irony, of course, was that nobody was more responsible for the Court's disrespect for the established principles of constitutional law than Roberts himself, an untheoretical pragmatist, yet he feared for a jurisprudence free from its past.

His fear was exaggerated as long as the Court truly practiced the judicial self-restraint that Holmes and Stone, among many others, had preached. But this was destined to give way; indeed, the impact of the Court-packing fight virtually assured it. Had President Roosevelt succeeded in his quest, even by adding as few as two additional justices, any of his successors might well have tried doing the same. Whenever a politically volatile decision loomed, the justices would have been inclined to look over their shoulders, to consider the potential of a backlash, to worry about becoming a target in the next election campaign—cast in a political role beyond Mr. Dooley's imagining. It would have meant a timid Court, a rubber stamp, one that was "so responsive to public opinion," historian Patrick Maney said many years later, "that it would not have had the independence to make a major unpopular, or at least explosively controversial, decision." But by facing down a powerful president and defeating him, the Court not only preserved its own independence but also underscored and reinforced it, in the public's eye as well as in its own. The Court, as an institution, was bound to feel emboldened. And it was a self-confident Court, sure of its authority, that stopped President Truman from seizing control of the nation's steel mills in 1952, that forced President Nixon to turn over the Watergate tapes that drove him from office in 1974, that assured constitutional protections to suspected terrorists at Guantánamo Bay in 2004 and again in 2008 over a wartime president's objections.

Unmoored from precedent, bold in its self-regard, lenient in its understanding of the Constitution's elastic terms, the Supreme Court was prepared to occupy the center of American political life. This had been foreseen by both sides in the battle over the Court. The adverse report of the Senate Judiciary Committee in 1937 had expressed the hope for "an independent Court, a fearless Court, a Court that will dare to announce its honest opinions in what it believes to be the defense of the liberties of the people." In 1941, Edward Corwin, who had testified on the Court bill's behalf, predicted that the Court would "give voice to the conscience of the country," having renounced its role as property's protector in favor of its guardianship of the general welfare.

Only thirteen years passed before Corwin's prophecy became true. A politician was seated again at the center of the Supreme Court bench, a former governor of California, Earl Warren. The plainspoken progressive Republican, ashamed that his chauffeur slept in the car on their overnight jaunt to Richmond, Virginia, because no hotel would rent a black man a room, applied his judicial statesmanship to bring a principle to life. Warren's politicking inside the Court produced a potent unanimity for its landmark 1954 decision in *Brown v. Board of Education*, which jettisoned a fifty-nine-year-old precedent, desegregated the nation's public schools, and touched off a turbulent era of social progress.

This was only the beginning. In 1957, the Court flaunted its disdain for precedent in reversing its ruling of the previous year about whether to court-martial a soldier's wife for his murder. Justice Roberts had offered his only contribution to the lasting literature of the law when, in a 1944 dissent from a decision that reversed an opinion he had written in 1935, he likened such jurisprudence to "a restricted railroad ticket, good for this day and train only." At the time, his statement "must have seemed extreme even to himself," Alpheus Thomas Mason, a Court historian, remarked. "His words became virtually a statement of fact in 1957." A series of historic decisions followed, ones that discovered in the Constitution a previously unnoticed array of individual rights. Criminal defendants were guaranteed a lawyer and a listing of their rights. Every citizen was to be accorded equal representation in the House of Representatives and state legislatures. Children could not be subjected to prayer or to Bible readings in public school. Americans were bequeathed a broader zone of privacy, after Justice William O. Douglas discerned a constitutional right in the "penumbras formed by emanations" arising from the guarantees of individual liberty in the First, Third, Fourth, Fifth, and Ninth amendments to the Constitution—half of the Bill of Rights. The judicial activism of the Warren Court became a mirror image of the laissez-faire jurisprudence of the pre-1937 Court—liberal rather than conservative, one that pushed the nation forward instead of holding it back.

After the crisis of 1937, "the Court emerged larger in influence, if not in numbers," concluded no less an authority than Sandra Day O'Connor. The first woman on the High Court was to serve in its highest tradition, as a judicial pragmatist who positioned the Court's jurisprudence (especially in calibrating another newfound constitutional right, to an abortion) wherever a fractured citizenry needed it to be. As the swing vote on a ruptured Court, she was a worthy successor to Owen J. Roberts.

The events of 1937, in the sesquicentennial year of the Constitution's birth, ruined the Court's cherished reputation as an impartial and principled institution, as somehow purer at its core than Congress or the president. For a public that had already suffered so much, this was simply one more lost illusion. However, as Burt Wheeler had understood, the emotional battle over the Court ended with the best of all possible outcomes. It left the world's oldest and most adaptable democratic republic with a surer-footed but less tyrannical president, a more skeptical Congress, and a vigorous and independent judiciary that took the American people's needs into account. The modern era of government, and of justice, had begun.

# ACKNOWLEDGMENTS

WRITING A BOOK requires long hours behind a closed door, but it goes more easily and turns out better if others help.

In telling a story in which all of the protagonists are dead, I've received invaluable insights from their descendants—notably from Burton K. Wheeler's surviving child, Marion Wheeler Scott; Owen Roberts's grandchildren, Owen Hamilton and Deborah Hamilton; and Willis Van Devanter's grandson, Willis Van Devanter II.

I am grateful beyond measure for the people who spent hours of their valuable time reading the manuscript and finding its weak spots. I am indebted to John Wiseman, history professor emeritus at Frostburg State University in Maryland, who read the manuscript twice; the eminent constitutional scholar Mark Tushnet of Harvard Law School; Allida Black, the Roosevelt scholar at George Washington University, who helped me understand the difference between journalism and history; seasoned congressional reporter Rich Cohen, my friend and colleague at *National Journal*; constitutional scholar Michael Ariens of St. Mary's University School of Law; and historian Patrick Maney, the dean of arts and sciences at Boston College. I'm beholden to people who have gone out of their way to help me in my research, notably the Senate's historians Dick Baker and Don Ritchie, and Nancy Kervin at the U.S. Senate library, FDR library archivists Virginia Lewick and Mark Renovitch, Karen Fishman and so many others at the Library of Congress, Franz Jantzen in the Supreme Court curator's office, Karlyn Bowman of the American Enterprise Institute, Alonzo Hamby at Ohio University, Stuart Taylor at *National Journal*, college chum Rich Feldman, law clerk Martin Hewett, author Jim Tobin, and my longtime friend Mark Iwry.

Let me add a word of thanks to the kind and capable staff in the Washingtoniana division at the D.C. Public Library, and to the Arlington Public Library for its electronic resources, which offer a pleasing return on my taxes. Thanks also to former Maryland senator Joseph Tydings, David Grove at the law firm of Montgomery, McCracken, Walker & Rhoads in Philadelphia, Dr. Richard Goldberg, Owen J. Roberts High School librarian Diane Geyer, Chester County (Pa.) Historical Society librarian Diane Rofini, neighbor Catherine Dowling, and labor historian Nelson Lichtenstein at the University of California (Santa Barbara) for their assistance.

I can't overstate my appreciation to Gail Ross, my literary agent, for her steadfastness and guidance in navigating the shoals of the publishing business, and to her editorial director, Howard Yoon, for his deft touch and unending patience. George Gibson has been a wonderful editor; his standards of excellence and finely pointed pencil have improved this book immeasurably.

More than anyone, my wife, Nancy Tuholski, has helped me through the ups and downs of book writing. She's a kind reader, a keen copy editor, and my best friend, and she knows how to encourage without saying a word.

Burt Solomon
Arlington, Virginia
August 2008

# NOTES

PROLOGUE

1 "If those people": Rex Collier, "Crowds Brave Downpour to Line Avenue," *Washington Evening Star*, January 20, 1937.

1 forsaking the traditional: He had done the same at his first inaugural, in 1933. "I am glad to have the suggestion that you repeat the oath in full instead of saying simply 'I do.' I think the repetition is the more dignified and appropriate course," Hughes wrote to "My dear President-elect." Hughes letter to Roosevelt, February 28, 1933, president's personal file 7590, box 85, Franklin D. Roosevelt library.

1 slowly and with emphasis: Harold L. Ickes, *The Secret Diary of Harold L. Ickes* (New York: Simon & Schuster, 1954), vol. 2, p. 53.

1 features were heavier: Arthur Krock, "President Speaks," *New York Times*, January 21, 1937.

1 eight thousand: "Weather Luck of Roosevelt Fails to Hold," *Washington Herald*, January 21, 1937.

2 cheerfulness: Damon Runyon, "Downpour Drenches Crowds," *Washington Herald*, January 21, 1937.

2 "*Today* we invoke": Master speech file, no. 1030, "Inaugural Address," January 20, 1937, FDR library. On the front page is written, "My reading copy FDR."

2 four months: William E. Leuchtenburg, *Franklin D. Roosevelt and the New Deal: 1932–1940* (New York: Harper & Row, 1963), p. 18.

3 The tuba player: Runyon, "Downpour Drenches Crowds."

3 Twice, the president brushed: Charles W. Hurd, "Downpour Fails to Depress Chief Executive's Spirits or Mar His Big Day," *New York Times*, January 21, 1937.

3 Dear President: A September 15, 1935, letter to FDR from an unidentified boy in Troy, New York, collected in *Down and Out in the Great Depression: Letters from the Forgotten Man*, edited by Robert S. McElvaine (Chapel Hill: University of North Carolina Press, 1983), p. 164. The letter writers were usually identified only by their initials and gender.

3 We will have to face: November 12, 1935, letter to FDR from Mr. Woodworth in Huntsville, Alabama; ibid., p. 91.

3 it is hard: November 15, 1935, letter to FDR from Mrs. F. O. S. in Miami, Oklahoma; ibid., p. 186.

3 My father he: February 1936 letter to FDR from an anonymous twelve-year-old boy in Chicago; ibid., p. 117.

3 I have no shoe: February 1, 1936, letter to Mrs. Roosevelt from an anonymous writer in St. Louis, Missouri; ibid., p. 118.

3 i have four boys: January 16, 1935, letter to Senator Matthew M. Neeley, a West Virginia Democrat, from Mr. J. T. C., Martinsburg, West Virginia; ibid., p. 76.

3 All I want: May 16, 1934, letter to FDR from an unidentified man in Cambridge (the state was unidentified); ibid., p. 158.

3  Mrs. Roosevelt this: August 15, 1936,
   letter from Mr. D. B. P. of Nashville,
   Tennessee; ibid., p. 194.
3  PRESIDENT ROSEFELT: March 22,
   1936, letter to FDR from an anonymous
   writer in San Francisco; ibid., p. 177.
3  frantic with depression: January 21, 1935,
   letter to Mrs. Roosevelt from an
   unidentified fifty-seven-year-old widow
   in Weldon, North Carolina; ibid., p. 110.
5  "Means must be found": Franklyn
   Waltman, "Extension of RFC and Power
   to Devalue Dollar Sought," *Washington
   Post*, January 7, 1937.
5  "will insist that *every*": Samuel I.
   Rosenman, *Working with Roosevelt*
   (New York: Da Capo Press, 1972), p.
   144; originally published by Harper in
   1952.
5  "there was no doubt": Ibid.

CHAPTER ONE:
*Nine Old Men*
7  martinis or old-fashioneds: Jean Edward
   Smith, *FDR* (New York: Random House,
   2007), p. 335.
7  his favorite room: Doris Kearns
   Goodwin, *No Ordinary Time: Franklin
   and Eleanor Roosevelt; The Home Front
   in World War II* (New York: Simon &
   Schuster, 1994), p. 33.
7  a young Eleanor: Frances Perkins, *The
   Roosevelt I Knew* (New York: Viking,
   1946), p. 77.
7  "The time for action": Rosenman,
   *Working with Roosevelt*, p. 153.
7  They drank a toast to: Ibid.
8  "financially and in other": A letter dated
   January 2, 1937, from W. Forbes Morgan,
   treasurer of the Democratic National
   Committee, to Marguerite LeHand at the
   White House, in the Office of Social
   Entertainment file, box 42, at the
   Franklin D. Roosevelt library.
8  a recent ill-natured best seller: Drew
   Pearson and Robert S. Allen, *The Nine
   Old Men* (Garden City, N.Y.: Doubleday,
   Doran, 1936).
8  "A great speech": Arthur Sears Henning,
   "Roosevelt Sets Age, 70; Law Deans
   Rebuke Bill," *Chicago Daily Tribune*,

February 6, 1937. Thanks to Nancy
Kervin at the U.S. Senate Library for
finding this clipping.
8  was wheeled into: A Filipino houseboy
   ordinarily pushed him inside the White
   House, according to Hugh Gregory
   Gallagher, *FDR's Splendid Deception*
   (New York: Dodd, Mead, 1985), p. 108.
8  loved his own voice: John Knox's letter to
   his parents dated November 11, 1936, in
   folder 10240-k, John Knox Collection,
   Special Collections, University of
   Virginia.
9  much talk of a "new Hughes": Verbatim
   from John H. Cline, "Hughes, 75 Today,
   Sees Court in Greatest Crisis Since '61,"
   *Washington Evening Star*, April 11,
   1937.
9  "First, is he human?": Everett Colby,
   "Charles E. Hughes," *Scribner's*, May
   1928, pp. 558–59.
9  following their physician's advice: The
   handwritten RSVP is in box 42, Social
   Entertainment file, FDR library.
9  "detested the very": *The Forgotten
   Memoir of John Knox: A Year in the Life
   of a Supreme Court Clerk in FDR's
   Washington*, edited by Dennis T.
   Hutchinson and David J. Garrow
   (Chicago: University of Chicago Press,
   2002), p. 106.
9  this was the only: Drew Pearson and
   Robert S. Allen, "How the Supreme
   Court Works," *Saturday Evening Post*,
   April 17, 1937, p. 98.
9  Roosevelt coat of arms: Writers' Program
   of the Work Projects Administration for
   the District of Columbia, *Washington
   City and Capital* (Washington, D.C.: U.S.
   Government Printing Office, 1937),
   p. 315.
9  waved his cigarette holder: James
   MacGregor Burns, *Roosevelt: The Lion
   and the Fox* (New York: Harcourt, Brace,
   1956), p. 293.
10 FDR had crossed party lines: Merlo J.
   Pusey, *Charles Evans Hughes* (New York:
   Macmillan, 1952), vol. 2, p. 732.
10 in Albany, Roosevelt: Richard Lee Strout,
   "The New Deal and the Supreme Court,"
   *North American Review* 236, no. 6
   (1933): 484.

10 often conferred: A. H. Ulm, "Behind Scenes of the Supreme Court," *New York Times*, January 18, 1925.

10 broached the idea: Burton K. Wheeler with Paul F. Healy, *Yankee from the West: The Candid, Turbulent Life Story of the Yankee-Born U.S. Senator from Montana* (Garden City, N.Y.: Doubleday, 1962), p. 330, and Charles Michelson, *The Ghost Talks* (New York: G. P. Putnam's Sons, 1944), pp. 185–86.

10 Hughes . . . later denied: Pusey, *Charles Evans Hughes*, vol. 2, p. 733.

10 without any real friend: Marquis W. Childs, "The Supreme Court To-Day," *Harper's Monthly Magazine* 176 (1938): 584.

10 "did not hesitate": Donald R. Richberg, *My Hero: The Indiscreet Memoirs of an Eventful but Unheroic Life* (New York: G. P. Putnam's Sons, 1954), p. 223. Richberg had been the general counsel and then the chairman of the National Recovery Administration until 1935.

11 "I wish this message": Rosenman, *Working with Roosevelt*, p. 154.

11 "I wish it were": Ibid.

11 over Eleanor's objections: Jonathan Daniels, *Washington Quadrille: The Dance Beside the Documents* (Garden City, N.Y.: Doubleday, 1968), p. 268.

11 "had fun with the Justices": The diary of James Roosevelt, entry for February 3, 1937, box 57, FDR library.

11 meant as a joke: Ibid., February 5, 1937.

12 Through the French doors: Rosenman, *Working with Roosevelt*, p. 1.

12 "our plan": The diary of Homer S. Cummings, entry for February 5, 1937, p. 25, papers of Homer S. Cummings, Albert and Shirley Small Special Collections Library, University of Virginia.

12 twirled his pince-nez: Joseph Alsop and Turner Catledge, *The 168 Days* (Garden City, N.Y.: Doubleday, Doran, 1938), p. 65.

13 "Of course, everyone": Cummings diary, February 5, 1937, p. 23.

13 swallowed the canary: Ibid., p. 24.

13 "Give me ten million": Ickes, *Secret Diary*, vol. 2, p. 65.

14 In 1863: According to the account delivered on the Senate floor by Senator Sherman Minton (D., Ind.), who was later a Supreme Court justice, 75th Cong., 1st sess., *Congressional Record* 81, part 6 (July 8, 1937): 6917–18.

14 screwed up: Verbatim from Cummings diary, February 5, 1937, p. 23.

14 "there is no doubt": Ibid.

14 "well-pleased": Ibid.

15 learned how to fawn: Smith, *FDR*, p. 306.

15 "in awe of": Paul Mallon, "News Behind the News: Roosevelt's Domination of Congress Forecasts Victory for His Ideas," *Evening Star*, January 5, 1937.

15 wheeled himself: Robert A. Caro, *Master of the Senate* (New York: Alfred A. Knopf, 2002), vol. 3 in *The Years of Lyndon Johnson*, p. 58.

15 "big news tomorrow": Arthur Krock, "Surprise Message," *New York Times*, February 6, 1937.

15 "the usual Rooseveltian": Arthur M. Schlesinger Jr., *The Coming of the New Deal, 1933–1935* (Boston: Houghton Mifflin, 1958), in *The Age of Roosevelt*, vol. 2, p. 512.

15 snow melting: Verbatim from "Democrats Open Peace Picnic; Effects on Party Are Watched," *Christian Science Monitor*, June 25, 1937.

16 a mournful shake of the head: Verbatim from Michelson, *The Ghost Talks*, p. 166.

16 "All in": This and the subsequent quotes from FDR's February 5, 1937, press conference, no. 342, are from *Complete Presidential Press Conferences of Franklin D. Roosevelt* (New York: Da Capo Press, 1972), pp. 130–49.

16 a Camel: This was FDR's brand, according to Jonathan Alter, *The Defining Moment: FDR's Hundred Days and the Triumph of Hope* (New York: Simon & Schuster, 2006), p. 235.

17 "an almost voluptuous pleasure": Mark Sullivan, "New Release Dramatized," syndicated column in the *Evening Star*, February 6, 1937.

18 tinted glasses: Hutchinson and Garrow, eds., *The Forgotten Memoir of John Knox*, p. 4.

18 "The Ark": J. H. Oppenheim, "The Supreme Court Grows Up," *American Mercury* 36, no. 143 (1935): 273.

19 "to soften the blow": Tommy Corcoran as quoted by Harry Hopkins, cited in Robert Sherwood, *Roosevelt and Hopkins: An Intimate History* (New York: Harper & Brothers, 1950), p. 90.

19 gymnasium-style green lockers: Pearson and Allen, "How the Supreme Court Works," p. 10.

19 stoop to his walk: Lewis J. Paper, *Brandeis* (Englewood Cliffs, N.J.: Prentice-Hall, 1983), p. 366.

20 the entire Old Testament: This list is from Richard L. Stokes, "Corcoran and Cohen: What They Do and Have Done," *St. Louis Post-Dispatch*, July 25, 1937.

20 to an extreme: Jeffrey Rosen, *The Supreme Court: The Personalities and Rivalries That Defined America* (New York: Times Books, 2006), p. 80. A classic, if perhaps apocryphal, story: when federal appeals court judge Learned Hand bid Holmes farewell after lunch, saying, "Do justice," Holmes replied, "That is not my job. My job is to play the game according to the rules." See Michael Ariens, "Dutiful Justice," *St. Mary's Law Journal* 22 (1991): 1019, 1022.

20 they took walks: Pearson and Allen, *Nine Old Men*, p. 180.

20 ten or fifteen minutes: Marquis W. Childs, *I Write from Washington* (New York: Harper & Brothers, 1942), p. 43.

21 "in a sense, the original": Robert H. Jackson, *The Struggle for Judicial Supremacy: A Study of a Crisis in American Power Politics* (New York: Alfred A. Knopf, 1941), p. 190.

21 emphasis on age: George Creel, "If the Court Please," *Collier's*, May 8, 1937, p. 26.

21 unfair, cruel: Verbatim from notes of an interview conducted for *The 168 Days* by Joseph Alsop, apparently with Charles Evans Hughes, as recorded in a notebook in box 53, papers of Joseph and Stewart Alsop, Library of Congress.

21 "Tell the president": Paper, *Brandeis*, p. 365, based on Paper's 1979 interview with Corcoran.

21 he kept them written: Pearson and Allen, "How the Supreme Court Works," p. 92.

22 Owen Roberts thumbed: Marian C. McKenna, *Franklin Roosevelt and the Great Constitutional War: The Court-Packing Crisis of 1937* (New York: Fordham University Press, 2002), pp. 288–89.

22 lawyer looked startled: Alsop and Catledge, *The 168 Days*, p. 135.

22 looked as glum: Turner Catledge, "New Act Opens in Court Bill's Stormy Drama," *New York Times*, July 18, 1937.

22 "We were all so stunned": Bascom N. Timmons, *Garner of Texas* (New York: Harper & Brothers, 1948), p. 23.

22 Only in the taxi: H. R. Baukhage, "What's Back of It All," *Evening Star*, July 16, 1937.

23 "cash in my chips": Alsop and Catledge, *The 168 Days*, p. 67.

23 in Missy LeHand's office: James Roosevelt diary, February 5, 1937. Marvin McIntyre was the other aide.

23 droned: "Congress Views on Court Hold to Party Lines," *Christian Science Monitor*, February 5, 1937.

23 line by line: Dewey L. Fleming, "Court Reform Bill Introduced in House; Senate Adjourns," *Baltimore Sun*, February 6, 1937.

23 more than a day: Rebecca L. Felton, a Democrat from Georgia, served a single day in 1922.

23 "eloquent advocates": Alexis de Tocqueville, *Democracy in America*, vol. 1 (New York: Vintage Books, 1990), p. 204.

24 "against the possibility": Caro, *Master of the Senate*, p. 23.

24 news would soon break: "15 Senators to Get $1,000 Apiece for Indorsing 'a Light Smoke,'" *Evening Star*, February 21, 1937.

24 *U.S. Senator Reynolds*: A display advertisement featuring Senator Robert R. Reynolds, Democrat of North Carolina, *Evening Star*, March 2, 1937.

24 "I ask that the message": 75th Cong., 1st sess., *Congressional Record* 81, part 1 (February 5, 1937): 881.

25 The sixteen Republicans: The Senate of the 75th Congress also included a Progressive Party member, Robert La Follette Jr. of Wisconsin, and an independent, George Norris of Nebraska, a former Republican.

25 "striking a blow": Marquis James, *Mr. Garner of Texas* (New York: Bobbs-Merrill, 1939), p. 111.

26 the second time: Author's interview with Donald A. Ritchie, the associate U.S. Senate historian.

26 No one exerted more influence: Alsop and Catledge, *The 168 Days*, p. 238.

26 assistant to the attorney general: Ibid., pp. 68–69. This was Joseph Keenan.

26 he smiled: Michelson, *The Ghost Talks*, p. 171.

CHAPTER TWO:
*Laissez-faire*

28 "Each year, since Versailles": George E. Sokolsky, "What of the Year 1937," *Evening Star*, January 3, 1937.

28 Seventy percent: Gallup poll no. 65, conducted January 20–25, 1937.

28 even more of them: By 73 percent to 27 percent, according to Gallup poll no. 91, conducted July 25–30, 1937.

28 "socialism or sovietism": www.spartacus .schoolnet.co.uk/USAcoughlinE.htm.

29 a clear majority: Verbatim from "Fortune Survey: VIII," *Fortune*, April 1937, p. 188. The report gave no percentages.

29 Mae West: Associated Press, "Hearst's $500,000 Tops Salary Lists; Mae West Second," *Philadelphia Record*, January 8, 1936. Mae West's 1934 paychecks amounted to $339,166.

29 "Bank-robbing ain't": Rex Collier, "Crime Front Is Held by G-Men After Relentless 1936 Warfare," *Evening Star*, January 1, 1937, quoting Eddie Bentz, of the Bentz-Doll bank-robbing gang, who was captured in Brooklyn, New York, on March 16, 1936, and sentenced to twenty years in Alcatraz.

29 the underlying deficiencies: See John Kenneth Galbraith, *The Great Crash, 1929* (Boston: Houghton Mifflin, 1954), pp. 182–88.

29 The pushcart peddlers: Henry F. Pringle, "It Was a Nice Depression," *Scribner's Magazine* 101, no. 6 (1937): 13.

30 "as men of vision": Frederick Lewis Allen, *Only Yesterday* (New York: Harper & Brothers, 1931), p. 148.

31 "Clearly a major cause": Robert S. McElvaine, *The Great Depression: America, 1929–1941* (New York: Times Books, 1984), p. 38.

31 Hoover labeled: Ibid., p. 72.

31 since the Civil War: Jackson, *The Struggle for Judicial Supremacy*, p. 125.

31 novels . . . about surviving: McElvaine, *The Great Depression*, p. 220. The four were *Gone with the Wind*, *God's Little Acre*, *The Good Earth*, and *The Grapes of Wrath*.

31 Between 1929 and 1933: David M. Kennedy, *The American People in the Great Depression*, vol. 1, *Freedom from Fear* (New York: Oxford University Press, 1999), p. 163.

32 "It was simply a gut": Studs Terkel, *Hard Times: An Oral History of the Great Depression* (New York: Pantheon Books, 1970), p. 207, quoting Edward Santander as he spoke of life in 1931 outside a small town in Illinois.

32 "the human wreckage": Kennedy, *The American People in the Great Depression*, p. 168.

32 "the terrible, crushing": Ibid., p. 190.

32 the election of 1932: McElvaine, *The Great Depression*, p. 94.

32 passengers on the *Mayflower*: Rita Halle Kleeman, *Gracious Lady: The Life of Sara Delano Roosevelt* (New York: D. Appleton-Century, 1935), pp. 5–6, cited in Smith, *FDR*, p. 10.

32 the Astors: Associated Press, "Franklin D. Roosevelt, Distantly Related to the Late Col. Theodore Roosevelt, Married a Niece of T. R.," *Washington Post*, July 7, 1920.

32 van Rozenvelt: Peter Collier with David Horowitz, *The Roosevelts: An American Saga* (New York: Simon & Schuster, 1994), p. 16.

33 Franklin's great-great-grandfather: Smith, *FDR*, pp. 3–4; "Col. Theodore Roosevelt, Married a Niece of T.R.," *New York Times*, July 7, 1920.

33  "The reason was born": Rosenman, *Working with Roosevelt*, p. 14.

33  "people in trouble": McElvaine, *The Great Depression*, p. 106.

33  "the seed": Rosenman, *Working with Roosevelt*, p. 15.

33  "saw the New Deal": Charles Peters, *Five Days in Philadelphia: Wendell Willkie, Franklin Roosevelt, and the 1940 Convention That Saved the Western World* (New York: PublicAffairs, 2005), p. 14.

33  "social duty": Smith, *FDR*, p. 251.

34  "You just hand me": "'Marchers' Parade, Petition Congress," *New York Times*, December 7, 1932.

35  Early in the New Deal: Schlesinger, *The Coming of the New Deal*, p. 333.

35  "if America could": Raymond Moley, cited by Kennedy, *The American People in the Great Depression*, p. 121.

35  "Philosophy? Philosophy?": Ibid., p. 131.

35  relying on managed capitalism: George Creel, "Roosevelt's Plans and Purposes," *Collier's*, December 26, 1936, p. 8.

35  "The whole": Ibid.

35  "was open to": Burns, *Roosevelt: The Lion and the Fox*, p. 238.

35  veer back and forth: McElvaine, *The Great Depression*, p. 142.

36  laissez-faire had made many lives worse: See Kennedy, *The American People in the Great Depression*, p. 199.

37  "It's neither fish": Alter, *The Defining Moment*, p. 288.

38  the humiliations of its means test: Kennedy, *The American People in the Great Depression*, p. 175.

38  "the most important": "Roosevelt Hails Goal," *New York Times*, June 17, 1933.

39  burlesque shows: Jonathan Alter, in remarks at the November 11–12, 2007, conference on "The Presidency and the Supreme Court" at the FDR library.

39  sense of national unity: Schlesinger, *The Coming of the New Deal*, p. 176.

39  "heaving toward": Mitchell Dawson, "The Supreme Court and the New Deal," *Harper's Monthly Magazine* 167 (November 1933): 642.

CHAPTER THREE:
*The Third Branch*

40  "has no influence": Publius (Alexander Hamilton), *Federalist* no. 78, in Alexander Hamilton, James Madison, and John Jay, *The Federalist, or, the New Constitution* (New York: E. P. Dutton, 1961), p. 395.

40  "An impenetrable bulwark": From James Madison's June 8, 1789, speech to the House of Representatives proposing a Bill of Rights, see http://www.jmu.edu/ madison/center/main_pages/madison_ archives/constit_confed/rights/ jmproposal/jmspeech.htm.

41  "the peace, the prosperity": Tocqueville, *Democracy in America*, vol. 1 (New York: Vintage Books, 1990), p. 151.

41  the only justice: Bernard Schwartz, *A History of the Supreme Court* (New York: Oxford University Press, 1993), p. 15. The justice was William Cushing.

41  the Federalist goals: Rosen, *The Supreme Court*, p. 36.

42  "a serious mistake": Charles Evans Hughes, *The Supreme Court of the United States: Its Foundation, Methods and Achievements* (New York: Columbia University Press, 1928), p. 52.

42  the Industrial Revolution: Mitchell Dawson, "The Supreme Court and the New Deal," *Harper's Monthly Magazine* 167 (November 1933): 642.

43  "the freedom of master": *Lochner v. New York,* 198 U.S. 45 (1905).

43  "among the several States": Article I, Section 8 of the Constitution.

44  hundreds of state laws: Peter Irons, *A People's History of the Supreme Court: The Men and Women Whose Cases and Decisions Have Shaped Our Constitution* (New York: Penguin Books, 1999), p. 236.

44  by century's end: Edward S. Corwin, *Constitutional Revolution, Ltd.* (Claremont, Calif.: Friends of the Colleges at Claremont, 1941), p. 10.

44  "judicial *review*": Alpheus Thomas Mason, *The Supreme Court from Taft to Burger* (Baton Rouge: Louisiana State University Press, 1979), p. 5.

44  "as though the Framers": Justice Felix Frankfurter's concurring opinion,

*American Federation of Labor v. American Sash Co.*, 335 U.S. 538, at 543 (1949), quoted in Schwartz, *A History of the Supreme Court*, p. 180.

44  "the bulwark": W. H. Taft, "Mr. Wilson and the Campaign," *Yale Review*, (October 1920): 19–20, cited in Mason, *The Supreme Court from Taft to Burger*, p. 41.

44  "super-legislature": Brandeis's 1924 dissent in *Burns Baking Co. v. Bryan*, 264 U.S. 504, at 534.

45  "The visit to Athens": A postcard dated June 4, 1927, in 3rd series, p. 2, William Howard Taft papers, Library of Congress.

45  "$9,000,000 Parthenon": Robert C. Albright, "Supreme Court Will Take Over New Structure," *Washington Post*, September 29, 1935.

45  answering only to the Court: Drew Pearson and Robert S. Allen, "How the Supreme Court Works," *Saturday Evening Post*, April 17, 1937, p. 98.

45  newspapermen: Associated Press, "Reporters Get Strict Notice of Seclusion," *Evening Star*, February 7, 1937. The number of trespassing "newspaper men" was not specified.

45  unpolished white oak: Ernie Pyle, "Supreme Court's New Home Inspires Sneezes as Well as Awe," *Washington Daily News*, October 7, 1935.

46  looked cheerful: Associated Press, "Reporters Get Strict Notice of Seclusion."

46  as stormy: Ray Tucker, "Court of the Last Guess," *Collier's*, July 7, 1934, p. 50.

46  "essentially unfair": Roberts's dissent in *Brush v. Commissioner of Internal Revenue*, 300 U.S. 352, at 377.

47  "three notable instances": Hughes, *The Supreme Court of the United States*, p. 50.

47  radiated authority: Almost verbatim from a dedication to Charles Evans Hughes written by then justice Felix Frankfurter in the 1949 Harvard Law School yearbook, reel 127, Frankfurter papers, Library of Congress.

47  photographic memory: Pusey, *Charles Evans Hughes*, vol. 2, p. 672.

47  "to rush our work": A February 10, 1936, letter from Stone to Felix Frankfurter, on reel 64 of the Frankfurter papers.

48  "You just didn't like to talk": Felix Frankfurter, "Chief Justices I Have Known," p. 36 of his notes for an informal talk delivered to University of Virginia law students on May 12, 1953, reel 127, Frankfurter papers, Library of Congress.

48  the middle of "if": Pusey, *Charles Evans Hughes*, vol. 2, p. 665.

49  met every week at Brandeis's apartment: Arthur M. Schlesinger Jr., *The Politics of Upheaval* (Boston: Houghton Mifflin, 1960), vol. 3, *The Age of Roosevelt*, p. 468.

49  irritation might cross: George Creel, "If the Court Please," *Collier's*, May 8, 1937, p. 26.

49  nineteenth-century men: Erwin N. Griswold, "Owen J. Roberts as a Judge," *University of Pennsylvania Law Review* 104 (December 1955): 334. Griswold was then the dean of Harvard Law School.

49  "the rules which govern": Jay S. Bybee, "George Sutherland 1922–1938," *The Supreme Court Justices: Illustrated Biographies, 1789–1995* (Washington, D.C.: *Congressional Quarterly*, 1995), p. 348.

50  "If it were not": *The Forgotten Memoir of John Knox*, edited by Dennis T. Hutchinson and David J. Garrow, p. 72.

50  "lady lawyers of both sexes": Associated Press, "Justice McReynolds Defends Views with Searing Fervor," *Evening Star*, February 26, 1937.

50  "savage": According to Frankfurter's notes of a conversation on July 3, 1923 or 1924, with Brandeis, who was quoting Holmes, on reel 142 in the Frankfurter papers.

50  The only Jew: Hutchinson and Garrow, eds., *Forgotten Memoir of John Knox*, pp. 36–37.

50  For three years: http://www.pbs.org/ wnet/supremecourt/personality/robes_ mcreynolds.html.

50  with Benjamin Cardozo: According to Harry Parker, McReynolds's black messenger and household assistant, Hutchinson and Garrow, eds., *Forgotten Memoir of John Knox*, p. 37.

50  "another one": http://www.pbs.org/wnet/
    supremecourt/personality/robes_
    mcreynolds.html.
51  morally offensive: Paper, *Brandeis*,
    p. 187.
51  When Hoover questioned: "The
    Honorable Supreme Court," *Fortune*,
    May 1936, p. 82.
51  "It is not a contest": An April 4, 1930,
    letter from Stone to Frankfurter, reel 64,
    Frankfurter papers, Library of
    Congress.
52  "the chief justice was even": John Knox,
    "Experiences as Law Clerk to Mr. Justice
    James C. McReynolds of the Supreme
    Court of the United States during the
    Year that President Franklin D. Roosevelt
    Attempted to 'Pack' the Court," a
    manuscript dated 1976, Oak Park,
    Illinois, pp. 309–10. Roughly two thirds
    of the manuscript was published as *The
    Forgotten Memoir of John Knox*
    (Hutchinson and Garrow, eds.).
52  "more successfully eluded": Samuel
    Hendel, "The 'Liberalism' of Chief
    Justice Hughes," *Vanderbilt Law Review*
    10 (1956–57): 261.
52  led the Court's liberal minority: Smith,
    *FDR*, p. 133.
52  "throne": "Memorandum of talk with
    HFS, Mar. 2, 1935," reel 64, Frankfurter
    papers, Library of Congress.
53  "Is Justice Roberts": *Christian Century*,
    June 10, 1931, p. 765.


CHAPTER FOUR:
*The Swing Vote*
54  Fisher's Lane: The address is now 207
    East Logan Street.
54  "an ambitious boy": "Roberts, as Boy,
    Scorned Lawyers," *Philadelphia Evening
    Bulletin*, February 16, 1924.
54  Germantown Academy: Edwin N.
    Probert II, "Owen Josephus Roberts: A
    Short Retrospective on a Favorite Son,"
    on Germantown Academy's Web site,
    http://www.ga.k12.pa.us/aboutga/history_
    traditions/profiles/Roberts/portrait
    .shtml.
54  "a school adapted": Francis N. Thorpe,
    "The University of Pennsylvania,"

    *Harper's New Monthly Magazine* 91, no.
    542 (1895): 303.
55  "the experience of the University": Ibid.,
    301.
55  "Roberts, our Pooh Bah": *The Record of
    the Class of '95, University of
    Pennsylvania*, University of Pennsylvania
    Archives, pp. 34, 134, 270.
55  "Your father is right": "Roberts, as Boy,
    Scorned Lawyers," *Philadelphia Evening
    Bulletin*, February 16, 1924.
56  the "University crowd": Pearson and
    Allen, *The Nine Old Men*, p. 143.
56  "a good big man": Jane S. McIlvaine,
    "Unretiring Justice," *Philadelphia
    Inquirer Magazine*, first of two parts,
    November 30, 1950.
56  "something big for my city": Ibid., second
    of two parts, December 7, 1950.
56  a law firm: Originally called Roberts,
    Montgomery & McKeehan, the firm is
    now Montgomery, McCracken, Walker &
    Rhoads, LLP.
56  exclusive clubs: "Coolidge Names Owen
    J. Roberts Oil Case Counsel,"
    *Philadelphia Evening Bulletin*, April 15,
    1924. He belonged to the Union League,
    Rittenhouse, University, Merion Cricket,
    and Philadelphia Cricket clubs.
56  He conducted civil trials: Robert T.
    McCracken, "Owen J. Roberts—Master
    Advocate," *University of Pennsylvania
    Law Review* 104 (December 1955):
    325.
56  $150,000: According to press estimates
    cited by David Burner, "Owen J.
    Roberts," in *The Justices of the United
    States Supreme Court, 1789–1969: Their
    Lives and Major Opinions*, edited by
    Leon Friedman and Fred L. Israel (New
    York: Chelsea House, 1969), vol. 3,
    p. 2254.
56  four-story town house: The address was
    1827 Delancey Street.
57  "very spoiled rotten": Elizabeth Roberts
    Hamilton, in a videotaped interview
    conducted in 1995, viewed in the Owen J.
    Roberts Archives at Owen J. Roberts
    High School in Pottstown, Pennsylvania,
    courtesy of librarian Donna Himmel.
57  "old-fashioned Anglo-Saxon
    individualism": "Defends High Pay for

Oil Officials," *New York Times*, February 16, 1923.

57  "noisy minorities": "Drys Won't Fight Roberts; What He Said in 1923 Talk," *New York World*, May 11, 1930. The newspaper obtained the text of Roberts's 1923 speech from the files of the American Banking Association.

57  summoned his protégé: "Who Is Owen J. Roberts, Oil Scandal Prosecutor?" *Literary Digest* 80 (March 22, 1924): 48.

58  turned down the job himself: William Allen White, *A Puritan in Babylon: The Story of Calvin Coolidge* (New York: Macmillan, 1938), p. 271.

58  seconded the choice: Pusey, *Charles Evans Hughes*, p. 566.

58  "He knows what I mean": George Wharton Pepper, *Philadelphia Lawyer: An Autobiography* (Philadelphia: J. B. Lippincott, 1944), p. 197.

58  "fame struck": "Who Is Owen J. Roberts, Oil Scandal Prosecutor?" *Literary Digest*, March 22, 1924.

58  "I think that in an hour's": 68th Cong., 1st sess., *Congressional Record* 65, part 3 (February 16, 1924): 2548.

59  "We will make haste": "Oil Counsel Get Commissions and Start Work; Promise to Lose No Time in Prosecution," *New York Times*, February 20, 1924.

59  "a Sherlock Holmes": "Justice Roberts Known as Fighter with Smile," *New York Times*, May 25, 1930.

59  club of conservatives: http://www.oyez .org/justices/edward_t_sanford/.

59  "the participation of the Negro": "Fight Over Parker Laid Before Hoover," *New York Times*, April 12, 1930, quoting from the *Greensboro (N.C.) News*.

60  as tolerable a nominee: Ernest Sutherland Bates, "McReynolds, Roberts and Hughes," *New Republic*, July 1, 1936, p. 235.

60  had discouraged friends: George Wharton Pepper wrote a September 23, 1942, letter to William Oscar Trapp, "The Constitutional Doctrines of Owen J. Roberts," Ph.D. diss., Cornell University, May 1943, pp. 65–66, in which he recounted: "I asked him, as did a number

of his other friends, whether it would be acceptable to him if there were a movement for his endorsement. He replied unequivocally that he desired no such step to be taken as he very much hoped that the appointment would not be tendered to him. If it were to be tendered he felt that he might have to accept and he was most reluctant to leave the ranks of the active bar."

60  "both a heart": A.F.C., "Backstage in Washington," *Outlook and Independent*, May 21, 1930, p. 100.

60  "Knowing him as I do": Recounted to Roberts in a May 10, 1930, letter from Jacob Bellikoff of Elkins Park, Pennsylvania, an NAACP supporter, in *Owen J. Roberts on His Appointment to the Supreme Court of the United States, May 20, 1930*, vol. 1, courtesy of Owen R. Hamilton, Roberts's grandson.

61  Roberts told his friends: Trapp, "The Constitutional Doctrines of Owen J. Roberts," p. 341.

61  travel to Baltimore: Representative Lindy Boggs (D., La.), in remarks as a new member of Congress about her arrival in Washington in 1941, 93rd Cong., 1st sess., *Congressional Record* 119, Part 10 (April 18, 1973): 13191.

62  lumberyards, garages: Keith Melder, *City of Magnificent Intentions: A History of Washington, District of Columbia* (Washington, D.C.: Intac Inc., 1997), p. 374.

62  Thirty-first and O: The house is still standing at 1401 31st St., NW, in Washington, D.C.

62  stop to gossip: J. H. Oppenheim, "The Supreme Court Grows Up," *American Mercury* 36, no. 143 (1935): 281–82, citing Albert Beveridge's *The Life of John Marshall* (Boston and New York: Houghton Mifflin, 1916–19).

63  "mystical halo": A. H. Ulm, "Behind the Scenes of the Supreme Court," *New York Times*, January 18, 1925.

63  briar pipe . . . clenched: Associated Press biographical sketch no. 2578, on Owen J. Roberts, issued on November 15, 1937, for newspapers to publish only in the event of his death.

63  "We shall look forward": A June 3, 1930, letter from Stone to Roberts, box 76, Harlan F. Stone papers, Library of Congress.

63  the two couples: Evelyn Peyton Gordon, "Six Members of the Highest Bench Attend Reception at White House," *Washington Post*, January 12, 1936.

63  "touched me deeply": A May 16, 1930, note from Roberts to Hughes, reel 59, Charles Evans Hughes papers, Library of Congress.

63  a father: David J. Danelski and Joseph S. Tulchin, eds., *The Autobiographical Notes of Charles Evans Hughes* (Cambridge, Mass.: Harvard University Press, 1973), p. xx.

64  "must be trained to think": "Roberts Assails Law Curriculum," *Philadelphia Public Ledger*, March 28, 1931, cited in Trapp, "The Constitutional Doctrines of Owen J. Roberts," p. 23.

64  "The Supreme Court's": *Literary Digest* 109 (June 13, 1931): 8.

64  "a tidy little case": Trapp, "The Constitutional Doctrines of Owen J. Roberts," p. 70. The speaker "may have been Mr. Justice Holmes."

64  "the use of the word 'of'": *Poe, Collector of Internal Revenue, v. Seaborn*, 282 U.S. 92, at 109, decided on November 24, 1930.

65  Rumor had it: Charles A. Leonard, *A Search for a Judicial Philosophy: Mr. Justice Roberts and the Constitutional Revolution of 1937* (Port Washington, N.Y.: Kennikat Press, 1971), p. 28.

65  pacing the floor: Corwin, *Constitutional Revolution, Ltd.*, pp. 75–76. "I have it on first-rate authority," he wrote.

65  "If I want to give": "Sustains State Milk Act," *New York Times*, March 6, 1934.

65  ecclesiastical air: Henry F. Pringle, "Profiles: Chief Justice—I," *New Yorker*, June 29, 1935, p. 22.

66  "During 1932": *Nebbia v. New York*, 291 U.S. 502, at 515.

66  seven hundred acres: Estimates of the size of the Robertses' farm in Chester County, Pennsylvania, ranged from 650 to 800 acres.

66  lost a good deal: Verbatim from Harold Ickes's paraphrasing of what Roberts told him at a luncheon on January 29, 1944, in Ickes's diary, p. 8587, reel 6, Harold L. Ickes papers, Library of Congress.

66  sold the milk: Judith A. Sultzer and Karen Hemighaus, *Owen J. Roberts: Our Namesake and Our Pride* (Pottstown, Pa.: Owen J. Roberts School District, 1977), p. 39.

66  "I'm a city farmer": Harold L. Wiand, "Farmer Off the Bench," *Country Gentleman* (December 1942): p. 14.

66  "[T]his court from the earliest": *Nebbia v. New York*, at 523–24.

66  the public good: Trapp, "The Constitutional Doctrines of Owen J. Roberts," p. 321.

66  "neither arbitrary": *Nebbia v. New York*, at 537.

67  Roberts's opinion heralded: Barry Cushman, *Rethinking the New Deal Court: The Structure of a Constitutional Revolution* (New York: Oxford University Press, 1998), pp. 80–81.

67  "Another historic liberalization": Elliott Thurston, "Supreme Bench Upholds New York's Milk Control Law," *Washington Post*, March 6, 1934.

67  "Certain fundamentals": *Nebbia v. New York*, at 546.

CHAPTER FIVE:
## The Conservative Court

68  the Court upheld: *Norman v. Baltimore & O.R.R.*, 294 U.S. 240 (1935).

69  "crudely drawn": Leon Dure Jr., "Roosevelt Signs Farm Mortgage, Rail Labor Bills," *Washington Post*, July 1, 1934.

69  "We search in vain": *Railroad Retirement Board v. Alton Railroad Co. et al.*, 295 U.S. 330, at 353, 368, and 374.

69  "The gravest aspect": Ibid., at 374–75.

69  "About the worst": A May 9, 1935, letter from Stone to Felix Frankfurter, reel 64, Frankfurter papers, Library of Congress.

70  His law clerk: Leonard, *A Search for a Judicial Philosophy*, p. 12, based on a 1962 interview with Albert J. Schneider, who served as Roberts's only law clerk

from 1931 until the justice retired in 1945.

70 Pierce Butler: Pearson and Allen, *Nine Old Men*, p. 160.

70 had also drawn close: Notes of Alsop's interview apparently with Hughes, box 53, Alsop papers, Library of Congress.

70 "under Justice Sutherland's influence": Corwin, *Constitutional Revolution, Ltd.*, p. 55. Corwin was an adviser to the Works Progress Administration in 1935 and a special assistant to Attorney General Homer Cummings in 1936–37.

70 1928 and 1932 national conventions: Thomas P. O'Neil, "Roberts Rebuffs Plan to Make Him GOP Candidate," *Philadelphia Record*, April 18, 1944.

70 "I figure that cost": Pearson and Allen, *Nine Old Men*, p. 162.

70 "the most important man": "Roberts: The Supreme Court's Hard-Working Balance-Wheel," *News-Week*, May 18, 1935, p. 15.

70 "Owen's duty": Pearson and Allen, *Nine Old Men*, p. 162.

70 Elsie disliked the New Deal: Author's interview with Deborah Hamilton, Roberts's granddaughter, August 12, 2006, in Hartford, Vermont. "But knowing my grandmother," she said, "she would have gotten it from him."

71 "soft": "Scout Council Raises Budget After Month's Finance Drive," *West Chester (Pa.) Daily Local News*, June 19, 1936. This was an account of a speech that Roberts delivered to the Chester County Council of Boy Scouts.

71 "and plunging them": Joseph Alsop's interview apparently with Chief Justice Hughes, box 53, Alsop papers. The phrase before the quotation is almost verbatim from Alsop's notes.

71 "In some people's minds": Perkins, *The Roosevelt I Knew*, p. 210.

71 instrument of monopoly: Ibid., p. 133.

72 NRA was unconstitutional: *Schechter Brothers v. U.S.*, 295 U.S. 495.

72 of kind and not of degree: Mason, *The Supreme Court from Taft to Burger*, p. 91.

72 "Hot dog!": "Filled Court Tense as Decision Is Read," *New York Times*, May 28, 1935.

73 black-winged angel of destruction: Verbatim from the paraphrased account in Schlesinger, *The Politics of Upheaval*, p. 280, which relied on an interview with Corcoran.

73 "This is the end": Ibid.

73 "a fool's paradise": McKenna, *Franklin Roosevelt and the Great Constitutional War*, p. 104.

73 "You mean it was": Robert H. Jackson, *That Man: An Insider's Portrait of Franklin D. Roosevelt* (New York: Oxford University Press, 2003), p. 66. Jackson, then a Treasury Department official, was meeting with President Roosevelt when Richberg telephoned.

74 The president feared: Ickes, *Secret Diary*, vol. 1, p. 495.

74 his usual smile: Felix Bruner, "Richberg Makes Plea to Business to Keep Fair Trade Practices," *Washington Post*, May 28, 1935.

74 "Today was a bad day": The diary of Homer S. Cummings, entry for May 27, 1935, pp. 64–66, papers of Homer S. Cummings, Albert and Shirley Small Special Collections Library, University of Virginia.

74 a French newspaper: William E. Leuchtenburg's remarks at the FDR library's conference on the presidency and the Supreme Court.

74 the AFL announced: Louis Stark, "Labor Demands New NRA, Scoring Any Surrender," *New York Times*, June 7, 1935.

75 "George says": Rosenman, *Working with Roosevelt*, p. 111.

75 "The implications": *Presidential Press Conferences*, vol. 5, no. 209, May 31, 1935, p. 315.

75 "The country was in": Ibid., p. 320.

75 " Since that time": Ibid., p. 322.

76 "Can we use": Ibid., p. 337. The transcript has Stephenson saying "stage" instead of "age."

76 "If we are Schechtered": "AAA: A New Dealer Salvages a Word Out of the NRA Wreck," *News-Week*, September 14, 1935, p. 11.

76 "I have number": "Crowd Is Thrilled in Supreme Court," *New York Times*, Jan. 7, 1936.

77  "to provide for": The opening paragraph in Article I, Section 8, reads in full: "The Congress shall have Power To lay and collect Taxes, Duties, Imposts and Excises, to pay the Debts and provide for the common Defence and general Welfare of the United States; but all Duties, Imposts and Excises shall be uniform throughout the United States;"

77  "This court has noticed": *United States v. Butler*, 297 U.S. 1, at 66 (1936).

77  "The power of Congress": Ibid.

77  Tenth Amendment: It reads, in its entirety: "The powers not delegated to the United States by the Constitution, nor prohibited by it to the States, are reserved to the States respectively, or to the people."

77  "means to an unconstitutional": *U. S. v. Butler*, at 68.

77  a sigh: "AAA Killed by Supreme Court as Invasion of States' Rights; New Deal Hit in 6–3 Decision," *Christian Science Monitor*, January 6, 1936.

78  "a novel approach": Editorial Board, "Notes," *Harvard Law Review* 50, no. 5 (1937): 808.

78  "[T]he Court while purporting": "Recent Cases," *University of Pennsylvania Law Review* 84, no. 4 (February 1936): 548.

78  "I think the judgment": *U. S. v. Butler*, at 78.

78  "Eat it up": Alpheus Thomas Mason, *Harlan Fiske Stone: Pillar of the Law* (New York: Viking Press, 1956), pp. 3, 37–41.

78  all-time gridiron greats: Wesley McCune, *The Nine Young Men* (New York: Harper & Brothers, 1947), p. 246.

78  blurting something: Drew Pearson and Robert S. Allen, "How the Supreme Court Works," *Saturday Evening Post*, April 17, 1937, p. 98.

78  "the warmth of Stone's": Hutchinson and Garrow, eds., *The Forgotten Memoir of John Knox*, p. 97. Knox was Justice McReynolds's law clerk for the Court's 1936–37 term.

79  "A tortured construction": *U. S. v. Butler*, at 87.

79  "sense of self-restraint": Ibid., at 78–79.

79  "The joke of it": January 9, 1936, letter from Stone to "Dear Youngsters," box 3, Stone papers, Library of Congress.

79  argued heatedly: Cummings diary, January 10, 1936, p. 11.

79  "must lead to absurd": *U. S. v. Butler*, at 85.

79  "House-that-Jack-Built": Trapp, "The Constitutional Doctrines of Owen J. Roberts," p. 307.

79  "a wretchedly argued": Leuchtenburg, *Franklin D. Roosevelt and the New Deal*, p. 170.

79  "a rather lumbering": Corwin, *Constitutional Revolution, Ltd.*, p. 58.

79  "to lay the article": *U. S. v. Butler*, at 62.

80  "slot machine": Roscoe Pound, *The Spirit of the Common Law* (Boston: Marshall Jones, 1921), pp. 170–71.

80  "Of the 6,000-odd words": Corwin, *Constitutional Revolution, Ltd.*, p. 13.

80  "is a living thing": Charles Beard, "The Living Constitution," *Annals of the American Academy of Political and Social Science*, May 1936, quoted in G. Edward White, *The Constitution and the New Deal* (Cambridge, Mass.: Harvard University Press, 2000), p. 216.

80  "national calamity": Associated Press, "Kansas Farmers Declared AAA End a 'Calamity,'" *New York Times*, January 8, 1936. The spokesman was O. O. Wolf, the president of the Kansas Farm Bureau Federation.

80  "Heartbreaking": "Mayor Urges Action," *New York Times*, January 7, 1936.

81  "I doubt if any": Stone's January 9, 1936, letter.

81  "Recreant": "The Honorable Supreme Court," *Fortune*, May 1936, p. 83.

81  barely taken their seats: "Supreme Court, 5-4, Voids State Minimum Wage Law; Another Blow, Says A.F. of L.," *New York Times*, June 2, 1936.

81  the most difficult man: Verbatim from Pusey, *Charles Evans Hughes*, vol. 2, p. 670.

81  "The right to make": *Morehead, Warden v. New York ex rel. Tipaldo*, 298 U.S. 587 (1936), at 610.

81  *Adkins* case: *Adkins v. Children's Hospital*, 261 U.S. 525 (1923).

82  "personal economic predilections": *Tipaldo*, at 632–35.

82  "a reasonable relation": Ibid., citing *Nebbia v. New York*, at 537.

82 "plausible on its face": Stone's February 17, 1936, letter to Frankfurter, reel 64, Frankfurter papers, Library of Congress.

82 "the most disastrous": Stone's June 2, 1936, letter to his sister, Helen Stone Willard, in the Stone papers, quoted in Mason, *The Supreme Court from Taft to Burger*, p. 96.

83 "instrument of oppression": "Ruling Disappoints Leaders Here," *New York Times*, June 2, 1936.

83 *Kiplinger's Letter*: Quoted in Frankfurter's June 9, 1936, letter to Stone, box 13, Stone papers.

83 "a shocking blow": Ibid.

83 "underfed girl employee": *Knickerbocker Press*, quoted in William E. Leuchtenburg, "Showdown on the Court," *Smithsonian Magazine*, May 2005, http://www.smithsonianmag.com/history-archaeology/showdown.html.

83 "something should be done": "Hoover Advocates Women's Wage Law," *New York Times*, June 7, 1936.

83 "done within the Constitution": Jackson, *The Struggle for Judicial Supremacy*, p. 174.


CHAPTER SIX:
*The Court Plan*

84 "within the existing": *Presidential Press Conferences* vol. 7, no. 300, June 1, 1936, pp. 280–81.

84 from an editorial: McKenna, *Franklin Roosevelt and the Great Constitutional War*, p. 216.

84 "By another 4 to 5": Quoted in William E. Leuchtenburg, *The Supreme Court Reborn: The Constitutional Revolution in the Age of Roosevelt*, p. 105.

85 a single timid reference: Almost verbatim from "The New Deal Versus the Old Courts," *Literary Digest*, February 13, 1937.

85 "Father Time": Henry Fountain Ashurst, *A Many-Colored Toga: The Diary of Henry Fountain Ashurst* (Tucson: University of Arizona Press, 1962), p. 168.

85 into eclipse: Jackson, *The Struggle for Judicial Supremacy*, p. 32.

85 "If the policy of the government": Quoted in "Nine Presidents on the Supreme Court," *Literary Digest*, April 17, 1937, p. 8.

85 "I may not know much": Jackson, *The Struggle for Judicial Supremacy*, p. 190.

86 "a man who would play ball": Howard L. Comstock, "Justice Homer?" *Bridgeport (Conn.) Herald*, July 25, 1937.

86 most passionate speech: William Allen White, "Convention Cheers Claque, Says White," *New York Times*, July 1, 1932.

86 campaigned even harder: Robert Shogan, *Backlash: The Killing of the New Deal* (Chicago: Ivan R. Dee, 2006), p. 67.

86 Missy LeHand's suggestion: McKenna, *Franklin Roosevelt and the Great Constitutional War*, p. 3.

86 "shrewd, level-headed": Quoted in Felix Frankfurter's memorandum about his March 8, 1933, conversation with FDR, in which Frankfurter was offered (and later turned down) the post of solicitor general, reel 60, Frankfurter papers, Library of Congress.

87 a conservative liberal: Verbatim from the paraphrasing by Leigh Danenberg, "Meet Our Homer Cummings," *Bridgeport Herald*, February 27, 1937.

87 It had been assumed: Smith, *FDR*, p. 380.

87 launched the War on Crime: Bryan Burrough, *Public Enemies: America's Greatest Crime Wave and the Birth of the FBI, 1933–34* (New York: Penguin, 2004), p. 518.

87 "I liked my handkerchiefs": Typewritten note dated August 26, 1937, from FDR to Mrs. Homer S. Cummings, 2700 Tilden St., Washington, D.C., president's personal file 270, FDR library.

87 "Personally, I cannot": The diary of Homer S. Cummings, entry for May 28, 1935, p. 68, papers of Homer S. Cummings, Albert and Shirley Small Special Collections Library, University of Virginia.

87 literally thousands: G. Gould Lincoln, "Roosevelt's Court Proposals Fruit of 18 Months' Study He Began After N.R.A. Reversal," *Evening Star*, February 12, 1937.

88  "implies a very": Cummings diary, December 24, 1936, p. 181.

88  "The real difficulty": A January 29, 1936, letter cited by Leuchtenburg, *The Supreme Court Reborn*, pp. 100–101, and McKenna, *Franklin Roosevelt and the Great Constitutional War*, p. 183.

88  "one supreme Court": Article III, Section 1 of the U.S. Constitution. Its first sentence reads, "The judicial Power of the United States, shall be vested in one supreme Court, and in such inferior Courts as the Congress may from time to time ordain and establish."

88  more than a hundred bills: Leuchtenburg, *The Supreme Court Reborn*, p. 102.

88  "a titanic struggle": David Lawrence, "Judging 1936 Is Task of Future," *Evening Star*, December 31, 1936.

89  allow his bitterness: Frederick Lewis Allen, *Since Yesterday: The 1930s in America, September 3, 1929–September 3, 1939* (Harper & Brothers, 1939), p. 243.

89  referendum on himself: Smith, *FDR*, p. 360.

89  "and the people must": Raymond Moley, *After Seven Years* (New York: Harper & Brothers, 1939), p. 343.

89  expression of the national will: George Creel, "Roosevelt's Plans and Purposes," *Collier's*, December 26, 1936, p. 7.

89  "weighing pro and con": Cummings diary, November 15, 1936, p. 165.

89  lunch a few days later: Ickes, *Secret Diary*, entry for November 13, 1935, vol. 1, p. 467.

90  "for the purpose of": Jackson, *That Man*, p. 65.

90  "1940 national election": Letter dated Feb. 9, 1937, from FDR to Felix Frankfurter, reel 60, Frankfurter papers, Library of Congress.

90  "violated a taboo": Leuchtenburg, *The Supreme Court Reborn*, pp. 118–19.

90  "an ingenious suggestion": Ibid., p. 118.

91  a mention of age: Alsop and Catledge, *The 168 Days*, pp. 32–33.

91  "insure at all times": Homer S. Cummings and Carl McFarland, *Federal Justice: Chapters in the History of Justice*

*and the Federal Executive* (New York: Macmillan, 1937), p. 531.

91  "a medieval gnome": "Aided Roosevelt in All His Offices," *New York Times*, April 19, 1936.

91  in recorded history: Gallagher, *FDR's Splendid Deception*, p. xiii.

91  never stopped calling: Smith, *FDR*, p. 235.

91  that Howe lacked: Ibid., p. 93.

91  the Lincoln Bedroom: Ibid., pp. 334–35.

91  argued the loudest: Rosenman, *Working with Roosevelt*, p. 25.

92  "After Louis' death": Schlesinger, *The Coming of the New Deal*, p. 515.

92  "I am 'bursting'": Handwritten note dated December 22, 1937, from Cummings to FDR, president's secretary's file no. 165, FDR library.

92  "one of the longest": Verbatim from paraphrasing in Cummings diary, December 26, 1936, p. 182.

92  "a very attractive volume": Ibid.

92  one request to make: Ibid., p. 186.

92  The real difficulty: Almost verbatim from the paraphrasing, ibid., p. 187.

92  "Go on": Ibid.

93  were probably unduly: Verbatim from the paraphrasing, ibid., p. 190.

93  "a maiden's prayer": Burns, *Roosevelt: The Lion and the Fox*, p. 296.

93  a veto over his prose: After Creel filed an article with *Collier's* about Tommy Corcoran and Ben Cohen, he sent a copy to Corcoran on August 31, 1937, and wrote, "Wire me if there is anything in it that you do not like," box 193, Thomas Corcoran papers, Library of Congress.

93  "Congress *can enlarge*": George Creel, "Roosevelt's Plans and Purposes," *Collier's*, December 26, 1936, p. 40. Italics in the original.

93  "Once again": Rosenman, *Working with Roosevelt*, p. 149.

93  would never fall back: Cummings diary, February 2, 1937, p. 18, and Paul A. Freund, "Charles Evans Hughes as Chief Justice," *Harvard Law Review* 81, no. 4 (1967–68): 24. Earlier in the drafting, the larger number of justices was to be temporary and would revert to nine once the elderly justices retired.

93   three other presidential advisers: McKenna, *Franklin Roosevelt and the Great Constitutional War*, pp. 275–77. These advisers are identified as speechwriter Sam Rosenman, Solicitor General Stanley Reed, and former NRA administrator Donald Richberg.

CHAPTER SEVEN:
An Ideal New Dealer

95   found him overbearing: Ickes, *Secret Diary*, vol. 2, p. 175, entry of July 27, 1937.

96   Joseph P. Kennedy: Richard L. Stokes, "Corcoran and Cohen: What They Do and Have Done," *St. Louis Post-Dispatch*, July 25, 1937.

96   met Missy LeHand: Draft by Joseph Alsop and Robert Kintner, *Men Around the President*, p. 36, box 95, Alsop papers, Library of Congress.

96   Gilbert and Sullivan: Alva Johnston, "White House Tommy," *Saturday Evening Post*, July 31, 1937, p. 6.

96   on Election Night: Leuchtenburg, *Franklin D. Roosevelt and the New Deal*, p. 195.

96   he had coined the phrase: Drew Pearson and Robert S. Allen, "Washington Daily Merry-Go-Round," *Washington Herald*, July 31, 1937.

96   on K Street: The address was 1610 K Street, NW, in Washington, D.C.

96   "He doesn't care": Wheeler, *Yankee from the West*, p. 322.

97   his dainty hands: Marion Wheeler Scott, Wheeler's youngest and only surviving child, in a March 24, 2007, interview with the author at her home in Rockville, Maryland.

97   "a sensation": Smith, *FDR*, p. 243.

97   "not visiting": G. Gould Lincoln, "Hughes Denies Larger Court More Efficient; Brandeis Shares View," *Evening Star*, March 22, 1937.

97   his son-in-law: Dudley Harmon, "Bridals Today Will Interest New Dealers," *Washington Post*, February 15, 1936. Edwin Colman, the husband of Wheeler's eldest daughter, Elizabeth, had worked at the AAA for "some months."

97   "was like a religion": Wheeler, *Yankee from the West*, p. 320.

98   in the northwestern quadrant: The address was 3757 Jocelyn St., NW, in Washington, D.C.

98   "Do you think": Wheeler, *Yankee from the West*, p. 321.

98   hunger for power: Elizabeth Wheeler Colman, *Mrs. Wheeler Goes to Washington* (Helena, Mont.: Falcon, 1989), p. 163.

98   "the concentration of power": McKenna, *Franklin Roosevelt and the Great Constitutional War*, p. 317.

98   Corcoran had learned: Johnston, "White House Tommy," p. 65.

98   naming two or three: Alsop and Catledge, *The 168 Days*, p. 100.

98   "It isn't a knowing": Colman, *Mrs. Wheeler Goes to Washington*, p. 163.

98   "and he'll put their people": Wheeler, *Yankee from the West*, p. 322.

98   "a fearful row": Richard L. Neuberger, "Wheeler of Montana," *Harper's Magazine* 180 (May 1940): 617.

98   "It's going to pass!": Alsop and Catledge, *The 168 Days*, p. 100.

99   "I tell you": Ibid.

99   Michelson asked: Michelson, *The Ghost Talks*, p. 178.

99   "Save the plate": Colman, *Mrs. Wheeler Goes to Washington*, p. 162.

99   washed dishes in a Negro restaurant: Verbatim from Neuberger, "Wheeler of Montana," p. 614.

99   "stultifying": Wheeler, *Yankee from the West*, p. 57.

99   Gaunt and asthmatic: Verbatim from Marion Wheeler Scott interview.

100   a well-established law firm: "American Messiahs by the Unofficial Observer: Installment XIII," *Washington Post*, May 31, 1935.

100   "scarred, charred": Gerald W. Johnson, "Wheeler Rides the Storm," *Collier's*, July 8, 1944, p. 11.

100   $30,000: Ibid., p. 72.

100   "in pure Montanese": Raymond P. Brandt, "Wheeler, Liberal Champion," part 2, *Washington Sunday Star*, April 21, 1940.

101   made a name: "American Messiahs."

101   trestle in Butte: Richard T. Ruetten, "Burton K. Wheeler of Montana: A Progressive Between the Wars," Ph.D. diss., University of Oregon, 1961, p. 11.

101   he was nearly lynched: Marion Wheeler
      Scott interview.
101   "in large measure because": Wheeler,
      *Yankee from the West*, p. 150.
102   almost tarred and feathered: Neuberger,
      "Wheeler of Montana," p. 615.
102   "I have suffered": U.S. Senate Committee
      on the Judiciary, *Reorganization of the
      Federal Judiciary: Hearings on S. 1392*,
      75th Cong., 1st sess., March 22, 1937,
      p. 498.
103   proclaimed his reluctance: Burton K.
      Wheeler, "How to Keep the Farmer on
      Farm Pointed Out by Senator Wheeler,"
      *New York Times*, November 4, 1923.
103   cover of . . . *Time*: Vol. 1, no. 16, June 18,
      1923.
103   "he is a bigger fool": 68th Cong., 1st sess.,
      *Congressional Record* 65, part 3
      (February 19, 1924): 2769.
103   "There is something soft": William Hard,
      "La Follette's Party: Will It Last?"
      *Nation*, vol. 119, August 6, 1924,
      pp. 142–43.
103   "the most sensational": "Daugherty Is
      Denounced in the Senate as Letting
      Friends Sell Immunity; Name of a
      Senator on Broker's Books," *New York
      Times*, February 20, 1924.
104   "this is pie": Neuberger, "Wheeler of
      Montana," p. 613.
104   "little green house": At 1625 K Street,
      NW, in Washington, D.C.
104   seven or eight ballots: Basil Manly,
      "Justice Stone and Senator Wheeler,"
      *New Republic*, May 13, 1925,
      p. 318.
104   "a pure and unadulterated": "Wheeler
      Calls It 'Frame-Up,'" *New York Times*,
      April 9, 1924.
104   "one of the most damnable": 68th Cong.,
      1st sess., *Congressional Record* 65, part 6
      (April 9, 1924): 5946.
104   "If I don't get": Walter Karig, "Burton K.
      Wheeler: Political Paradox," *Christian
      Science Monitor*, May 16, 1940.
105   had changed his mind: Reminiscences of
      Burton K. Wheeler (March 18, 1968),
      Columbia University Oral History
      Research Office Collection, pp. 15–16.
105   a fighting campaigner: Verbatim from
      Associated Press, "Wheeler Accepts

      Place on Ticket with La Follette,"
      *Christian Science Monitor*, July 19,
      1924.
105   the personal pronoun: Oswald Garrison
      Villard, "Wheeler Invades New York,"
      *Nation*, September 24, 1924, p. 303.
105   "I am a Democrat": "Ticket Completed,
      Independents Get Ready for Battle,"
      *Washington Post*, July 20, 1924.
105   "Christ was the greatest": "Wheeler
      Arraigns Both Old Parties," *New York
      Times*, September 7, 1924.
106   "I have always pointedly avoided":
      Wheeler, *Yankee from the West*,
      p. 46.
106   "believing that capitalism": "Wheeler:
      Montana Senator; His Hat in Ring for
      Silver," *News-Week*, May 6, 1933,
      p. 18.
106   "has been grouchy": Michelson, *The
      Ghost Talks*, p. 140.
106   "She thought him": Colman, *Mrs.
      Wheeler Goes to Washington*, p. 151.
107   "unwavering": Associated Press, "New
      Deal Test Is Expected in Montana Vote,"
      *Washington Post*, June 24, 1934.
107   an ideal New Dealer: Alsop and
      Catledge, *The 168 Days*, p. 53.
107   "You can't fix": Karig, "Burton K.
      Wheeler: Political Paradox."
107   "Wheeler's liberalism": Paul Mallon,
      "News Behind the News," *Evening Star*,
      February 24, 1937. Mallon had covered
      Wheeler's 1924 vice presidential
      campaign as a United Press reporter.
107   "I discovered": Wheeler, *Yankee from the
      West*, p. 313.
107   *Dear Bert*, misspelled: Marquis W.
      Childs, *I Write from Washington* (New
      York: Harper & Brothers, 1942), p. 189.
108   "This working relationship": Ibid.

CHAPTER EIGHT:
*Leader of the Opposition*

109   "'packing' the Supreme Court": "Aim to
      Pack Court, Declares Hoover," *New York
      Times*, February 6, 1937.
109   the tersest: Dewey L. Fleming, "Court
      Reform Bill Introduced in House; Senate
      Adjourns," *Baltimore Sun*, February 6,
      1937.

110 "primarily a device": Charles S. Collier, "Precedent Peril on Court Scouted," *Evening Star*, March 9, 1937. Collier was a professor at George Washington University.

110 A 1936 opinion poll: "The *Fortune* Quarterly Survey: IV," *Fortune*, April 1936, p. 210. In the survey, 39.2 percent of the respondents answered "protected the people," and 21.7 percent said the Court stood "in the way of the people." Some 6.5 percent said "neither," and 32.8 percent answered "don't know." *Fortune*'s quarterly surveys carried no byline, but according to Karlyn Bowman, an expert on polling at the American Enterprise Institute for Public Policy Research, they were written by Elmo Roper.

110 "the great mystery": A February 15, 1937, letter from Harvard law professor Felix Frankfurter to FDR, president's secretary's file, subject: Felix Frankfurter: 1937, at the FDR library.

110 The dozen senators: Robert C. Albright, "Surprise Move Splits Congress; Majority Noncommittal," *Washington Post*, February 6, 1937.

111 FDR's boldest step: J. Fred Essary, "Roosevelt's Court Proposal Arouses Doubt in Congress," *Baltimore Sun*, February 6, 1937.

111 "The people are": Alsop and Catledge, *The 168 Days*, pp. 74, 79.

111 panoramic view: Turner Catledge, "The Liberal Who Fights New Deal Liberalism," *New York Times Magazine*, August 8, 1937.

111 the heating plant: "New Capital Mall Near Completion," *New York Times*, October 4, 1936.

112 "Go ahead": Colman, *Mrs. Wheeler Goes to Washington*, p. 164.

112 "Another hysteria": Wheeler, *Yankee from the West*, p. 150.

112 Two weeks before: The diary of Homer S. Cummings, entry for January 24, 1937, the day FDR informed Cummings he had spoken to Lewis and Corcoran, p. 13, papers of Homer S. Cummings, Albert and Shirley Small Special Collections Library, University of Virginia.

112 a thousand telegrams: "Bill to Permit U.S. to Intervene in Suits Reported by House Group," *Evening Star*, February 9, 1937.

112 "The senators rival": "Congress Hears from the Nation on Supreme Court," Hearst's *News of the Day*, shot March 24, 1937, vol. 8, issue 254, from the UCLA Film & Television Archive.

113 only seven of them: Robert C. Albright, "Missouri Senator Says 'Sack of High Bench Is Involved,'" *Washington Post*, February 13, 1937. The senator was Royal S. Copeland, a Democrat from New York.

113 arouse such vehemence: Almost verbatim from the paraphrasing of Maverick's comment in an Associated Press article, "Fightin' Words Fly in Letters For and Against Court Change," *Evening Star*, March 4, 1937.

113 "Asinine": Ibid., excerpts from letters sent to Senator James Pope, an Idaho Democrat.

113 A syndicated columnist: Paul Mallon, "News Behind the News," *Evening Star*, February 11, 1937.

113 "The chicken farmers": Associated Press, "President on Norris' Idea," *New York Times*, February 13, 1937.

113 more than two thirds: "President Opposed on Court by Large Part of Own Press; Public Opinion Still Molding," *Christian Science Monitor*, February 17, 1937.

113 "too much power": Associated Press, "Don't Join Unions, Henry Ford Says," *Evening Star*, February 20, 1937.

114 "comes perilously near": Associated Press, "Nine Leaders Give Views," *Evening Star*, February 7, 1937.

114 "Our family is with": A handwritten letter dated March 7, 1937, from Ed M. and Margueritte Eby of Shubert, Nebraska, office file 41, FDR library.

114 "any thing you do": Ibid., a handwritten letter dated March 2, 1937, signed "Mr. Ernest Shanks & Family" of Sullivan, Ind.

114 "if we the common people": Ibid., a typed letter dated March 20, 1937, signed "E. L. Eaton & family," Route 6, Sacramento, California.

114 "It is high time": Ibid., a handwritten
letter dated March 31, 1937, from John
H. Achey of St. Paul, Minnesota.

114 "PLEASE ACCEPT": Ibid., from E. E.
Echols, 2921 South Boulevard, Dallas,
Texas, dated March 13, 1937.

114 scores of newspapers: Sixty newspapers
by December 1935 and seventy-eight by
October 1936. "Dr. Gallup Tells How
Institute Gauges Opinion," *Washington
Post*, December 8, 1935, and "Election to
Test New Idea in Polls," *Washington Post*,
October 11, 1936.

114 "a new technique": "The *Fortune*
Quarterly Survey: V," *Fortune*, July 1936,
p. 83.

114 "with mathematical care": "The *Fortune*
Quarterly Survey: VII," *Fortune*, January
1937, p. 86.

114 "mature people": Ibid.

115 foretold the outcome: FDR took 60.7
percent of the popular vote
in 1936. Roper predicted 59.4 percent
and Gallup, 53.8 percent. Gallup said
that three states were sure for Landon—
New Hampshire, besides the two states
the Republican won, Maine and
Vermont.

115 "infant science": George Gallup and Saul
Forbes Rae, *The Pulse of Democracy:
The Public-Opinion Poll and How It
Works* (New York: Simon & Schuster,
1940), p. vii.

115 "Unless the ordinary citizen": Ibid., pp.
14–15.

115 53 percent: A Gallup poll conducted
February 17–22, 1937.

115 almost equal proportions: A Gallup poll
conducted February 24–March 1, 1937,
found 38 percent wanted the president's
plan passed, 39 percent wanted it
defeated, and 23 percent wanted it
modified.

115 At the Women's City Club: Crete Cage,
"Forum Discussion Covers Proposed
Supreme Court Changes," *Los Angeles
Times*, February 17, 1937.

115 the Earnest Workers Club: Joseph
Williams, "Lancaster, Ky.," *Chicago
Defender*, May 1, 1937.

116 Mrs. Charles Evans Hughes: Ruth de
Young, "Mrs. Roosevelt Table Partner of

Mrs. Hughes," *Chicago Daily Tribune*,
April 23, 1937.

116 a sound truck: "Women Open Drive for
'Hands Off Court'; Sound Truck Tours
City with Message," *New York Times*,
February 25, 1937.

116 Jim Farley discussed: "Elks Hear Farley
Support Court Bill," *Washington Post*,
July 14, 1937.

116 $1,250 a year: According to the Bureau of
Labor Statistics, the average wage for all
manufacturing workers in 1937 was
$24.05 a week, which amounted to
$1,250.60 for fifty-two weeks.

116 Lightly regarded by: Laura Hillenbrand,
*Seabiscuit: An American Legend* (New
York: Ballantine Books, 2001), p. 141.

117 for fifteen strides: Ibid., p. 145.

117 *Little Orphan Annie*: "Fortune
Survey: VIII," *Fortune*, April 1937,
pp. 190, 194.

117 W. C. Fields's everyman: *It's a Gift*,
directed by Norman Z. McLeod
(1934, Universal Home Entertainment,
2000).

117 eighty million movie tickets: "The
*Fortune* Quarterly Survey: VIII,"
*Fortune*, April 1937, p. 190.

117 as ordinary men: Verbatim from Thomas
Sugrue, "The Newsreels," *Scribner's
Magazine* 51, no. 4 (1937): 17.

118 on Massachusetts Avenue: At 2941
Massachusetts Avenue, NW, in
Washington, D.C. It is now the residence
of the ambassador from Saudi Arabia.

118 as "Mi-Lord": James T. Patterson,
*Congressional Conservatism and the
New Deal: The Growth of the
Conservative Coalition in Congress,
1933–1939* (Westport, Conn.: Greenwood
Press, 1981), pp. 24–25.

118 redheaded Aunt Polly: Joseph Tydings,
the senator's son (and himself a senator
from Maryland from 1965 to 1971), in an
interview with the author. He was eight
years old at the time.

119 "Burt, we can't": Wheeler, *Yankee from
the West*, pp. 322–23.

119 Wheeler admired Borah: Verbatim from
Marion Wheeler Scott interview.

119 "if you're honest": Reminiscences of
Burton K. Wheeler (March 18, 1968),

Columbia University Oral History Research Office Collection, p. 102.

119 stay in the background: Verbatim from Michelson, *The Ghost Talks*, p. 179.

120 "Who's trying to muzzle": Alsop and Catledge, *The 168 Days*, p. 98. Hoover was talking to Senator Arthur Vandenberg, Republican of Michigan.

120 "outsphinxing the sphinx": Frederic William Wile, "Washington Observations," *Evening Star*, March 29, 1937.

120 asked Wheeler to lead: Colman, *Mrs. Wheeler Goes to Washington*, p. 163.

120 pollsters had named: "The *Fortune* Quarterly Survey: XIV," *Fortune*, January 1938, p. 91. Jack Benny led for the fourth straight year, with the votes of 10.7 percent of respondents, and his Jell-O broadcast led with 8.7 percent.

120 press agent's ploy: "Allen-Benny Radio Gag War Reaches 'Let-Down,'" *Evening Star*, February 28, 1937.

120 five hours a day: Michele Hilmes, *Radio Voices: American Broadcasting, 1922–1952* (Minneapolis: University of Minnesota Press, 1997), p. 183.

121 George Gallup: "For Business Men Who Listen In," *Wall Street Journal*, February 18, 1937.

121 haughty tenor: From listening to a CD of Cummings's speech, kindly prepared for the author by the University of Virginia libraries.

121 "Hello, folks": These quotations come from Wheeler's speech as delivered, from listening to a tape of the February 19, 1937, broadcast at the Motion Picture, Broadcasting, and Recorded Sound Division of the Library of Congress. The exclamation points were used in "Abstract of Wheeler's Speech," *Washington Post*, February 20, 1937.

121 lacked the warmth: Colman, *Mrs. Wheeler Goes to Washington*, p. 51.

122 65 percent: Gallup survey no. 71, question no. 13, from February 24 to March 1, 1937, asked, "Would you vote for Franklin Roosevelt today?" Some 65.2 percent of respondents said yes.

122 Kremer was suspected: Ickes diary, p. 2404, October 31, 1937, reel 2, Ickes papers, Library of Congress.

123 $5,500 a year: Box 167, Homer Cummings papers, University of Virginia. Alf Kremer was hired on January 21, 1935.

## CHAPTER NINE:
### King Franklin

124 had remained worryingly silent: "President Tightens Court Grip," *Christian Science Monitor*, February 11, 1937.

124 carved the baked pheasant: Ashurst, *A Many-Colored Toga*, p. 369. This luncheon took place on February 8, 1937.

124 face kept changing expression: James A. Farley, *Behind the Ballots* (New York: Harcourt, Brace, 1938), p. 65.

124 "I think it quite": Handwritten February 8, 1937, note from Bankhead, president's secretary's file, box 165, FDR library. Sumners met with the president alone on February 10 and again on February 14.

124 "infamous": February 8, 1937, "confidential memorandum" from Stephen Early to FDR, box 165, president's secretary's file, FDR library.

125 inscribing in his schoolbook: Frederic William Wile, "Washington Observations," *Evening Star*, March 5, 1937.

125 "acidly eloquent": Wheeler, *Yankee from the West*, p. 212.

125 "My faults are": 75th Cong., 1st sess., *Congressional Record* 81, part 2 (February 19, 1937): 1411.

125 "I may be driven": "House Democrats to Await Action on Court," *Evening Star*, February 23, 1937.

125 "prelude to tyranny": Merlo J. Pusey, *The Supreme Court Crisis* (New York: Macmillan, 1937), p. 67.

125 "moderation": *Congressional Record*, (February 19, 1937): 1406.

125 "Which stand?": Alsop and Catledge, *The 168 Days*, p. 194.

125 "and take down": The diary of James Roosevelt, entry for February 14, 1937, box 57, FDR library.

126   seventy minutes: "FDR: Day by
        Day—The Pare Lorentz Chronology for
        February 10 and 14, 1937," FDR library.
126   "things like that": James Roosevelt diary,
        February 11, 1937, FDR library.
127   The president laughed: Alsop and
        Catledge, *The 168 Days*, p. 78.
127   "Would you bring": Dewey L. Fleming,
        "President Calls for Curb 'Now' on Power
        of Courts to Halt New Deal Policies,"
        *Baltimore Sun*, March 5, 1937. The guest
        was unidentified.
127   was often nervous: Rosenman, *Working
        with Roosevelt*, p. 122.
127   eminence in the Elks: Alter, *The Defining
        Moment*, p. 86.
127   knew more people: Goodwin, *No
        Ordinary Time*, p. 107.
128   "in the bag": Michelson, *The Ghost Talks*,
        p. 174.
128   "The simple job": Ibid., p. 22.
128   seemed so earnest: Franklyn Waltman,
        "Roosevelt Charges Courts Veto Help for
        Farmer, Flood Victim, Laborer;
        Demands Action Now," *Washington Post*,
        March 5, 1937.
129   "the usual number": The diary of Homer
        S. Cummings, entries for February 15,
        1937, to March 2, 1937, p. 29, papers of
        Homer S. Cummings, Albert and Shirley
        Small Special Collections Library,
        University of Virginia.
129   "unfortunately timed": Jackson, *That
        Man*, p. 51.
129   twenty-one drafts: FDR speech files,
        February 8 to May 11, 1937, at the FDR
        library.
129   last nine words: FDR speech files, box
        32, FDR library. Roosevelt also added "so
        long and no longer" to the fourth draft of
        the speech.
130   "If three well-matched": President
        Roosevelt, "Now!," *Vital Speeches of the
        Day*, vol. 3, no. 11, March 15, 1937,
        corrected by listening to a recording of
        the speech prepared for the author by
        archivist Mark Renovitch at the FDR
        library.
130   bobbed in time: A newsreel excerpt of the
        speech by Paramount News, FDR library.
131   no one he admired more: Almost
        verbatim from William J. Vanden Heuvel,

"FDR's Place in History," *Prologue* 38,
        no. 4 (2006): 41.
131   he shouted "Bully!": Collier with
        Horowitz, *The Roosevelts*, pp. 103,
        107–8.
131   "I'm not Teddy": James MacGregor Burns
        and Susan Dunn, *The Three Roosevelts:
        Patrician Leaders Who Transformed
        America* (New York: Atlantic Monthly
        Press, 2001), p. 116.
131   the defining event: Gallagher, *FDR's
        Splendid Deception*, p. 214.
132   openly discussed his disease: Ibid., p. 15.
132   "Burt, when you": Marion Wheeler Scott
        interview.
132   was commonly known, but: James Tobin,
        who is writing a book about FDR's polio,
        in a July 31, 2008, e-mail to the author.
132   more patient: Gallagher, *FDR's Splendid
        Deception*, p. 120.
133   "No one could be a dictator": "Young
        Democrats Toast Roosevelt," *Evening
        Star*, March 5, 1937.
133   forced to spike rumors: "Mrs. Roosevelt
        Spikes Rumors She Will Run for
        Presidency," *Evening Star*, March 1, 1937.
133   immediately after the banquet: Jessie Ash
        Arndt, "Notables of District and Nation
        Among 1,300 Attending Victory Dinner
        for President Roosevelt at Mayflower,"
        *Washington Post*, March 5, 1937.
134   "If Landon had": "Willard Strikers
        Return to Posts," *Evening Star*, March
        10, 1937.
134   the judicial precedents: Shogan,
        *Backlash*, p. 46.
135   "Nine old men!": Hutchinson and
        Garrow, eds., *The Forgotten Memoir of
        John Knox*, p. 174.
135   three fourths of Americans: "The
        *Fortune* Quarterly Survey: IX," *Fortune*,
        July 1937, p. 98.
135   "mass lawlessness": A July 1, 1937, letter
        from Garner to Farley, quoted in James
        A. Farley, *Jim Farley's Story: The
        Roosevelt Years* (New York: Whittlesey
        House, 1948), p. 85.
135   she started to cry: Raymond Clapper
        diary, December 28, 1937, box 17,
        Library of Congress, cited in Patterson,
        *Congressional Conservatism and the
        New Deal*, p. 136.

136 a picket line: "The Line John L. Lewis Wouldn't Buck," *Washington Post*, March 9, 1937.

136 nasal announcement: From listening to a recording (RWC 5442 A2-3) of the March 9, 1937, fireside chat, Library of Congress.

136 "upon which much": James Roosevelt diary, February 26, 1937, FDR library.

136 Poughkeepsie newspaper editor: Smith, *FDR*, p. 65. The editor was Richard E. Connell of the *Poughkeepsie News-Press*, who ran unsuccessfully for Congress in 1896 and for the state assembly in 1898 and 1900. He was elected to Congress as a Democrat in 1910 and died the next year.

136 more than twenty million people: Thomas Sugrue, "The Newsreels," *Scribner's Magazine* 51, no. 4 (1937): p. 9.

137 especially at upstate New Yorkers: Burns, *Roosevelt: The Lion and the Fox*, p. 118.

137 workman who was disassembling: Alter, *The Defining Moment*, p. 263.

137 "toothpaste and patent medicines": "Radio Waves and Ripples," *Washington Post*, October 19, 1933.

137 the effect of a friend: Almost verbatim from Charles Hurd, *When the New Deal Was Young and Gay* (New York: Hawthorn Books, 1965), p. 249. Hurd was a correspondent in 1937 for the *New York Times*.

137 Tommy Corcoran, Ben Cohen: Rosenman, *Working with Roosevelt*, p. 158, and James Roosevelt diary, entries for March 6 and 7, 1937, FDR library.

137 canceled his engagements: J. Russell Young, "Roosevelt Bars All Visitors in Rewriting 'Chat,'" *Evening Star*, March 9, 1937.

137 reasonable in tone: "President Denies 'Spineless Puppet' Court Is Intended," *Christian Science Monitor*, March 10, 1937.

137 preferred Anglo-Saxon: Jackson, *That Man*, p. 160.

137 80 percent: Seventy to 80 percent, according to an analysis cited by Kenneth D. Yeilding and Paul H. Carlson, *Ah, That Voice: The Fireside Chats of Franklin D. Roosevelt* (Odessa, Tex.: John Ben Shepperd Jr. Library of the Presidents, Presidential Museum, 1974), p. xviii. Commonly used words accounted for 88.5 percent of the Gettysburg Address.

138 his original arguments: "Suggestions for the Starting of the March Ninth Speech," in Samuel I. Rosenman papers, box 20, FDR library.

139 "plausible": David Lawrence, "'Packing' Foes Fear Chronic Changes," *Evening Star*, March 11, 1937.

139 interpretation of the Constitution: Arthur Sears Henning, "Roosevelt Hits Court; C.I.O. Wars on A.F. of L.," *Chicago Daily Tribune*, March 10, 1937.

139 *Whereas, Franklin*: "Yale Group Votes Roosevelt Crown," *New York Times*, March 9, 1937.

139 "a jackass": "'Roosevelt for King' Clubs Started by Harvard Satirists," *Christian Science Monitor*, March 10, 1937.

140 "silly, idle talk": "Roosevelt-for-King," *Lexington (Ky.) Herald*, March 11, 1937, FDR library. The clipping was signed by L.W.A., who was otherwise unidentified.

140 "He was totally incapable": Perkins, *The Roosevelt I Knew*, p. 156.

140 "Dictator" was not: Alter's remarks at the FDR library's conference on the presidency and the Court.

140 "may have no alternative": Alter, *The Defining Moment*, pp. 5, 187.

CHAPTER TEN:
## The Voice from Olympus

141 Turkish bath: Ashurst, *A Many-Colored Toga*, p. 372.

141 "absolutely important": "Memo for the President" from J.R., dated February 19, 1937, in the president's secretary's file, box 165, at the FDR library.

142 Ashurst saw his task: Ashurst, *A Many-Colored Toga*, p. 373.

142 a dignified committee: Ibid.

142 Feeling the importance: "At the Supreme Court Hearings," *Evening Star*, March 21, 1937.

142 loving the limelight: Almost verbatim from Ickes, *Secret Diary*, vol. 2, p. 135, entry for May 9, 1937.

142 "the committee is here": Transcript of the March 10, 1937, hearing, in *Senate Committee Hearings: 1937*, vol. 536, "Reorganization of the Federal Judiciary," 75th Cong., 1st sess., part I, March 10–16, 1937, p. 3.

142 until four o'clock that morning: The diary of Homer S. Cummings, entry for March 9, 1937, p. 30, papers of Homer S. Cummings, Albert and Shirley Small Special Collections Library, University of Virginia.

142 "damnable acoustics": Ashurst, *A Many-Colored Toga*, p. 372.

142 "reading *Gone with the Wind*": Hearing transcript, p. 7. Cummings exaggerated the length of the 1936 best seller by a factor of eight. He calculated that if a justice worked for 10 hours every day in the year and read the briefs and records for every case for the 1935 term (totaling 51,695 pages) and for all 869 petitions for writs of certiorari (totaling 344,232 pages), it would require reading at the rate of 122 pages an hour. *Gone with the Wind* runs more than 1,000 pages.

142 "That would require": Ibid., pp. 12–14.

143 annoy the senators: Joseph Alsop Jr., "Cummings Parries Sharp Attack on Court Plan as First Witness at Judiciary Hearing of Senate," *New York Herald Tribune*, March 11, 1937. "He took the whole business very calmly, cracking little jokes all the while, much to the annoyance of some of the Senators."

143 felt even angrier: In a reporter's notebook, box 53, Alsop papers, Library of Congress. Alsop's source was unidentified.

143 she organized and managed: Paper, *Brandeis*, pp. 247–49.

144 juvenile court judge: Colman, *Mrs. Wheeler Goes to Washington*, pp. 165–66.

144 caused a splash: Dudley Harmon, "Wheelers Visit Gallery to Hear Senator Speak," *Washington Post*, July 14, 1937.

145 She was flattered: Colman, *Mrs. Wheeler Goes to Washington*, p. 166.

145 "Tell your father": Ibid.

145 "A very destructive blow": Paper, *Brandeis*, p. 367, based on a 1979 interview with Marquis Childs.

145 California Street: The Brandeises' address was 2205 California St., NW, apartment 505.

145 in Alice's eyes: Paper, *Brandeis*, p. 1. See also George L. Knapp, *Uncle Sam's Government at Washington* (New York: Dodd, Mead, 1933), p. 178.

146 The justice ushered Wheeler: Leonard Baker, *Back to Back: The Duel Between FDR and the Supreme Court* (New York: Macmillan, 1967), p. 154.

146 He asked if the justice: Wheeler, *Yankee from the West*, p. 328.

146 "You call up": Ibid.

146 At first Hughes: Paul A. Freund, "Charles Evans Hughes as Chief Justice," *Harvard Law Review* 81, no. 4 (1967–68): 27. Freund was a former law clerk to Brandeis.

146 chief justice's door: The address was 2223 R St., NW, which is now the embassy of Myanmar.

146 "Did Brandeis tell you": Wheeler, *Yankee from the West*, p. 329.

147 George Washington had: McKenna, *Franklin Roosevelt and the Great Constitutional War*, p. 149.

147 The early justices: Oppenheim, "The Supreme Court Grows Up," *American Mercury*, November 1935, p. 273.

147 corresponded secretly with James Buchanan: Ibid., p. 280.

147 represented President Coolidge: C. Herman Pritchett, *The Roosevelt Court: A Study in Judicial Politics and Values, 1937–1947* (New York: Macmillan, 1948), p. 18.

148 "the poorest darky": "'Good Sportsmanship' Asked by McReynolds, Ending Court Silence on Proposed Changes," *Washington Post*, March 17, 1937. The Associated Press, the *Christian Science Monitor*, and the *Evening Star* reported it as "the backwoodsman in the hills of Georgia."

148 "He did not seek": Erman J. Ridgway, "Hughes," *Everybody's Magazine* 18, no. 3 (1908): 355–56.

149 "In private life he": Ida M. Tarbell, "How About Hughes?" *American Magazine* 65, no. 5 (1908): 463.

149 "At an early age": Burton J. Hendrick, "Governor Hughes," *McClure's Magazine*, part 1, March 1908, p. 3.

149 inadvertent: Henry F. Pringle, "Chief Justice," part 2, *New Yorker*, July 6, 1935, pp. 21–22.

149 probably argued more cases: John Shure, "Hughes to Enter Office Facing Great Questions," *Philadelphia Inquirer*, February 16, 1930.

149 Hoover had wanted: Pringle, "Chief Justice," part 3, *New Yorker*, July 13, 1935, p. 19.

150 "Each went over it": Danelski and Tulchin, eds., *The Autobiographical Notes of Charles Evans Hughes*, pp. 20–21.

150 "The baby is born": Wheeler, *Yankee from the West*, p. 329. Unless otherwise noted, the rest of the dialogue is from the same source, pp. 329–30.

150 "They are the Court": Freund, "Charles Evans Hughes as Chief Justice," p. 27. Hughes said this to Wheeler at their meeting on Sunday, March 21, according to a December 21, 1962, letter from Wheeler to Freund.

151 "a super-government": Senate Judiciary Committee hearing transcript, "Reorganization of the Federal Judiciary," March 10, 1937, p. 39.

151 Edward Corwin: A March 18, 1937, letter from Corwin to Thomas Corcoran, in Corcoran's papers, box 269, Library of Congress, accompanying Corwin's original hotel and train receipts. He remitted expenses to the White House of $19.65, including $4.00 for a room at the Dodge Hotel, $5.40 for the train, and $1.00 for a Pullman.

151 "unpack": G. Gould Lincoln, "Educator Views 'Economic Bias' Swaying Court," *Evening Star*, March 17, 1937.

151 filibuster of sorts: Alsop and Catledge, *The 168 Days*, p. 124.

151 "Senators, we are signally": Senate Judiciary Committee hearing transcript "Reorganization of the Federal Judiciary," March 22, 1937, p. 485. All of the quoted testimony is from the transcript, to p. 519.

152 Excitement rippled: Joseph Alsop Jr., "Hughes Opposes Extra Justices as Impairing Court's Efficiency; Brandeis, Van Devanter Concur," *New York Herald Tribune*, March 23, 1937.

152 clinched his case: Sandra Day O'Connor, in her remarks on the conference on the presidency and the Court, FDR library.

153 "a comma drop": Ibid.

153 since John Marshall: Smith, *FDR*, p. 386.

153 "the most powerful": Bernard Kilgore, "Brandeis' Opposition to Court Plan Seen Senate Bloc's Best Argument," *Wall Street Journal*, March 23, 1937.

153 was irate: Paul Mallon, "News Behind the News: Point-by-Point Rebuttal Seen in Hughes' Letter Opposing Court Packing," *Evening Star*, March 24, 1937.

153 "I never thought": Paper, *Brandeis*, p. 368, based on an interview with Corcoran.

154 blamed Alice Brandeis: This is almost verbatim from Ickes's paraphrasing of Corcoran's remarks, Ickes diary, July 16, 1938, reel 2, Ickes papers, Library of Congress.

154 never . . . again: Paper, *Brandeis*, p. 368.

CHAPTER ELEVEN:
*A Switch in Time*

155 "Do I eat it?": "50,000 Seen at White House for Easter Egg Rolling Fete," *Evening Star*, March 29, 1937.

156 most foul-tempered: James Roosevelt with Bill Libby, *My Parents: A Differing View* (Chicago: Playboy, 1976), p. 316.

156 savor the provocation: James Roosevelt, *Affectionately, F.D.R.* (New York: Harcourt, Brace, 1959), p. 305.

156 four thousand people: John Knox, "Experiences as Law Clerk to Mr. Justice James C. McReynolds of the Supreme Court of the United States during the Year that President Franklin D. Roosevelt Attempted to 'Pack' the Court," a manuscript dated 1976, Oak Park, Illinois, p. 727.

156 double line of spectators: Jackson, *The Struggle for Judicial Supremacy*, p. 207.

156 more likely: Lewis Wood, "Wage Law Issue Puts Amendment to Fore," *New York Times*, October 18, 1936.

157   "This case": *West Coast Hotel Co. v. Parrish et al.*, 300 U.S. 379, at 386.

157   "We are of": Ibid., at 389–90.

158   "absolute and uncontrollable": Ibid., at 391. Subsequent quotations at 398–99.

158   lawmakers' assessments of society's needs: See, for example, White, *The Constitution and the New Deal*, p. 223–25.

158   his eyes flashing: Almost verbatim from Hutchinson and Garrow, eds., *The Forgotten Memoir of John Knox*, p. 201.

158   "Our conclusion is that": *West Coast Hotel v. Parrish*, at 400.

158   in a footnote: *Burnet v. Coronado Oil & Gas Co.*, 285 U.S. 393 (1932).

158   a serious mistake: Hughes, *The Supreme Court of the United States*, p. 52.

159   "character and conscience": In a July 6, 1924, conversation with Felix Frankfurter, according to Frankfurter's typewritten recollection, reel 142, Frankfurter papers, Library of Congress.

159   the multiplication tables: Leonard, *A Search for a Judicial Philosophy*, p. 15.

159   "Mr. Justice Van Devanter": *West Coast Hotel v. Parrish*, at 400.

159   a defense of his fourteen and a half years: Joel Paschal, *Mr. Justice Sutherland, a Man Against the State* (Princeton, N.J.: Princeton University Press, 1951), p. 202, cited by John W. Chambers, "The Big Switch: Justice Roberts and the Minimum-Wage Cases," *Labor History* 10, no. 1 (1969): 62.

159   "ebb and flow of economic events": *West Coast Hotel v. Parrish*, at 402.

159   "fixed when it is adopted": Ibid., at 404, quoting from Thomas M. Cooley, *A Treatise on the Constitutional Limitations: Which Rest Upon the Legislative Power of the States of the American Union*, vol. 1, 8th ed. (Boston: Little, Brown, 1927), p. 124.

159   "exceeds the fair value": *West Coast Hotel v. Parrish*, at 409.

160   "we do not understand": Ibid., at 406.

160   pressed a handkerchief: Franklyn Waltman, "Judicial 'No Man's Land' Between Governments Is Wiped Out," *Washington Post*, March 30, 1937.

160   "another Saul at another Tarsus": Corwin, *Constitutional Revolution, Ltd.*, p. 75.

160   "Opens the Way": "Minimum Wage Act and Railroad Law Pass High Court," *Christian Science Monitor*, March 29, 1937.

161   "the Constitution": Arthur Krock, "In Washington: Flexibility of Constitution Conceded by High Court," *New York Times*, March 30, 1937.

161   its biblical sound: Trapp, "The Constitutional Doctrines of Owen J. Roberts," pp. 2–3.

161   "The traitor of Jerusalem": G. A. Williamson's introduction to Flavius Josephus, *The Jewish War* (New York: Penguin, 1959), p. 11, quoting Dr. Cecil Roth.

161   "Roberts' somersault": Frankfurter's letter to Stone dated March 30, 1937, in box 13, Stone papers, Library of Congress.

161   "A sad chapter": Ibid., Stone's April 2, 1937, letter to Frankfurter.

161   swept the capital: William E. Leuchtenburg, "FDR's Court-Packing Plan: A Second Life, A Second Death," *Duke Law Journal*, 1985, nos. 3 and 4 (1985): 673.

162   The best guess: Remarks of G. Edward White, a law professor at the University of Virginia, at the FDR library conference on the presidency and the Court.

162   letter to Homer Cummings: Leuchtenburg, "FDR's Court-Packing Plan," p. 673. The letter, from Corwin's papers at Princeton, was dated May 19, 1937.

162   "Mr. Justice Roberts's theory": "High Court Assailed at Labor Institute," *New York Times*, June 15, 1937.

162   Thomas Reed Powell: According to historian Arthur M. Schlesinger and others. See, for example, Charles Poore, "The Founder of the House of Schlesinger Historians," *New York Times*, November 12, 1963, a review of Arthur M. Schlesinger, *In Retrospect: The History of a Historian* (New York: Harcourt, Brace, & World, 1963).

162   "The liberal margin": "Is the Supreme Court Going Liberal?" *Nation*, April 3, 1937, p. 368.

162 "soundproof room": "Of All Things," *New Yorker*, April 10, 1937, p. 34, clipped to an April 9, 1937, letter from Felix Frankfurter to Harlan Stone, Stone papers, box 13, Library of Congress.

CHAPTER TWELVE:
*The Heat of Democracy*

163 "It is the economic royalists": 75th Cong., 1st sess., *Congressional Record* 81, part 3 (March 29, 1937): 2816. The quotes that follow are from pp. 2810–21.

163 shook a fist: Robert C. Byrd, *The Senate 1789–1989* (Washington, D.C.: U.S. Government Printing Office, 1988), p. 470.

164 "Senator Robinson's wrath": Edwin D. Canham, "Majority Leader Was Loved by Friends and Foes Alike," *Christian Science Monitor*, July 14, 1937.

164 never broken a promise: Sidney Olson, "Senator Robinson, Arkansas Lawyer, Became a Supreme Court Possibility," *Washington Post*, July 15, 1937.

164 house within their means: Frederic William Wile, "Washington Observations," *Evening Star*, July 16, 1937.

164 ordered the man off the premises: Ibid.

164 "There is something": The diary of James Roosevelt, entry for February 8, 1937, box 57, FDR library.

164 almost without exception, loved: Michelson, *The Ghost Talks*, p. 176.

165 brown and freckled fists: Sidney Olson, "Law-Making Order of Day in Congress," *Washington Post*, April 18, 1937.

165 "what the judges say it is": White, *The Constitution and the New Deal*, p. 357.

165 "From 1922 until": *Congressional Record* (March 29, 1937): 2832.

166 "Dear Christian friend": Robert C. Albright, "'Propaganda' Charges Flare as Senators Discuss Court," *Washington Post*, March 2, 1937.

166 "easily increase the number": "Winrod States His Views," *New York Times*, March 2, 1937. The Reverend Gerald B. Winrod was the editor of a Wichita religious publication, *The Defender*.

166 A front-page editorial: Franklyn Waltman, "Court Change Needed to Save Constitution, Cummings Tells U.S.," *Washington Post*, February 15, 1937.

166 Jewish congressmen: Paul Mallon, "News Behind the News: Religious Groups Oppose Court Program, Fearing Tampering with Freedom of Worship," *Evening Star*, February 24, 1937.

166 "Fascism, in essence": "Judiciary Reform Debated in Pulpits," *New York Times*, February 15, 1937.

167 held the balance of political power: Almost verbatim from Elmo Roper, "The *Fortune* Quarterly Survey: IV," *Fortune*, April 1936, p. 208.

167 "unfair with him": M. W. Thatcher, "Release for Tuesday Morning Papers February 23, 1937," box 269, Thomas Corcoran papers, Library of Congress. Thatcher was identified as the Washington representative for the Farmers National Grain Corp. and the Northwest Farmers Union Legislative Committee and as the chairman of the Wheat Conservation Conference.

167 "the capitalistic system": G. Gould Lincoln, "Judiciary Plan Backing Demand of Labor Group," *Evening Star*, February 18, 1937. Wallace was speaking at a press conference.

167 "No threats exactly": Joseph Alsop's handwritten notes from an interview with Fred Brenckman, legislative director of the National Grange, box 53, Alsop papers, Library of Congress.

167 larger commercial farmers: Burns, *Roosevelt: The Lion and the Fox*, p. 194.

168 twenty-nine to nine: Alsop's notes from an interview with John D. Miller of the National Cooperative Council.

168 "doubts the wisdom": L. J. Taber, the National Grange master, quoted by Robert C. Albright, "Farm Group to Battle Supreme Court Plan; Labor with President," *Washington Post*, February 17, 1937.

168 "Personally": Robert C. Albright, "Senate Foes Forecast Court Change Defeat by Margin of 10 Votes," *Washington Post*, February 25, 1937. The Farmers Union president, E. H. Everson, issued the statement to South Dakota newspapers.

168   The mildest epithet: "Washington Notes,"
      *New Republic*, April 7, 1937, p. 261.
168   number of sit-down: Shogan, *Backlash*,
      p. 138.
169   "Lincoln freed": Associated Press, "Ford
      Sit-ins Weld Gates, Hold Plant as Peace
      Parleys Reopen in Detroit," *Evening Star*,
      April 3, 1937.
169   "the revolutionary quality": Mark
      Sullivan, "Sit-Downism's New Test,"
      *Evening Star*, March 16, 1937.
169   "an insuperable": Shogan, *Backlash*,
      p. 151.
170   New Deal's labor policies: Nelson N.
      Lichtenstein, a professor of labor history
      at the University of California, Santa
      Barbara, in an interview with the author.
170   "There is no doubt": Letters to Norris
      from the Nebraska Federation of Labor,
      dated March 28, 1937, and from George
      Jackson of Litchfield, Nebraska, dated
      June 9, 1937, George W. Norris papers,
      box 117, Library of Congress.
171   "was extremely unfair": May 10, 1937,
      letter from Wheeler to Farley, as
      chairman of the Democratic National
      Committee, president's personal file,
      box 723, FDR library.
171   "indignation meetings": "Democratic
      Ranks Split by Dispute over Court,"
      *Washington Post*, March 8, 1937.
172   "Repugnant scheme": "Senator Carter
      Glass's Radio Attack on President's
      Proposals for Court Change," *New York
      Times*, March 30, 1937.
172   "a Jeffersonian Democrat": S. J. Woolf,
      "An 'Unreconstructed Rebel' Speaks
      Out," *New York Times Magazine*, August
      2, 1936, p. 15.
172   "indefensible libel": "Glass Sees an
      Attempt to Deprave Court," *Christian
      Science Monitor*, March 30, 1937.
173   "had gone far enough": James T.
      Patterson, *Congressional Conservatism
      and the New Deal: The Growth of the
      Conservative Coalition, 1933–1939*
      (Lexington, Ky.: University of Kentucky
      Press, 1967), p. 75.
173   had already confided: Schlesinger, *The
      Coming of the New Deal*, pp. 504–5.
      FDR had said this to Harold Ickes, his
      interior secretary, in 1936.

174   seven holes of golf: Marion Wheeler Scott
      interview and Wheeler, *Yankee from the
      West*, p. 337. The Wheelers' eldest
      daughter, Elizabeth Colman, wrote in
      *Mrs. Wheeler Goes to Washington*,
      p. 166, that they played nine holes.
174   "Burton": Marion Wheeler Scott
      interview.
174   "frightening, in a way": A relative of Mrs.
      Wheeler who asked not to be named, in
      an interview with the author.
174   occasional mint julep: Marion Wheeler
      Scott interview.
174   considered him a self-seeker: Colman,
      *Mrs. Wheeler Goes to Washington*, pp.
      163, 167.
174   Joseph Kennedy: Reminiscences of
      Burton K. Wheeler (March 22, 1968),
      Columbia University Oral History
      Research Office Collection, p. 44.
      Wheeler said, "I think it was Joe
      Kennedy."
174   "Wheeler's all right": Wheeler, *Yankee
      from the West*, pp. 369–70.
174   "I'm glad that he thinks": Reminiscences
      of Wheeler, p. 44.
174   Sam Rosenman phoned: Ibid.
174   "Frances, there is only": Colman, *Mrs.
      Wheeler Goes to Washington*, p. 165.
174   "There is more than one": Associated
      Press, "Daughter of Wheeler Favors
      Court Change," *Washington Post*, March
      18, 1937.
175   almost a Communist: Marion Wheeler
      Scott interview.
175   Lulu Wheeler spoke her piece: Hope
      Ridings Miller, "Mrs. Wheeler Is Image
      of Abigail Adams," *Washington Post*,
      April 21, 1940.
175   "morally unsound": Associated Press,
      "Court Plan Foe Barred from Film," *New
      York Times*, April 17, 1937.
175   "I thought you knew": A letter from
      Farley to Wheeler dated May 6, 1937,
      president's personal file, box 723, FDR
      library.
176   "a long and very intimate": The diary of
      Homer S. Cummings, entry for April 10,
      1937, papers of Homer S. Cummings,
      Albert and Shirley Small Special
      Collections Library, University of
      Virginia.

176 Seven seats: Gridiron Club records, box 35, vol. 40, p. 55, manuscript division, Library of Congress.

176 the remotest idea: Verbatim from paraphrasing in Cummings diary, April 10, 1937, p. 182.

176 built a bridge for Roberts: Ibid.

177 "These sit-down strikes": "Court Fight Is Satirized by Gridiron," *Washington Post*, April 11, 1937.

177 "There were some sketches": Cummings diary, April 10, 1937, p. 40.

177 "Dictator Gould Lincoln": Gridiron Club's 1937 records, p. 153, from a transcript of President Roosevelt's remarks that White House press secretary Stephen Early sent to G. Gould Lincoln on April 12, 1937.

177 "to four hours of": Erwin D. Canham, "The Wide Horizon: Wit for Democracy," *Christian Science Monitor*, April 12, 1937.

CHAPTER THIRTEEN:
*No Compromise*

179 caused concern throughout Washington: Alsop and Catledge, *The 168 Days*, p. 145.

179 "any other union": Associated Press, "'Will Never Recognize Any Union,' Ford Asserts as New Strike Ends," *New York Times*, April 8, 1937.

179 Roberts had not even glanced: The diary of Homer S. Cummings, entry for April 9, 1937, p. 39, papers of Homer S. Cummings, Albert and Shirley Small Special Collections Library, University of Virginia.

180 waited since dawn: "Judiciary: Four 5–4; One 9–0," *Time*, April 19, 1937, p. 14.

180 tipping off: Hutchinson and Garrow, eds. *The Forgotten Memoir of John Knox*, p. 209.

180 The courtroom was hushed: Franklyn Waltman, "Roberts' Switch Strengthens U.S. Control in Industry," *Washington Post*, April 13, 1937.

180 The first case: *Associated Press v. National Labor Relations Board*, 301 U.S. 103.

180 "The New York office": Ibid., at 127.

180 Greyhound bus line: *Washington, Virginia & Maryland Coach Co. v.*

*National Labor Relations Board*, 301 U.S. 142.

180 "Seldom has the Supreme Court": Ernest K. Lindley, "Justices Split 5–4, Upon 4 of 5 Test Cases," *New York Herald Tribune*, April 13, 1937. In the original, "chamber" is capitalized and the second reference to "Court" is lower-case.

181 "a completely integrated": *National Labor Relations Board v. Jones & Laughlin Steel Corp.*, 301 U.S. 1, at 26.

181 "are not controlling": Ibid., at 41.

181 "most serious": Ibid.

181 "It is idle": Ibid., at 41–42.

182 done more to knit: The biographer Albert J. Beveridge was quoted in Franklyn Waltman, "Supreme Court's Wagner Act Decisions Follow 150-Year Controversy," *Washington Post*, April 18, 1937, p. B3.

182 a pivotal case: Almost verbatim from Leuchtenburg's remarks at the FDR library conference on the presidency and the Court.

182 "Chief Justice Hughes has saved": Franklyn Waltman, "Politics and People," *Washington Post*, April 13, 1937. Neither speaker was identified.

182 "Off the record": *Presidential Press Conferences*, vol. 9, no. 360, April 13, 1937, pp. 259–61. The publicity man FDR quoted was Eddie Roddan.

183 "an old-fashioned fit": Alsop and Catledge, *The 168 Days*, p. 153.

183 They were lucky: Cummings diary, April 12, 1937, p. 44.

183 "Hooey": Albert L. Warner, "Court Scheme Slowed Down by Decisions," *New York Herald Tribune*, April 13, 1937.

184 "nobody can tell": Cummings diary, April 12, 1937, p. 45.

184 "The thing to do": Alsop and Catledge, *The 168 Days*, p. 153. Their source was presumably Joe Keenan.

184 "Now, Lyndon": Robert A. Caro, *The Path to Power*, vol. 1, *The Years of Lyndon Johnson* (New York: Vintage Books, 1981), p. 396.

185 a vote of confidence: Associated Press, "Johnson, Backing Roosevelt's Court Plan, Wins Seat in Congress in Texas Election," *New York Times*, April 11, 1937.

185  president was only too pleased: Baker, *Back to Back*, pp. 189–90.

185  as Woodrow Wilson had: Smith, *FDR*, p. 86.

185  "the Duke of Alba": Arthur Krock, "Roosevelt's Prestige Rocked by Court Fight," *New York Times*, July 25, 1937.

185  asserted in a speech: David Lawrence, "Fate Decrees Court Bill's Defeat," *Evening Star*, July 15, 1937.

185  only twenty-two senators: Baker, *Back to Back*, p. 186.

185  Jackson advised the president: Jackson, *That Man*, p. 53.

185  "If you're going to pack": Alsop and Catledge, *The 168 Days*, p. 159.

185  president would become responsible: So said Corcoran, quoted in Alsop's notes of his interview, box 53, Alsop papers, Library of Congress.

185  opening term: Turner Catledge, "Robinson Leads for Court Place; Compromise Seen," *New York Times*, May 20, 1937, said the promise was "reliably reported" to have been made in 1933. *The 168 Days*, p. 156, which Catledge coauthored, dated the promise to 1935 and described Farley and Robinson at lunch.

186  The high-ceilinged room: Marion Wheeler Scott interview.

186  every night: Patterson, *Congressional Conservatism and the New Deal*, p. 118.

186  Leslie Biffle: Wheeler, *Yankee from the West*, p. 323.

186  "Court has reformed": Robert C. Albright, "Congressional Factions United in Hailing Wagner Decisions," *Washington Post*, April 13, 1937.

187  "You don't run so fast": Albert L. Warner, "Roosevelt Presses Fight for Court Plan, Delays Labor Bill for Showdown," *New York Herald Tribune*, April 14, 1937. The senator was unidentified.

187  "Apparently, the destiny": Louis Stark, "Labor Will Drive for a New Power," *New York Times*, April 13, 1937.

187  senators suggested: Albert L. Warner, "Court Scheme Slowed Down by Decisions," *New York Herald Tribune*, April 13, 1937.

187  buttonholing his friends: Alsop and Catledge, *The 168 Days*, p. 200.

187  seven hundred thousand copies: Alsop's notes from an unidentified source, box 53, Alsop papers, Library of Congress.

187  "those nine old men": "Eleven-Justice Plan Is Offered by McCarran," *Washington Post*, April 16, 1937.

187  filibuster all summer: Russell Smith, "Court Bill Foes Plan Filibuster in Compromise," *Washington Post*, May 10, 1937.

187  "We've got it licked": Robert C. Albright, "Congress Waits for Roosevelt to Chart Plans," *Washington Post*, May 9, 1937.

188  "For several years": "Text of Hughes' Speech," *Evening Star*, May 6, 1937.

188  "Go ahead": "'Not Too Close,' Says Hughes," *Evening Star*, May 6, 1937.

189  craned their necks: "Great Crowds Here Watched Ship, with Many Notables Aboard, Sail to Her Doom," *New York Times*, May 7, 1937.

189  "not much to say": Associated Press, "Mrs. Roosevelt Flies," *Evening Star*, May 7, 1937.

189  62 percent: "If someone paid your expenses would you like to go by airplane to Europe and back?" Yes, 38 percent; No, 62 percent. Gallup survey no. 90, question no. 1, interviewing date July 7–12, 1937, issued on July 25, 1937, according to George H. Gallup, *The Gallup Poll: Public Opinion, 1935–1971* (New York: Random House, 1972), p. 65.

189  "you and the German people": "Roosevelt Sends Hitler Message of Sympathy," *New York Times*, May 7, 1937.

189  leaned on Harold Ickes: Burns, *Roosevelt: The Lion and the Fox*, p. 385.

190  "a Garbo bob": Clintie Winfrey, "Writer Learns Why F.D.R., Wife Are Popular," *Cleveland Press*, April 22, 1937.

190  broad smile: Sigrid Arne, Associated Press, *Galveston News*, January 31, 1937.

190  Robinson could speak privately: Donald C. Bacon, "Joseph Taylor Robinson: The Good Soldier," in *First Among Equals: Outstanding Senate Leaders of the Twentieth Century*, edited by Richard A.

Baker and Roger H. Davidson
(Washington, D.C.: Congressional
Quarterly, 1991), pp. 73–74.

190    "Mr. Roosevelt": Alsop and Catledge, *The 168 Days*, p. 203.

191    "Let him do it": Farley, *Jim Farley's Story*, p. 82.

191    "And good riddance": Ibid.

191    "Why compromise?": William V. Nessly, "Roosevelt Adamant Against Court Truce, Slash in Relief Fund," *Washington Post*, May 15, 1937.

191    "The whole mess": McKenna, *Franklin Roosevelt and the Great Constitutional War*, p. 379.

192    "They are getting desperate": Sidney Olson, "Straight Vote on Court Bill Is Threatened," *Washington Post*, May 16, 1937.

192    "For fourteen months": 75th Cong., 1st sess., *Congressional Record* 81, part 3 (March 29, 1937): 2837.

192    visibly furious: Verbatim from Joseph Alsop Jr., "Keenan Dangled Federal Judgeship for Support of President's Scheme, West Virginian Asserts," *New York Herald Tribune*, March 30, 1937.

192    Reporters had been tipped: Sidney Olson, "Bloc of 15 Senate Democrats Announces Last-Ditch Fight Against Roosevelt Court Bill," *Washington Post*, May 18, 1937.

193    "We're all taking": Ibid.


CHAPTER FOURTEEN:
*Out of the Impasse*

194    comfortable but somber: Willis Van Devanter II, the justice's grandson and namesake, in a March 4, 2008, interview with the author in Arlington, Virginia.

194    "What I really wanted": Associated Press, "Reporter, Confidant of Justices, Scored Beat with Resignation," *Evening Star*, May 24, 1937.

195    "annual summer's sojourn": "Mrs. Van Devanter Funeral in Germany," *Washington Post*, September 5, 1934.

195    fixed up the old house: "Not Influenced by Court Fight, Van Devanter Tells His Friends," *New York Herald Tribune*, May 19, 1937.

195    His close friendship: Willis Van Devanter II interview.

195    "lord chancellor": Quoted by Felix Frankfurter in his prepared remarks, p. 27, for an NBC broadcast on June 30, 1941, in honor of Charles Evans Hughes's retirement, reel 127, Frankfurter papers, Library of Congress.

195    "matter of local experiment": "The Honorable Supreme Court," *Fortune*, May 1936, p. 182.

195    "The Great Assenter": Sidney Olson, "Foe of New Deal Laws Content to Become Maryland Farmer," *Washington Post*, May 19, 1937.

195    "perspicacity and common sense": Quoted by Paul A. Freund, "Charles Evans Hughes as Chief Justice," *Harvard Law Review* 81, no.1, (1967): 16.

195    "brains of the Court": Willis Van Devanter II interview. Frankfurter told him this in a private conversation.

195    "My dear Van": Ibid. The note was dated March 2, 1935. Brandeis also met with Van Devanter personally to urge him to stay.

195    "undignified": Willis Van Devanter II interview.

195    assured his full salary: By retiring rather than resigning, an ex-justice technically remained a member of the Supreme Court and was therefore protected by the constitutional provision (in Article III, Section 1) that justices' "Compensation . . . shall not be diminished during their Continuance in Office."

195    he told Brandeis: Paper, *Brandeis*, p. 371.

196    refused to quit: "Justice Retired," *Time*, May 31, 1937.

196    Connecticut Avenue: The address was 2101 Connecticut Avenue, NW.

196    Borah had hinted: Alsop and Catledge, *The 168 Days*, p. 206.

196    "a little too large": Perkins, *The Roosevelt I Knew*, p. 65.

196    "One up and": Turner Catledge, "A New Deal Foe," *New York Times*, May 19, 1937.

196    had really ended: Edward C. Stone, "Deposits Climb to New All-Time Peak in Capital," *Evening Star*, December 31, 1936.

196 her Hope Diamond: "$50,000 McLean Party Paces Riotous New Year Eve Here," *Evening Star*, January 1, 1937.

197 "and what's more": "Washington Considers 1936—and Likes It," *Evening Star*, January 1, 1937.

197 "Business recovery": "The Menace of Prosperity," *New Republic*, January 27, 1937, p. 370.

197 The outlook was bright: "Outlook: Uncertainties of Economic Horizon Fail to Dim Optimism of the Year-End Forecasters," *News-Week*, January 2, 1937, citing a report by investment analyst Peter B. B. Andrews in *Barron's*.

197 An opinion survey: "The *Fortune* Quarterly Survey: VII," *Fortune*, January 1937, p. 150. In the survey, 25.5 percent said the Depression was over; 34.8 percent, getting over; 31.9 percent, not over; and 7.8 percent didn't know.

197 only a third: Ibid., pp. 86–87. Forty percent said a young man still had the opportunity; 18 percent said "yes, if he's lucky"; 35 percent said no, and 8 percent said "don't know."

198 1,150,000 words: "High Lights in Seven Weeks' Hearings on Supreme Court Bill," *Evening Star*, April 25, 1937.

198 More and more: Ibid.

198 "coherent citizen": "Democratic Ranks Split by Dispute Over Court," *Washington Post*, March 8, 1937.

198 "show must go on": Frederic William Wile, "Washington Observations," *Evening Star*, April 7, 1937.

199 opponents named four: Besides Pat McCarran of Nevada and Joseph O'Mahoney of Wyoming, both Democrats, the writing subcommittee included William King of Utah and William Borah of Idaho, the committee's ranking Democrat and Republican, respectively.

199 "another five-to-four": Associated Press, "'Another 5 to 4 Decision' Makes Senators Laugh," *New York Times*, May 19, 1937.

199 "They are begging": Franklyn Waltman, "Invalidation of Social Security Act Seen as Only Hope," *Washington Post*, May 19, 1937.

199 called him "Mr. Justice": Alsop and Catledge, *The 168 Days*, p. 209.

199 "I will personally move": Sidney Olson, "4 Democrats Seeking Robinson's Post After Slating Him for Court," *Washington Post*, May 20, 1937.

199 "Each side": "Robinson Boomed by Senate Friends for Court Vacancy," *Christian Science Monitor*, May 20, 1937.

200 "Do you intend": *Presidential Press Conferences*, vol. 7, no. 368, May 21, 1937, p. 380.

200 his ordinary mind: Alsop and Catledge, *The 168 Days*, p. 220.

200 "did not know enough corporate": "The Senator from Arkansas," *Fortune*, January 1937, p. 102.

200 led the Senate battles: Cecil Edward Weller Jr., *Joe T. Robinson: Always a Loyal Democrat* (Fayetteville: University of Arkansas Press, 1998), pp. 36–39, 66–69, 110–11.

200 "I don't know why": S. J. Woolf, "Robinson's Last Interview, Given Day Before His Death," *New York Times*, July 15, 1937.

201 growing disaffected: Bacon, "Joseph Taylor Robinson," p. 83.

201 "a conservative at heart": Ickes, *Secret Diary*, vol. 2, p. 144, entry for May 22, 1937.

201 Robinson had enraged him: Verbatim from Alsop's notes on an interview with Tommy Corcoran, box 53, Alsop papers, Library of Congress.

201 "What are you going": Henry Morgenthau papers, diary entry for May 24, 1937, p. 308, roll 19, box 69, FDR library. The rest of this dialogue is from the same source.

201 it fell to Farley: Farley, *Behind the Ballots*, p. 332.

201 "Think no more": Alsop and Catledge, *The 168 Days*, pp. 212–13.

202 keen but gentle face: Knapp, *United Sam's Government at Washington*, p. 178.

202 "This is the justice": John Knox, "Experiences as Law Clerk to Mr. Justice James C. McReynolds of the Supreme Court of the United States

during the Year that President Franklin
D. Roosevelt Attempted to 'Pack' the
Court," a manuscript dated 1976, Oak
Park, Illinois, p. 208.

202 rescue a lawyer befuddled: George Creel,
"If the Court Please," *Collier's*, May 8,
1937, p. 22.

202 at Columbia Law: Theodore C. Wallen,
"The Supreme Court—Nine Mortal
Men," *Literary Digest*, April 7, 1934, p. 9.

202 read Greek and Latin for pleasure:
Verbatim from "The Honorable Supreme
Court," p. 82.

202 he made interesting: Felix Frankfurter,
"Remarks of Justice Frankfurter at
Broadcast (NBC) in Honor of the
Termination of the Service of Charles
Evans Hughes as Chief Justice of the
United States," p. 37, June 30, 1941,
Frankfurter papers, reel 127, Library of
Congress.

202 "I have here": "New Deal Victory," *New
York Times*, May 25, 1937.

203 "your Court tells us": Perkins, *The
Roosevelt I Knew*, p. 286.

203 "provide for the common Defence":
Article I, Section 8, in the opening
sentence.

203 would always regard: Perkins, *The
Roosevelt I Knew*, p. 301.

203 an instrument of government:
Schlesinger, *The Coming of the New
Deal*, p. 314.

203 Cardozo's voice: Franklyn Waltman, "Job
Insurance Upheld, 5–4 U.S. Old-Age
Pensions, 7–2," *Washington Post*, May 25,
1937.

204 "There is need to remind": *Steward
Machine Co. v. Davis, Collector of
Internal Revenue*, 301 U.S. 548, at 586.

204 *The Congress shall*: Article I, Section 8.

204 directly to a case: Hutchinson and
Garrow, eds., *The Forgotten Memoir of
John Knox*, p. 234.

204 "Nor is the concept": *Guy Helvering v.
Davis, Collector of Internal Revenue*, 301
U.S. 619, at 641.

204 "More like economic": Franklyn
Waltman, "Politics and People:
Supreme Court Approval of Security
Program Was Foregone Conclusion
Several Weeks Ago," *Washington Post*,

May 25, 1937. The spectator was
unidentified.

205 "The hope behind": *Helvering v. Davis*,
at 641.

205 "The final cause": James Reston, "A
Sociological Division," *New York Times*,
May 18, 1954, cited in Jim Newton,
*Justice for All: Earl Warren and the
Nation He Made* (New York: Riverhead
Books, 2006), p. 327.

205 leaned forward, smiled: "Unemployment
Insurance, Old-Age Pensions Are Ruled
Legal," *Christian Science Monitor*, May
24, 1937.

205 hardly on speaking terms: Hutchinson
and Garrow, eds., *The Forgotten Memoir
of John Knox*, p. 37.

205 "Strange that they could not": The diary
of Homer S. Cummings, entry for
January 13, 1936, p. 18, Homer
Cummings papers, Albert and Shirley
Small Special Collections Library,
University of Virginia. This anecdote had
reached FDR's ears, and he related it to
Cummings at a judicial reception on
January 9, 1936.

206 "contempt and alarm": Hutchinson and
Garrow, eds., *The Forgotten Memoir of
John Knox*, p. 239.

206 "No volume of words": "Unemployment
Insurance, Old-Age Pensions Are Ruled
Legal," *Christian Science Monitor*, May
24, 1937.

206 "Neither can we": "New Deal Victory,"
*New York Times*, May 25, 1937.

206 constitutional revolution: Edward S.
Corwin, more precisely, titled his 1941
book *Constitutional Revolution, Ltd.*

207 "I do realize it": McKenna, *Franklin
Roosevelt and the Great Constitutional
War*, p. 135.

207 "It gives me chills": John Knox, "Some
Comments on Chief Justice Charles E.
Hughes," dated February 1980, an
unpublished manuscript in the John Knox
Collection, folder 10240-m, Special
Collections, University of Virginia Library.

207 "It was, in fact": Knox, "Experiences as
Law Clerk," p. 967. These sentences did
not appear in the edited version, *The
Forgotten Memoir of John Knox*
(Hutchinson and Garrow, eds.), but

were reduced to a single sentence, p.
247, that said Roberts, "more than any
other Justice, was responsible for the
change in the trend of the Court's
decisions" and mentioned that,
otherwise, the conservatives "would
have permanently wrecked the Supreme
Court."

CHAPTER FIFTEEN:
A Good Man's Mind

209 "because he did not want": A letter dated
February 26, 1976, from Paul Bruton, a
retired law professor at the University of
Pennsylvania, box 2257, University of
Pennsylvania archives.

209 drafted a memorandum: Felix
Frankfurter, "Mr. Justice Roberts,"
University of Pennsylvania Law Review
104, no. 3 (1955): 311–17.

209 "I had to wheedle": Letter dated March
19, 1956, from Frankfurter to Professor
Wallace Mendelson, box 181, Frankfurter
papers, Library of Congress.

209 "disingenuous and born": Frankfurter,
"Mr. Justice Roberts," p. 314.

210 "call for a reconsideration": "Petition for
Writ of Certiorari and Motion to
Advance," signed by New York attorney
general John J. Bennett Jr. and New York
solicitor general Henry Epstein, filed at
the Supreme Court on March 16, 1936, in
the case of Frederick L. Morehead v.
People ex rel. Joseph Tipaldo and
stamped No. 838, p. 9.

210 "assumed": The petition for rehearing,
submitted on June 22, 1936, p. 3, said, "it
was assumed that the Adkins case and
the principles therein enunciated would
necessarily be reconsidered in the
determination of this case."

210 "a hidden rather": Frankfurter, "Mr.
Justice Roberts," p. 312.

210 "the major cause": The diary of Homer S.
Cummings, entry for May 4, 1937, p. 59,
papers of Homer S. Cummings, Albert
and Shirley Small Special Collections
Library, University of Virginia.

210 await his return: A four-to-four vote
would have sustained the Washington
State Supreme Court's ruling, which the

U.S. Supreme Court's Parrish decision
upheld, but it would not have been
considered a precedent.

210 Hughes waited a while: Pusey, Charles
Evans Hughes, vol. 2, p. 757, based on a
1947 interview with Hughes.

210 Sutherland had practically accused:
Chesly Manly, "Wage, Debt Holiday and
Rail Labor Laws Validated," Chicago
Daily Tribune, March 30, 1937.

211 "president and a stick": Reminiscences of
Charles E. Wyzanski (1954), Columbia
University Oral History Research Office
Collection, p. 291.

211 "What is the matter": Roberts
memorandum in Frankfurter, "Mr.
Justice Roberts," p. 315.

211 "Hughes is the best": William O.
Douglas, Go East, Young Man: The Early
Years (New York: Random House, 1974),
p. 327.

211 felt so bitter: Robert S. Allen, "Hughes
Checkmates the President," Nation, May
29, 1937.

211 "the wee small voice": 75th Cong., 1st
sess., Congressional Record 81, part 6
(July 9, 1937): 6987.

211 grew to adore: Owen J. Hamilton, the
justice's grandson, in an August 12, 2006,
interview with the author in Hartford,
Vermont.

211 son or a younger brother: Verbatim from
the paraphrasing of a statement "years
later" by Roberts, quoted in John Knox,
"Some Comments on Chief Justice
Charles E. Hughes," dated February 1980,
an unpublished manuscript in the John
Knox Collection, folder 10240-m, Special
Collections, University of Virginia Library.

211 "In most ways": A letter dated September
4, 1948, from Roberts to Felix
Frankfurter, box 59, Frankfurter papers,
Library of Congress.

211 chief justice visited him: Pusey, Charles
Evans Hughes, vol. 2, p. 669.

211 "his amiability and talent": Phoenixville
(Pa.) Daily Republican, May 18, 1935.

211 Hughes and his wife motored: Elizabeth
Hamilton videotaped interview.

212 "stickler for proprieties": Owen Roberts,
"Charles Evans Hughes: The
Administrative Master," Memorial

*Address Before the Association of the Bar of the City of New York*, December 12, 1948, cited in Leonard, *A Search for a Judicial Philosophy*, p. 21.

212 almost hugged him: Pusey, *Charles Evans Hughes*, vol. 2, p. 757.

212 surveyed law journals: John W. Chambers, "The Big Switch: Justice Roberts and the Minimum-Wage Cases," *Labor History* 10, no. 1 (1969): 55.

212 "dose of presidentialitis": Drew Pearson and Robert S. Allen, "Washington Daily Merry-Go-Round," *Washington Herald*, August 19, 1939.

212 "a matter of common knowledge": U.S. Senate Committee on the Judiciary, Subcommittee on Constitutional Amendments, *Composition and Jurisdiction of the Supreme Court: Hearing on S.J. Res. 44*, 83rd Cong., 2nd sess., January 29, 1954, p. 8.

213 Cardozo had once explained: Benjamin N. Cardozo, *The Nature of the Judicial Process* (New Haven, Conn.: Yale University Press, 1921), p. 113, cited in Leonard, *A Search for a Judicial Philosophy*, p. 106.

213 "There is nothing": Richard A. Posner, "A Political Court," foreword to "The Supreme Court: 2004 Term," *Harvard Law Review* 119, no. 31 (2005): 40, 56.

213 "from reading life": Hendel, "The 'Liberalism' of Chief Justice Hughes," p. 260.

213 "lurid detective stories": "Roberts Chose Teaching Over Law in Early Days," *New York World*, May 10, 1930.

213 invariably guessed the solution: Jane S. McIlvaine, "Unretiring Justice," *Philadelphia Inquirer Magazine*, December 7, 1950.

214 "untheoretical": Paul Edward Nelson, "The Constitutional Theory of Mr. Justice Roberts," dissertation for a master's degree in political science, University of Chicago, March 1960, p. 126.

214 organic constitutional philosophy: A letter dated March 19, 1956, from Frankfurter to Professor Wallace Mendelson, Frankfurter papers, box 181, Library of Congress.

214 "conservative with liberal": "Justice Roberts," *Outlook and Independent*, June 4, 1930, p. 175.

214 "flexibility of mind": Erwin N. Griswold, "Owen J. Roberts as a Judge," *University of Pennsylvania Law Review* 104 (December 1955): 340.

214 "original or innovating mind": Ibid., p. 333.

214 "I have no illusions": Quoted in David Burner, "Owen J. Roberts," in Friedman and Israel, eds., *The Justices of the United States Supreme Court 1789–1969*, vol. 3, p. 2263. Roberts was referring to Chief Justices John Marshall and Roger B. Taney and Associate Justices Joseph P. Bradley, Oliver Wendell Holmes Jr., Louis D. Brandeis, and Benjamin Cardozo.

214 "His beliefs were not": George Wharton Pepper, "Owen J. Roberts—The Man," *University of Pennsylvania Law Review* 104, no. 3 (1955): 374.

214 "the way to stop": "To Seek Development of the United Nations into a World Federation," House Foreign Affairs Committee hearing on H.R. Concurrent Resolution 64, October 12–13, 1949, p. 141.

214 "George Washington in disguise": Ibid., p. 147.

215 "a higher ideal": Owen Hamilton interview.

215 scythed along the fence: Ibid.

215 "a humble, calm": Sultzer and Hemighaus, *Owen J. Roberts: Our Namesake and Our Pride* (Pottstown, Pa.: Owen J. Roberts School District, 1977), p. 4.

215 too thrifty: Elizabeth Hamilton videotaped interview.

215 the most generous tip: Pearson and Allen, "How the Supreme Court Works," *Saturday Evening Post*, April 17, 1937, p. 10.

215 Clumsy on the tennis: Elizabeth Hamilton videotaped interview.

215 "We can learn much": "Brundage Extols Hitler's Regime," *New York Times*, October 5, 1936.

216 front-page news: "30 Held at Bay 2 Hours in Row over Debt Sale," *Philadelphia*

*Inquirer*, October 3, 1936, and Associated Press, "Pennsylvania Farmer Kills 1, Wounds 3 in Battle Over Auction for $75 Debt," *New York Times*, October 3, 1936. Both articles were on page one.

216  "We live today": Owen J. Roberts, "American Constitutional Government: The Blueprint and the Structure," *Boston University Law Review* 29, no. 1 (1949): 27.

216  "fully conscious": *Composition and Jurisdiction of the Supreme Court*, Senate Judiciary Committee hearings on S.J. Res. 44, 83rd Cong., 2nd sess., January 29, 1954, p. 9.

217  "The continual expansion": Owen J. Roberts, *The Court and the Constitution* (Cambridge, Mass.: Harvard University Press, 1951), pp. 61–62.


**CHAPTER SIXTEEN:**
*Jefferson's Last Stand*

218  "In fact, he's rather": Alsop and Catledge, *The 168 Days*, p. 215. According to the Pare-Lorentz day-by-day diary, Robinson visited the White House on the evening of June 3, 1937.

219  "is to be a bride": McKenna, *Franklin Roosevelt and the Great Constitutional War*, p. 472.

219  was not a candidate: William V. Nessly, "Retreat on Court Stand by Roosevelt Indicated; Compromise Is Sought," *Washington Post*, June 4, 1937.

219  "Mr. Justice": Farley, *Jim Farley's Story*, p. 86.

219  "clearly unconstitutional": Memorandum dated June 11, 1937, from FDR to Robinson, Joseph T. Robinson papers, box 11:114, Special Collections, University of Arkansas Libraries, Fayetteville.

219  The public's support: George Gallup, "Sharp Drop Recorded Since Wagner Decision," *Washington Post*, May 23, 1937.

219  "the first time": "The *Fortune* Quarterly Survey: IX," *Fortune*, July 1937, pp. 96–97. The poll found that 36.9 percent of respondents favored the president's plan "to add six new younger justices to

the Supreme Court," 18.9 percent favored an alternative reform, and 38.1 percent preferred the status quo. The rest said they didn't know or had mixed feelings.

220  "wriggled out of doing": Alsop's notes from an interview with Corcoran, box 53, Alsop papers, Library of Congress.

220  stunned the capital: McKenna, *Franklin Roosevelt and the Great Constitutional War*, p. 484.

220  "as an invasion": Quotes from "Reorganization of the Federal Judiciary: Adverse Report [To accompany S. 1392]," Senate Judiciary Committee, 75th Cong., 1st sess., Senate Report no. 711, pp. 11, 14, and 23.

220  Robinson . . . canvassed his colleagues: Alsop and Catledge, *The 168 Days*, pp. 222–26.

221  ten minutes' deliberation: Gerald G. Gross, "Secret Rift in Jefferson Shrine Board Is Disclosed," *Washington Post*, April 21, 1937. The alternative design was "a cruciform structure adapted from the Villa Rotunda near Vicenza, Italy." Both were designed by John Russell Pope.

221  "[T]he 'Great Republican'": Daniel Boon of Washington, D.C., letter to the editor, *Washington Post*, April 22, 1937.

222  women threatened to chain: http://www .nps.gov/nama/planyourvisit/cherry-blossom-history.htm.

222  "not built to serve": "Wright's Lance Hurled at D.C.," *Evening Star*, October 26, 1938.

222  been Roosevelt's idea: Christopher Weeks, *AIA Guide to the Architecture of Washington, D.C.* (Baltimore: Johns Hopkins University Press, 1994), p. 61.

222  "real inventor": "Court Bill Needed, Farley Declares," *New York Times*, April 14, 1937.

222  exercised powers: Dean Alfange, *The Supreme Court and the National Will* (Garden City, N.Y.: Doubleday, Doran, 1937), p. 20.

222  "Hello, Burt!": Frederic William Wile, "Washington Observations," *Evening Star*, June 30, 1937.

223 the Jefferson Islands: Individually they were called Jackson, Wilson, and Roosevelt islands.

223 "The men might feel": William V. Nessly, "Roosevelt Calls Parley to Heal Party Breach," *Washington Post*, June 17, 1937.

223 "You know, there's": "Ten Democrats Decline Bids to Roosevelt Rally," *Washington Post*, June 22, 1937.

223 efforts of Sam Rayburn: Alsop's notes from an interview, apparently with Attorney General Homer S. Cummings, box 53, Alsop papers, Library of Congress.

223 shady back porch: James, *Mr. Garner of Texas*, p. 119.

223 "The Mystery of Jack Garner": Frederic William Wile, "Washington Observations," *Evening Star*, June 21, 1937.

223 great row: Alsop's notes from an interview, apparently with Jim Farley, box 53, Alsop papers, Library of Congress.

223 Garner had urged: Smith, *FDR*, p. 388.

223 "This is a fine time": Farley, *Jim Farley's Story*, p. 84.

224 had never met him: Turner Catledge, "Congress Guests of President Find Politics Tabooed," *New York Times*, June 26, 1937, and Paul Mallon, "News Behind the News: White House Guests Discover They Are Committee on Reorganization Plan," *Evening Star*, May 29, 1937.

224 to two minutes: Turner Catledge, "Rift Among Democrats Has Deep-Laid Causes," *New York Times*, June 27, 1937.

224 "dispensed wisdom": The diary of Homer S. Cummings, entry for June 28, 1937, p. 94, papers of Homer S. Cummings, Albert and Shirley Small Special Collections Library, University of Virginia.

224 swam in the nude: Leuchtenburg, "FDR's Court-Packing Plan: A Second Life, A Second Death," *Duke Law Journal* 1985, nos. 3 and 4 (1985): 278.

224 New York congressman: Representative Matthew J. Merritt (D., N.Y.).

224 disapproved of gossip and jokes: Colman, *Mrs. Wheeler Goes to Washington*, p. 73.

224 "only reinforced her belief": Ibid., pp. 167–68.

225 Wheeler had been quoted: "Court Plan Due for Compromise After Holidays," *Christian Science Monitor*, June 28, 1937.

225 "Well, can you jump": Wheeler, *Yankee from the West*, p. 334.

225 "Burt, I just want": Wheeler, *Yankee from the West*, pp. 334–36, for the ensuing dialogue, unless otherwise noted.

226 "It is the difference": Carlisle Bargeron, "White House Raps Wheeler in Subterfuge," *Washington Herald*, July 8, 1937.

226 the cruelty: Alsop and Catledge, *The 168 Days*, p. 253.

226 "How can I be sure?": Burton K. Wheeler, "Borah of Idaho, Senate Giant," *Washington Post*, June 4, 1961, a book review of *Borah* by Marian C. McKenna (Ann Arbor: University of Michigan Press, 1961).

CHAPTER SEVENTEEN:
*Death Knell*

227 "How did you": Wheeler, *Yankee from the West*, p. 336.

227 "I move that": 75th Cong., 1st sess., *Congressional Record* 81, part 6 (July 6, 1937): 6787. The rest of the dialogue is from the same source, pp. 6791–98.

229 his fingers burned: Sidney Olson, "Senator Robinson, Arkansas Lawyer, Became a Supreme Court Possibility," *Washington Post*, July 15, 1937.

229 rushed to his side: Verbatim from the remarks of Capitol physician George Calver, quoted in "Senator Robinson Found Dead of Heart Attack in Apartment; Fight over Court Bill Halted," *Evening Star*, July 14, 1937.

229 "Joe, take it easy": Franklyn Waltman, "Copeland Warns Senate as Leader Succumbs to Heart Attack," *Washington Post*, July 15, 1937.

229 So many autograph hounds: Eddie Brietz, "Diz Dean's Rebellion Is Labeled Just an 'Act,'" *Evening Star*, July 7, 1937.

229 "Play the game": Pat Frank, "Roosevelt Hurls First Ball; Nearly Hit by Foul," *Washington Herald*, April 20, 1937.

230  most magnetic: http://www.baseball
     -almanac.com/asgbox/yr1937as.shtml.

230  "I am tired": Shirley Povich, "30,000 to
     See 'Dizzy' Battle Gomez in All-Star Tilt
     Today," *Washington Post*, July 7, 1937.

231  "McCarthy packed": Shirley Povich,
     "Americans Win Battle of Stars, 8–3,"
     *Washington Post*, July 8, 1937.

231  "Let me say": *Congressional Record* (July
     8, 1937): 6895.

232  "I do not know anybody": Ibid., p. 6896.

233  "fusillade of 'dead cats'": Arthur Krock,
     "Court Bill Is Obscured in Senate Battle
     Haze," *New York Times*, July 11, 1937.

233  nervous excitement: "Wheeler Urges
     Referendum on Changing Court,"
     *Christian Science Monitor*, July 9,
     1937.

233  "It was *cheap*": *Congressional Record*
     (July 9, 1937): 6972–73.

233  Wheeler turned beet red: Robert C.
     Albright, "Wheeler Denounces Court Bill
     as 'Cheap' in Three-Hour Speech,"
     *Washington Post*, July 10, 1937.

233  "a Patrick Henry": Sidney Olson, "Oratory
     on Capitol Hill Is Fast Approaching End
     of Long Decline," *Washington Post*, April
     18, 1937.

233  that "the judicial power": *Congressional
     Record* (July 9, 1937): pp. 6974–77.

235  her ill brother: Ashurst, *A Many-Colored
     Toga*, p. 377.

235  "People in Washington": Leuchtenburg,
     "FDR's Court-Packing Plan," p. 683,
     quoting Representative Thomas Amlie (R.,
     Wis.) in a July 10, 1937, letter to Alfred M.
     Bingham, in Bingham manuscripts, box 1,
     Yale University Library.

235  subsisting mostly on buttermilk: Alsop
     and Catledge, *The 168 Days*, p. 260.

235  "You could never tell": Ibid., p. 245. The
     "intimate" could only have been Tommy
     Corcoran or Vice President Garner.

235  shared with Joe Keenan: Ibid.

235  "Pretty Sure Pro": Dated June 17, in the
     president's secretary's file, box 165, FDR
     library.

235  "slow packing": *Congressional Record*
     (July 9, 1937): 6980.

236  "Webster-Calhoun-Clay era": Frederic
     William Wile, "Washington

237  Observations," *Evening Star*, July 16,
     1937.

237  shaking a preacher's finger: Albert L.
     Warner, "Plan to Shelve Court Scheme
     Needs 3 Votes," *New York Herald
     Tribune*, July 12, 1937.

237  finished an early lunch: Alsop and
     Catledge, *The 168 Days*, p. 261.

237  "Bailey's in there": Ibid., p. 262.

237  sharp pain in his breast: Verbatim from
     Ashurst's paraphrasing, *A Many-Colored
     Toga*, p. 376.

237  "the hot air hit me": Edward Jamison,
     "Flags Lowered as Washington Mourns
     Death," *Arkansas Democrat*, July 14,
     1937. Robinson was speaking to Senator
     Carl Hatch of New Mexico, a Democrat.

237  "I am unwilling": *Congressional Record*
     (July 9, 1937): p. 6987.

237  What Minton saw: Alsop and Catledge,
     *The 168 Days*, p. 263.

238  "a little flurry": Associated Press, "Had
     Heart Attack Monday," *New York Times*,
     July 15, 1937.

238  Methodist Building: He lived in
     apartment 402 at 110 Maryland Avenue,
     NE.

238  blow to his brain: Almost verbatim from
     Arthur Krock, "In Washington: Senator
     Robinson and the Court Bill Struggle,"
     *New York Times*, July 15, 1937,
     paraphrasing what Robinson had told an
     unnamed friend.

238  an old friend: "Found Dead Alone," *New
     York Times*, July 15, 1937. The friend's
     name was Homer Adkins.

238  "I would hate to think": S. J. Woolf,
     "Robinson's Last Interview, Given Day
     Before His Death," *New York Times*, July
     15, 1937.

238  forty-three senators in favor: Robert C.
     Albright, "Sen. McCarran Risks Party
     Ouster, Urges Defeat of Court Bill,"
     *Washington Post*, July 11, 1937.

239  "cutting [it] to pieces": Ashurst, *A
     Many-Colored Toga*, p. 376. The
     following quotes are from the same
     source.

239  "Joe, I wish": H. R. Baukhage, "What's
     Back of It All: Death Ends Constitutional
     Amendment Compromise Efforts of

Robinson on Court," *Evening Star,* July 15, 1937.

239 "quite all right": "Found Dead Alone," *New York Times,* July 15, 1937.

CHAPTER EIGHTEEN:
*Burial*

240 "It is with deep grief": 78th Cong., 1st sess., *Congressional Record* 81, part 7 (July 14, 1937): 7153. The other remarks are on pp. 7153–54, 7156.

240 had been strained: Diane D. Kincaid, ed., *Silent Hattie Speaks: The Personal Journal of Senator Hattie Caraway* (Westport, Conn.: Greenwood Press, 1979), p. 55.

240 ten of their number: "Robinson is 23rd Official Lost to Roosevelt; Ten of Senate Have Died in New Deal Regime," *New York Times,* July 15, 1937. Senator Bronson Cutting of New Mexico, a Republican, was killed in a plane crash on May 6, 1935, and automobile accidents took the lives of senators Thomas Schall, Republican of Minnesota, on December 23, 1935, and Louis Murphy, Democrat of Iowa, on July 16, 1936.

241 William Borah's wife: Evelyn Peyton Gordon, "Mrs. Borah Attributes Death of Robinson to Broken Heart," *Washington Daily News,* July 15, 1937.

241 intermittent heart afflictions: Associated Press, "Robinson's Death Is Held Due to Strain of Senate Leadership," *Montana Standard,* a daily newspaper in Butte, July 15, 1937.

241 "Joe Robinson was both": Turner Catledge, "Want Bill Dropped," *New York Times,* July 15, 1937.

241 "positively ghoulish": Ickes, *Secret Diary,* vol. 2, p. 162, entry for July 16, 1937.

241 two or three days: Richard L. Neuberger, "Wheeler of Montana," *Harper's Magazine* 180 (May 1940): 614.

241 "I was so emotionally": Wheeler, *Yankee from the West,* p. 337.

241 at eight fifteen: "FDR: Day by Day—The Pare Lorentz Chronology," July 14, 1937, at the FDR library.

241 "I am shocked": Undated note from FDR to Mrs. Robinson, Joseph T. Robinson papers, box 12:119, Special Collections, University of Arkansas Libraries, Fayetteville.

241 "conscience that knew": FDR's speech file, box 33, FDR library.

241 "He suggested that": The diary of Homer S. Cummings, entry for July 15, 1937, p. 86, papers of Homer S. Cummings, Albert and Shirley Small Special Collections Library, University of Virginia.

242 "Mr. President, it's the hardest": Alsop and Catledge, *The 168 Days,* pp. 269–70.

242 "sort of last-minute help": Alsop's notes from an interview with Homer Cummings, box 53, Alsop papers, Library of Congress.

242 as "dear Alben": Smith, *FDR,* p. 392.

242 "a few members of": A draft of the July 15, 1937, letter to Barkley, with FDR's changes, FDR library.

243 "I cannot believe": United Press, "Wheeler Says Roosevelt Was Badly Counseled," *New York Herald Tribune,* July 16, 1937.

243 "ceased to rebel against reality": Alsop and Catledge, *The 168 Days,* p. 272.

243 "Joe" and "Burt": Edwin D. Canham, "Majority Leader Was Loved by Friends and Foes Alike," *Christian Science Monitor,* July 14, 1937.

244 gray and drawn: Verbatim from "Capitol Honors Robinson at State Funeral," *New York Herald Tribune,* July 17, 1937.

244 Robinson's heavily veiled widow: "President Leads Officialdom in Paying Robinson Tribute," *Evening Star,* July 16, 1937.

244 misspelled his name: Franklyn Waltman, "Sen. Robinson Given Honors by Colleagues," *Washington Post,* July 17, 1937.

245 sweet hymns: Ibid.

245 *For I reckon: Congressional Record* (July 16, 1937): 7201. This was from Romans 8:14.

245 "Is it Harrison?": Turner Catledge, "New Compromise Offered on Court by Roosevelt Men," *New York Times,* July 18, 1937.

246 averted his head: "Robinson Laid to Rest
While State Mourns," *Arkansas
Democrat*, July 19, 1937.

246 laughing and jovial Joe: Franklyn
Waltman, "Sen. Robinson Laid to Rest in
Rainstorm at Little Rock," *Washington
Post*, July 19, 1937.

246 brushed away the water: Ibid.

246 an antimonopolist: "Mr. Roosevelt's
Party," *Fortune*, June 1938, p. 88.

246 "a labor-baiting": Louis Stark, "Ovation to
Garner in House Follows Attack by
Lewis," *New York Times*, July 28, 1939.

246 always tell the truth: James, *Mr. Garner
of Texas*, p. 26.

246 "Boy, bring me": Franklyn Waltman,
"Garner Shows U.S. He's No
Throttlebottom by Canny Strategy in
Ending Court Battle," *Washington Post*,
July 23, 1937.

246 at Chillicothe: Franklyn Waltman,
"Opponents Drop Plan to End Long-
Drawn Battle Today," *Washington Post*,
July 20, 1937. Alsop and Catledge, in *The
168 Days*, p. 279, report that the news
reached the train in Parkersburg, West
Virginia.

247 But his brother: Reminiscences of Samuel
I. Rosenman (July 18, 1958), Columbia
University Oral History Research Office
Collection, pp. 9–10.

247 "incensed and hurt": Ibid.

247 disapproved of each other: Peters, *Five
Days in Philadelphia*, p. 15.

247 "that sphinx of sphinxes": Frederic
William Wile, "Washington Observations,"
*Evening Star*, May 10, 1937.

247 understood the uses of silence: Almost
verbatim from James, *Mr. Garner of
Texas*, p. 144.

247 convene a Board of Education: Ibid.,
p. 143.

248 breakfasts and dinners: Ibid., p. 137.

248 "fifth wheel": Associated Press, " 'Silent
Partner' Jack Garner Doing a Lot of
Talking on Court," *Evening Star*, July 21,
1937.

248 "told a few cronies": Perkins, *The
Roosevelt I Knew*, p. 134.

248 "Do you want it": Alsop and Catledge,
*The 168 Days*, p. 279. Their source
presumably was Garner.

248 Wheeler had rejected: Ickes, *Secret
Diary*, vol. 2, p. 172, diary entry for July
25, 1937. Roosevelt had told this to
Ickes.

248 authorized Garner: Ibid., p. 171.

249 Richard Russell: "Barkley Elected
Majority Leader; Court Bill Fades,"
*Christian Science Monitor*, July 21, 1937.

249 "the *coup de grace*": Ickes, *Secret Diary*,
vol. 2, p. 171, diary entry for July 25,
1937.

249 "Court Change to Be Shelved": *New York
Times*, July 21, 1937.

249 "Swing of 7 Senators": *Washington Post*,
July 21, 1937. The full headline included
"Insist on Action;" between the two
quoted clauses.

249 "I bit my pipe stem": "Secret Poll Taken,"
*New York Times*, July 22, 1937.

249 Tommy Corcoran claimed: Ickes, *Secret
Diary*, vol. 2, p. 174, entry for July 27,
1937.

249 he rode the elevator: Turner Catledge,
"The Liberal Who Fights New Deal
Liberalism," *New York Times Magazine*,
August 8, 1937.

250 "Burt, you're a real": McKenna, *Franklin
Roosevelt and the Great Constitutional
War*, p. 319.

250 The vice president stared: Catledge, "The
Liberal Who Fights New Deal
Liberalism."

250 "Jack, I won't give": Wheeler, *Yankee
from the West*, p. 338. The rest of this
conversation is from the same source
unless otherwise noted.

250 "All right, Jack.": Catledge, "The Liberal
Who Fights New Deal Liberalism."

250 "The best bargain": Cummings diary, July
22, 1937, p. 98.

250 "Some persons of a cynical": Ibid., p. 103,
July 24 entry.

250 dropped from the list: "John Nance
Garner, 98, Is Dead; Vice President
Under Roosevelt," *New York Times*,
November 8, 1967.

250 Twenty-seven senators: Alsop and
Catledge, *The 168 Days*, pp. 287–88.

251 starched sheets of wrapping paper:
30–32 [pseudonyms], *High Low
Washington* (Philadelphia: J. B.
Lippincott, 1932), p. 51.

251 Against all precedent: Ickes, *Secret Diary*, vol. 2, July 25, 1937, p. 171.

251 "kicks in the face": Robert C. Albright, "Epic Battle Is Concluded to Prevent Party Split," *Washington Post*, July 23, 1937.

251 "I think that's very": Alsop and Catledge, *The 168 Days*, p. 289.

251 loopy cursive: Reproduced in "Historic Court Compromise Memo," *Washington Post*, July 23, 1937.

252 reduced the new majority leader to silence: Alsop and Catledge, *The 168 Days*, p. 289.

252 "You'll get the party harmony": Albright, "Epic Battle Is Concluded."

252 "Senators, senators": Alsop and Catledge, *The 168 Days*, p. 290.

252 *Bestow upon us*: *Congressional Record* (July 22, 1937): 7353. It was delivered by the Reverend Richard A. Cartmell, assistant rector, Church of the Epiphany, located at 1317 G Street, NW, in Washington, D.C.

252 All but five: Ninety-two senators answered to their names in the day's first quorum call, and only ninety to the second one. Senators Key Pittman of Nevada and James Hughes of Delaware, both Democrats, had momentarily vanished.

253 "with the understanding": *Congressional Record* (July 22, 1937): 7375.

253 Barkley had refused: Turner Catledge, "A Full Surrender," *New York Times*, July 23, 1937.

253 struggled to his feet: Alsop and Catledge, *The 168 Days*, p. 293.

253 "I desire to know": *Congressional Record* (July 22, 1937): 7381.

253 Garner let them: Caro, *Master of the Senate*, p. 63.

254 "You'll need both": Albright, "Epic Battle Is Concluded."

254 "I wish some day": Ibid.

CHAPTER NINETEEN:
*Victory*

255 "Oh, I don't know": *Presidential Press Conferences*, vol. 10, no. 383, July 23, 1937, pp. 59–60.

255 the sarcasm: "Much of Goal Won, President Asserts; More Must Follow," *Christian Science Monitor*, July 23, 1937.

255 a memorandum: President's secretary's file, box 165, FDR library.

256 shifting power: Corwin, *Constitutional Revolution, Ltd.*, pp. 96, 104.

256 "A good part": *Presidential Press Conferences*, vol. 10, no. 383, July 23, 1937, p. 60.

256 "We lost the battle": See Richberg, *My Hero*, p. 226. See also Michelson, *The Ghost Talks*, p. 185, and Rosenman, *I Worked with Roosevelt*, p. 161.

257 "The thing that killed": Reminiscences of Samuel I. Rosenman (July 18, 1958), Columbia University Oral History Research Office Collection, p. 11.

257 "the day of grace": The diary of Homer S. Cummings, entry for July 25, 1937, p. 97, papers of Homer S. Cummings, Albert and Shirley Small Special Collections Library, University of Virginia.

257 acknowledged that they: Turner Catledge, "A Full Surrender," *New York Times*, July 23, 1937. "[I]t can be seen how much more closely was the Senate divided than was expressed in any of the rival claims; that enlargement of the court by the legislative method had escaped from Mr. Farley's 'bag'; and that Mr. Wheeler's frequent assertions of certain victory, before the death of Mr. Robinson, were not strongly based," Arthur Krock wrote in "In Washington: As Senate Decreed Death (or Exile) of Court Bill," *New York Times*, July 23, 1937.

257 seething inside: Farley, *Jim Farley's Story*, pp. 95–96.

257 "a terrific defeat": Ickes, *Secret Diary*, vol. 2, July 25, 1937, entry, p. 170.

257 "It was a bitter": Rosenman, *I Worked with Roosevelt*, p. 161.

257 "that growing ego": Robert A. Wilson, ed., *Character Above All: Ten Presidents from FDR to George Bush* (New York: Simon & Schuster, 1995), p. 35, quoted in McKenna, *Franklin Roosevelt and the Great Constitutional War*, p. 560.

258  6o percent of Americans: Gallup survey no. 94, conducted Aug. 4–9, 1937. Asked "Are you for or against President Roosevelt?" 6o.4 percent of respondents said "for" and 39.6 percent said "against."

258  "[H]is prestige": "The *Fortune* Quarterly Survey: XII," *Fortune*, April 1938, p. 104. The percentage of respondents who favored a third term for FDR was measured at 52.6 percent in April 1937, 45.0 percent in July, and 43.3 percent in October.

258  was credited more: Smith, *FDR*, p. 390.

258  "Most of the congressmen": Perkins, *The Roosevelt I Knew*, p. 263.

258  "already ample signs": "The Pack in Full Cry," *Nation*, July 31, 1937, p. 116.

259  "consider a message": 75th Cong. 1st sess., *Congressional Record* 81, part 8 (August 12, 1937): 8732.

259  A gasp: Franklyn Waltman, "'Dark-Horse' Nomination of Alabaman Facing Study," *Washington Post*, August 13, 1937.

260  "Hugo," the president said: Alsop and Catledge, *The 168 Days*, p. 307. The same source described FDR's meeting with Black, which evidently was recounted by Black.

260  The Constitution had authorized: According to Article II, Section 2 of the Constitution, "The President shall have Power to fill up all Vacancies that may happen during the Recess of the Senate, by granting Commissions which shall expire at the End of their next Session."

260  Because he had demonized: Alsop and Catledge, *The 168 Days*, p. 303.

260  "will certainly stir up": Cummings diary, August 12, 1937, p. 138.

260  Hugo's Negro playmate: "Justice Black, Champion of Civil Liberties for 34 Years on Court, Dies at 85," *New York Times*, September 26, 1971.

261  a book a day: Rosen, *The Supreme Court*, p. 136.

261  works of Thomas Jefferson: Ibid., p. 138.

261  twenty-four for twenty-four: United Press, "Black's Voting Record," *Washington Daily News*, August 13, 1937.

261  judicial temperament: Arthur Krock, "Senate Held to Invite Nominating of Black," *New York Times*, August 15, 1937.

261  not a soul: Verbatim from paraphrasing in Cummings diary, August 12, 1937, p. 139.

261  laughed about the surprise: Alsop and Catledge, *The 168 Days*, p. 307.

261  "Jesus Christ": Henry J. Abraham, *Justices and Presidents: A Political History of Appointments to the Supreme Court* (New York: Oxford University Press, 1974), p. 200.

261  "a complete surprise": Waltman, "'Dark-Horse' Nomination of Alabaman Facing Study."

261  "It is an immemorial": *Congressional Record* (August 12, 1937): 8732.

262  ashen-faced: Turner Catledge, "Senate Is Startled," *New York Times*, Aug. 13, 1937.

262  implied to his colleagues: Roger K. Newman, *Hugo Black: A Biography* (New York: Fordham University Press, 1994), p. 241.

262  offices and cloakrooms: Franklyn Waltman, "Politics and People: 'Devil's Advocate' Urges Scrutiny of Senator Black's Reputed Ku Klux Klan Connection," *Washington Post*, August 14, 1937.

262  "according to ex-Klansmen": Scripps Howard Alliance, "F.D. Strikes at Foes by Nominating Black," *Washington Daily News*, August 13, 1937.

262  "to withdraw this name": *Congressional Record* (August 17, 1937): 9070.

263  Carter Glass's "no": Robert C. Albright, "Black Voted to Supreme Court Despite Klan Charge," *Washington Post*, August 18, 1937.

263  in Klan regalia: Roger K. Newman, *Hugo Black: A Biography* (New York: Pantheon Books, 1994), p. 94.

263  "I did join": Lewis Wood, "Radio Talk Is Brief," *New York Times*, October 2, 1937.

263  "stuck with a Kluxer": Westbrook Pegler, "Fair Enough: Plight of the Pinks," *Washington Post*, October 2, 1937.

263  "Get out your pencils": *Presidential Press Conferences*, vol. 10, no. 398, September 14, 1937, p. 208.

264 The president decided: Smith, *FDR*, pp. 410–13.

264 the "purge": Rosenman, *Working with Roosevelt*, p. 176.

264 Tommy Corcoran's efforts: "John O'Connor, 74, Legislator, Dies," *New York Times*, January 27, 1960.

264 two-to-one margin: Gallup and Rae, *The Pulse of Democracy*, p. 297. The July 1938 poll found 69 percent in opposition and 31 percent in favor.

264 "It's a terrible thing": Rosenman, *Working with Roosevelt*, p. 167.

265 "Roosevelt saw leadership": Ibid., p. 171.

265 "Suppose my neighbor's": http://www .fdrlibrary.marist.edu/odlendls.html. He addressed the nation by radio on March 11, 1941.

265 shrewd from beginning to end: Patrick J. Maney, a specialist in U.S. political history in the 1930s and now dean of arts and sciences at Boston College, in an interview with the author.

265 had already taken steps: "Roosevelt's success in mobilizing the nation to this extraordinary level of collective performance rested on his uncanny sensitivity to his followers, his ability to apprise public feeling and to lead the people one step at a time." Goodwin, *No Ordinary Time*, p. 608.

EPILOGUE

266 FDR detested him: Joseph Alsop and Robert Kintner, "Farley and the Future," *Life*, September 19, 1938, p. 56.

266 through . . . Bruce Kremer: Joseph Alsop and Robert Kintner, "The Capital Parade," *Evening Star*, June 6, 1938.

266 Agriculture Department's own records: Memorandum titled "Patronage: Department of Agriculture," on U.S. Senate stationery, marked "1938" (though with no specific date) in Wheeler file, box 169, president's secretary's file, FDR library.

266 "married a du Pont heiress": "He Ought to Know," an interior headline in an undated 1938 column of "Washington Merry-Go-Round," in Wheeler file, box 169, president's secretary's file, FDR

library. The details about Wheeler's relatives are from the same source.

266 Jimmy Roosevelt admitted: W. Davenport, "I'm Glad You Asked Me: Interview," *Collier's*, August 20 and 27, 1938.

267 "all the people": Telegram dated October 2, 1937, to FDR from Wheeler in Gerber, California, in president's personal file 723, FDR library.

267 "has transformed the raw-boned": Ray Tucker, "Capitol Leaders in Revolt: No. 4—Burton K. Wheeler," *Evening Star*, May 18, 1938.

267 he was boasting: "White House Wins on Reorganization," *New York Times*, May 19, 1938.

267 "an ornament": Syndicated columnist Marquis Childs, "Washington Calling," *Washington Post*, July 20, 1946.

268 The original name: Douglas W. Churchill, "News of the Screen," *New York Times*, May 27, 1939.

268 vetoed by Will Hays: Raymond P. Brandt, "Wheeler, Liberal Champion," part 2, *Washington Sunday Star*, April 21, 1940.

268 was loosely based: Ibid.

268 three-quarters scale: Richard A. Baker, U.S. Senate historian, in an interview with the author.

268 Using a statistical composite: Mayme Ober Peak, "Jim Preston Goes to Hollywood to Help Make a Picture on Washington," *Washington Post*, May 28, 1939.

268 shots had been filmed: Byrd, *The Senate 1789–1989*, vol. 2, p. 484.

269 the audience cheering: James J. Cullinane, "4,000 Welcome 'Mr. Smith' at Gala Premiere," *Washington Times-Herald*, October 18, 1939.

269 "grotesque distortion": Richard L. Strout, "Now, 'Mr. Capra Goes to Washington' But the Senators Are Not Amused," *Christian Science Monitor*, October 27, 1939.

269 Capra alleged: Richard A. Baker, *200 Notable Days: Senate Stories, 1787 to 2002* (Washington, D.C.: U.S. Government Printing Office, 2006), p. 148.

269  "Exceedingly fraudulent": Nelson B. Bell,
     "New Capra Picture Has Faulty Story
     Excellently Acted; Brief Stage Bill,"
     *Washington Post*, October 21, 1939.

269  "a fairyland": Richard L. Strout,
     "Intimate Message from Washington:
     Washington Sees 'Mr. Smith Goes to
     Washington' and Is Impressed by
     Hollywood's Genius for Hokum and
     Misrepresentation," *Christian Science
     Monitor*, October 19, 1939.

269  "The Capra caper": Frederic William
     Wile, "Washington Observations,"
     *Evening Star*, October 20, 1939.

270  "To work under you": Pusey, *Charles
     Evans Hughes*, vol. 2, p. 802.

270  deferred his departure: Lewis Wood,
     "Sutherland Quits Supreme Court; Past
     75, He Notes," *New York Times*, January
     6, 1938.

270  emotion in place of logic: McCune, *The
     Nine Young Men*, p. 242.

270  His fiercest dissent: Kermit L. Hall,
     "Owen Josephus Roberts," in Melvin I.
     Urofsky, ed., *The Supreme Court
     Justices: A Biographical Dictionary* (New
     York: Garland, 1994), p. 386.

271  "to shut our eyes": *Toyosaburo
     Korematsu v. U.S.*, 323 U.S. 214, at
     232.

271  Privately, he accused Black: Ickes diary,
     p. 9733, May 23, 1945, reel 6, Ickes
     papers, Library of Congress. Roberts had
     lunched with Ickes on May 15.

271  Black's, William Douglas's, and Frank
     Murphy's: Ibid.

271  "Stone dreaded conflict": Mason, *Harlan
     Fiske Stone*, p. 769. Then justice Robert
     H. Jackson said this to author Mason in
     1953.

271  "uncharted sea of doubt": "Roberts
     Denounces Inconsistent Rulings of
     Supreme Court," *Evening Star*, February
     2, 1944.

271  an average age: McCune, *Nine Young
     Men*, p. 270.

271  resigning, not retiring: A letter dated
     April 13, 1953, to John Knox from
     Gertrude (Mrs. Charles L.) Regis, who
     had been Stone's and then Frankfurter's
     social secretary, in folder 10240-M, Knox
     papers, University of Virginia.

271  "I will not come": A handwritten letter
     dated September 9, 1946, from Roberts
     to Frankfurter, in the Frankfurter
     papers, box 59, Library of Congress.

271  "not too cordial": A letter dated
     September 8, 1945, from Robert H.
     Jackson, who was serving as the chief
     American prosecutor at the Nazi trials in
     Nuremberg, Germany, to Stone at the
     Wambauk Inn in Jefferson, New
     Hampshire, in box 119, Jackson papers,
     Library of Congress.

271  "that our association": Box 82, Stone
     papers, Library of Congress. The
     proposed letter in its entirety, with
     Black's proposed excisions:

     *Dear Justice Roberts:*
         *The announcement of your
     resignation as a Justice of this Court
     brings to us a profound sense of regret
     [that our association with you in the
     daily work of the Court must now come
     to an end].*
         *During the more than fifteen years
     since you took office you have given to
     the work of the Court the benefit of your
     skill and wide knowledge of the law,
     gained through years of assiduous study
     and practice of your profession. You have
     faithfully discharged the heavy
     responsibility which rests on a Justice of
     this Court with promptness and
     dispatch, and with untiring energy. [You
     have made fidelity to principle your
     guide to decision.]*
         *At parting we who have shared that
     responsibility with you, and who have
     shared in the common endeavor to make
     the law realize its ideal of justice, give
     you the assurance of our continued good
     will and friendly regard. In the years to
     come we wish for your good health,
     abiding strength and, with them, the full
     enjoyment of those durable satisfactions
     which will come from the continued
     devotion of your knowledge and skill to
     worthy achievement.*
         *Yours faithfully,*

271  "derogatory excisions": Ibid., a letter
     dated September 7, 1945, from
     Frankfurter to Stone.

272 "serious intellectual limitations": A letter dated August 20, 1945, from Frankfurter to Stone, in box 119, Jackson papers, Library of Congress.

272 "If there's one thing": Ibid.

272 with their implication: Frankfurter's retelling to Jackson in diary form, dated October 2, 1945, box 119, Jackson papers, Library of Congress.

272 his eyes blazing: Ibid.

272 "did not vote his prejudices": John Knox, "Experiences as Law Clerk to Mr. Justice James C. McReynolds of the Supreme Court of the United States during the Year that President Franklin D. Roosevelt Attempted to 'Pack' the Court," a manuscript dated 1976, Oak Park, Illinois, p. 975.

273 "He was, if not": A handwritten letter dated February 13, 1956, to Justice Frankfurter from Charles Edward Wyzanski Jr. in Cambridge, Massachusetts, box 181, Frankfurter papers, Library of Congress.

273 "All in all": Catledge, "The Liberal Who Fights New Deal Liberalism," New York Times Magazine, August 8, 1937.

273 "With the arrival": M. Ramaswamy, The Creative Role of the Supreme Court in the United States (New York: Russell & Russell, 1970), p. 12. Originally published in 1956 by Stanford University Press.

274 The Roosevelt Court: Pritchett, The Roosevelt Court, p. 264.

274 "an intolerance": Ibid., p. 69, quoting Roberts's dissent in Smith v. Allwright, Election Judge et al., 321 U.S. 649 (1944).

274 "so responsive to": A December 7, 2006, e-mail to the author from Patrick J. Maney, then the chairman of the history department at the University of South Carolina.

275 "give voice to": Corwin, Constitutional Revolution, Ltd., p. 112.

275 ashamed that his chauffeur: Newton, Justice for All, p. 315.

275 "a restricted railroad ticket": Smith v. Allwright, at 669.

275 "became virtually a statement": Mason, The Supreme Court from Taft to Burger, p. 212.

275 "formed by emanations": Griswold v. Connecticut, 381 U.S. 479, at 484.

276 "the Court emerged larger": Sandra Day O'Connor's remarks, November 11, 2007, conference on the presidency and the Supreme Court, FDR library.

# BIBLIOGRAPHY

Abraham, Henry J. *Justices and Presidents: A Political History of Appointments to the Supreme Court.* New York: Oxford University Press, 1974.

Alfange, Dean. *The Supreme Court and the National Will.* Garden City, N.Y.: Doubleday, Doran, 1937.

Allen, Frederick Lewis. *Only Yesterday: An Informal History of the Nineteen-Twenties.* New York: Harper & Brothers, 1931.

————. *Since Yesterday: The 1930s in America, September 3, 1929–September 3, 1939.* New York: Harper & Brothers, 1939.

Alsop, Joseph, and Turner Catledge. *The 168 Days.* Garden City, N.Y.: Doubleday, Doran, 1938.

Alter, Jonathan. *The Defining Moment: FDR's Hundred Days and the Triumph of Hope.* New York: Simon & Schuster, 2006.

Ashurst, Henry Fountain. *A Many-Colored Toga: The Diary of Henry Fountain Ashurst.* Tucson: University of Arizona Press, 1962.

Baker, Leonard. *Back to Back: The Duel Between FDR and the Supreme Court.* New York: Macmillan, 1967.

Baker, Richard A. *200 Notable Days: Senate Stories 1787 to 2002.* Washington, D.C.: U.S. Government Printing Office, 2006.

Baker, Richard A., and Roger H. Davidson, eds. *First Among Equals: Outstanding Senate Leaders of the Twentieth Century.* Washington, D.C.: Congressional Quarterly, 1991.

Brinkley, David. *Washington Goes to War.* New York: Ballantine Books, 1988.

Burns, James MacGregor. *Roosevelt: The Lion and the Fox.* New York: Harcourt, Brace, 1956.

Burns, James MacGregor, and Susan Dunn. *The Three Roosevelts: Patrician Leaders Who Transformed America.* New York: Atlantic Monthly Press, 2001.

Burrough, Bryan. *Public Enemies: America's Greatest Crime Wave and the Birth of the FBI, 1933–34.* New York: Penguin, 2004.

Byrd, Robert C. *The Senate 1789–1989.* Washington, D.C.: U.S. Government Printing Office, 1988.

Caro, Robert A. *The Years of Lyndon Johnson.* Vol. 3, *Master of the Senate.* New York: Alfred A. Knopf, 2002.

Childs, Marquis W. *I Write from Washington.* New York: Harper & Brothers, 1942.

Clark, Delbert. *Washington Dateline.* New York: Frederick A. Stokes, 1941.

Collier, Peter, with David Horowitz. *The Roosevelts: An American Saga.* New York: Simon & Schuster, 1994.

Colman, Elizabeth Wheeler. *Mrs. Wheeler Goes to Washington.* Helena, Mont.: Falcon Press, 1989.

*Complete Presidential Press Conferences of Franklin D. Roosevelt.* New York: Da Capo Press, 1972.

Corwin, Edward S. *Constitutional Revolution, Ltd.* Claremont, Calif.: Friends of the Colleges at Claremont, 1941.

Cushman, Barry. *Rethinking the New Deal Court: The Structure of a Constitutional Revolution.* New York: Oxford University Press, 1998.

Danelski, David J., and Joseph S. Tulchin, eds. *The Autobiographical Notes of Charles Evans Hughes.* Cambridge, Mass.: Harvard University Press, 1973.

Daniels, Jonathan. *Washington Quadrille: The Dance Beside the Documents.* Garden City, N.Y.: Doubleday, 1968.

Farley, James A. *Behind the Ballots.* New York: Harcourt, Brace, 1938.

———. *Jim Farley's Story: The Roosevelt Years.* New York: Whittlesey House, 1948.

Friedel, Frank. *Franklin D. Roosevelt: A Rendezvous with Destiny.* Boston: Little, Brown, 1990.

Friedman, Leon, and Fred L. Israel, eds. *The Justices of the United States Supreme Court 1789–1969: Their Lives and Major Opinions.* New York: Chelsea House, 1969.

Galbraith, John Kenneth. *The Great Crash, 1929.* Boston: Houghton Mifflin, 1954.

Gallagher, Hugh Gregory. *FDR's Splendid Deception.* New York: Dodd, Mead, 1985.

Gallup, George, and Saul Forbes Rae. *The Pulse of Democracy: The Public-Opinion Poll and How It Works.* New York: Simon & Schuster, 1940.

Goodwin, Doris Kearns. *No Ordinary Time: Franklin and Eleanor Roosevelt; The Home Front in World War II.* New York: Simon & Schuster, 1994.

Hendel, Samuel. *Charles Evans Hughes and the Supreme Court.* New York: Russell & Russell, 1951.

Hillenbrand, Laura. *Seabiscuit: An American Legend.* New York: Ballantine Books, 2001.

Hilmes, Michele. *Radio Voices: American Broadcasting, 1922–1952.* Minneapolis: University of Minnesota Press, 1997.

Hughes, Charles Evans. *The Supreme Court of the United States: Its Foundation, Methods and Achievements.* New York: Columbia University Press, 1928.

Hurd, Charles. *Washington Cavalcade.* New York: E. P. Dutton, 1948.

———. *When the New Deal Was Young and Gay.* New York: Hawthorn Books, 1965.

Hutchinson, Dennis T., and David J. Garrow, eds. *The Forgotten Memoir of John Knox: A Year in the Life of a Supreme Court Clerk in FDR's Washington.* Chicago: University of Chicago Press, 2002.

Ickes, Harold L. *The Secret Diary of Harold L. Ickes.* Vols. 1 and 2. New York: Simon & Schuster, 1953 and 1954.

Irons, Peter. *A People's History of the Supreme Court: The Men and Women Whose Cases and Decisions Have Shaped Our Constitution.* New York: Penguin, 1999.

Jackson, Robert H. *The Struggle for Judicial Supremacy: A Study of a Crisis in American Power Politics.* New York: Alfred A. Knopf, 1941.

———. *That Man: An Insider's Portrait of Franklin D. Roosevelt.* New York: Oxford University Press, 2003.

James, Marquis. *Mr. Garner of Texas.* New York: Bobbs-Merrill, 1939.

Kennedy, David M. *Freedom from Fear.* Vol. 1, *The American People in the Great Depression.* New York: Oxford University Press, 1999.

Kim, David George. *The Plot Against America: Senator Wheeler and the Forces Behind Him.* Missoula, Mont.: John F. Kennedy, 1946.

Kincaid, Diane D., ed. *Silent Hattie Speaks: The Personal Journal of Senator Hattie Caraway.* Westport, Conn.: Greenwood Press, 1979.

Kiplinger, W. M. *Washington Is Like That.* New York: Harper & Brothers, 1942.

Knapp, George L. *Uncle Sam's Government at Washington.* New York: Dodd, Mead, 1933.

Leonard, Charles A. *A Search for a Judicial Philosophy: Mr. Justice Roberts and the Constitutional Revolution of 1937.* Port Washington, N.Y.: Kennikat Press, 1971.

Leuchtenburg, William E. *Franklin D. Roosevelt and the New Deal: 1932–1940.* New York: Harper & Row, 1963.

———. *The Supreme Court Reborn: The Constitutional Revolution in the Age of Roosevelt*. New York: Oxford University Press, 1995.

Maroon, Fred J., and Suzy Maroon. *The Supreme Court of the United States*. New York: Thomasson-Grant & Lickle, 1996.

Mason, Alpheus Thomas. *Harlan Fiske Stone: Pillar of the Law*. New York: Viking, 1956.

———. *The Supreme Court from Taft to Burger*. Baton Rouge: Louisiana State University Press, 1979.

McCune, Wesley. *The Nine Young Men*. New York: Harper & Brothers, 1947.

McElvaine, Robert S. *Down and Out in the Great Depression: Letters from the Forgotten Man*. Chapel Hill: University of North Carolina Press, 1983.

———. *The Great Depression: America, 1929–1941*. New York: Times Books, 1984.

McKean, David. *Tommy the Cork: Washington's Ultimate Insider from Roosevelt to Reagan*. South Royalton, Vt.: Steerforth Press, 2004.

McKenna, Marian C. *Franklin Roosevelt and the Great Constitutional War: The Court-Packing Crisis of 1937*. New York: Fordham University Press, 2002.

Melder, Keith. *City of Magnificent Intentions: A History of Washington, District of Columbia*. Washington, D.C.: Intac, 1997.

Michelson, Charles. *The Ghost Talks*. New York: G. P. Putnam's Sons, 1944.

Newton, Jim. *Justice for All: Earl Warren and the Nation He Made*. New York: Riverhead Books, 2006.

Paper, Lewis J. *Brandeis*. Englewood Cliffs, N.J.: Prentice-Hall, 1983.

Patterson, James T. *Congressional Conservatism and the New Deal: The Growth of the Conservative Coalition in Congress, 1933–1939*. Westport, Conn.: Greenwood Press, 1981.

Pearson, Drew, and Robert S. Allen. *The Nine Old Men*. Garden City, N.Y.: Doubleday, Doran, 1936.

Pepper, George Wharton. *Philadelphia Lawyer: An Autobiography*. Philadelphia: J. B. Lippincott, 1944.

Perkins, Frances. *The Roosevelt I Knew*. New York: Viking Press, 1946.

Peters, Charles. *Five Days in Philadelphia: Wendell Willkie, Franklin Roosevelt, and the 1940 Convention That Saved the Western World*. New York: PublicAffairs, 2005.

Powell, Jim. *FDR's Folly: How Roosevelt and His New Deal Prolonged the Great Depression*. New York: Three Rivers Press, 2003.

Pritchett, C. Herman. *The Roosevelt Court: A Study in Judicial Politics and Values, 1937–1947*. New York: Macmillan, 1948.

Pusey, Merlo J. *Charles Evans Hughes*. New York: Macmillan, 1952.

———. *The Supreme Court Crisis*. New York: Macmillan, 1937.

Ramaswamy, M. *The Creative Role of the Supreme Court in the United States*. New York: Russell & Russell, 1956.

Richberg, Donald R. *My Hero: The Indiscreet Memoirs of an Eventful but Unheroic Life*. New York: G. P. Putnam's Sons, 1954.

Roberts, Owen J. *The Court and the Constitution*. Cambridge, Mass.: Harvard University Press, 1951.

Roosevelt, James. *Affectionately, F.D.R.* New York: Harcourt, Brace, 1959.

Roosevelt, James, with Bill Libby. *My Parents: A Differing View*. Chicago: Playboy Press, 1976.

Rosen, Jeffrey. *The Supreme Court: The Personalities and Rivalries That Defined America*. New York: Times Books, 2006.

Rosenman, Samuel I. *Working with Roosevelt*. New York: Da Capo Press, 1972.

Ruetten, Richard T. "Burton K. Wheeler of Montana: A Progressive Between the Wars." Ph.D. diss., University of Oregon, 1961.

Schlesinger, Arthur M. Jr. *The Age of Roosevelt*. Vol. 2, *The Coming of the New Deal, 1933–1935*. Boston: Houghton Mifflin, 1958.

———. *The Age of Roosevelt*. Vol. 3, *The Politics of Upheaval*. Boston: Houghton Mifflin, 1960.

Schwartz, Bernard. *A History of the Supreme Court*. New York: Oxford University Press, 1993.

Shogan, Robert. *Backlash: The Killing of the New Deal*. Chicago: Ivan R. Dee, 2006.

Smith, Jean Edward. *FDR*. New York: Random House, 2007.

Sultzer, Judith A., and Karen Hemighaus, *Owen J. Roberts: Our Namesake and Our Pride*. Pottstown, Pa.: Owen J. Roberts School District, 1977.

Terkel, Studs. *Hard Times: An Oral History of the Great Depression*. New York: Pantheon Books, 1970.

Timmons, Bascom N. *Garner of Texas*. New York: Harper & Brothers, 1948.

Trapp, William Oscar. "The Constitutional Doctrines of Owen J. Roberts." Ph.D. diss., Cornell University, 1943.

Urofsky, Melvin I., ed. *The Supreme Court Justices: A Biographical Dictionary*. New York: Garland, 1994.

Weller, Cecil Edward Jr. *Joe T. Robinson: Always a Loyal Democrat*. Fayetteville: University of Arkansas Press, 1998.

Wheeler, Burton K., with Paul F. Healy. *Yankee from the West: The Candid, Turbulent Life Story of the Yankee-Born U.S. Senator from Montana*. Garden City, N.Y.: Doubleday, 1962.

White, G. Edward. *The Constitution and the New Deal*. Cambridge, Mass.: Harvard University Press, 2000.

Wilson, Robert A., ed. *Character Above All: Ten Presidents from FDR to George Bush*. New York: Simon & Schuster, 1995.

Writers' Program of the Work Projects Administration for the District of Columbia. *Washington City and Capital*. Washington, D.C.: U.S. Government Printing Office, 1937.

Yeilding, Kenneth D., and Paul H. Carlson. *Ah, That Voice: The Fireside Chats of Franklin D. Roosevelt*. Odessa, Tex.: John Ben Shepperd Jr. Library of the Presidents, Presidential Museum, 1974.

# INDEX

# A NOTE ON THE AUTHOR

BURT SOLOMON HAS written about the nation's capital and its history for three decades. A longtime staff correspondent for *National Journal*, he won the Gerald R. Ford Prize for Distinguished Reporting on the Presidency. He is the author of *The Washington Century: Three Families and the Shaping of the Nation's Capital*; and *Where They Ain't: The Fabled Life and Untimely Death of the Original Baltimore Orioles, the Team That Gave Birth to Modern Baseball*, named one of the twenty best books of the millennium by *GQ*. He lives inside the Capital Beltway.